Software Architecture with Kotlin

Combine various architectural styles to create sustainable
and scalable software solutions

Jason (Tsz Shun) Chow

Software Architecture with Kotlin

Copyright © 2024 Packt Publishing

Group Product Manager: Kunal Sawant
Publishing Product Manager: Teny Thomas
Book Project Manager: Manisha Singh
Content Development Editor (CDE): Rosal Colaco
Technical Editor: Kavyashree K S
Copy Editor: Safis Editing
Proofreader: Rosal Colaco
Indexer: Rekha Nair
Production Designer: Joshua Misquitta

First published: December 2024
Production reference: 1031224

Published by Packt Publishing Ltd.
Grosvenor House
11 St Paul's Square
Birmingham
B3 1RB, UK

ISBN 978-1-83546-186-0
www.packtpub.com

To Marta and Mieszko Yin-jo.

Contributors

About the author

Jason (Tsz Shun) Chow has been working in the software industry since 2001. He is a Senior Vice President at CAIS, an alternative investment platform, with a focus on the complex domain modeling of private equity and hedge funds, combined with unified design and the use of artificial intelligence. Prior to this, Tsz Shun was a Principal Engineer at 11:FS, a digital fintech consultancy focused on building digital strategies and lovable products aimed at changing the fabric of financial services. In the early 2010s, Tsz Shun worked at IG Index on several latency-sensitive financial exchange services and authored the public APIs in the FIX protocol.

I want to thank the people who have been close to me and supported me, especially my wife and my parents.

About the reviewers

Jose Coll is an experienced Financial Services IT professional with over 20 years of experience in systems implementation, specializing in electronic trading, risk management, and valuation systems for OTC and exchange-traded derivatives. He has worked with JVM languages, middleware messaging, and distributed, parallelizable compute technologies. For the past 7 years, Jose has focused on Blockchain and **Distributed Ledger Technology (DLT)** as a lead engineer, building the Corda platform using Kotlin and exploring various aspects of Blockchain, Crypto, and Web3.

Alexei Timofti, with over 18 years of experience spanning startups and global enterprises, specializes in building complex and scalable systems. Currently a Principal Engineer at N26, he has spent the past five years leveraging Kotlin to craft a banking experience people love to use. Starting his programming journey with Java, he discovered Kotlin at N26 and quickly fell in love with its concise and clean syntax. Since then, Kotlin has become his preferred language for backend development.

Alexei is passionate about designing clean architecture, data engineering, and championing test-driven development to deliver robust and maintainable solutions. In his free time, he enjoys traveling, reading, and spending time with his closest ones.

Table of Contents

5

Exploring MVC, MVP, and MVVM   107

6

Microservices, Serverless, and Microfrontends   129

9

Event Sourcing and CQRS   217

10

Idempotency, Replication, and Recovery Models   247

11

Auditing and Monitoring Models   271

12

Performance and Scalability   299

13

Testing   327

14

Security   353

Preface

Welcome to *Software Architecture with Kotlin*, a comprehensive guide designed to equip you with the knowledge and skills needed to build robust software systems using Kotlin. As the demand for efficient and scalable applications continues to grow, understanding architectural principles becomes indispensable for engineers and architects.

In this book, we will break down a selection of software architecture styles into basic components by the first principle, so these components can be rearranged and combined to solve real-world problems. Each chapter focuses on specific areas, introducing key concepts, best practices, and real-world examples illustrating how to apply these principles in Kotlin.

Whether you are a seasoned engineer looking to deepen your understanding of software architecture or a newcomer eager to learn, this book provides practical insights that can be immediately applied. You will find hands-on exercises, code snippets, and case studies that will help you grasp complex ideas and implement them in your projects.

As you embark on this journey, I encourage you to experiment with the concepts presented here. Software architecture is more than patterns and styles – it is about creativity, problem-solving, flexibility, and adapting solutions to meet the unique challenges of your applications. Happy reading!

Who this book is for

This book is for software engineers who want to enhance their architectural knowledge and mindset to solve daily engineering problems. Prior experience in engineering will be useful but not essential.

If you have just started learning how to write Kotlin code, are expanding your technical experience from Android development to backend, or are transitioning from writing Java code, you will find this book useful.

If you are a software architect interested in discussing and exploring unique architectural ideas, this is the book for you.

What this book covers

Chapter 1, The Essence of Software Architecture, revisits the importance of software architecture and the role of software architects in an organization. It covers how the structure of an organization affects architectural decisions. Then it discusses choosing a framework and the factors to consider in the process. Several industry-standard documents and diagrams are introduced, which will be used for illustrations in subsequent chapters.

Chapter 2, Principles of Software Architecture, explores multiple ways to visualize and quantify software architectures, extracting quality attributes for measurement and analysis. It then delves into three key concepts: the separation of concerns, cohesiveness, and coupling. Popular architecture principles such as SOLID, the Law of Demeter, YAGNI, and future-proofing are also covered. These principles lay the foundation for further exploration of architecture styles in the following chapters.

Chapter 3, Polymorphism and Alternatives, uses a real-life problem and solves it using multiple styles in Kotlin code. It starts with a polymorphic solution, then explores two solutions involving Kotlin sealed classes. Next, a solution using delegation is presented, followed by a functional approach. Finally, all approaches are compared based on system quality attributes.

Chapter 4, Peer-to-Peer and Client-Server Architecture, focuses on network communication in distributed systems. It includes a step-by-step guide to implementing a client-server solution with an API-first approach using OpenAPI specifications and the Http4K framework in Kotlin. The chapter then implements a peer-to-peer solution to the same problem and compares the two approaches, discussing which is suitable for different situations.

Chapter 5, Exploring MVC, MVP, and MVVM, shifts focus to frontend applications. Using a sample Android application, we apply MVC, MVP, and MVVM to observe the evolution of the implementation with different architecture styles. The three patterns are compared along with other commonly used styles.

Chapter 6, Microservices, Serverless, and Microfrontends, moves the focus to the backend. This chapter shows how monolithic applications and service-oriented architectures evolve into microservices and nanoservices. It explains how serverless architectures impact modern software systems through cloud provider services. Finally, the frontend counterpart of microservices, the micro-frontend, is discussed.

Chapter 7, Modular and Layered Architectures, starts with three layered architectures—Clean architecture, Hexagonal architecture, and Functional Core Imperative Shell—that have similarities and differences. They are demonstrated and compared using Kotlin code for the same real-life problem. Later, the chapter explores the Connect pattern, providing a modular approach to integrate with remote systems.

Chapter 8, Domain-Driven Design (DDD), takes a deep dive into DDD design activities. It starts with basic concepts and terms, then looks at the bigger picture of the domain with Strategic Design. A bounded context is selected for Tactical Design. The chapter also walks through three popular domain modeling activities with a real-life example.

Chapter 9, Event Sourcing and CQRS, extends the DDD practices from the previous chapter into two powerful architecture patterns. It first illustrates the use of Event Sourcing with a real-life example, then explains how CQRS can be applied. Finally, it combines Event Sourcing and CQRS as a solution to the same problem to unlock the potential of both architecture styles.

Chapter 10, Idempotency, Replication, and Recovery Models, discusses three related architectural concepts. It starts with idempotency in distributed systems, providing practical examples of how to implement it. Next, several replication models are explored and compared using the CAP Theorem. The chapter concludes with system recovery, using RAFT leader election as a case study.

Chapter 11, Auditing and Monitoring Models, demonstrates a sample audit trail structure in Kotlin that can be used by multiple services but centrally recorded. It also discusses various monitoring data formats and approaches for collecting data for monitoring purposes. The chapter covers structural and contextual logging with Kotlin code, as well as automated alerts, incident management, and metrics.

Chapter 12, Performance and Scalability, focuses on measuring performance using defined metrics. It showcases performance testing through basic approaches and micro-benchmarking. The chapter guides you through performance testing workflows while discussing strategies for performance improvement using Kotlin code. Additionally, a voting system is used to illustrate the process of enhancing performance and scaling the system.

Chapter 13, Testing, explores the role of Quality Assurance. It examines various testing methods within the Testing Pyramid and highlights best practices for each type. The chapter includes a step-by-step journey through a Test-Driven Development exercise with the Kotest framework.

Chapter 14, Security, focuses on safeguarding software systems and their data from malicious attacks. It starts with securing network communication using Transport Layer Security (TLS). Then, the chapter covers Multi-Factor Authentication (MFA) for user identity verification. It also addresses common methods of authorization and data entitlement, techniques for hiding and anonymizing sensitive data, and various network security approaches. The chapter concludes with a discussion of DevSecOps and a Threat Modeling exercise.

Chapter 15, Beyond Architecture, covers various engineering topics beyond software architecture. First, it explores several Kotlin language features that help engineers achieve better code quality and software architecture. Next, it discusses the transition from Java to Kotlin with the help of IDE features. The chapter compares two CI approaches: feature-based and trunk-based development. It then covers release strategies, briefly touches on Developer Experience, and concludes with a look at current trends in software architecture.

To get the most out of this book

It is essential to approach the material with an open mind and a willingness to experiment. Start by revisiting the foundational concepts presented in the first two chapters, as they serve as the building blocks for more advanced topics. Engage with the hands-on examples and coding exercise, which are designed to materialize your understanding for practical application. Reflect on how each architecture style can meet the needs of your projects. In addition, consider exploring external resources to further enrich your learning experience.

Software covered in the book	Operating system requirements
IntelliJ IDEA (Community or Ultimate version)	Windows, macOS, or Linux
Android Studio	Windows, macOS, Linux, or ChromeOS
OpenJDK 17+	Windows, macOS, or Linux
Git CLI tool	Windows, macOS, or Linux

You will need to configure IntelliJ and Android Studio to use the installed JDK and Git CLI tool.

If you are using the digital version of this book, we advise you to type the code yourself or access the code from the book's GitHub repository (a link is available in the next section). Doing so will help you avoid any potential errors related to the copying and pasting of code.

After reading the book, I would recommend you start a new project to try to solve the real-life example problem of household exchanging services in a village, or to solve a problem that you know a lot about, e.g. a problem that you face in your day-to-day life or work. Meanwhile, apply the architecture styles, analyze them with your knowledge of the problem, and explore the frameworks that were mentioned in the book. Solving a well-understood problem helps us focus on addressing non-functional concerns and hands-on coding.

Download the example code files

You can download the example code files for this book from GitHub at `https://github.com/PacktPublishing/Software-Architecture-with-Kotlin`. If there's an update to the code, it will be updated in the GitHub repository.

We also have other code bundles from our rich catalog of books and videos available at `https://github.com/PacktPublishing/`. Check them out!

Conventions used

There are a number of text conventions used throughout this book.

`Code in text`: Indicates code words in text, database table names, folder names, filenames, file extensions, pathnames, dummy URLs, user input, and Twitter handles. Here is an example: "The `Person` class directly accesses the `city` property inside the `Address` class."

A block of code is set as follows:

```kotlin
class Person(val name: String, val address: Address) {
    fun getAddressCity(): String {
        return address.city
    }
}
class Address(val city: String)
```

Bold: Indicates a new term, an important word, or words that you see onscreen. For instance, words in menus or dialog boxes appear in **bold**. Here is an example: "The **Business** package uses the **Persistence** package to perform the actual relational database operations for service contracts and households."

> **Tips or important notes**
> Appear like this.

Get in touch

Feedback from our readers is always welcome.

General feedback: If you have questions about any aspect of this book, email us at customercare@packtpub.com and mention the book title in the subject of your message.

Errata: Although we have taken every care to ensure the accuracy of our content, mistakes do happen. If you have found a mistake in this book, we would be grateful if you would report this to us. Please visit www.packtpub.com/support/errata and fill in the form.

Piracy: If you come across any illegal copies of our works in any form on the internet, we would be grateful if you would provide us with the location address or website name. Please contact us at copyright@packt.com with a link to the material.

If you are interested in becoming an author: If there is a topic that you have expertise in and you are interested in either writing or contributing to a book, please visit authors.packtpub.com.

Share your thoughts

Once you've read *Software Architecture with Kotlin*, we'd love to hear your thoughts! Scan the QR code below to go straight to the Amazon review page for this book and share your feedback.

https://packt.link/r/1835461867

Your review is important to us and the tech community and will help us make sure we're delivering excellent quality content.

Download a free PDF copy of this book

Thanks for purchasing this book!

Do you like to read on the go but are unable to carry your print books everywhere?

Is your eBook purchase not compatible with the device of your choice?

Don't worry, now with every Packt book you get a DRM-free PDF version of that book at no cost.

Read anywhere, any place, on any device. Search, copy, and paste code from your favorite technical books directly into your application.

The perks don't stop there, you can get exclusive access to discounts, newsletters, and great free content in your inbox daily

Follow these simple steps to get the benefits:

1. Scan the QR code or visit the link below

https://packt.link/free-ebook/978-1-83546-186-0

2. Submit your proof of purchase
3. That's it! We'll send your free PDF and other benefits to your email directly

1

The Essence
of Software Architecture

Software architecture is the blueprint of a software system. It may not contain a single line of code but it describes how different structures work together so that systematic behaviors emerge from these structures, and thus the system serves its intended functions.

This is a book for those who wish to boost their architectural knowledge and mindset to solve daily engineering problems. In this chapter, we will discuss the essential values of software architecture and its position in an organization. We are going to cover the following topics:

- The importance of software architecture
- The role of an architect
- Conway's law
- Choosing a framework
- Documentation and diagrams

The importance of software architecture

Why should we bother with software architecture? In theory, a good engineer can simply jump into coding. Given time and effort, a software system can be produced to start functioning. This is a typical example of jumping to the result without extracting the value from the process.

A software system is a living entity that needs to adapt to the changes in the environment. Let us use a real-life example to illustrate this concept.

Real-life use case – community service exchange as a contract

In a village community, every household offers help to each other. One household's members have certain skills lacking in another household. A member in household A is good at plumbing but not good at making clothes, while a member in household B is a tailor but the household needs pipes fixing.

So, household A offers to fix the pipes of household B in exchange for household B making clothes for a newborn baby in household A.

Each household uses bookkeeping software to keep records of the exchange of services in each household's file. Each copy of the software in each household does not communicate with the other.

It works well for a while until some households have a dispute over what was agreed in their exchange of services. Both households claimed their records were correct in the software; however, the records in each copy of the software are slightly different. Since each copy of software does not communicate with the other, the dispute cannot be easily resolved.

One of the possible enhancements of the bookkeeping software would be to keep the records in a central data store so that households can view and agree on the details of the exchange of services before carrying out their services.

However, the bookkeeping software was written without architecture. All we have are lines and lines of codes, scattered in multiple files, and with some duplicated logic in multiple places. The code itself may be well-written and organized, but the original engineer has left the village, and the new engineer does not understand the rationale behind the code.

Software architecture as a means of communication

Software architecture is fundamentally a way of communication. Firstly, it defines what problems it solves in an abstract manner that stakeholders from non-engineering backgrounds can understand and reason about the software system.

Stakeholders use specific terms in describing the problem. Sometimes, different stakeholders use different terms that mean the same thing, or they might use the same term but mean different things. Engineers will also need to align with the terms and usage in the engineering structures. Software architecture acts as a common language and understanding so that all stakeholders and engineers can communicate with well-defined terms.

Usually, stakeholders make use of software architecture to integrate with their operation workflows. They may have other systems to interact with, or they need teams of people to work in various parts of the system. Software architecture becomes a visualization of the automated part of the workflow.

Software architecture as training materials

Secondly, software architecture provides an abstract view of how different structures work together and focuses on certain concerns at a time. A new engineer joining the team usually has a lot to learn to understand how the current system works. Source code is the ultimate source of truth; however, it could be laborious and time-consuming to read it all. Source code is usually cluttered with language syntax and layers of function invocations. Building up an understanding of the system from the code bottom-up is certainly possible, but it would take a long time.

Learning is much more effective with architectural documents that guide new members directly to the areas they care about. It is less overwhelming than source code, and it avoids engineers treating the bugs in code as the correct behaviors. New engineers can learn one aspect of the system at a time, with the aid of architectural documents.

Software architecture to manifest system quality attributes

System quality attributes, also known as system non-functional attributes, are the characteristics of a software system that define its overall behaviors, and operational and performance aspects. They are non-functional in that they are agnostic to the functional or business problems the system solves.

System quality attributes, such as availability, scalability, security, testability, extendability, and maintainability, are difficult to measure with only code. Software architecture provides at least one view to manifest each of these attributes so we can tune the system accordingly.

In the given example, the software could be lacking redundancy in the sense that each copy of the software stores the data in its own local storage and does not communicate with any other. If a copy has stopped working, the household would lose all data. Also, because each copy does not communicate with the other, there is no reliable way to guarantee that two households who exchanged services have the same records in their own software copies.

By having software architecture to describe the system attributes, engineers will be able to identify the issue and design a change to improve the given attributes. Moreover, it enables us to measure and monitor how these attributes change over time and correlate them with software changes. We are even able to project and predict these attributes when we plan a change to the current software architecture.

Software architecture as a change management tool

Usually, problems change and evolve over time. In the example, separated records of the exchange of services in each copy of the software were sufficient, as there was not a dispute. Software architecture provides a foundation for changes and enhancements. In many cases, different stakeholders have different priorities in their minds. Software architecture facilitates the discussion of how the system could evolve and at what cost, so the enhancement can be prioritized in order.

Also, with system attributes being described in software architecture, we can identify and mitigate risks since we understand which part of the architecture is being changed.

Software architecture as records of reusable solutions

Software architecture documents a series of concerns raised and decisions made. In the example of the bookkeeping software, since the original engineer has left the village, no one really knows the thinking process and why certain design choices were made at the time. It becomes very risky to enhance the system as no one knows the impact of changing one line of code. The idea of a central data store was planned and we are just one step behind it, or it was never designed to share data. We simply do not know.

This leaves us unable to safely improve the software, or even just to fix a bug. We might end up making the same mistake. We might misunderstand the original intent of the software and even create a bug. It becomes difficult to continue using the software if the problem evolves like the given example.

Software architecture acts as a set of records of decisions made to solve the problem. It explains the rationale of what drove the decisions and what factors were considered to make the choice. It also records any alternatives considered and why they were not eventually chosen.

Software architecture also identifies any constraint the system is bound to. It is important to include constraints because any new technological advancement may eliminate such constraints, such as new frameworks, and thus create new opportunities for improvement.

All this information provides solid ground if, one day, we decide to start a new system from scratch to solve the problem. We will not need to start from zero. We can start from what we have learned and the journey behind it. We can reuse a lot of the concepts from previous architecture if the context is applicable. We can significantly improve the next system with fewer constraints imposed on the previous system.

The role of a software architect

It may seem obvious that a software architect (the *architect*) is someone who creates software architecture. However, software architecture is the result of multi-dimensional thought processes that involve a lot of people. There is no single architect who would produce architecture alone and require no input from others.

It is important to point out that, although a software architect can be a job title in some organizations, the role of a software architect is not restricted to only someone who has the title.

Interface between engineers and stakeholders

Software architects align and translate the language used by engineers and non-technical people (the *stakeholders*). They facilitate communication using documentation and diagrams to illustrate key topics in the software system for discussion. There are variations in how the interface works between engineers and different stakeholders with the facilitation of software architects. We are going to explore these variations now.

Engineers and product managers

Software architects translate product requirements into technical designs. Engineers can do the same, but software architects apply a broader view in the sense of how certain implementations may impact system quality attributes. Software architects do not dictate the choice of implementation; however, they define non-functional requirements that predict system quality attributes. The non-functional requirements provide directions and constraints on the implementation.

In the example given previously, if a software architect were involved in the technical design process, they could have required the records of the exchange of service between neighbors to be replicated in both software copies and thus could have avoided the dispute of inconsistent records.

Software architects also take part in translating technical constraints, bugs, and implementations into information that product managers can digest and engage in. Software architects provide an abstract view of the code implementation to facilitate communication with product managers.

Imagine there is a new framework that facilitates two software copies to synchronize records of service exchange between neighbors, which permanently solves the dispute problem. Software architects can document this new approach and abstract the interaction to provide a foundation to discuss with product managers how this improves user experience.

Engineers and delivery managers

There is often tension when it comes to engineers developing features and delivery managers managing the timeline for when those features can be released. It is common for engineers to not deliver the full features in time. Software architects can facilitate the discussion of how the features may be delivered in phases and still be operational. In each phase, software architects determine the impact on system quality attributes and how users can operate in the meantime.

This is just an example of how software architects are involved when full features will not be available in time.

Regulators and compliance

Software systems, particularly in regulated industries, must address compliance concerns. The range is wide, and it may include the processing of personal data, auditing of persisted data, or complying with regulatory procedures.

Software architects are not only involved in designing an architecture that complies with regulations but also in illustrating how it was implemented. Regulatory bodies will examine technical documents, including architecture diagrams, as part of their due diligence process.

Security professionals

People who specialize in the fields of information security or cybersecurity work with software architects in multiple areas.

They provide security requirements in line with security policies, procedures, and guidelines. The requirements might include authentication, access control, and even the choice of encryption algorithms.

Software architects work with security analysts to perform threat modeling and risk assessment. They analyze the system architecture, identify vulnerabilities and risks, and discover potential attacks. The likeliness and impact of threats drive architectural choices.

Software architects may also work with penetration testers or ethical hackers to discover security holes and potential fixes.

Security architects collaborate with software architects to identify and choose the approach to address identified risks and meet security requirements.

Stakeholders

Stakeholders usually come from multiple departments of the organization, and they are likely to have different requirements and priorities for how the system is required to work. Software architects can navigate these tangled requirements and ensure that the system can fulfill these requirements in an agreed priority order.

Software architects also play the part of extracting common terms from multiple domain experts and stakeholders so the terms can be used in the architecture documents in a clear and unambiguous manner.

Balancing appropriate architecture and budget

While some software architects might be keen on having the most state-of-the-art technology and the latest and the fastest, realistically, they are more balanced with the budget the organization can afford.

Financial constraints on technology choice do not necessarily result in bad architecture; on the contrary, they encourage software architects to find more cost-effective ways to solve problems, and they could lead to a leaner and simpler architecture. If two architectures can address an identical set of concerns, the simpler and cheaper one is always better.

The decision of whether to buy or build is often affected by multiple factors, and the technical factor is only one of them. Although software architects may not have the power to decide which way to go, they provide technical and operational analysis so the organization can make an informed choice.

When the organization cannot afford the most technically sound system or service, software architects are there to bring out compromise, trade-offs, and impact analysis for the "second-class solution." It may seem not ideal initially, but software architects can design the system in a way that leaves room for enhancement and expansion in the future.

Vision and roadmap to technical evolution

Legacy systems are outdated software systems that are still in use by the organization. They are legacy because their technology has very little room for improvement, and it is likely at least a few years backward.

There are systems that became legacy due to external factors such as discontinued technology support and severe limitations. And there are no feasible or cost-effective ways to evolve.

Legacy systems can also be the result of the lack of technical vision and roadmaps, in which software architects are heavily involved. Some small start-ups may not have someone taking the role of software architect, or there is no one championing software architecture continuously. These can all be reasons for systems to become legacy.

However, software architects can still jump in at any point to modernize the current architecture. They start by understanding what the current system does and what the organization really needs. Then, they decompose the system into autonomous parts, modernize them individually, and recombine them in a separate way so the whole technical ecosystem can be up to date again.

Usually, a technical vision includes inspiration in achieving a software architecture that manifests certain system quality attributes, such as highly available and scalable systems. While a technical roadmap includes small steps to achieve short- to medium-term goals, and some more dramatic changes to long-term goals, it requires meticulous planning and thought toward how the system evolves. Also, the technical roadmap must interact with the external technological evolution to pivot and adapt to a better alternative.

Cross-cutting concerns in a technical ecosystem

Cross-cutting concerns are typically the concerns that require multiple software components to work together to derive the desired outcome.

One example can be standardizing logging messages so they can facilitate cross-service log searches.

Engineers are often divided into teams and each team looks after a certain area of business. They do not necessarily have the bandwidth to ensure that services in other teams conform to the same convention to achieve cross-cutting outcomes.

Software architects engage these cross-cutting concerns in a holistic manner. They consult, engage, and discuss with multiple teams to form a consensus or convention so cross-cutting concerns can be addressed.

Software architects also drive common infrastructures, frameworks, and tooling to address these cross-cutting concerns. These concerns are closely related to the system quality attributes.

Let us say there are multiple services that need to communicate with each other, and REST endpoints are chosen to be the way of communication. However, without establishing standards among teams, the system quickly falls into a collection of inconsistent APIs. The URI resource hierarchy can be inconsistent, as can the error response payload. All these impact the maintainability and reusability of the system.

Software architects can be involved in understanding each team's requirements and their concerns about using REST endpoints. Then, a guideline of REST endpoints can be created so that there is a pattern that engineers align with. A typical example would be to define a general payload structure for error responses to contain information in addition to the HTTP response status:

```
{
    "resource": "/users/32039/address/0",
    "shortMessage": "first line of address must be present",
    "longMessage": "A valid address must contain the first line",
    "details": {
        "addressLine1": null,
        "city": "London",
        "postCode": "EC12 10ED",
    }
}
```

This sample payload represents an error of an address input; it contains general fields such as `resource`, `shortMessage`, and `longMessage` that every service can conform to, while also having a `details` section to be customized by each service.

By having this standard, we can achieve overall observability of these errors and persist them in a universal format for audit purposes. Engineers can reuse this structure to reduce the time needed to develop a new REST endpoint. Engineers will also find it easier to maintain a REST endpoint even if it was developed by other engineers.

In a sense, standardizing the REST error payload has addressed the cross-cutting concerns of observability, auditability, maintainability, and reusability in the whole technical ecosystem.

Conway's law

Conway's law is an observation that the system design of an organization mirrors the organizational structure. A computer programmer called Melvin Conway introduced this idea in 1967, and his original wording is as follows:

> *"Any organization that designs a system (defined broadly) will produce a design whose structure is a copy of the organization's communication structure."*

In the context of software systems, software architecture mirrors the organization structure. The classic example can be illustrated in this diagram:

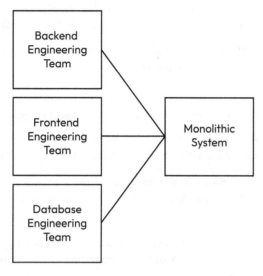

Figure 1.1 – A company organized by skill set

The company has a **backend engineering** (**BE**) team, a **frontend engineering** (**BE**) team, and a **database engineering** (**DE**) team. This organization groups people by their skill set. Everyone in a team is responsible for all business functions. This structure is likely to produce a monolithic system, which usually manifests in a single source code repository or one single logical process.

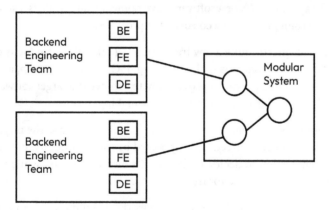

Figure 1.2 – A company organized by business functions

The organization in *Figure 1.2* groups people by their business functions. So, everyone in a team is responsible for a designated business function, but each member may not have the same skill set. This structure is likely to produce a modular system, which contains multiple logical processes that interact with each other. Usually, there are dedicated source code repositories for each team.

Systems scale better when the team size is small because the number of communication channels required for people to talk to each other is $n (n - 1) / 2$ so it is exponentially scaled up. Jeff Bezos from Amazon proposed his two-pizza rule:

"If you can't feed your team with two large pizzas in a meeting, you're in trouble."

So, if teams cannot be too big to scale the organization as well as the system, then it usually ends up with many teams. This resonates a lot with the architectural concepts we will cover very soon.

On the other hand, despite best efforts in modernizing the architecture of a legacy system, if the organization structure refuses to align with it, it is likely that the new architecture will eventually fall back to its old habitual structure.

This is something that should be solved by engineering management and upward. It is beyond what software architects can solve. However, it is worth understanding this phenomenon so the issue can be escalated as soon as possible.

Some big organizations found it extremely difficult to change their structures. And they even created start-up companies to run with modern organization structures alongside modern software architecture.

Choosing a software framework

A software framework (a *framework*), or a software development framework, is a standardized set of tools that aim to solve certain problems by consistent approaches.

A software system typically needs quite a few frameworks, so that they can focus on the business functions instead of lower-level concerns such as logging, JSON transformation, and configuration management. These frameworks provide a proven way to achieve the target software architecture. Choosing a framework is a part of architectural decision-making.

It is rare that organizations build every framework themselves these days. The major reason is that most of the frameworks are open-sourced and supported by the community. It would take a lot of justifications for an organization to decide to develop its own framework while there are similar competing frameworks that can be used for free.

Some technology companies develop their own frameworks when there are no existing ones that suit their needs. Some companies develop their own frameworks with the intent to compete with the other frameworks, and to potentially monetize from consulting business or to cross-sell their other products. It would take a lot of research effort and talent to achieve that.

The other option would be to choose a framework that already exists in the market, commercial or open-sourced.

The new framework paradox

New frameworks are released every month with the intent to solve the age-old problems of existing frameworks. Usually, there are one or two popular frameworks on the market, and the new frameworks advertise that they solved the old ones with an approach that everyone has always wanted.

Of course, there are true paradigm-shifting new frameworks that made engineers more productive and really have moved the industry forward with an innovative approach. For example, **Ruby on Rails** has transformed the repetitive and boilerplate code configuration of web development into inference and conventions, hence vastly reducing the number of lines of code.

But there are also a lot of cases where the new frameworks started with innovative approaches that did not go too well. And here comes the new framework paradox.

If a new framework aims to replace a framework that has been around for many years, the new framework will need to cover a lot of areas and keep the "new approach" in each area. This is a huge undertaking for the contributors.

For example, the **Spring frameworks** were created in 2002 to simplify dependencies of code by using **Dependency Injection** (**DI**) and **Inversion of Control** (**IOC**). But now, the frameworks have evolved to cover an extensive range of features, such as web, messaging, security, persistence, and so on. A next-generation framework to replace Spring frameworks would have to cover over 20 years of development, with a very comprehensive coverage of technical areas.

The most significant risk is that the new framework may have solved one of the longest-standing problems of a framework but it falls short of the areas that are fundamental and essential. It traps the engineers who adopt the new framework and makes them face the dilemma of whether to fix the new framework or return to the old one.

Another risk is that the community may not agree on what the "new approach" should be, and therefore, multiple new frameworks are created to solve the same age-old problem of the old framework. Engineers who want to try a new framework face the choice overload problem. And sometimes, it becomes a choice paralysis as there is no single definitively better choice to choose from.

Let us say your team has chosen a framework and everyone is quite happy with it. However, for whatever reason, the major contributor has decided to not work on this project anymore. Then, your team is at risk of the framework not being kept up to date with the fixes and planned enhancements. Not to mention that most open-sourced frameworks are contributed by normal engineers who spend their personal time for free on this.

How to compare and decide between software frameworks

However, in a real situation, the team would still need to choose some frameworks to move forward. An example situation would be a framework for logging messages for a Java application. Do we use the **Java Logging** framework that comes with the standard **Java Development Kit** (**JDK**), **Apache Log4J**, or **Logback**? How could we make the most sensible choice? Unfortunately, there are no golden rules that guarantee the best choice, but there are several aspects that the team should consider before making the decision.

Community

Community is the most crucial factor in your consideration. People are the reasons the framework is created, used, and maintained. Without people, the framework will not continue. There are at least three areas of the community for the framework to look for:

- Firstly, the bigger the community, the more likely the framework will have someone to continuously support and enhance the framework. A framework should be like a living being, powered by the people in the community. Also, reasons for having a large community for a framework are likely that the framework is universally applicable and of acceptable quality for general usage.

- Secondly, we need to look at how well the framework is supported by the community. It could be as simple as getting help from another user on how to use the framework. It could also be the quality and quantity of technical blogs written by the members of the community to share their tips on how to apply the framework to problems. It could be measured by suggestions the community made for new features and enhancements.

- Thirdly, we need to see how the members of the community communicate with each other. Do they have a Slack channel, a Discord server, an email distribution list, or any instant messaging platform? How responsive are the members of the community when people post their questions out there? Are the people helpful and positive in receiving feedback?

Contribution

Every commit to the source code repository made up the framework the way it is now. It is worth checking some statistics to understand how actively the framework is being maintained.

When was the last commit? Was it recently updated? How many commits have been made so far? Also, we can check the number of commits in the last month, the last 6 months, or the last year. Moreover, we can look at the variety of contributors. A good sign is that the commits are done by a variety of contributors, not only the usual ones. It indicates a diverse and healthy growth from contributors putting their efforts into the framework.

How many forks and branches are there? Bigger numbers usually indicate healthy growth that either some members of the community are working on a change or there could be a variant of the framework soon. It is likely that there are useful features already in the code base that people are willing to spend their effort on.

The number of tags indicates historical releases and may give a hint about the evolution and growth of the framework. However, be careful of versions under 1.0 (e.g., 0.67), or simply just build numbers. The contributors in this case may not want to commit to the current shape of the framework, and there may be breaking changes in the future.

Versions under 1.0 also could mean contributors may not have confirmed their commitment to keep the framework running for long yet. Extra caution must be taken if you intend to put a *0.x* library dependency in your production system. It is going to be difficult if the library discontinues or introduces breaking changes.

We should also look at the source code and get an impression of the code's quality and test cases. We should glance at the test coverage to understand how deep and broad the code was tested. This would help us predict the reliability and stability of the framework.

Tooling and documentation

We should also consider whether the framework uses mature tooling to manage itself. It may include an issue tracking system that members of the community can submit bugs and track how long it takes for a bug to go from reported to fixed.

The framework may also use an established **Continuous Integration** (**CI**) system. This is also a good sign of a healthy, long-running, and mature framework since there is a need to automate builds to handle the number of commits, control the quality, and release the framework.

Documentation is a key factor to consider since this is where engineers learn how to use the framework. The documentation does not necessarily need to be polished or automatically generated. It is the quality of the content that matters. And diagrams would be nice if they help engineers understand the concepts.

Interoperability with other frameworks

Many frameworks were designed to work with other frameworks, and some of them have innate dependencies on other frameworks. This is common and not a bad sign; however, caution must be taken on the impact.

Adopting a framework that uses or works with another framework implies we are also indirectly adopting the other framework. Is the other framework compatible with the engineering approach the team has taken? Do we allow engineers in the team to use the transitive dependencies directly in the code?

Even if we are OK with the other framework, we still need to ensure that the versions are compatible. For example, framework A may have used the Apache Commons IO library, version 2.14.0, and our project currently uses 1.4. Importing framework A to our project would bring version 2.14.0 as a dependency to the project. Luckily, build frameworks such as Gradle and Maven provide a graceful way to explicitly specify a version and exclude a particular version from the transitive dependency. In this example, we will upgrade our dependency on Apache Commons IO to 2.14.0 from 1.4 to use framework A.

Building instead of choosing a framework

Engineers might want to build their own framework instead of choosing an existing one. Under certain conditions, this could be beneficial.

If the software has unique requirements that cannot be met by existing frameworks, then it would justify building a bespoke framework. It could be a very specific domain, or it could have very strict non-functional requirements. For instance, engineers for **High-Frequency Trading** (HFT) software might write their own framework to meet ultra-low-latency requirements.

Building a bespoke proprietary framework might also be justified if the organization treats it as a competitive advantage in the market with cutting-edge technology.

It may also be the start of a new open-sourced framework in the community if no such framework has existed before. In this case, it may be beneficial to gather engineering talents among the communities and collaborate.

What if we made the wrong choice?

Despite all our best efforts, we might still have chosen the wrong framework. The framework may not have delivered the intended behaviors. The contributors may have given up on the project. The framework may have taken a novel approach that no longer suits our needs.

The adoption of the wrong framework becomes technical debt. Unfortunately, we need to source a replacement framework and plan the refactoring works to remove this dependency.

The technique of refactoring is beyond the scope of this book, though. And it is not always possible to avoid choosing the wrong framework. All we can do is exercise our due diligence in the process of decision. If appropriate, we can also create interfaces so that only minimal classes in the code base have direct reference to the framework, while the framework usage to the rest of the code base is transparent.

Documentation and diagrams

Software architecture as a blueprint of the system is captured in documentation and diagrams. Some of them could be captured in configuration files and templates, but when software architects need to present the system or communicate with stakeholders, documentation and diagrams are still the most used formats. Some of these diagrams will be used in upcoming chapters.

Business Process Model and Notation

Software systems, at a high level, can be seen as automated business processes that can be visualized in diagrams. **Business Process Model and Notation** (BPMN) standardizes graphical notations and provides a common language for modeling business processes. It is commonly used among engineers and stakeholders for communication and documentation purposes.

Taking the example of two households coming to a mutual agreement on the contract of services they exchange (the *service contract*), the business process could be modeled as follows:

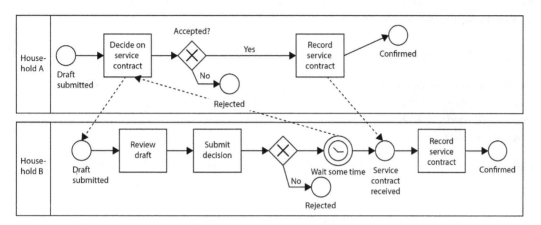

Figure 1.3 – Example of a BPMN diagram

Household A and **Household B** have their own swimlanes to illustrate the process on each side. **Household A** submits a draft of the service contract and **Household B** receives it. **Household B** reviews the draft and submits its decision. If **Household B** rejects the service contract, then both processes at **Household A** and **Household B** end. Otherwise, **Household B** waits for **Household A**'s response; meanwhile, **Household A** records the service contract, and the process ends. Finally, **Household B** receives the service contract from **Household A** and records the service contract, and the process ends.

BPMN has a rich collection of notations to describe business processes. They can be categorized into four groups.

Flow objects – activities, events, and gateways

Activities can be tasks and sub-processes that happen in the business process. **Events** are outcomes that have happened. **Gateways** are the points where a decision is made or the process splits into branches.

Connecting objects – sequences and associations

Sequences illustrate the flow of control and the messages communicated among flow objects. **Associations** describe the relationship among objects, such as inputs, outputs, or dependencies.

Swimlanes

Swimlanes are the groupings of flow and connecting objects based on the roles and responsibilities of participants involved in the business process.

Artifacts

Artifacts are additional information to the diagrams, and they provide context such as the data objects involved or simply free-text annotations.

Architecture decision record

Software architecture can be seen as a journey from problem discovery to solution implementation. Along the journey, there are a lot of decisions made to move the system forward. An **Architecture Decision Record** (**ADR**) is a document that captures the decision made based on the context at that time and the consequences coming with it.

There are many ADR templates available on the internet, which conceptually cover the following sections.

Status

This is typically just a single word to describe the current state of the ADR in the process. Here is an example of the ADR process:

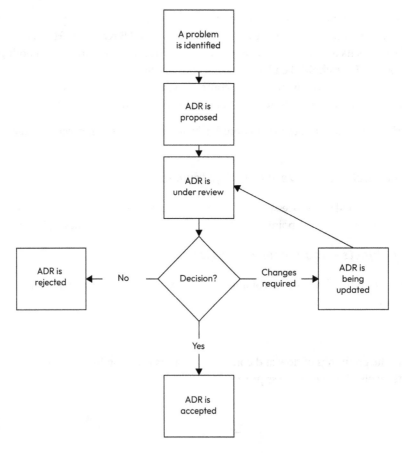

Figure 1.4 – An example of the ADR process

The basic possible states are **Proposed**, **Accepted**, and **Rejected**. In this example, there are other states, such as **Under Review** and **Changes Required**. It varies from one organization to another.

Context

This section should introduce the background where the discussions started. A good introduction would bring the needs of the change to the current situation e.g., pain points of the current operations, organization restructuring, business expansion, etc.).

It also introduces the terms that are used throughout the discussion so they can be easily referred to without ambiguity. A bit of the current organizational structure and technical infrastructure would also be helpful.

If applicable, this section can mention the current system quality attributes and why we want to change them. For instance, if our system can only handle 100 concurrent logins and the company wants to support 10,000 in the new technical design, then scalability is the system attribute this ADR proposes to change.

It should also mention the desired outcomes. This sets up a target state we want our change to achieve. The motivation here should refer to the problems mentioned previously and elaborate on how the outcome could improve business results.

Decision

This section describes the proposed change in detail. It should focus on how the change would produce the desired outcome described in the previous section. It may also mention the concerns raised and how the decision was driven by the discussion.

In some cases, alternative changes are mentioned. If they are mentioned, there should be a comparison between the proposed change and the alternatives. One way to compare is to list the pros and cons of each option. Another way could be to compare each option against a list of factors and conclude why an option is proposed.

Consequences

This section describes the impact of choosing the proposed change. Does it change the way the team operates? Which system attribute would it change and how? Does it optimize one aspect of the system but sacrifice another aspect? Which part of the system may become obsolete?

Request for Comments

Request for Comments (**RFC**) is a series of documents in which standards, protocols, procedures, and guidelines are proposed, discussed, agreed, and defined. **Internet Engineering Task Force** (**IETF**), a **standard development organization** (**SDO**), defined the numerous significant standards for the internet via the RFC processes, such as **Internet Protocol (IP)** version 4 (RFC 791) and 6 (RFC 2460), and **Hypertext Transfer Protocol (HTTP)** version 1.1 (RFC 2616).

RFCs can be submitted by anyone, and anyone is allowed to comment on existing RFCs. They go through an iterative review and feedback process in an open and transparent manner. They are usually initiated by subject experts but are maintained by the wider community. The outcome of an RFC can be standards and protocols adopted by the industry, which are useful for framework extension, further research, or the basis for the next RFC.

The format of an RFC document varies among organizations. In general, the document should cover the following sections.

Status

There are several possible statuses: **Drafted**, **Collecting Feedback**, **Accepted**, **Rejected**, and **Abandoned**.

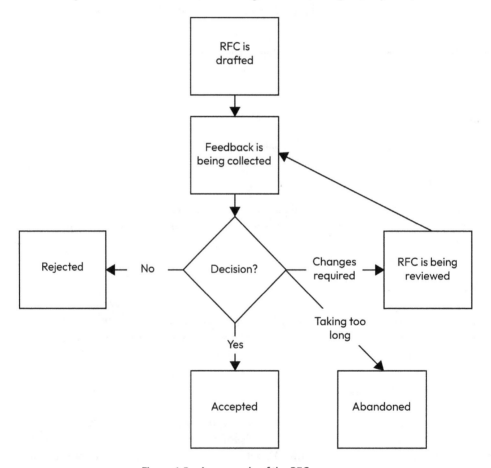

Figure 1.5 – An example of the RFC process

Once an RFC is drafted, it goes through a review and feedback iterative process. The RFC exits the iteration when it is either accepted, rejected, or abandoned.

Context

This section explains the need to submit this RFC. An example may be presented to illustrate the need for standardization or the problems caused by the lack of consistent protocols.

Approach

This section explains the approach agreed with the community after the review-feedback process. It should be as detailed as possible to capture the consensus of the approach.

Pros and cons

The benefits and drawbacks of the approach should be covered in detail so that it is clear to the community whether there should be another round of feedback collection, or at least the community is informed about the consequences of the approach.

Alternatives

This section mentions any alternative approach that was considered and discussed, but not adopted.

References

This section includes any previous RFCs mentioned, an academic paper, or any additional materials that give more context to the discussion.

Update log

As an RFC is likely to result in a lengthy review-feedback process, an update log is useful in keeping each meaningful change of the RFC in chronological order.

RFC and ADR

RFC and ADR share many similarities in their document formats, but they are also different in terms of usage. RFC focuses on industry standards and protocols among large communities, while ADR focuses on conventions within an organization. RFC tends to be closer to best practices, while ADR tends to be closer to solutions and code.

Despite the difference, RFC and ADR can work in collaboration. For topics that require consensus, expect long discussion, or have significant impacts, an RFC can be written first to come to an agreement on the approach. Then, an ADR can be written as a record of the decision and as a detailed technical specification of the approach.

UML diagrams

Unified Modeling Language (UML) is a software modeling language standardized from different modeling languages and notations since 1994. UML 1.0 was adopted as a standard by an international standards consortium called the **Object Management Group** (OMG) in 1997.

UML has a diverse collection of well-defined software elements that can form various diagrams that help engineers model business problems in a structural and visual manner. There are 14 UML diagrams, grouped into two categories.

Structural diagrams

Structural diagrams represent the static structure of a system. They focus on elements such as classes, objects, components, and packages. They emphasize how these elements are organized and connected with each other in a system. The following diagram is an example of a class diagram:

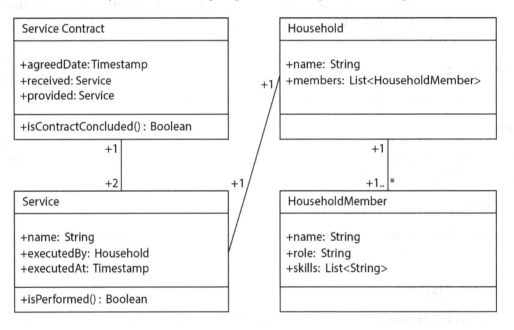

Figure 1.6 – An example of a UML class diagram

A class diagram usually contains classes and interfaces. Each class can contain a few attributes and a few functions. For example, the `ServiceContract` class has three attributes: `agreedDate`, `received`, and `provided`. The class also has one function, `isContractConcluded`, that returns a `boolean` value. The `received` and `provided` fields of the `ServiceContract` class references the other class, `Service`. We could say the multiplicity of the `ServiceContract` class to the `Service` class is one-to-two, as depicted in the diagram.

From the business perspective, a `ServiceContract` class is a contract of exchanged services modeled as two instances of the `Service` class: one is a `received` service and the other is a `provided` service. If the contract is mutually agreed, then the `agreedDate` field should capture the time when it was agreed.

There are seven UML structural diagrams, and there is a specific use for each, depending on which element is under the spotlight:

- **Class diagrams**, as illustrated, depict the static structure of classes, and their attributes, functions, and relationships with other classes.

- **Object diagrams** visualize the instances of classes and their relationships at a point in time, usually from a real-life example, to represent a snapshot of the system runtime structure.

- **Package diagrams** show how classes and components are organized into packages and the relationship among packages.

- **Component diagrams** represent the high-level logical or physical components that make up a system and their relationships.

- **Deployment diagrams** depict the software components physically deployed to hardware infrastructure and their connections to other physical nodes.

- **Composite structure diagrams** describe the internal structure of a class or a component, with a focus on how the internal fields and functions collaborate.

- **Profile diagrams** are extensible and customized diagrams that combine other UML diagrams. They facilitate UML language being extended to be domain-specific.

Behavioral diagrams

Behavioral diagrams represent the dynamic interactions of a system. They include elements such as actors, messages, activities, states, and transitions. The key focus in these diagrams is how the system's behavior emerges from the flow of control, interactions, or state transitions. The following is an example of a state diagram:

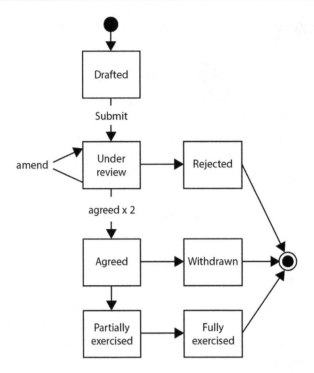

Figure 1.7 – Example of a UML state machine diagram

This state machine diagram describes the life cycle of a service contract between two households. It begins with the submission of a service contract drafted by one household. Then, while the service contract is under review, the service contract can be amended by either household, until it is either rejected or mutually agreed. Afterward, the service contract may still be withdrawn. Otherwise, the households involved exercise the services in the contract until both services are exercised and the service contract reaches the end of the life cycle.

There are seven UML behavioral diagrams. It is technically possible to use any of them to describe the same system behavior. The difference is the aspect of the behaviors shown in the diagram:

- **State machine diagrams**, as visualized, model how the system responds differently in each state and how the state transitions from one to another.

- **Communication diagrams**, also known as **collaboration diagrams**, emphasize the messages exchanged between objects or components.

- **Activity diagrams** represent a business or operational workflow of a component in a system as a sequence.

- **Interaction overview diagrams** represent a business or operational workflow of a component in a system, with a focus on interactions among components in a system.

- **Sequence diagrams** visualize the messages exchanged between objects and components in chronological order.

- **Timing diagrams** visualize the messages exchanged between objects and components within a period with a focus on time constraints and the ordering of events.

- **Use case diagrams** capture the interactions between actors and the system. Actors can be users or external systems, so actors can achieve their goals through the functions of the system.

The C4 model

The C4 model is a visual modeling approach developed in the 2010s. This approach originated from the observation that many software architecture diagrams were either lacking details (too high level) or overwhelmed with details (too low level). This approach aims to provide a set of guidelines and conventions to document architectures at the right level of abstraction.

It gained popularity over time among software architects and engineers who wanted a simple and effective way to document their systems. The **Structurizr** tool was developed by the C4 model creator, Simon Brown, to allow the creation of architecture models as code.

The C4 model can be described using the metaphor of maps: from a street view, where we could see pedestrians and cars on the roads, then zoom out to see a city map of how the main roads are connected in the city, then zoom out to see a country map, where we see the main cities and towns of the country, then to the world map, where we see the Earth.

The C4 model has four levels of abstraction. Each level helps different people to communicate and collaborate with the subject in question highlighted. It is helpful to bring up the right diagram in a meeting or workshop to start a conversation.

Level 1 – System context diagram

The **system context diagram** is the "big picture" diagram, and the major focus is the "system." The diagram should be centered around the system, and it interacts with actors, business operations, and external systems. This diagram is particularly useful for communication with non-technical stakeholders and external organizations.

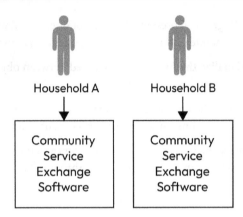

Figure 1.8 – An example of a system context diagram (C4 level 1)

The Community Service Exchange software is a standalone software installed as an isolated copy in each household. The copies of the software do not communicate with each other.

Level 2 – Container diagram

The **container diagram** zooms in on the "system" and focuses on how multiple containers inside the system work together. Each container here refers to a deployable process and has its own role, responsibility, and boundary in the system.

The container diagram can also be used to illustrate any middleware or infrastructure used in the system, such as messaging brokers, data stores, or filesystems.

This diagram is useful for communication with technical stakeholders such as platform engineers, database administrators, network engineers, or security engineers.

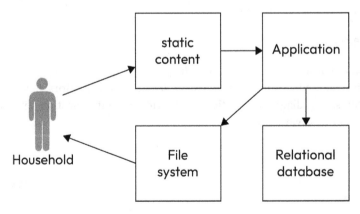

Figure 1.9 – An example of a container diagram (C4 level 2)

The Community Service Exchange software contains a module to organize all the static content such as images and fonts. There is an application module to validate data and run checks. The application module uses the relational database to persist the data required. The application module also retrieves report data from the relational database and exports it to the filesystem. The household can read the report file from the filesystem.

Level 3 – Component diagram

The **component diagram** zooms in a container and provides a view of how different components constitute a container.

It describes the input to the component (e.g., REST endpoints, message consumers, or a scheduler) and the output from the component (e.g., events, response to a request, etc.).

Another important function of this diagram is to demonstrate the logical packages inside the container that serve business operations. They typically load, transform, combine, and compute functions on multiple representations of entities modeled for the business purpose.

This diagram is closer to the software engineers, so they understand the context where they write code and scripts.

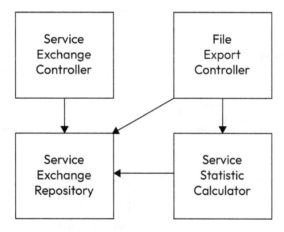

Figure 1.10 – An example of a component diagram (C4 level 3)

The application module of the Community Service Exchange software has a service exchange controller that operates a service contract (the "contract") between two households. It is business logic that manages the life cycle of a contract from the beginning till the end. It passes the contracts to the service exchange repository for persistence logic such as translating the contract entities into database tables and columns.

On the other hand, the file export controller serves a request from the household to generate a report of the contracts the household was involved in. The file export controller validates the request and generates the file ready to be available in the filesystem, which is outside of this application module. There is part of the statistical data on the contracts, and the calculations are done by the service statistic calculator.

Level 4 – Code diagram

Finally, we come to the lowest level of abstraction – the **code diagram**. This is a microscopic view of a component for engineers to understand the design patterns used, and how source code is represented in an abstract view in relation to other source files.

We could describe the entities modeled in the component and the relationship among them. That can be translated into a relational database schema.

We could be describing a process that involves multiple classes in the object-oriented style. We could demonstrate the fields captured in each class and how classes interact with each other.

It is not mandatory to have a code diagram for every part of the system because simple logic can be expressed directly in the source code. Typically, code diagrams are used to capture more complex interactions so engineers can be mindful when they are coding. This is also where you will see UML diagrams.

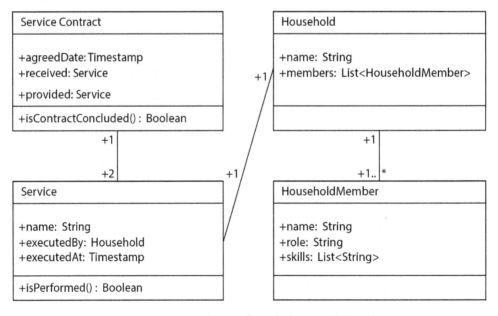

Figure 1.11 – An example of a code diagram (C4 level 4)

Inside `ServiceExchangeController`, there is a data class called `Household` that contains a list of `HouseholdMember` objects. The `HouseholdMember` data class models a household member who has the skills to execute a contract.

There is a `Service` class that captures the execution details of a contract from a household. It provides an `isExecuted` function that returns a Boolean value of `true` if its `executedBy` and `executedAt` fields are both not null.

The `ServiceContract` class models a service contract between two `Service` objects. It captures the date when the contract was agreed by both households. The receiver and the provider of the contract is a `Service` object. It provides an `isContractConcluded` function that returns a Boolean value of `true` if the result of the `isExecuted` function from both objects returns `true`.

Summary

We have covered the importance of software architecture with a real-world example. We discussed how software architecture plays a role in communication, training, budgeting, defining visions, and addressing cross-cutting concerns in the technology ecosystems.

We have discussed Conway's law and how the structure of an organization affects the architecture of systems.

We have navigated the topic of choosing a software framework in multiple scenarios with pros and cons.

We have also covered the documentation and diagrams that are often used in software architecture, such as ADRs, RFC, UML diagrams, and the C4 model.

In the next chapter, we will introduce some fundamental architectural principles that drive modern software architecture. We will break down and combine multiple concepts and illustrate them with the same real-world example.

2

Principles of Software Architecture

In this chapter, we are going to cover the fundamental principles of software architecture. They are vitally important to every part of software architecture. We should constantly remind ourselves of these, just like professional pianists practice scales every day.

We'll go through different ways to describe and view software architecture first. Then we'll cover a few important principles that will be referenced in later chapters. It is intended that you might go back to this chapter anytime and contemplate again some of these key concepts.

- Perspectives, dimensions, and qualities
- Separation of concerns, cohesiveness, and coupling
- SOLID principles
- YAGNI and future-proof architecture
- The Law of Demeter

Technical requirements

You can find all the code files used in this chapter on GitHub: `https://github.com/Packt Publishing/Software-Architecture-with-Kotlin/tree/main/chapter-2`

Perspectives, dimensions, and qualities

Software systems are not physical objects that we can easily see or touch. At their roots, they are instructions that are interpreted by a machine. So, we will need to visualize software systems in other ways.

The major purpose of visualizing software systems is to demonstrate how stakeholder concerns are addressed. There is usually a lengthy list of concerns. Each stakeholder usually has multiple concerns at various levels of abstraction. It is not possible to address all concerns from all angles in one visual representation.

The concept of **View** was introduced in the 1970s to describe software architecture. Since then, there have been numerous efforts to codify and standardize methods in describing software architecture. **ISO/IEC/IEEE 42010:2022** is the current standard in specifying software architecture, by which the architectural concepts, structure, and language are defined.

In a View, only selected perspectives of software architecture are portrayed. The selection aims at addressing certain stakeholder concerns. Moreover, there are multiple Views so each View can target specific concerns and specific stakeholders.

A **View Model** is a collection of Views wherein each View has a dedicated focus, purpose, and language for visualization.

The **4+1 architecture view model** was created by Philippe Kruchten in 1995. It includes four views of a software system, plus selected scenarios that help different stakeholders understand the software system from the perspectives of other stakeholders.

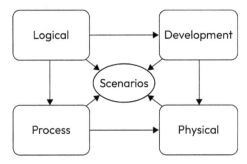

Figure 2.1 – A 4+1 architecture view model

Let's look at each view from the 4+1 architecture view model in the upcoming sections.

Logical view

The **logical view** focuses on the business functionality of the system and how it is implemented. It is agnostic to the technical concerns. It is an abstract view of how a business feature works without involving technical terms, using the language that both technical and non-technical stakeholders understand. It is suitable for communication with non-technical stakeholders.

In the example of the state transition of a service exchange contract between households, the logical view is expressed in the UML state diagram that follows:

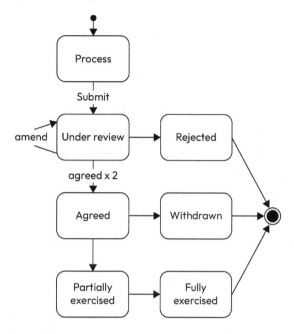

Figure 2.2 – A 4+1 architecture view model – logical view

A service contract between two households is first drafted by one household. The contract is of the **Drafted** state. Once the draft is complete, the household submits the contract to be reviewed by the other household.

The contract could be amended by both households before they reach an agreement. Both households must agree to the terms before going further. However, in some cases, the contract may be rejected by a household and thus enter the **Rejected** terminal state.

Assuming that both households agreed to the terms, there is still a chance that the contract could be withdrawn due to other circumstances. Assuming that the contract goes ahead, both households then exercise and fulfill the terms of the contract. This concludes the contract and reaches the end of its life cycle.

Physical view

The **physical view** focuses on the deployable software components and the interconnections between them. It is also called the **deployment view**. It is suitable for communication with system engineers, platform engineers, and infrastructure engineers.

Imagine that the ADR example we demonstrated in the previous chapter was approved. There is a central service to keep the master records of service exchange contracts. The physical view may look something like the following:

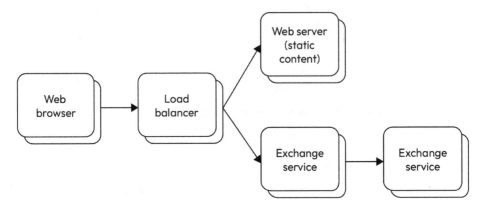

Figure 2.3 – A 4+1 architecture view model – physical view

The software has been moved to a browser-based web application. Users access the system via a web browser as a client and submit requests for service. The load balancer is the first component to receive these requests and distribute them to the appropriate instance of the **Exchange service** based on the load of each instance. Any static content such as images is fetched from a web server. The **Exchange service** processes the request and persists the result in the **Relational database**.

Process View

The **process view** focuses on the real-time behaviors of the system. It is usually close to the system's operation, where internal employees or other systems are involved. It is useful in showcasing issues involving concurrency, performance, and scalability. This view facilitates communication among technical stakeholders.

UML diagrams such as sequence diagrams, interaction diagrams, activity diagrams, communication diagrams, and timing diagrams are useful to represent a process view. **Business Process Modeling and Notation (BPMN)** diagrams are also useful in describing how the system behaves in the context of business processes.

If the service contract exchange system has an email notification function, it may look like the figure that follows:

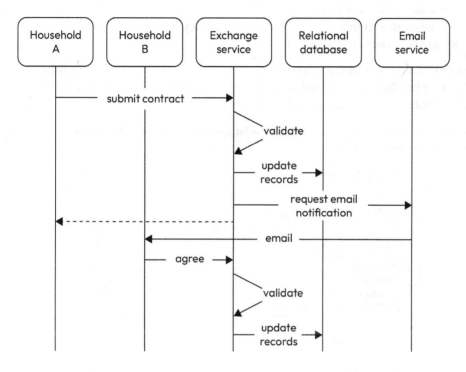

Figure 2.4 – A 4+1 architecture view model – process view

When **Household A** submits a draft contract, the **Exchange service** validates the request and updates the corresponding records in the **Relational database**. Afterward, the **Exchange service** makes a call to the **Email service** to send an email notification to **Household B** for the service contract submitted by **Household A**.

Household B, in this case, is notified of the service contract in the email. Then **Household B** submits a request to agree to the contract terms to the **Exchange service**. The **Exchange service** then updates the records in the **Relational database**.

Development view

The **development view** concentrates on software management. The target audience is programmers who are coding hands-on in the system.

The view focuses on the static organization of the software in the development environment. This includes how multiple components collaborate to form a software system at various levels, such as packages of source code, call hierarchies from higher-order business functions to lower-level utility functions, inheritance hierarchies of classes, and dependency trees of software artifacts. The details of this view can be found in the source code repository.

UML package and component diagrams can be used to represent this view. An organized source code repository may find these diagrams redundant. However, these diagrams are good at highlighting any dependency issues between packages and modules.

The **Exchange service** in the service contract exchange system may be expressed in a UML package diagram, as in the figure that follows:

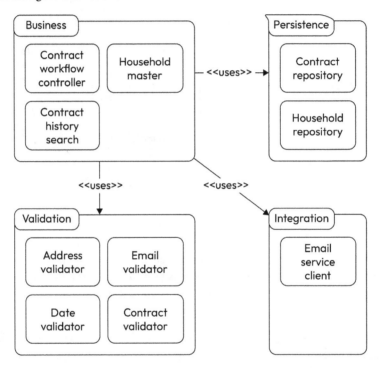

Figure 2.5 – A 4+1 architecture view model – development view

The **Exchange service** has a business package that includes the following:

1.   A module that controls the workflow of a service contract

2.   A module that master's the records of households

3.   A module that searches the history of service contracts

The **Business** package uses the **Persistence** package to perform the actual relational database operations for service contracts and households.

The **Business** package has a dependency on the **Validation** package, which contains a few standalone validators for addresses, emails, dates, and service contracts.

The **Integration** module is responsible for communicating with other services such as the **Email service**. This module is used by the **Business** module to notify households.

Scenarios

In the 4+1 architecture view model, scenarios are represented by the *+1* because only important scenarios would be chosen to be documented. It focuses on user-system interactions and on how the system facilitates users in their workflow. It is often used in communication with users, both internal and external.

UML use case diagrams are used for scenarios. In the example of the service contract exchange system, the drafting and exercising of the service contract are selected use cases.

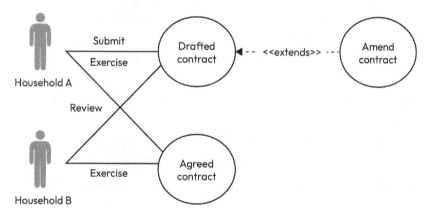

Figure 2.6 – A 4+1 architecture view model – scenario

Household A submits a drafted contract to be reviewed by **Household B**. The contract can be amended before it is agreed to. Once the households agree to the contract terms, they exercise the service contract to completion.

We have discussed the 4+1 architecture view model, which visualizes the architecture of a system from at least five perspectives. Each perspective visualizes the system using different dimensions to highlight certain aspects at a time. Each view is useful in communicating with its own audience.

Next, we are going to explore system quality attributes, which can be used to describe, measure, and predict how well a system can perform.

System quality attributes

If there are two functionally identical systems, how might we compare and evaluate which system performs better? We can use system quality attributes to measure and compare the two systems.

System quality attributes exist independently of the business functions that the system provides. They are purely technical attributes that determine whether a system runs smoothly or not. The requirements to have certain system quality attributes are called **Non-Functional Requirements (NFRs)** or **Cross-Functional Requirements (CFRs)**.

It is important to differentiate between functional requirements and NFRs. Functional requirements define what the system does, while NFRs define how the requirements are fulfilled. Functional requirements specify the features of a system, while NFRs define its qualities, behaviors, and performance characteristics.

There are many dimensions for system quality attributes. Here we will highlight several system quality attributes that we will cover in later chapters:

- **Correctness**: This measures whether the system behaves as described in the specifications. This could be referred to as **Application Programming Interface (API)** documentation, operation manuals, or simply function contracts.

- **Availability**: This measures the uptime of the system or the time when it can operate and serve its purpose.

- **Robustness**: This refers to the level of service the system can provide when the system has faulty parts and/or is under heavy traffic.

- **Resilience**: This refers to how quickly the system can recover from faults, continue to operate, and bounce back from unexpected disruption to a fully functional state.

- **Performance**: This measures how quickly the system can respond to requests and how many requests the system can process at a time.

- **Scalability**: This measures how flexibly the system can scale to cope with changing the volume and latency requirements. It is the ability of the system to expand or shrink.

- **Observability**: This refers to how well the external view of the system helps us determine its internal state. The external view can be represented by log messages, charts, alerts, files, or the payload of a system remote call.

- **Manageability**: This measures how easy it is to manage and control a system in terms of operations, monitoring, configuration, and administration.

- **Maintainability**: This measures how easy it is to maintain a working system. This can include source code, updating infrastructure, modifying build pipelines, and tweaking environments.

- **Extensibility**: This measures the ease of extending the current capability of the system to include new functions as the business grows. It includes the time, complexity, and effort required to modify and enhance the current system.

- **Testability**: This measures the extent to which tests can cover the functionality of the system. It is not limited to the business functions to be tested but also includes the assessment of other system quality attributes.

- **Reusability**: This refers to the extent to which the individual components of the system can be reused for other purposes. This includes not only the software modules and source code but also the business functions and processes.

- **Usability**: This translates to how good the user experience is while working with the system. It is not limited to end users who treat the system as a black box but also includes other stakeholders such as internal users, system operators, administrators, and programmers.

We have covered a few important system quality attributes that we will mention in later chapters. We are going to discuss the fundamental architecture principles that drive modern software architecture and help us improve current systems.

Separation of concerns, cohesiveness, and coupling

A system is composed of many components and the interconnections among them. The ability to group and separate elements in the system has become a crucial factor in ensuring it is maintainable, reusable, and extendable. We are going to cover three fundamental concepts that will help us group and separate elements appropriately, namely **separation of concerns**, **cohesiveness**, and **coupling**.

Separation of concerns

Separation of concerns is a fundamental principle that we should apply in every corner of the system. It is a principle that advocates segregating the system into independent components and having each component address a specific concern. Separation of concerns aims at creating a system that is easier to maintain, reason, and update, and which can adapt to changes in requirements over time.

Let us take the following scenario as an example: the submission of a draft service exchange contract from a household's browser to **Exchange service** via **Representational State Transfer (REST)** with payload in the **JavaScript Object Notation (JSON)** format.

The first concern will likely be to ensure that **Exchange service** only takes the correct information to create a draft service in the **Relational database**.

Within the correctness category, there are multiple levels:

1. The request payload needs to conform to the agreed structure; otherwise, an HTTP 400 (Bad request) status should be returned.

2. The services to be exchanged must not be empty; otherwise, an HTTP 400 (Bad request) status should be returned.

3. The households in the contract must already exist in the system records; otherwise, an HTTP 404 (Not found) status should be returned.

4. The household that submitted the draft contract must already have logged on; otherwise, an HTTP 401 (Unauthorized) status should be returned.

5. The household that submitted the draft contract must already have been verified; otherwise, an HTTP 403 (Forbidden) status should be returned.

6. If the request passes all validation checks and the contract persists, an HTTP 200 (OK) status should be returned with the payload of the persisted record.

7. If the request passes all validation and the contract persists, the contract should be in the **Drafted** state.

The list goes on. However, we could see that, for example, the payload is at the syntactical level. Returned HTTP statuses, on the other hand, are at the contractual communication level, while being in the correct state is at a semantic level.

If a change addressing one concern for a part of the system is made without affecting the other concerns, then this change is aligned with the separation of concerns principle.

To be able to separate concerns when modifying a system, some parts of the system will need to be grouped together and other parts need to be separated.

The degree to which the software elements within a component are closely related can be measured by cohesiveness. The degree of independence of each component can be measured by coupling.

Cohesiveness

Software components that are strongly related to each other have a few properties. Firstly, they share similar responsibilities and most likely have a common objective. Secondly, if you change one component, it is likely that the rest of the components will require changes as well. Finally, they coordinate and cooperate in at least one manner. Chained function calls are examples of cohesive components.

Software components can be cohesive in the following ways.

Horizontal cohesiveness

Horizontally cohesive components are grouped together to provide features related to a certain implementation. For example, components related to integration with a particular external system are grouped together to separate the concerns of vendor-specific implementation from the functional behaviors that the system provides. In the case of reviewing vendor choices, engineers can replace this group of components with another group that targets a different vendor system. This cohesive approach supports a plug-and-play structure that is easy to maintain and understand.

Vertical cohesiveness

Vertically cohesive components are grouped together based on the functional behaviors that they collectively provide. Vertical cohesiveness usually involves **encapsulation** of data and behaviors shared among components in the group. For example, components responsible for providing **Create, Read, Update, Delete (CRUD)** operations for managing households can be grouped together. This grouping provides clarity on how the system behaves. When the behaviors must be modified, engineers can focus on a small area and lower the risk of change.

Linear cohesiveness

Linearly cohesive components are grouped together due to the sequence of their execution or the flow of control. This could be manifested by chains of function calls or by a chained reaction of event communication. This grouping provides clarity and visibility for how smaller tasks or processes emerge into a larger workflow.

Interactive cohesiveness

Interactively cohesive components are grouped based on the frequency of communication and interaction patterns among them. For example, the HTTP service and the client library of a certain function are grouped under a project of different modules. When there is a change in communication protocol, engineers can find most of the necessary changes in one project. This reduces the cost and effort of making a change. It also keeps the change contained in one area.

Look at the example of household validation that follows:

```
data class Household(
    val name: String,
    val members: List<Person>,
)

data class Person(
    val firstName: String,
    val lastName: String,
    val age: Int,
    val skills: List<String>,
)

fun Household.validate(): List<String> =
    listOfNotNull(
        if (name.isBlank()) "name must not be empty" else null,
    ) + members.flatMap { it.validate() }

fun Person.validate(): List<String> = listOfNotNull(
    if (firstName.isBlank()) "first name must be non-empty" else null,
    if (lastName.isBlank()) "last name must be non-empty" else null,
    if (age < 0) "age must be non-negative" else null,
)
```

A household has a name and a list of members. Each member has a few basic fields such as first and last names. A basic household validation would involve ensuring that the household name is not empty; moreover, it also requires that each person in the household passes the validation. For example, age cannot be a negative number.

In this example, the validation of a household depends on the validation of a person in that household. The functions to validate both the household and the person are vertically cohesive because they behave as a validation feature in the form of a higher-order function. They are also linearly cohesive because the validation function of a household invokes the validation function of a person.

High cohesiveness concentrates related components in one place. This illustrates the overall behavior of the components and makes the behavior easier to understand. It also promotes better testability as engineers can test the components' overall behavior in one place. Keeping related components in one place also means fewer moving parts when making a change, which lowers risk. The overall behavior can be treated as one unit that other parts of the system can reuse.

On the other hand, low cohesiveness results in related components being scattered around, making them difficult to understand, modify, and maintain. It creates inappropriate coupling between components, making it riskier to make changes without affecting unrelated parts of the system. Attempting to modify one system quality attribute can result in the unintended effect of changing the others. You are also more likely to create bugs when making a change. It then becomes difficult to reuse the component as it brings dependencies that are unlikely to be suitable for the use case.

Coupling

Coupling is a bad idea in the context of cohesiveness, but the measurement of coupling is not bad at all. It provides a view of how interdependent the software components in the system are.

Coupling is inevitable, but it can be minimized in a way that promotes better maintainability, reusability, and understanding. It is preferable to limit the interactions among components as much as possible.

Functional coupling

To limit the interactions among components, we must separate what needs to be done from how to do it. In the previous example, the "what" is the validation of households including their members; the "how" is that the validation functions run through each field and add violated conditions to a list to be returned. The household is valid if the returned list is empty.

The definition of the work performed by a software component is a contract between the provider and the invoker. It typically consists of an input, an optional state, and an output. The invoker is concerned with the input to supply and the output to receive, but not with what happens internally within the software component. On the other hand, the provider is concerned with how to compute the output and optionally update the state based on the given input.

This contract is often referred to as an interface between the provider and the invoker. It gives a good foundation for loosely coupled software components. With the interaction of both parties centered around the interfaces, the invoker now has the flexibility to switch to a different provider who can fulfill the contract. The provider need not do anything extra for another invoker who wants to reuse this functionality.

This type of coupling is called **functional coupling**. It is based on the contracts or interfaces among software components.

Data coupling

A software component may require the data that it shares with another to function properly. The ownership of data is a topic in itself. However, in a simple sense, if there is only one component that creates, updates, or deletes a category of data, then that component owns the data.

It is almost guaranteed that if more than one component owns the same piece of data, there will be a big problem in keeping the data reliable and consistent. In this situation, it is better for the two components to truly own their data.

There are several options to consider:

1. Should the components that share the same data be merged into one component?

2. Can the ownership of the data be split among the components so they no longer share the same data?

3. Can a new component be extracted to own the data, while other components become the listeners of the data change?

4. Should one of the components take all the responsibility of creating, updating, and deleting the data, effectively becoming the owner of the data? This would mean that the other components become the listeners of the data change.

5. Should each component own a copy of the data and let each copy be diverse in each component?

6. Can each component keep a separate copy of the data owned by another component while there are reconciliation processes in place to process the difference?

Given that a software component can own the data, it is important for the component to decide how much of the data should be exposed externally. The component should encapsulate the data to hide any internal data and only expose the fields that are related to the interface to other components.

Moreover, it is often useful to separate the internal and external representations of the data. For instance, a list of internal error enumeration values may contain information that exposes the internal state of the component unintentionally.

For example, given that there are several internal error enumeration values for a log-on operation, then the Kotlin enum class would look like the following code:

```
enum class InternalError {
    WRONG_PASSWORD,
    USERNAME_NOT_FOUND,
    FAILED_CAPTCHA,
    TIMED_OUT,
    INVALID_REQUEST
}
```

If we expose all these values externally, the invoker of the component will be able to understand whether a username exists even if the log-on operation failed, or if both were valid but failed the captcha challenge. These are unnecessary details to the outside of the component and should be hidden. This is without mentioning the obvious security concern that is also at play. So, we could create a list of external error enumeration values to only show what is of interest to the invoker:

```
enum class ExternalError {
    FAILED_AUTHENTICATION,
    TIMED_OUT,
    INVALID_REQUEST
}
```

Temporal coupling

Two software components can be temporally coupled if they both need to be available for the whole operation to run through. Component A might need to invoke a synchronous remote call to component B to continue to handle its incoming requests, for example. An even worse situation would be a chain of multiple remote cascading calls to multiple components. An example of temporally coupled components is described in the UML sequence diagram that follows:

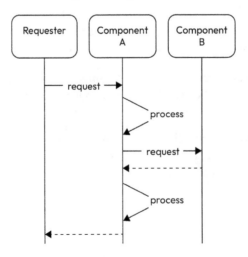

Figure 2.7 – A Synchronous pull interaction

Each time a synchronous call is made, it blocks the thread until there is an answer returned or until it times out. This is also called the **pull-based** approach. If we had multiple of these calls, it would be quite easy to cause a timed-out error to the original request.

Synchronous remote calls have the nature of blocking the thread, pulling data, and depending on the component's availability. There are cases where synchronous remote calls may be necessary due to time sensitivity, such as when the service must authenticate a user within a given number of seconds or time out.

If all the synchronous remote calls are only there to provide data, then we can consider an asynchronous and **push-based** approach. Using this approach, component A subscribes to a topic whereby component B publishes an event when the data changes. Component A then keeps a copy of the data locally. Then component A no longer requires component B to be available to handle requests; component A uses the last known value instead. An example of asynchronous push interactions among components is illustrated as a UML sequence diagram in *Figure 2.8*:

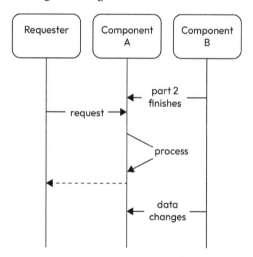

Figure 2.8 – An asynchronous push interaction

If the interaction between components A and B is more procedural and sequential, then the components can still be loosely coupled by being reactive and asynchronous using events. In this scenario, component A has processed up to the point where it needs component B, so component A sends an event, and component B receives it. Then component B performs the work. When component B finishes its part, it sends an event that component A receives. Component A then continues the rest of the work. An example of the asynchronous reactive event-driven interaction among components can be expressed by a UML sequence diagram as follows:

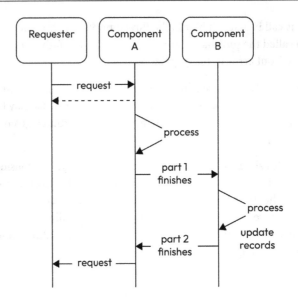

Figure 2.9 – An asynchronous reactive event-driven interaction

We have discussed the principles of separation of concerns, cohesiveness, and coupling. We went through why they are important and how the application of these concepts affects system quality attributes. We also covered the sub-categories of cohesiveness and coupling with real-time world examples. They are three different concepts but relate to each other often.

Next, we are going to cover the **SOLID principles**. These principles encourage software architecture with separate concerns, highly cohesive components, and low coupling between components.

SOLID principles

The SOLID principles are a set of five software architecture principles that advocate for creating maintainable, understandable, flexible, and modular software. Though they were originally targeted at object-oriented software, the concepts behind them are useful and can be applied to systems other than object orientation.

These concepts were first introduced by Robert J. Martin in his *Design Principles and Design Patterns* paper in 2000. However, the SOLID acronym was introduced later by Michael Feathers.

The acronym SOLID stands for the following:

- **Single Responsibility Principle (SRP)**
- **Open-Closed Principle (OCP)**
- **Liskov Substitution Principle (LSP)**

- **Interface Segregation Principle (ISP)**

- **Dependency Inversion Principle (DIP)**

We will walk through each of them and use the concepts that we have covered for discussion.

SRP

The SRP states that a class should have one responsibility or concern, and only one. There is only one reason to change. If a class conforming to this principle has a clear and well-defined purpose and it is then easier to understand, test, and maintain, it can be counted as an exception.

Let us have a look at a class that violates the SRP:

```
interface HouseholdService {
    fun create(household: Household): Household
    fun draftContract(contract: Contract)
    fun notifyHouseholds(contract: Contract)
}
```

The HouseholdService interface is responsible for creating a household, drafting a contract, and notifying the households involved in a contract. This class can change due to a change in any one of these operations.

We can refactor the example to conform to SRP:

```
interface HouseholdService {
    fun create(household: Household): Household
}
interface ContractService {
    fun draftContract(contract: Contract)
}
interface NotificationService {
    fun notifyHouseholds(contract: Contract)
}
```

Now HouseholdService is only responsible for managing households. The ContractService interface is solely responsible for drafting a contract. NotificationService only aims to notify the households involved in a contract. Now each class only has one responsibility and one reason to change.

There are a few more benefits that come with this change. Each class is now more testable, easier to understand, and easier to maintain. Each class can evolve and extend its functions independently. A concern in a single class can be addressed without impacting the others. Other classes can also reuse one of these classes easily without pulling in some never-to-be-used functions.

OCP

The OCP states that software components such as classes, modules, and functions should be open for extension but closed for modification.

A component is *open* if its behaviors can be extended without modifying the existing code. A highly cohesive component already contains all strongly related elements, so an extension of the behavior only needs to use what is already provided and does not need to modify the code inside.

A component is *closed* if it can be used by other components. We should be able to modify the implementation without changing the behaviors. A loosely coupled component offers a simple and straightforward way for it to be used by other components without pulling in dependencies that others may not wish to include.

In the following example, there is a `NotificationService` that notifies households of the status of the contract in which they are involved:

```
interface NotificationService {
    fun notifyHouseholds(contract: Contract)
}
class SmsNotificationService : NotificationService {
    override fun notifyHouseholds(contract: Contract) {
        // send SMS messages to household's phone numbers
    }
}
class EmailNotificationService : NotificationService {
    override fun notifyHouseholds(contract: Contract) {
        // send messages to household's email addresses
    }
}
```

We have an interface that defines a `notifyHouseholds(contract: Contract)` function. `SmsNotificationService` and `EmailNotificationService` are concrete implementations of the interface.

If we want to extend the behavior by adding a new medium of communication, such as phone app notifications, we can create a new concrete implementation without modifying any existing code. This interface is *open* for extension.

We can reuse this interface in other situations where we need to notify households about their contract. We can update the way in which `EmailNotificationService` is authenticated with the **Simple Mail Transfer Protocol (SMTP)** server without changing the interface. This interface is *closed* for modification.

LSP

The LSP states that the objects of a superclass can be replaced by objects of its subclasses with no change in the correction of the system.

In other words, all subclasses should behave functionally identically to their superclasses.

From the previous example, NotificationService specifies that the notifyHouseholds function would notify the households involved in the given contract. From a behavioral function point of view, it can do this via emails, text messages, or any other ways of communication. However, all these subclasses should notify the households that are involved in the given contract.

On the contrary, if there is a PhoneNotificationService that not only notifies households involved in a contract but also updates the contract status to UNDER_REVIEW, it would violate the LSP. This is because if EmailNotificationService is replaced by PhoneNotificationService, the contract status will be updated, which would not happen before the replacement:

```
class PhoneNotificationService : NotificationService {
    override fun notifyHouseholds(contract: Contract) {
        // ring an automated message to household's phone
    // also update contract status to UNDER_REVIEW
    }
}
```

If we adhere to the LSP, then we will have classes that are highly cohesive, as it only focuses on classes being behaviorally equivalent to their superclasses and nothing else.

ISP

The ISP states that clients should not be forced to depend upon interfaces that they do not use.

This principle promotes that interfaces should be designed to be specific to the needs of the clients that use them. This could result in a few outcomes:

- **Small and numerous interfaces**: The interface is small, so the clients do not need to depend on functions from an interface that they do not use. Since each interface is smaller, there are likely to be more interfaces to cover the same scope of functionalities.

- **Relevance**: The interface is relevant and specific to the needs of the clients. Different clients may have unique needs. Therefore, there may be a few specific interfaces for different clients. There may be an overlap of functionalities and some clients may want unique behaviors that are only relevant to them for different clients.

- **Higher cohesiveness**: Each interface shall contain only related functions and ideally focus on one responsibility.

- **Looser coupling**: Since the interfaces are smaller, the coupling with other components is also looser.

This is an example of a violation of the ISP:

```kotlin
interface Human {
    fun logOn()
    fun exerciseContract()
}
data class User(val username: String) : Human {
    override fun logOn() {
        // user log on
    }
    override fun exerciseContract() {
        throw UnsupportedOperationException("user cannot exercise
contract")
    }
}
data class HouseholdMember(val name: String) : Human {
    override fun logOn() {
        throw UnsupportedOperationException("household members do not
log on")
    }
    override fun exerciseContract() {
        // exercise contract
    }
}
```

The Human interface has two functions: `logOn` and `exerciseContract`. There are two concrete implementations: `User` and `HouseholdMember`. While both users and household members are human, they have nothing in common functionally. Both subclasses were forced to implement functions that they had no use for. The interface should be segregated so that they are specifically targeted toward the functions for users and household members.

DIP

The DIP consists of two parts:

1. High-level components should not depend on low-level components directly. Both should depend on abstractions.

2. Abstractions should not depend on details; details should depend on abstractions.

Abstractions can be referred to as interfaces and details can be referred to as concrete implementations. The rationale behind the principle is that the user of a component should only care about the behaviors of the component, not its implementation.

For example, if we want to reuse the component that notifies the households involved in a contract in a workflow, then the principle suggests that we reference the component as the NotificationService type, even if we know that EmailNotificationService is the concrete implementation.

This approach brings a few benefits:

- The NotificationService interface can be mocked or replaced by a **test double** easily during unit testing. There is no need to set up an EmailNotificationService. Our unit tests focus on how to interact with NotificationService, handling several types of outcomes from the notifyHouseholds function.

- The dependency on NotificationService can be injected or looked up at runtime. This gives us the flexibility to swap it with a different concrete implementation and have the function still run correctly. An **Inversion of Control (IoC)** container framework can support the implementation of the injection.

- Coupling with NotificationService is loosened to only care about the behaviors.

- The code is easier to maintain as swapping the concrete implementation of NotificationService requires no code changes.

- It is easier to extend NotificationService by providing a different concrete implementation.

Let us look at the ensuing example and see whether it adheres to the DIP:

```
class ContractWorkflowService(
    val emailNotificationService: EmailNotificationService,
) {
    fun agree(contract: Contract): Contract {
        return contract.copy(agreedAt = Instant.now()).also {
  emailNotificationService.notifyHouseholds(contract)
        }
    }
}
interface NotificationService {
    fun notifyHouseholds(contract: Contract)
}
class EmailNotificationService : NotificationService {
    override fun notifyHouseholds(contract: Contract) {
        // send messages to household's email addresses
    }
}
```

ContractWorkflowService has a function to mark a contract as agreed. After the contract is agreed to, it invokes EmailNotificationService to notify households about the agreement. However, ContractWorkflowService uses the function from the interface NotificationService and not the subclass.

There is no need for ContractWorkflowService to reference the concrete implementation as the service does not concern itself with whether the notification is sent via email or another channel. This is a violation of the DIP.

The Law of Demeter

The **Law of Demeter**, or the principle of least knowledge, states that a software component should have limited knowledge about the inner details of other components. More specifically, a component should not know about the internal details of another component.

Let us say there is a function that returns the city in the address of a person:

```
class Person(val name: String, val address: Address) {
    fun getAddressCity(): String {
        return address.city
    }
}
class Address(val city: String)
```

The Person class directly accesses the city property inside the Address class. The Person class should not have this knowledge, as this is a violation of the **Law of Demeter**.

This creates a coupling between Person and Address. The coupling dictates that if the city property changes its data type, then both classes will need to change. It also means that the code change is bigger than it needs to be, hence making it less maintainable and testable.

To conform to the Law of Demeter, the getAddressCity function should be provided by the Address class. This reduces the responsibility of the Person class for getting the city of an address and thereby reduces the complexity of the code base.

YAGNI and future-proof architecture

You Ain't Gonna Need It (YAGNI) is a principle that states that functionalities should not be implemented until they are needed. This principle came from **Extreme Programming (XP)** as an approach to improve software quality and respond to changing business requirements.

This principle is also related to the idea of minimalism in software development, which states that we should avoid unnecessary code and complexity in exchange for clean, easy-to-understand, and extensible software.

Another way to describe YAGNI is as the imperative to do the simplest thing that works. This is by no means an incomplete design or unfulfilled user requirement. It still promotes complete and functional software that satisfies user requirements with the simplest design available.

YAGNI aims at a few practices:

- **Simple and lean code base**: By implementing only what is necessary now, a lot of complexity can be avoided. As a result, the code base is simple, clean, and maintainable.

- **Prevention of over-engineering**: Over-engineering happens when an engineer anticipates future requirements and includes unused features in the system. It not only results in wasted time on unnecessary work but also becomes a dead weight in the code base, which is then made harder to maintain. Over-engineered code also implies a design choice made before there is sufficient information to make that choice, locking in the approach prematurely.

- **Adaptive and flexible implementation**: By delaying the implementation of a feature until it is needed, engineers have more options to adapt to changes when the feature is finally needed. It also encourages a more organic evolution of the system whereby engineers respond more effectively to changing requirements.

- **Productivity**: By focusing on the absolute must-have requirements, engineers can deliver changes more quickly and efficiently. Any unnecessary features can be postponed, saving time and resources.

There is also an opposite idea though: **future-proof architecture**. It aims at creating systems that are unlikely to be obsolete or to fail in the future. This sounds very appealing. If we can build a system that can fulfill future requirements, we will have saved time and effort that would otherwise be spent continuously evolving it.

However, there is an assumption behind this. You need to predict the new requirements and you need to be right. That is equivalent to knowing the future. It rarely happens.

If you are certain about requiring a feature in the future, then it is neither a prediction nor a future requirement. It is simply a requirement now.

This does not mean that we should build systems based on short-term objectives or take shortcuts. Instead, we should build systems that are ready to adapt to new requirements but not have these implemented.

Capacity planning should not be mistaken for future-proof architecture. Capacity planning is an operational concern related to deployment and physical resources. For instance, building a road to handle twice the current traffic is different from building a branch of the road that goes nowhere. Leaving headroom for expansion, extra volume, and extra traffic is part of the readiness for evolution. Capacity planning is an NFR, not a future requirement. We would not want the system to run on edges that may collapse in response to a fluctuation in the volume of requests.

This mindset leads to a few outcomes. The software architecture aims for modular, extensible, and flexible components that are ready to make changes when they become necessary.

It implies that each component is highly cohesive but loosely coupled. It means that interfaces are small and specific. It also means that interactions among components are based on abstract interfaces and not concrete implementations. It further means that subclasses conform to the behaviors of their superclasses and are ready to be extended. Furthermore, it means that each component has only one reason to change. It also means that modifying a component does not require recompiling the entire system. It also means that concerns are separated so that when we want to adjust system quality attributes, we can address the particular concern in isolation.

Summary

We have covered the 4+1 architecture view model, as well as system quality attributes, separation of concerns, cohesiveness, coupling, the SOLID principles, and the Law of Demeter. We have demonstrated them with code examples. These demonstrated that adhering to these principles lets the code become modular, flexible, maintainable, extensible, and easy to understand.

We have also discussed the conflicting concepts of the YAGNI principle and future-proof architecture. We clarified what future-proofing is and how it is different from capacity planning.

In the next chapter, we will explore polymorphism and its alternative approaches.

Polymorphism and Alternatives

In this chapter, we are going to take a real-life example and solve the problem by implementing various solutions using different approaches. We will use **polymorphism** as a baseline for the solution. Afterward, we will use other approaches that are powered by the Kotlin language. Finally, we will compare them and try to understand which one is suitable under which circumstances.

We will cover the following topics in this chapter:

- Why Kotlin?
- Real-life example – revisited
- Polymorphic solution
- Sealed class solution
- Delegation solution
- Functional solution
- Comparison and summary

Technical requirements

You can find all the code files used in this chapter on GitHub: `https://github.com/PacktPublishing/Software-Architecture-with-Kotlin/tree/main/chapter-3`

Why Kotlin?

Kotlin is chosen to be the primary programming language for all the examples in this book. There are several reasons for this choice:

- Kotlin has gained significant popularity since it was released in 2011
- It can be used for both frontend and backend applications, which allows for a wide range of architecture topics to be illustrated with the same language

- It has a concise, readable, and expressive syntax that helps us understand the implementation without a deep understanding of the language

- It is interoperable with Java so code examples can leverage existing numerous libraries in both Java and Kotlin if applicable

Real-life example – revisited

We are using the same real-life example as in *Chapters 1* and *2*. This example is as follows. In a village, households provide services to and receive services from other households. To provide clarity to the exchange of services among households, software was created to keep records of the contract for exchanged services (the "contract").

After both households have agreed on the services to be exchanged in the contract, each household will need to perform the service. Here are a few examples:

- Repairing a piece of furniture

- Making a dress

- Babysitting a toddler for x hours

- Performing a trick at a party

- Donating a used piece of clothing

- Providing food and drinks

- Cleaning n rooms in the house

We need to be able to capture the details of these services and to be able to verify that the service has been performed. Once both services in a contract have been performed, the contract is concluded and reaches its terminal state. Let us focus on one scenario, in which Household A performed a service for Household B and Household B confirmed that Household A performed the service as per the contract. The sequence of interactions can be briefly described in the following UML sequence diagram:

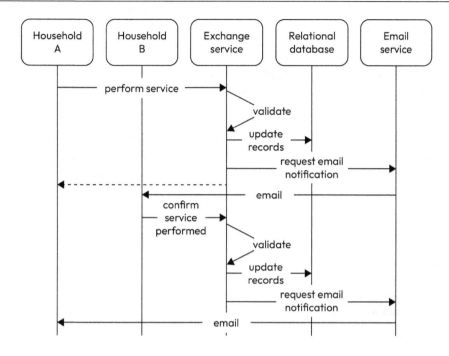

Figure 3.1 – Revisiting the real-time example

Inside the **Exchange Service**, we need to provide two functions. One function is provided for a household performing a service for the other household. Another function is provided for a household to confirm that the service was performed by the other household as per the contract. The problem is that distinct types of services would require different ways to claim and confirm completion.

For example, if the service is to repair an item, then it only takes the repairer household to acknowledge that the item has been repaired. The receiver household would confirm that the item was repaired. If the service is to babysit a toddler, then the babysitter household may instead log the hours spent babysitting to confirm that the service was performed. Sometimes, the service is an aggregation of multiple sub-services.

Minimally, there should be two functions to perform a service and to check whether a service was performed:

```
interface Service {
    fun performService(time: Instant)
    fun wasServicePerformed(): Boolean
}
```

For this exercise, let us assume that we need to support three types of services: plumbing, babysitting, and room cleaning:

- The plumbing service requires the plumber household to report the service as started and completed; the other household then confirms this

- The babysitting service requires the babysitter household to log the start of the session and track it until the other household picks up the toddler and logs the total duration of the service

- The room cleaning service requires the cleaner household to log the start of the service and the rooms cleaned, then the other household to confirm that all rooms, as per the contract, have been cleaned

Let us start by solving this exercise with a polymorphic approach.

Polymorphic solution

In object-oriented programming, polymorphism provides a powerful way to abstract an interface of many forms. Polymorphism literally means *many forms* in Greek.

The common interface of the households contains a function called `performService` to signal the start of the service, as well as a function called `wasServicePerformed` to return true if the service was performed as per the agreement:

```
interface Service {
    fun performService(time: Instant)
    fun wasServicePerformed(): Boolean
}
```

This solution can be illustrated in the following UML class diagram:

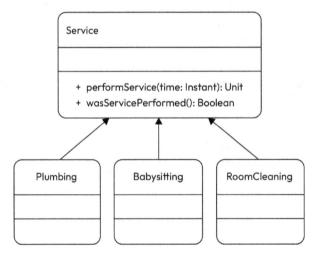

Figure 3.2 – Polymorphic solution

The `Plumbing` class is relatively simple. It provides a function for the household to start the service, a function to report the service completed, and a function for the other household to confirm that the service has been performed. Meanwhile, timestamps are recorded that indicate when the service was performed, completed, and confirmed:

```
class Plumbing : Service {
    var startedAt: Instant? = null
    var completedAt: Instant? = null
    var confirmedAt: Instant? = null
    override fun performService(time: Instant) {
        startedAt = time
    }
    fun completeService(time: Instant) {
        completedAt = time
    }
    fun confirmService(time: Instant) {
        confirmedAt = time
    }
    override fun wasServicePerformed(): Boolean {
        return startedAt != null && completedAt != null && confirmedAt
!= null
    }
}
```

The `Babysitting` class is different because the completion criterion is based on the duration of the service. The class's constructor takes an agreed number of hours to determine whether the service has been completed. There is one function for the babysitter household to start the job and another for the other household to confirm the end of the job. If the duration is the same as or longer than the agreed hours, the service is considered performed:

```
class Babysitting(val agreedHours: Int) : Service {
    var startedAt: Instant? = null
    var endedAt: Instant? = null
    override fun performService(time: Instant) {
        startedAt = time
    }
    fun endService(time: Instant) {
        endedAt = time
    }
    override fun wasServicePerformed(): Boolean {
        return if (startedAt == null || endedAt == null) {
            false
        } else {
```

```
                    Duration.between(startedAt, endedAt).toHours() >=
    agreedHours
            }
        }
    }
```

The RoomCleaning class has performed the service when all the rooms in agreement have been cleaned. The constructor takes a Set of room names, which is later used to check whether all of the rooms in the agreement have been cleaned. It has one function for the cleaner to start the job and another for the other household to confirm whether each room has been cleaned:

```
class RoomCleaning(val agreedRooms: Set<String>) : Service {
    var startedAt: Instant? = null
    val roomCleaned: MutableSet<String> = mutableSetOf()
    var endedAt: Instant? = null
    override fun performService(time: Instant) {
        startedAt = time
    }
    fun cleaned(
        time: Instant,
        room: String,
    ) {
        roomCleaned.add(room)
        if (allAgreedRoomsCleaned()) {
            endedAt = time
        }
    }
    private fun allAgreedRoomsCleaned() = roomCleaned.
containsAll(agreedRooms)
    override fun wasServicePerformed(): Boolean =
allAgreedRoomsCleaned()
}
```

There is a main function to have all these households perform the service and the results are printed:

```
fun main() {
    val now = Instant.now()
    val plumbing = Plumbing()
    plumbing.performService(now)
    plumbing.completeService(now.plus(2, HOURS))
    plumbing.confirmService(now.plus(2, HOURS).plus(3, MINUTES))
    println("Was plumbing service performed? ${plumbing.
wasServicePerformed()}")
    val babysitting = Babysitting(3)
    babysitting.performService(now)
```

```
    babysitting.endService(now.plus(3, HOURS))
    println("Was babysitting service performed? ${babysitting.
wasServicePerformed()}")
    val roomCleaning = RoomCleaning(setOf("Kitchen", "Bathroom"))
    roomCleaning.performService(now)
    roomCleaning.cleaned(now.plus(3, HOURS), "Kitchen")
    println("Was room cleaning service performed? ${roomCleaning.
wasServicePerformed()}")
}
```

The program should print something like this:

```
Was plumbing service performed? true
Was babysitting service performed? true
Was room cleaning service performed? false
```

The plumbing service starts with a timestamp. Then it is completed with a timestamp after two hours. After three minutes, it is then confirmed as complete with a timestamp. Since all three timestamps exist, the service has been performed.

The babysitting service has a duration of three hours in the agreement. It started with a timestamp and ended time with a timestamp three hours later. The duration is exactly three hours. This matches the agreed hours, so the service has been performed.

The room-cleaning service lists both the kitchen and the bathroom in the agreement. Only the kitchen was reported to be cleaned with a timestamp, so the service has not been performed yet.

This approach results in a homogeneous yet polymorphic style and facilitates three different services that have certain shared behaviors.

Sealed class solution

The Kotlin language has a feature called **sealed class**, which restricts the class hierarchy and requires that all subclasses be defined at compile time. All subclasses need to be in the same package and module where the sealed class is defined. This also means that no third-party classes can be inherited from sealed classes.

Here are a few observations from the polymorphic solution mentioned previously. Firstly, all subclasses have a startedAt field and an implementation of the performService function that sets the startedAt field. So, the sealed class solution can be modified from the polymorphic solution. The interface can be changed to a sealed class with the startedAt field and the performService function:

```
sealed class Service {
    var startedAt: Instant? = null
    fun performService(time: Instant) {
        startedAt = time
```

```
    }
    abstract fun wasServicePerformed(): Boolean
}
```

The subclasses can be simplified by using the sealed class implementation as follows:

```
class Plumbing : Service() {
    var completedAt: Instant? = null
    var confirmedAt: Instant? = null
    fun completeService(time: Instant) {
        completedAt = time
    }
    fun confirmService(time: Instant) {
        confirmedAt = time
    }
    override fun wasServicePerformed(): Boolean {
        return startedAt != null && completedAt != null && confirmedAt
!= null
    }
}
```

The performService function has been implemented by the Service superclass, so there is no need to implement it in the subclasses:

```
class Babysitting(val agreedHours: Int) : Service() {
    var endedAt: Instant? = null
    fun endService(time: Instant) {
        endedAt = time
    }
    override fun wasServicePerformed(): Boolean {
        return if (startedAt == null || endedAt == null) {
            false
        } else {
            Duration.between(startedAt, endedAt).toHours() >=
agreedHours
        }
    }
}
```

The same simplification applies to the RoomCleaning subclass:

```
class RoomCleaning(val agreedRooms: Set<String>) : Service() {
    val roomCleaned: MutableSet<String> = mutableSetOf()
    var endedAt: Instant? = null
    fun cleaned(
```

```
        time: Instant,
        room: String,
    ) {
        roomCleaned.add(room)

        if (allAgreedRoomsCleaned()) {
            endedAt = time
        }
    }
    private fun allAgreedRoomsCleaned() = roomCleaned.
containsAll(agreedRooms)
    override fun wasServicePerformed(): Boolean =
allAgreedRoomsCleaned()
}
```

The sealed `Service` class has the `startedAt` field and the `performService` function to facilitate the starting of the service, while the subclasses have their own variations to complete it.

The power of the Kotlin sealed classes is not the restriction of having all subclasses known at compile time. The power lies in what the compiler does with the restriction. If we use the `when` construct together with sealed classes, we can reduce our program to be as follows:

```
sealed class Service {
    var startedAt: Instant? = null
    fun performService(time: Instant) {
        startedAt = time
    }
    fun wasServicePerformed(): Boolean {
        return when (this) {
            is Babysitting -> durationCoversAgreedHours()
            is Plumbing -> areAllDatesPresent()
            is RoomCleaning -> allAgreedRoomsCleaned()
        }
    }
}
```

As the `Service` class has the implementation of the `wasServicePerformed` function using the `when` construct, the subclasses do not need to implement this function at all:

```
class Plumbing : Service() {
    var completedAt: Instant? = null
    var confirmedAt: Instant? = null
    fun completeService(time: Instant) {
        completedAt = time
    }
}
```

```
    fun confirmService(time: Instant) {
        confirmedAt = time
    }
    internal fun areAllDatesPresent(): Boolean {
        return startedAt != null && completedAt != null && confirmedAt
!= null
    }
}
```

Like the Plumbing subclass, other subclasses will now only contain the body of functions related to completing the service in various forms:

```
class Babysitting(val agreedHours: Int) : Service() {
    var endedAt: Instant? = null
    fun endService(time: Instant) {
        endedAt = time
    }
    internal fun durationCoversAgreedHours(): Boolean {
        return if (startedAt == null || endedAt == null) {
            false
        } else {
            Duration.between(startedAt, endedAt).toHours() >=
agreedHours
        }
    }
}
class RoomCleaning(val agreedRooms: Set<String>) : Service() {
    val roomCleaned: MutableSet<String> = mutableSetOf()
    var endedAt: Instant? = null
    fun cleaned(
        time: Instant,
        room: String,
    ) {
        roomCleaned.add(room)
        if (allAgreedRoomsCleaned()) {
            endedAt = time
        }
    }
    internal fun allAgreedRoomsCleaned() = roomCleaned.
containsAll(agreedRooms)
}
```

The compiler enforces that all subclasses are included in branches of the when construct. If they are not, it will not compile. In addition, the `this` instance is automatically cast (**smart cast**) to the specific subclass in each branch, so we can directly access the fields defined in the subclass.

In this implementation, all variations of the check for services performed are grouped together in the when construct as branches. It is better than an enum implementation because you will not overlook a subclass, given that we do not use `else` as a branch.

Also, as these are subclasses of a sealed class, all the subclasses are known and we can easily compare the variations in a single function.

However, this pattern is useful only when there are a small number of subclasses and they have similar implementations. Also, this pattern does not support the extension of functionality outside the package.

Delegation solution

Delegation is often considered an alternative to the polymorphic solution. In this approach, an extension of a function is implemented by delegating part of the responsibility to other classes and then extending its behaviors. As a result, there is no mandatory requirement to create a subclass. There are several reasons for that:

- Loose coupling and high cohesion
- Separation of concerns
- Easy substitution
- Refactoring to the delegation solution

Loose coupling and high cohesion

Using delegation, code can be reused and composed only for the parts that are needed. It is more flexible than inheriting a class that is likely to give the subclasses more than it needs. This results in looser coupling to the reused code while still maintaining high cohesion within the class.

Separation of concerns

With the use of delegation, classes can be broken into small classes (sub-classes) that only have a single responsibility. These classes are only delegated on demand. As a result, each class has a clear focus and responsibility. Classes are therefore easier to maintain, test, and understand.

We are also able to break away from any change of superclass in unrelated implementation that may cause unintended changes in behaviors. We simply separate unrelated implementations from what is really needed.

Easy substitution

If we need to have a different behavior, it is easier to swap the delegate object than to swap an inherited superclass. Not only are there fewer functions to implement in delegate objects than a different superclass but it is also possible to swap to delegate objects at runtime dynamically.

As long as the subclasses conform to the **Liskov Substitution Principle (LSP)**, there is no behavioral change in substituting subclasses.

Refactoring to the delegation solution

To refactor to the delegation solution, we will break down responsibilities into smaller interfaces. We will have an interface that starts a service and another interface that checks whether a service was performed:

```
interface ServiceStarter {
  fun start(time: Instant)
}
interface ServiceChecker {
  fun wasServicePerformed(): Boolean
}
class Started : ServiceStarter {
  var startedAt: Instant? = null
  override fun start(time: Instant) {
    startedAt = time
  }
}
```

Plumbing, babysitting, and room cleaning are three services that are completed very differently.

The plumbing service has three phases: *Started*, *Completed*, and *Confirmed*.

Figure 3.3 – A three-phase service

It can be expressed as a `ThreePhaseService` that is also a `ServiceStarter` and `ServiceChecker`. However, we already have the concrete `Started` class as an implementation of `ServiceStarter`, so we can use the Kotlin delegation feature to specify that the implementation of `ServiceStarter` is realized by the `started` field provided in the constructor with a `Started` default value:

```kotlin
interface ThreePhaseService : ServiceStarter, ServiceChecker {
  fun complete(time: Instant)
  fun confirm(time: Instant)
}
class ThreePhaseServiceImpl(val started: Started = Started()) :
    ThreePhaseService, ServiceStarter by started {
  var completedAt: Instant? = null
  var confirmedAt: Instant? = null
  override fun complete(time: Instant) {
    completedAt = time
  }
  override fun confirm(time: Instant) {
    confirmedAt = time
  }
  override fun wasServicePerformed(): Boolean {
    return started.startedAt != null && completedAt != null &&
confirmedAt != null
  }
}
```

Then, `Plumbing` is merely a specialization of `ThreePhaseServiceImpl` that we can define as a one-liner by Kotlin delegation:

```kotlin
class Plumbing : ThreePhaseService by ThreePhaseServiceImpl()
```

The babysitting service has only two phases: *Started* and *Ended*. The duration, or the amount of time between the start and end times, determines whether the service has been performed. Here is a simple UML state diagram to capture the phase transition.

Figure 3.4 – Hourly service phase transition

It can be expressed as an `HourlyService`. Again, we can make use of the Kotlin delegation to avoid code duplication:

```
interface HourlyService : ServiceStarter, ServiceChecker {
    fun end(time: Instant)
}
class HourlyServiceImpl(val agreedHours: Int, val started: Started =
Started()) :
    HourlyService, ServiceStarter by started {
    var endedAt: Instant? = null
    override fun end(time: Instant) {
        endedAt = time
    }
    override fun wasServicePerformed(): Boolean =
        if (started.startedAt == null || endedAt == null) {
            false
        } else {
            Duration.between(started.startedAt, endedAt).toHours() >=
agreedHours
        }
}
```

After that, `Babysitting` is declared as a one-liner delegated class:

```
class Babysitting(agreedHours: Int) : HourlyService by
HourlyServiceImpl(agreedHours)
```

Lastly, the room cleaning service is repeated in a loop until all agreed items have been completed. Here is a simple UML state diagram to capture the phase transition.

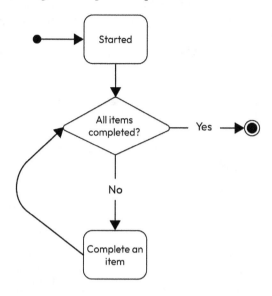

Figure 3.5 – Itemized service phase transition

We can treat each room as an item that is completed individually in the name of ItemizedService. We also use the generic T type to make it flexible:

```
interface ItemizedService<T> : ServiceStarter, ServiceChecker {
  fun complete(time: Instant, item: T)
}
class ItemizedServiceImpl<T>(val agreed: Set<T>) : ItemizedService<T>,
ServiceStarter by Started() {
  val completed: MutableSet<T> = mutableSetOf()
  var endedAt: Instant? = null
  override fun complete(time: Instant, item: T) {
    completed.add(item)
    if (allAgreedItemsCleaned()) {
      endedAt = time
    }
  }
  private fun allAgreedItemsCleaned() = completed.containsAll(agreed)
  override fun wasServicePerformed(): Boolean =
allAgreedItemsCleaned()
}
```

RoomCleaning can now be defined as follows:

```
class RoomCleaning(agreedRooms: Set<String>) :
    ItemizedService<String> by ItemizedServiceImpl(agreedRooms)
```

This example of a delegation solution can be illustrated by the following UML class diagram:

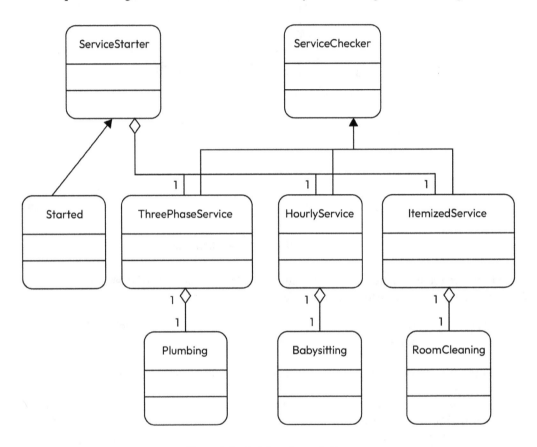

Figure 3.6 – A delegation solution

Putting them all together, we need to modify a bit of the main function only because the function names are different. The program behaves in the same way:

```
fun main() {
    val now = Instant.now()
    val plumbing = Plumbing()
    plumbing.start(now)
    plumbing.complete(now.plus(2, HOURS))
    plumbing.confirm(now.plus(2, HOURS).plus(3, MINUTES))
```

```
    println("Was plumbing service performed? ${plumbing.
wasServicePerformed()}")
    val babysitting = Babysitting(3)
    babysitting.start(now)
    babysitting.end(now.plus(3, HOURS))
    println("Was babysitting service performed? ${babysitting.
wasServicePerformed()}")
    val roomCleaning = RoomCleaning(setOf("Kitchen", "Bathroom"))
    roomCleaning.start(now)
    roomCleaning.complete(now.plus(10, MINUTES), "Kitchen")
    println("Was room cleaning service performed? ${roomCleaning.
wasServicePerformed()}")
}
```

From this example, we can see how easy it is to reuse the code. For example, if there is another service that needs to run for an agreed hour, we can reuse the `HourlyService` using delegation without the need to implement the same logic again. We also need not write the same test.

This pattern reduces duplicated code and testing. It also promotes each class to be more specific and focused on its responsibility. It makes any extension of existing features easier, since it does not impose inheriting a concrete superclass.

Functional solution

Functional programming uses a completely different mindset in approaching the problem. The fundamental elements can be categorized into **immutable data structures** and **pure functions**.

Immutable data structures

An immutable data structure cannot be changed once it has been created. If a new value is needed to capture a change, new data structure instances are created and usually transformed from the existing ones. This approach makes data reliable and thread-safe.

Kotlin provides the **data class** construct that comes with standard functions such as `toString`, `hashcode`, and `equals` for free. Combined with the use of the `val` keyword and exclusive refereces to other immutable data, we can easily create an immutable data structure.

Here are the equivalent data structures for the example:

```
data class Plumbing(
    val startedAt: Instant? = null,
    val completedAt: Instant? = null,
    val confirmedAt: Instant? = null,
)
data class Babysitting(
```

```
    val agreedHours: Int,
    val startedAt: Instant? = null,
    val endedAt: Instant? = null,
)
data class RoomCleaning(
    val agreedRooms: Set<String>,
    val startedAt: Instant? = null,
    val completed: Set<String> = emptySet(),
    val endedAt: Instant? = null,
)
```

It is worth noting that all fields are declared with `val`, so the references cannot be changed. Also, the `Instant` class that is used in many fields is also immutable.

The `Set` interface has no mutable functions declared. Although a mutable concrete implementation could be injected that makes the data class not strictly immutable, if we only use the functions declared in the interface and the concrete implementation conforms to the LSP, there should be no behavioral change.

Also, the fields that may have a different value in another instance come with either a nullable declaration (?) or default values. Kotlin constructors can provide these values if they are not specified during invocation.

Kotlin provides a `copy` function for data classes to be mutable as a separate instance. For example, a plumbing service can be started by the following code:

```
val plumbing = Plumbing()
val started = plumbing.copy(started = Instant.now())
```

However, merely using the `copy` function may seem too low-level and does not help communicate the intent of the code. It may be better to have a function with a better name such as `start` that invokes `copy` to make the intent obvious.

Pure functions

Functions are said to be pure if, when they are given the same input, they always produce the same output and have no side effects. To achieve this, the function does not mutate any external data or state. It does not use any randomization or system clock functions either. It does not invoke any function that creates side effects, such as making a database update or calling an external system remotely. It is deterministic, predictable, testable, and thread-safe.

In the real-life example of the households used in this chapter, all three services need to start the service despite all of them having different forms. Also, we want to have a better function name to communicate intent. Kotlin supports **parametric polymorphism** through generics so that our `start` function can work with multiple types. In addition, we use **lambda expressions** so that each type can specify its own way to create a new instance of new values.

The `start` function looks something like the following:

```
fun <T> T.start(time: Instant, transform: T.(Instant) -> T): T =
transform(time)
```

It declares a generic T type as the function receiver so we can invoke the function in the style of `T.start` as an **extension function**. The function also requires a transform lambda expression in order to transform the T type to create a new instance of T with the `startAt` time. This is an example of the invocation of the `start` function:

```
Plumbing().start(now) { startedAt -> copy(startedAt = startedAt) }
```

`Plumbing()` creates a new instance of `Plumbing` without a `startAt` time. Then the `start` function is invoked by supplying an `Instant` object and a lambda expression specifying the creation of a new `Plumbing` instance with a `startedAt` field set using the `copy` function.

The rest of the functions

Other functions that are specific to the types of services can be declared separately:

```
fun Plumbing.complete(time: Instant): Plumbing = copy(completedAt =
time)
fun Plumbing.confirm(time: Instant): Plumbing = copy(confirmedAt =
time)
fun Babysitting.end(time: Instant): Babysitting = copy(endedAt = time)
fun RoomCleaning.complete(
    time: Instant,
    room: String,
): RoomCleaning {
    val newCleaned = completed + room
    val newEnded = if (completed.containsAll(agreedRooms)) time else
endedAt
    return copy(completed = newCleaned, endedAt = newEnded)
}
```

Note that it is not mandatory to use extension functions for the preceding functions. They can be declared inside the body of their corresponding data classes. Declaring them as extension functions, however, does provide flexibility in that they can be in a different package than the data classes.

The functions to determine whether the service was performed are also different for each type of service.

```
fun Plumbing.wasServicePerformed(): Boolean = startedAt != null &&
completedAt != null && confirmedAt != null
fun Babysitting.wasServicePerformed(): Boolean =
    if (startedAt == null || endedAt == null) {
        false
```

```
    } else {
        Duration.between(startedAt, endedAt).toHours() >= agreedHours
    }
fun RoomCleaning.wasServicePerformed(): Boolean = endedAt != null
```

Lastly, the main function looks different from other solutions, mainly because every change in the service would end up in a new instance when using the main function:

```
fun main() {
    val now = Instant.now()
    val plumbing =
        Plumbing()
            .start(now) { startedAt -> copy(startedAt = startedAt) }
            .complete(now.plus(2, HOURS))
            .confirm(now.plus(2, HOURS).plus(3, MINUTES))
    println("Was plumbing service performed? ${plumbing.
wasServicePerformed()}")
    val babysitting =
        Babysitting(3)
            .start(now) { startedAt -> copy(startedAt = startedAt) }
            .end(now.plus(3, HOURS))
    println("Was babysitting service performed? ${babysitting.
wasServicePerformed()}")
    val roomCleaning =
        RoomCleaning(setOf("Kitchen", "Bathroom"))
            .start(now) { startedAt -> copy(startedAt = startedAt) }
            .complete(now.plus(10, MINUTES), "Kitchen")
    println("Was room cleaning service performed? ${roomCleaning.
wasServicePerformed()}")
}
```

Since every function uses the data class or the generic type as the receiver, the calls can be chained in the sense that the output of the current function is the input of the next.

The code could end up like the **Domain-Specific Language (DSL)** style of expression. DSL is a specialized language designed only for a specific domain or problem. It is different from general programming languages like Kotlin or Python, which are designed to solve a wide range of problems. Powered by Kotlin's concise and expressive syntax, it is possible to produce DSL code that is close to natural language. For example, the construction of the Babysitting object can be refactored to look like the following:

```
val babysitting = Babysitting()
        .withAgreedHoursOf(3)
        .startAt(startTime)
        .endAt(endTime)
```

Comparing all the solutions

All these solutions are valid, though their styles vary a lot. It is important to understand the pros and cons of each approach so we can make an informed decision to apply the solution wherever appropriate:

- **Extensibility**:

  - **Polymorphic**: Extensible outside package and module

  - **Sealed classes**: Not extensible outside package or module

  - **Delegation**: Extensible outside package and module

  - **Functional**: Extensible outside package and module

- **Readability and code cleanness**:

  - **Polymorphic**: Subclasses may inherit unnecessary features from superclasses, creating noise while reading code; classes can be big

  - **Sealed classes**: All subclasses are known at compile time; no missing branches; not suitable for too many subclasses

  - **Delegation**: Small interfaces; multiple behavioral delegations can be complicated; promotes single responsibility per interface; only delegates behaviors on demand

  - **Functional**: Small classes and functions; easy to reason about immutable data and pure functions; not so easy readable when it uses recursion, monads, and higher-level abstractions

- **Testability**:

  - **Polymorphic**: Each subclass would require testing of all behaviors to ensure it behaves like its superclass, that is, that it conforms to the LSP; also, each subclass would require testing on subclass-specific logic

  - **Sealed classes**: Behaviors implemented in superclass only need to be tested once; any when clause and subclass-specific logic need to be tested

  - **Delegation**: Each small behavioral unit can be tested individually and need not repeat in its delegation

  - **Functional**: All small classes and functions can be tested individually without the need for repetition; each test would only need to verify the output given the input

- **Thread safety**:

  - **Polymorphic**: Not thread-safe by nature

  - **Sealed classes**: Not thread-safe by nature

- **Delegation**: Not thread-safe by nature
- **Functional**: Thread-safe due to immutable data classes and pure functions

Summary

We used the example of three types of services (plumbing, babysitting, and room cleaning) that households can perform for each other, focusing on the start, completion, confirmation, and checks for whether the service was performed.

We presented a solution that uses traditional polymorphism in object-oriented programming. An interface was defined and implemented by three subclasses, one for each type of service. The `main` function uses these subclasses in a homogeneous yet polymorphic manner.

We then used the Kotlin sealed class feature to restrict all subclasses to be known. A further variation was that the sealed class was used together with the `when` construct to handle all branches within the `when` block. It resulted in a function containing all variations of the service check behaviors suitable for a small and fixed number of subclasses in a package.

We presented an alternative solution that uses Kotlin delegation over polymorphism. We defined smaller interfaces for each responsibility and identified a service starter class. Then we created three classes that use the service starter class by delegation. Plumbing, babysitting, and room cleaning services were then declared as one-liners using delegation. This style allowed us to reuse code without inheriting a superclass that might have provided more than the subclasses needed.

Then we used the functional approach to create immutable data classes for each type of service. We used parametric polymorphism and lambda expressions to create a `start` function for shared behavior among the three types of services. We declared several extension functions with the service as the receiver to enable chains of calls in the `main` function.

Lastly, we compared all the solutions in terms of extensibility, code readability, testability, and thread safety. We also briefly mentioned when a particular solution is suitable and when it is not.

In the coming chapters, we will go through several architectural patterns commonly used in today's industry. We will group similar patterns together and compare them so you will be able to customize them to solve real-life problems.

Peer-to-Peer and Client-Server Architecture

This chapter explores two fundamental architectural patterns for organizing and structuring communication systems: **peer-to-peer** (**P2P**) and **client-server** architectures. These architectural patterns have significantly impacted the way we design and implement various modern network systems.

This chapter provides a comprehensive understanding of the P2P and client-server architectures, in terms of their principles, characteristics, and applications. Afterward, we will compare and identify the crucial differences between these two approaches and analyze their respective strengths and limitations.

We will cover the trade-offs and pros and cons of the P2P and client-server architectures. More importantly, we will discuss factors to consider when deciding between these two models, with the desired system quality attributes such as scalability, fault tolerance, security, and control. We will also explore the possibility of a hybrid model for flexibility and adaptability.

In this chapter, you will learn about the following topics:

- A real-life example of a networked system
- Client-server architecture
- P2P architecture
- Comparison between client-server and P2P architectures

Technical requirements

You can find all the code files used in this chapter on GitHub: `https://github.com/PacktPublishing/Software-Architecture-with-Kotlin/tree/main/chapter-4`

A real-life example of a networked system

We will use the same real-life example that we have been using in previous chapters. Households in a village exchange services with each other. Each household has an isolated copy of the software that keeps the records of the contract for exchanged services.

They are suffering an ongoing problem; that is, sometimes two households that exchanged services have a discrepancy between the contract records kept in their own copy of the software. This has caused a few disputes among households.

An engineer wants to eliminate these disputes by synchronizing the contracts between two copies of the software. The synchronization requires two copies of the software to be connected. An oversimplified interaction of the synchronization is illustrated in *Figure 4.1*:

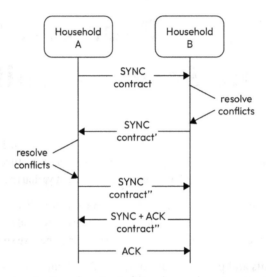

Figure 4.1 – Synchronization of contracts for exchanged services among households

In the diagram, *Household A* sends the details of the contract to *Household B*. The received contract is compared against the contract stored locally in *Household B*. *Household B* resolves the conflicts for any differences found. The revised contract (*contract'*) is then sent to *Household A*. *Household A* also compares the contracts and resolves any conflicts. *Household A* sends another revised contract (*contract"*) to *Household B*. This time, *Household B* does not find any differences and therefore acknowledges *Household A* with the contract. *Household A* receives the acknowledgment from *Household B* and sends a final acknowledgment that both households have synchronized the contract.

Given that we have a way to synchronize contracts between two copies of the software, we still need a way for them to discover each other and communicate.

We are going to explore the P2P and client-server architectures in the next section and relate them to the context of solving the problem in this example.

Client-server architecture

Client-server architecture is a model for organizing distributed systems and computer networks. In this architecture, the roles of the client and the server are clearly defined, and each component plays at least one of them.

Clients are devices or components that request resources or services, and servers are the devices or components that serve requests or provide services. An example of client-server architecture over the internet is illustrated in *Figure 4.2*:

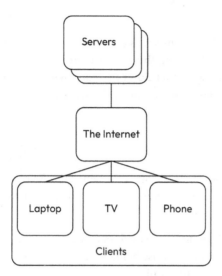

Figure 4.2 – Client-server architecture (C1)

Usually, clients are everyday user-facing devices such as laptops, phones, and televisions. They tend to be lightweight devices with limited computation power, and they usually only need to be available during communication with servers.

Servers are devices dedicated to serving requests and are usually hosted in the cloud or data centers. They usually have more computational power, more storage, and more network bandwidth, and are highly available to serve requests from clients. Systems with client-server architecture start with servers being available to serve requests from clients.

Interactions between clients and servers

Interactions between clients and servers fall into a request-response model. Clients send to servers a request that identifies a resource or specifies the details of the service needed. Servers receive the request, validate it, process it, and send back a corresponding response containing the requested resources or the outcome of the service.

Note that clients always initiate the interaction and have the knowledge of how to locate the servers. On the contrary, servers only know the location of the client within the context of the corresponding request.

As a result, the resources or services provided are centralized in servers. Clients do not directly communicate with other clients. Any resource that might need to be shared among clients is hosted on servers and is available to be requested by clients instead.

This architecture results in much higher and broader non-functional requirements for servers compared to clients. We are now going to discuss some of the key system quality attributes in servers.

Availability

Servers usually need to be available as much as possible, so they are operational to serve requests from clients whenever required. Typically, this means there are redundant instances of the servers running at the same time. There might be a failover mechanism to route requests to an available server, a backup system to recover the last known state of the server, and monitoring tools to proactively ensure servers are up.

Performance

Servers are centralized to serve numerous clients at the same time. Being fast and efficient is paramount to sustaining servers to be operational. Latency and throughput are the two major system quality attributes for performance.

Latency under client-server architecture is the total time that has elapsed between a request being sent from a client and the corresponding response being received by a client. Throughput is the number of requests that arrive in servers per time unit.

The performance of servers depends on multiple factors, such as processing power, memory, network bandwidth, and disk I/O. There are usually multiple components in servers that contribute to performance-related system quality attributes, such as filesystems, databases, messaging middleware, and even third-party systems.

Scalability

Servers sometimes need to cope with a growing and shrinking number of client requests. Here are some common approaches to managing this.

A load balancer can be deployed to distribute the requests from clients to a pool of servers. It keeps track of the health and traffic of each server instance so it can aim to route requests to the less busy server and archive an equal workload among servers.

Servers can be horizontally scaled by running more instances to distribute the load, or vertically scaled by upgrading the hardware capabilities of servers.

There should also be a configuration of a minimum or desired number of running server instances, so the number of servers can drop when the load is not heavy.

Security

The requests are centralized to be served in servers and the corresponding data is also centralized in servers. Security becomes of significant importance. There are at least four major areas to address.

Firstly, servers should only process incoming requests that come from identifiable clients. Clients need to be authenticated by various means, such as passwords or multi-factor verifications. The details of the approaches will be covered in *Chapter 14*.

Servers should also have control over which requests can be accepted by which client. For example, a normal client cannot access system settings while an administrator client can. Clients are usually authorized by internal processes not visible outside servers, so clients are not able to bypass the checks.

The data in the request and response payload may contain personal or sensitive information that requires protection. In these cases, the communication between clients and servers may require encryption in an agreed-upon protocol. The encryption method may be personalized so that a client's data cannot be read by other clients.

Servers will also need to have a basic defense against common malicious attacks, for example, **denial of service (DOS)**, **cross-site scripting (XSS)**, and **man in the middle (MitM)**.

Server discovery

Clients need to locate an available server to send their requests. There are several common discovery mechanisms:

1. Static and hardcoded addresses as client configurations
2. **Domain Name System (DNS)**, which translates server IP addresses into human-readable domain names
3. Dynamic DNS services that dynamically change the server addresses
4. Service registry services that allow clients to query the appropriate server to connect to
5. Load balancers that distribute requests from clients to a pool of available servers
6. Service mesh, which abstracts service discovery, load balancing, and other network concerns with a dedicated infrastructure layer

Common client-server architectures

There are many variations of architecture styles that handle the communication between clients and servers:

1. **As an exchange of representations of resources: Representational state transfer (REST)** is a popular client-server architecture that focuses on the exchange of resources using standard HTTP methods such as GET, POST, PATCH, and DELETE.
2. **As remote procedure calls (RPCs):** An RPC sees a request from a client as an action to perform, and therefore the URLs usually end with a verb (e.g. /place or /update) while using mostly only the GET and POST HTTP methods.
3. **As asynchronous messages:** In this architecture, clients and servers do not directly contact each other. Instead, they communicate through messaging infrastructure as queues and topics.

4.   **As two-way dedicated connections**: Clients and servers open a dedicated channel over a **Transmission Control Protocol** (TCP) connection to communicate. This style of communication is usually seen in systems that require lower latency and frequent messaging.

The client-server solution

We are going to apply the client-server architecture to solve the real-life example of service contract synchronization between two households. It is recommended to draft the interactions between clients and servers before coding. Let us assume HTTP as the communication protocol.

We will use REST architecture in this solution. We need to define endpoints that are provided by servers so clients can use these endpoints to facilitate the necessary communication.

Step 1 – defining client-server communication

Let us illustrate a sample scenario of client-server communication:

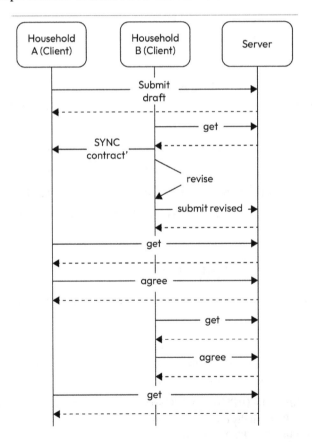

Figure 4.3 – Sample client-server interaction for service contract synchronization

The following are the messages sent between clients and servers:

1. *Household A* submits a draft of a service contract to servers.

2. *Household B* gets the service contract drafted by *Household A* from servers.

3. *Household B* revises the service contract and submits it to servers.

4. *Household A* gets the service contract revised by *Household B* from servers.

5. *Household A* acknowledges to the servers that it agrees with the service contract.

6. *Household B* gets the service contract agreed by *Household A* from servers.

7. *Household B* acknowledges to the servers that it agrees with the service contract.

8. *Household A* gets the service contract agreed upon by both households from the servers.

From these messages, we can define a few HTTP endpoints to be called by clients:

- `PUT /contracts/{id}`: Submit a draft or revised service contract

- `GET /contracts/{id}`: Get a service contract

- `PATCH /contracts/{id}/agreedAt`: Acknowledge agreeing to a service contract

Here, `{id}` is the unique identifier of the resource as the service contract.

Step 2 – defining a message payload

The message payload used for `PUT` and `GET` endpoints needs to be defined. The service contract itself is the resource, so its model is the payload. The `PATCH` endpoint does not need to return a payload. The payload will be defined using the **OpenAPI 3.0** model, as shown here:

```
Party:
  type: object
  properties:
    householdName:
      type: string
    service:
      type: string
    agreedAt:
      type: string
      format: date-time
ServiceContract:
  type: object
  properties:
    id:
      type: integer
      format: int32
```

```
        partyA:
          $ref: '#/components/schemas/Party'
        partyB:
          $ref: '#/components/schemas/Party'
```

For simplicity's sake, the `ServiceContract` class is defined by an integer ID and two parties. Each party has the name of the household, the service provided, and an optional time when the household agrees with the service contract.

Step 3 – defining API specifications

Even though the three HTTP endpoints were identified in *step 1*, it is necessary to go into the details of each endpoint and define them as API specifications.

Let us assume that only the two households in the service contract can see the service contract. This means we need certain ways to authenticate and authorize the `GET` endpoint. In this example, we enforce that the `GET` request should include a header to specify which household requests it. In production systems, it should use something more secure, such as a **JSON Web Token (JWT)** issued by a trusted **identity and access management (IAM)** system and the decoded token contains claims that would reveal the household name.

Therefore, there are two input parameters for the `GET` endpoint, as described here in the OpenAPI 3.0 model:

```
    parameters:
      - in: path
        name: id
        required: true
        schema:
          type: integer
      - in: header
        name: household
        required: true
        schema:
          type: string
```

The first input parameter is the identifier of the service contract, shown in the URI path. The second input parameter is the household name, found in the header.

As for the response, we need to consider the success and failure cases. The possible outcomes should be captured as HTTP status codes in the response, documented in the OpenAPI 3.0 model shown here:

```
    responses:
      '200':
        description: Successful operation
```

```
      content:
        application/json:
          schema:
            $ref: '#/components/schemas/ServiceContract'
      '400':
        description: Failed request validation
      '403':
        description: Not authorized
      '404':
        description: Service contract not found
```

The request can be valid, and the service contract exists, therefore an HTTP status code of 200 (OK) and the payload of the service contract are returned. The request could be initiated by a household not mentioned in the service contract, and therefore it is not authorized and an HTTP status code of 403 (Forbidden) is returned. Or the service contract of the given ID simply does not exist, and an HTTP status code of 404 (Not Found) is returned.

The PUT endpoint uses the same URI path variables and header values as the GET endpoint, and in addition, a request body, which is the service contract itself:

```
      requestBody:
        description: The service contract to be created or updated
        content:
          application/json:
            schema:
              $ref: '#/components/schemas/ServiceContract'
        required: true
```

The request body is the ServiceContract component itself, so the schema refers to the specification of the component.

The response of the PUT endpoint is quite different from the GET endpoint. All the different scenarios are captured by the HTTP status codes in the response:

```
      responses:
        '200':
          description: Service contract updated
          content:
            application/json:
              schema:
                $ref: '#/components/schemas/ServiceContract'
        '201':
          description: Service contract created
          content:
            application/json:
```

```
                schema:
                    $ref: '#/components/schemas/ServiceContract'
        '400':
          description: Failed request validation
        '403':
          description: Not authorized
```

Firstly, the service contract in the request payload may have used the same household names for both parties, and therefore it is not valid and an HTTP status code of 400 (Bad Request) is returned. Also, if the household name in the header does not appear in the service contract's party section, then it is not authorized, and an HTTP status code of 403 (Forbidden) is returned. If the request is valid, there are two outcomes. If a new service contract is created in servers, the HTTP status code 201 (Created) is returned with the service contract as the payload. If an existing one is updated, then the HTTP status code 200 (OK) is returned instead, together with the service contract as the payload.

The final endpoint, the PATCH endpoint, is simple. It uses the exact same set of input parameters as the GET endpoint, as there is no need for a request body and the request merely needs to identify an existing service contract. All responses are specified here:

```
        responses:
          '204':
            description: Agreed service contract
          '400':
            description: Failed request validation
          '403':
            description: Not authorized
          '404':
            description: Service contract not found
```

The failed outcomes in the response of the PATCH endpoint are the same as the GET endpoint, in identifying an existing service contract. But the successful outcome of the PATCH endpoint is different from the other two endpoints, because it has no request body, and therefore an HTTP status code of 204 (No Content) is returned.

Step 4 – server development

Now that we have the API specifications, we are ready to develop server endpoints. The corresponding entities need to be defined in Kotlin:

```
data class ServiceContract(
    val id: Int,
    val partyA: Party,
    val partyB: Party,
)
data class Party(
```

```
    val householdName: String,
    val service: String,
    val agreedAt: Instant? = null,
)
```

Note that this is semantically equivalent to the OpenAPI 3.0 component definitions.

It is recommended to use a highly available storage system to keep service contracts permanently, for example, a database. However, in this example, we simplify the repository to keep service contracts in memory:

```
val contracts = ConcurrentHashMap<Int, ServiceContract>()
```

This thread-safe in-memory map uses the integer IDs of the service contract as the keys and the `ServiceContract` objects as the values.

In this example, **http4k** is used as the server framework because of its small code footprint. We need to set up the means to read and write different values. This is achieved by declaring a couple of **http4k Lenses** to validate and transform the payload into type-safe structures:

```
val serviceContractLens = Body.auto<ServiceContract>().toLens()
val householdHeader = Header.required("household")
```

Here, we have the Lens for `ServiceContract` objects as the body and the household name in the header. They will be used in the actual endpoint implementations.

http4k configures endpoint routing by simply declaring an `HTTPHandler` using the `route()` function:

```
val app: HttpHandler =
    routes(
    ...
    )
```

Inside the `route()` function, a list of endpoints is declared and the details of the implementation are defined. The following are the implementation details of the `GET` endpoint:

```
"/contracts/{id}" bind GET to { request ->
    val household = householdHeader(request)
    val id = request.path("id")?.toInt()
    val contract = id?.let { contracts[it] }
    if (contract == null) {
        Response(NOT_FOUND).body("Service contract of ID $id not
found")
    } else if (contract.partyA.householdName != household && contract.
partyB.householdName != household) {
        Response(FORBIDDEN).body("Household $household is not allowed
to see the service contract of ID $id")
```

```
    } else {
        Response(OK).with(serviceContractLens of contract)
    }
}
```

This implementation defines the routing URI of GET /contracts/{id}. Then, it uses the http4k Lens defined previously to read the household name from the header. The service contract ID is also read from the path variable.

Then there is an attempt to get the ServiceContract object from the in-memory map we defined previously. If the object is not found, an HTTP status of 404 (Not Found) is returned. If the service contract is found, but the household name in the header is not that of either party of the service contract, then an HTTP status of 403 (Forbidden) is returned. Otherwise, everything is fine, and an HTTP status of 200 (OK) is returned with the response body transformed from the ServiceContract object by the http4k Lens defined previously.

The PUT endpoint is also defined similarly:

```
"/contracts/{id}" bind PUT to { request ->
    val household = householdHeader(request)
    val lens = Body.auto<ServiceContract>().toLens()
    val id = request.path("id")?.toInt()
    val contract = lens(request)°
    if (id == null || id != contract.id) {
        Response(BAD_REQUEST).body("Service contract ID in the payload
and the URI path do not match")
    } else if (contract.partyA.householdName == contract.partyB.
householdName) {
        Response(BAD_REQUEST).body("Service contract must have two
different household: $household")
    } else if (contract.partyA.householdName != household && contract.
partyB.householdName != household) {
        Response(FORBIDDEN).body("Household $household is not allowed
to update the service contract of ID $id")
    } else {
        val previous = contracts.put(contract.id, contract)
        val status = if (previous == null) CREATED else OK
        Response(status).with(serviceContractLens of contract)
    }
}
```

However, the PUT endpoint transforms the request body into a ServiceContract object with the http4k Lens.

The service contract ID from the URI path variable is checked against the ServiceContract object to ensure that the ID is the same as the id field inside the object. Also, there is a validation to ensure that household names in each party of the `ServiceContract` object are different. Any validation failures here would result in returning an HTTP status code of 400 (Bad Request).

Like the `GET` endpoint, there is a check to ensure the household name in the header matches that of one of the parties in the `ServiceContract` object; otherwise, an HTTP status code of 403 (Forbidden) is returned.

Afterward, the `ServiceContract` object is put into the in-memory map. The `put` function returns the previous value associated with the key. If the previous value is `null`, then an HTTP status of 201 (Created) is returned; otherwise, an HTTP status of 200 (OK) is returned. Both cases come with the response body transformed from the `ServiceContract` object by the http4k Lens defined previously.

The last endpoint, `PATCH`, has a very similar implementation to the `GET` endpoint in the first half. The same input parameters are read, and the servers attempt to get the `ServiceContract` object from the in-memory map. The first part of the implementation ends with the necessary validations:

```
"/contracts/{id}/agreedAt" bind PATCH to { request ->
    val household = householdHeader(request)
    val id = request.path("id")?.toInt()
    val contract = id?.let { contracts[id] }
    if (contract == null) {
        Response(NOT_FOUND).body("Service contract of ID $id not
found")
    } else if (contract.partyA.householdName != household && contract.
partyB.householdName != household) {
        Response(FORBIDDEN).body("Household $household is not allowed
to see the service contract of ID $id")
```

After validating the request, the household that agrees to the contract is located. An `agreedAt` timestamp is set to the relevant party of the contract. Also, the revised contract is put to the shared `ConcurrentHashMap` previously declared:

```
    } else {
        val now = Instant.now()
        val revisedContract =
            if (contract.partyA.householdName == household) {
                contract.copy(partyA = contract.partyA.copy(agreedAt =
now))
            } else {
                contract.copy(partyB = contract.partyB.copy(agreedAt =
now))
            }
        contracts[contract.id] = revisedContract
        Response(NO_CONTENT).with(serviceContractLens of contract)
    }
}
```

The second part of the implementation focuses on adding the agreedAt timestamp to the correct party of the ServiceContract object. Since validation has passed to ensure that the household is either one of the two, the servers determine which one it is and create a variant of the original ServiceContract object, with the agreedAt timestamp set to the current timestamp, using the copy function. The value in memory is then updated. An HTTP status code of 204 (No Content) is then returned.

Finally, there is the main function:

```
fun main() {
    val printingApp: HttpHandler = PrintRequest().then(app)
    val server = printingApp.asServer(Undertow(9000)).start()
}
```

The main function launches the server and starts listening to requests incoming on port 9000.

Step 5 – client development

As mentioned earlier, clients always initiate interactions with servers. So, the client implementation in this example reflects the client-server interaction in the sequence diagram in *Figure 4.3*. For simplicity reasons, we use a main function to simulate both households in this example. We start with creating an HTTP client using **OKHTTP**:

```
val client: HttpHandler = OkHttp()
val printingClient: HttpHandler = PrintResponse().then(client)
```

Then, the initial service contract drafted by *Household A* is created:

```
val initialContractDraftedByHouseholdA =
    ServiceContract(
        id = 1,
        partyA = Party("A", "Plumbing"),
        partyB = Party("B", "Cleaning"),
    )
printingClient(
    Request(PUT, "http://localhost:9000/contracts/1").with(
        householdHeader of "A",
        Body.json().toLens() of
            initialContractDraftedByHouseholdA.asJsonObject(),
    ),
)
```

Then, the initial service contract is submitted to servers by calling the PUT endpoint. Subsequently, *Household B* received the initial service contract by calling the GET endpoint:

```
val contractReceivedByB =
    serviceContractLens(
```

```
            printingClient(
                    Request(GET, "http://localhost:9000/contracts/1").
        with(householdHeader of "B"),
                ),
        )
    val contractRevisedByB =
        contractReceivedByB.copy(
                partyB = contractReceivedByB.partyB.copy(service =
        "Babysitting"),
        )
    printingClient(
        Request(PUT, "http://localhost:9000/contracts/1").with(
            householdHeader of "B",
            Body.json().toLens() of
                    contractRevisedByB.asJsonObject(),
            ),
    )
```

Household B revises the contract and submits the revised contract to the server by calling the PUT endpoint. Then, *Household A* receives the revised contract by calling the GET endpoint:

```
val contractReceivedByA =
    serviceContractLens(
            printingClient(
                    Request(GET, "http://localhost:9000/contracts/1").
        with(householdHeader of "A"),
                ),
        )
printingClient(Request(PATCH, "http://localhost:9000/contracts/1/
agreedAt").with(householdHeader of "A"))
```

Household A is happy with the revised contract. *Household A* acknowledges its agreement to the service contract through the servers, by calling the PATCH endpoint. Now it is *Household B*'s turn to receive and acknowledge the service contract:

```
val revisedContractReceivedByB =
    serviceContractLens(
            printingClient(
                    Request(GET, "http://localhost:9000/contracts/1").
        with(householdHeader of "B"),
                ),
        )
if (revisedContractReceivedByB.partyA.agreedAt != null) {
    printingClient(Request(PATCH, "http://localhost:9000/contracts/1/
agreedAt").with(householdHeader of "B"))
}
```

Household B sees that *Household A* agreed to the service contract. *Household B* then also acknowledges its agreement to the service contract through the servers, by calling the PUT endpoint. Finally, it comes back to *Household A* to receive the service contract agreed by both households:

```
val contractAgreedByBoth =
    serviceContractLens(
        printingClient(
            Request(GET, "http://localhost:9000/contracts/1").
with(householdHeader of "A"),
        ),
    )
```

The client-service interaction in this example has concluded. The service contract between *Household A* and *Household B* is mutually agreed upon and synchronized.

Throughout this example implementation, we demonstrated how to divide the roles of clients and servers in solving the service contract synchronization problem with the client-server architecture.

What systems use client-server architecture?

Client-server architecture is widely used in many systems. Here are a couple of examples:

- **B2C systems**: Most **business-to-customer** (B2C) systems use client-server architecture, where the client is either a web browser or a mobile application. A client holds very little data, only data about the user. Meanwhile, servers hold most of the data of all clients.

- **B2B systems**: Most **business-to-business** (B2B) systems use client-server architecture, where a part of the business system of a firm acts as a client to servers of another business system of another firm. These systems share some data because of the communication between clients and servers.

- **Online gaming**: Many online games use client-server architecture to maintain a shared state of the game among multiple players. The game client runs on players' devices and communicates with the game server to synchronize states and interact with other players.

- **Financial service systems**: Finance services are heavily regulated by various authorities and there are strict rules on how the data is stored and distributed. Client-server architecture can keep unnecessary data away from clients and have servers keeping sensitive data and complying with regulatory and audit controls.

- **Instant messaging, chat, and email systems**: Popular messaging platforms such as Slack, WhatsApp, Discord, and Microsoft Outlook use the client-server architecture. Clients connect to the servers to send and receive messages to other clients, broadcast messages to a group of clients, share files, and participate in real-time chat.

Coming next, we will explore another option, P2P architecture, and how the same problem of the households and their service contracts can be solved differently.

P2P architecture

P2P architecture is rooted in the idea of the absence of a centralized authority for coordination. A P2P network is formed of numerous nodes ("peers") that have equal roles in communicating with one another.

Each node can request resources or services from other nodes, while also providing resources or services to other nodes. This distributed nature of P2P networks enables efficient resource sharing and collaboration among participants.

There is no hard non-functional requirement on the computational power, storage, and network bandwidth for each node coming from the P2P architecture. However, consistency is a major non-functional concern in many P2P systems.

Consistency

There is no central authority or server that controls the data in a P2P system. Each node stores and manages its own data, and the nodes communicate directly with each other to share and synchronize information. This distributed nature of P2P systems brings several consistency challenges:

- **Data replication and concurrency control**: A node in a P2P system often replicates its data across multiple nodes to improve availability and fault tolerance. This replication can lead to inconsistencies if the data is modified at different nodes at the same time. It is crucial that updates are propagated to all relevant nodes in a timely manner.

  Moreover, if multiple nodes update the same data at the same time, there is a conflict about which update should take place. Implementing effective concurrency control mechanisms, such as locking, versioning, or conflict resolution strategies, is necessary to maintain data consistency.

- **Eventual consistency**: In a distributed network where nodes are spread out, delays and partitions can occur, making it difficult to achieve strong and immediate consistency. Instead, **peer-to-peer (P2P)** systems focus on eventual consistency, meaning that a consistent state will eventually be reached after some time, even in the presence of network disruptions or node failures.

- **Causal consistency**: Another option for consistency is causal consistency, where related events are received by all nodes in the same order, and unrelated events are received in any order.

- **Consensus and Quorum**: In some P2P systems, all nodes must reach a specific state or be updated before changes are accepted. This is known as the consensus approach. Alternatively, a quorum-based approach requires agreement from only a majority of nodes. Both methods help maintain a certain level of consistency but introduce extra coordination and communication overhead.

- **Merkle trees and hashing**: Merkle trees or hash-based approaches can be used to efficiently detect and resolve inconsistencies in the distributed data, allowing nodes to quickly identify and synchronize their data. These approaches are widely used in decentralized systems such as blockchain networks.

Bootstrapping and node discovery

A P2P network starts with the first node available, and then other nodes join. This process is called **bootstrapping**. Before a new node joins an existing P2P network, the new node must somehow discover at least one other node in the network. We will now cover several node discovery mechanisms.

Static

The most basic way to discover a node is that each node has the addresses of all other nodes in static configurations. The obvious limitation of this approach is the number of nodes that can be configured. The limitation of IP addresses can be overcome by techniques such as **relay servers**, **network address translation** (**NAT**), and **hole-punching**. This is about storage and memory limitations to hold the addresses of all nodes in each node.

A P2P network with static node discovery can be bootstrapped by attempting to connect each node from the static configuration.

Centralized directory

Contrary to the concept of decentralization, some P2P networks have a centralized directory that maintains a list of active nodes in the network. That means the network starts with the centralized directory being available. When a node joins the network, it lists itself as available in the directory. Also, each node can get a list of available nodes from the centralized directory.

The centralized directory falls into the category of servers, which requires very different system quality attributes from other nodes. For example, the centralized directory must be highly available; otherwise, it cannot accept new nodes or provide a list of available nodes.

Multicast or broadcast

In a private or **local area network** (**LAN**), a P2P network can be established by having each node send broadcast or multicast messages to all other nodes. A couple of nodes can decide to respond, and the originator node is able to discover them. The network is started the first time a node is discovered. This discovery mechanism is suitable only for small networks with a limited number of nodes.

Multicast networks usually use **User Datagram Protocol** (**UDP**) as the transport protocol. This is usually configured in a designated subnet to avoid broadcast floods and limit security risks.

Kademlia

Kademlia is a specification of the network structure and message protocol that is used in P2P networks. A **distributed hash table** (**DHT**) emerges across multiple nodes in the network. The network usually uses multicast UDP as the transport protocol.

Each node has a node ID, which is usually an unsigned big random integer number. The node ID prefix is used to calculate a hash value using a universal hash function. The hash value translates to a bucket in the hash table, and this is how each node maintains the IDs of other nodes in its local hash table and uses it as a routing table.

When a node joins the network, it broadcasts its node ID to all nodes in the network. Then, other nodes find a bucket to keep the ID of the new node in their routing tables.

Node IDs that are close to each other have their buckets close to each other as well. The "distance" between two node IDs calculated by the **exclusive OR (XOR)** function is used for node discovery. When a node wants to discover another node in the network, it starts from the bucket that is closest to its node ID and iteratively finds a responsive node by traversing buckets, from the closest to the farthest away.

Exchanging information with other nodes

Nodes can share their own nodes among themselves as well. The exchange among nodes comes with a few variations.

If the P2P network has a well-known structure, such as a DHT, a node can crawl the structure using a certain protocol to query nodes for information about other nodes. The downside is that a newly joined node would still need another mechanism to get an initial list of nodes.

A newly joined node can also contact a few bootstrapping nodes to query information about other nodes. This does, however, rely on the availability of the well-known bootstrapping nodes.

A gossip protocol can also be employed among nodes to periodically share information with a few random neighbor nodes. The information should collectively spread like gossiping or an epidemic, though it takes some time to emerge. This protocol scales very well from small to big networks. It is also fault-tolerant, which means if a neighbor node fails, other neighbor nodes would still be able to provide alternative information.

Communication among nodes

Once a node has information on how to contact other nodes in the network, it can initiate communication.

Direct communication with IP addresses

The most basic form of communication between two nodes is to have one node directly contact another node using an IP address. This approach is often used in small networks or LANs. Nodes in the network use transport protocols such as TCP for more reliable and ordered messages, or they use UDP for faster and unordered messages.

Hole-punching

For a node under one local network to connect to another node under another local network, the nodes are not able to use IP addresses for direct communication. Let us consider the situation in the following sample network topology. See *Figure 4.4*:

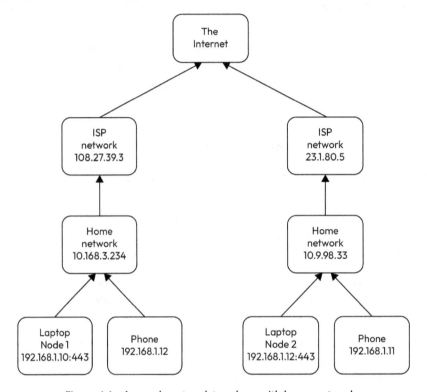

Figure 4.4 – A sample network topology with home networks

Node 1 has no direct way to communicate with *Node 2* via the internet, since both nodes are behind their own home networks. However, if the home networks and **internet service provider (ISP)** networks support NAT, then **hole-punching** can be employed to allow *Node 1* to indirectly communicate with *Node 2* with this relay mechanism.

NAT is a mechanism that translates local network addresses to public and global IP addresses. As a result, both *Node 1* and *Node 2* have their own global IP addresses, and they can communicate with each other. This is illustrated in the diagram here:

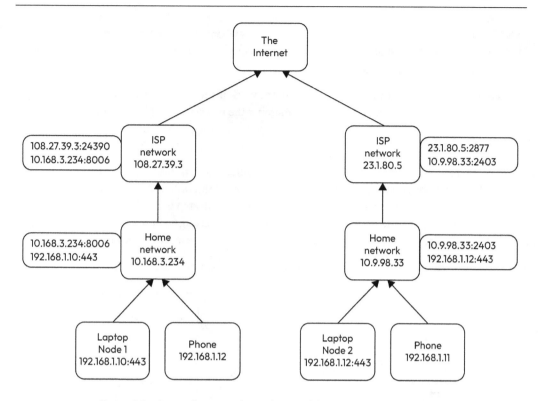

Figure 4.5 – A sample network topology with home networks and NATs

Node 1 has opened its port 443 to receive messages and can be located by the private IP address 192.168.1.10 under its home network. Its home network has a NAT mapping of 192.168.1.10:443 (as an internal address) to 10.168.3.234:80006 (as an external address). Then, the ISP network also has a NAT mapping of an internal address of 10.168.3.234:80006 to a global address of 108.27.39.3:24390. *Node 2* has a similar NAT mapping path except its global address is 23.1.80.0:2877.

From this point, we can start the hole-punching in steps, and assume *Node 1* has already discovered *Node 2*'s global address. Firstly, *Node 1* contacts its home network with the source local address (*Node 1*) and the target global address (*Node 2*). Then, the home network relays this information and contacts its ISP network similarly.

The ISP network where *Node 1* originated then contacts another ISP network where *Node 2* originated, using the global address.

The ISP network where *Node 2* originated contacts the target local home network with the translated address local to the ISP network. Then, the home network contacts the target *Node 2* in its network with the translated address local to the home network.

The NATs punch temporary *holes* in their respective tables where they translate internal and external addresses. As a result, *Node A* and *Node B* can establish communication with multiple networks and NATs in the middle to relay messages.

Note that hole-punching behind firewalls would not work if the firewalls were stateless. Stateless firewalls do not track connections and do not remember the translations of addresses.

Publish-subscribe

Publish-subscribe is an alternative model for P2P communication, where node discovery is not necessary. Instead, nodes publish messages to specific topics of interest, and other nodes subscribed to those topics would receive the messages. If the messages are delivered with a broker, then nodes still need to know the address of the broker to publish and receive messages. Publish-subscribe removes the need for node discovery and spreads information efficiently to relevant receivers.

An example of a publish-subscribe architecture with a broker is shown in *Figure 4.6*:

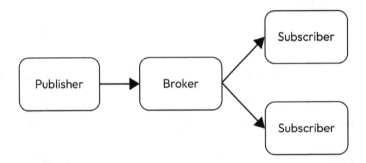

Figure 4.6 – Publish-subscribe architecture

The publisher does not know the subscribers. It knows the address of the broker and the topic where a message should be published. Subscribers register their interests in certain topics with the broker and receive messages associated with the topics.

The broker is a type of infrastructure middleware that receives messages from publishers. It stores the messages and manages subscriptions by subscribers. Most importantly, it routes messages to the appropriate subscribers based on their registered interests.

Now, we are going to delve into the implementation of the P2P solution.

The P2P solution

We are going to apply the P2P architecture to solve a real-life example of service contract synchronization between two households. For simplicity's sake, let us assume the two households have already discovered each other and their devices run in the same local network.

Step 1 – defining P2P communication

We are going to draft the interactions between nodes before coding. Let us assume that UDP is used as the communication protocol. Nodes communicate directly with each other, using IP addresses and ports. See *Figure 4.7*:

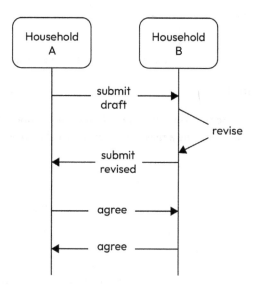

Figure 4.7 – Sample P2P interaction service contract synchronization

The following are the messages sent between the nodes of *Household A* and *Household B* as described in *Figure 4.7*:

1. *Household A* submits a draft of a service contract to *Household B*.
2. *Household B* revises the service contract and submits it to *Household A*.
3. *Household A* acknowledges to *Household B* that it agrees with the service contract.
4. *Household B* acknowledges to *Household A* that it agrees with the service contract.

After the communication protocol is defined, the message's payload should be defined as the next step.

Step 2 – defining the message payload

From the communication defined previously, the only message that passes around is the service contract itself. The model of the service contract remains the same:

```
data class ServiceContract(
    val id: Int,
    val partyA: Party,
```

```
    val partyB: Party,
)
data class Party(
    val householdName: String,
    val service: String,
    val agreedAt: Instant? = null,
)
```

In this example, we externalize the `ServiceContract` class as a byte array to be sent across the wire.

Step 3 – peer development

Let us start with scaffolding some necessary transport functions for nodes to communicate using UDP. As a node can produce and consume a message, it seems sensible to define a generic UDP node class as follows:

```
class UdpNode<T>(
    val address: SocketAddress,
    val convertor: DtoConvertor<T>,
    val transformer: (T) -> T?,
) {
    private val inbound: ByteBuffer = convertor.allocate()
    private val outbound: ByteBuffer = convertor.allocate()
    private var channel: DatagramChannel? = null
```

The UdpNode class uses the **Non-Blocking Input/Output (NIO)** package to support three major functions:

- Bootstrapping the node
- Sending a message to a target node
- Receiving a message from another node

While supporting these functions, the `UdpNode` class should only be changed if the transport mechanism needs to change, leaving it with a single responsibility of addressing concerns at the transport level, and conforming to the **single-responsibility principle**.

Therefore, the serialization and deserialization of the `ServiceContract` class is delegated to the `DtoConvertor` interface with generic type T, so the UdpNode class is not coupled to the `ServiceContract` class.

The handling of and responding to a `ServiceContract` object is an application-level concern, and this concern is delegated to a transformer lambda from the constructor.

The start function of the UdpNode class is simple. It binds the node to the configured address and gets it ready to consume a message:

```
fun start() {
    channel =
        DatagramChannel.open()
            .bind(address)
}
```

The produce function clears the outbound buffer before it calls DtoConvertor to write on it. Then, the buffer is sent to the channel:

```
fun produce(
    payload: T,
    target: SocketAddress,
): Int {
    outbound.clear()
    convertor.toBuffer(payload, outbound)
    outbound.flip()
    return channel!!.send(outbound, target)
}
```

The consume function clears the inbound buffer first, then the channel receives the byte array and writes it to the buffer. Then, DtoConvertor is called to convert the byte array into a ServiceContract object:

```
fun consume(): Int {
    return channel?.let { c ->
        inbound.clear()
        val address: SocketAddress = c.receive(inbound)
        inbound.rewind()
        val received = convertor.fromBuffer(inbound)
        transformer(received)?.let { transformed ->
            produce(transformed, address)
        }
    } ?: 0
}
```

The transformer lambda is called to determine the response to the ServiceContract object. If the response is null, then nothing happens. If the response is another ServiceContract object, then the produce function is called to send the response back to the node that sends the original message.

Another important class in this example is `DtoConvertor`. It is designed to be generic and to encapsulate the serialization and deserialization of a generic type, E, to a byte array. There are only three functions:

```
interface DtoConvertor<E> {
    fun allocate(): ByteBuffer
    fun toBuffer(dto: E, buffer: ByteBuffer)
    fun fromBuffer(buffer: ByteBuffer): E
}
```

The `allocate` function creates a `ByteBuffer` that is large enough to hold the designated type. The `toBuffer` function writes a **data transfer object (DTO)** of type E to `ByteBuffer`, and the `fromBuffer` function reads a DTO of type E from `ByteBuffer`.

A Kotlin singleton, `ServiceContractConvertor`, is declared to implement the `DtoConvertor` interface with the `ServiceContract` type:

```
object ServiceContractConvertor : DtoConvertor<ServiceContract> {
    override fun allocate(): ByteBuffer {
        return ByteBuffer.allocate(1024)
    }
```

The `toBuffer` function writes each field in a `ServiceContract` object in a certain order:

```
    override fun toBuffer(dto: ServiceContract, buffer: ByteBuffer) {
buffer.putInt(dto.id).putParty(dto.partyA).putParty(dto.partyB)
    }
    private fun ByteBuffer.putParty(dto: Party): ByteBuffer =
putString(dto.householdName).putString(dto.service).putInstant(dto.
agreedAt)
    private fun ByteBuffer.putInstant(dto: Instant?): ByteBuffer =
        if (dto == null) {
            putChar(ABSENT)
        } else {
            putChar(PRESENT).putLong(dto.epochSecond)
        }
    private fun ByteBuffer.putString(dto: String): ByteBuffer =
putInt(dto.length).put(dto.toByteArray())
```

The `fromBuffer` function reads from a `ByteBuffer` each field of the `ServiceContract` object in the same order and returns the object:

```
    override fun fromBuffer(buffer: ByteBuffer): ServiceContract =
ServiceContract(buffer.getInt(), buffer.getParty(), buffer.getParty())
    private fun ByteBuffer.getParty(): Party = Party(getString(),
getString(), getInstant())
    private fun ByteBuffer.getInstant(): Instant? =
```

```
            if (getChar() == PRESENT) {
                Instant.ofEpochSecond(getLong())
            } else {
                null
            }
        private fun ByteBuffer.getString(): String {
            val bytes = ByteArray(getInt())
            get(bytes)
            return String(bytes)
        }
}
```

Finally, there are two `main` functions, one for *Household A* and one for *Household B*, to represent how each of them negotiates the service contract.

Household A's behaviors are defined in the following code block, and then the node starts listening:

```
fun main() {
    val node =
        UdpNode(
            InetSocketAddress(HOST_A, PORT_A),
            ServiceContractConvertor,
        ) { it.receivedByHouseholdA() }
    node.start()
```

Household A does not respond to a `ServiceContract` object under the following circumstances:

1. The same household name appears in both parties

2. Both households have already agreed to the contract

3. *Household A* is not involved in any party

Otherwise, *Household A* agrees with `ServiceContract`:

```
    val contract =
        ServiceContract(
            id = 1,
            partyA = Party(HOUSEHOLD_A, PLUMBING, null),
            partyB = Party(HOUSEHOLD_B, CLEANING, null),
        )
    node.produce(contract, InetSocketAddress(HOST_B, PORT_B))
    println("Submitted service contract: ${contract.id}")
    loopForever(1000) { node.consume() }
}
private fun ServiceContract.receivedByHouseholdA() =
    if (bothPartiesHaveDifferentNames().not() ||
```

```
        partyAgreed(HOUSEHOLD_A) ||
        isHouseholdInvolved(HOUSEHOLD_A).not()
    ) {
        println("No response to service contract: $this")
        null
    } else {
        println("Agreed to service contract: $id")
        agree(HOUSEHOLD_A) { Instant.now() }
    }
```

Then, *Household A* sends the draft contract to *Household B*. At the end, *Household A* enters an infinite loop to try to consume any further messages.

On the other hand, *Household B* has its behaviors defined in another `main` function and then it starts listening:

```
fun main() {
    val node =
        UdpNode(
            InetSocketAddress(HOST_B, PORT_B),
            ServiceContractConvertor,
        ) { it.receivedByHouseholdB() }
    node.start()
    loopForever(1000) { node.consume() }
}
fun ServiceContract.receivedByHouseholdB() =
    if (bothPartiesHaveDifferentNames().not() ||
        partyAgreed(HOUSEHOLD_B) ||
        isHouseholdInvolved(HOUSEHOLD_B).not()
    ) {
        println("No response to service contract: ${this}")
        null
    } else if (serviceReceivedBy(HOUSEHOLD_B) == CLEANING) {
        println("Submitted revised service contract: $id")
        withReceivedService(HOUSEHOLD_B, BABYSITTING)
    } else if (serviceReceivedBy(HOUSEHOLD_B) == BABYSITTING) {
        println("Agreed to service contract: $id")
        agree(HOUSEHOLD_B) { Instant.now() }
    } else {
        println("No response to service contract: $id")
        null
    }
```

Similarly, *Household B* does not respond to a `ServiceContract` object under the following circumstances:

- The same household name appears in both parties as it is not valid
- Both households have already agreed to the contract
- *Household B* is not involved in any party

Household B would revise the service received in the contract from *Cleaning* to *Babysitting*, and *Household B* would accept if the service received were *Babysitting*.

When both `main` functions run, we should see the two nodes representing *Household A* and *Household B* negotiating the service contract. Eventually, the service contract is mutually agreed upon and synchronized. We should see an output like this:

Household A:

```
Started on $localhost/127.0.0.1:7001
Submitted service contract: 1
Agreed to the service contract: 1
No response to service contract: ServiceContract
```

Household B:

```
Submitted to revised service contract: 1
Agreed to service contract: 1
```

At this point, we have demonstrated how to solve the service contract synchronization problem using UDP. To fully demonstrate the P2P network, there must be numerous nodes available to send and receive messages in a multicast UDP network. Moreover, there should be a data replication and consistency mechanism among the nodes.

What systems use P2P architecture?

P2P architecture is used in a few common systems, such as the following:

- **Napster** was one of the earliest P2P systems that was commonly used by people to share files on the internet. Napster used a centralized directory server to maintain an index of available files and their locations.
- **BitTorrent** is a popular P2P protocol used to distribute large files on the internet. It breaks down large files into smaller pieces and allows each piece to be shared independently. Users download and upload these pieces simultaneously. Upon completion, BitTorrent combines the pieces back into a file for users. BitTorrent has reduced the need for centralization for file sharing.

- **Decentralized finance (DeFi)** is a more recent example. Cryptocurrencies such as **Bitcoin** and **Ethereum** operate on P2P networks. Nodes in the network communicate and validate transactions without relying on a central authority, using a consensus algorithm. This distributed and synchronized share state enables decentralized and trustless digital currency systems.

We are now going to compare the two architectures, client-server and P2P, to see which architecture is more useful in certain circumstances.

Comparison between client-server and P2P architectures

Client-server and P2P architectures should be seen as a spectrum of models ranging from centralization to decentralization, with a lot of viable hybrid models in between the two. See *Figure 4.8*.

Figure 4.8 – The spectrum from decentralized to centralized architectures

Centralized architectures have simpler ways of achieving strong consistency, and decentralized architectures have more complex ways of achieving usually weaker consistency.

Client-server architectures are useful in the following circumstances:

- There is a need for central control and management, typically applicable to industries under regulations
- There are mission-critical processes that require systems to be highly available, resilient, and consistent
- There is a lot of data to be collected and correlated, and the data needs to be consistent, replicated, secure, and accessed in a secure manner

On the contrary, P2P architectures are useful in the following circumstances:

- There is a need to avoid the high cost of hosting servers and to make use of the existing resources of the peer nodes
- There is a need to share resources freely without central control or censorship
- There is a need to avoid relying on a subset of processing that could result in total system failure

Summary

We have delved into two important architectures, **client-server** and **P2P**, with the context of solving the synchronization problem of a real-life example of a service contract between households.

We have covered how systems of each architecture can be bootstrapped, and which system quality attributes are required for each architecture.

We have also demonstrated in Kotlin code how the synchronization problem can be solved by each architecture.

We have described a couple of real-life systems that employ client-server and P2P architectures. We have also compared the two.

You should now have a brief understanding of the two architectures and what problems they solve, and also be able to reason which architecture can be used in different situations.

In the coming chapter, we are going to explore the architecture patterns often used in the frontend.

5

Exploring MVC, MVP, and MVVM

This chapter aims to provide a comprehensive comparison of **Model-View-Controller (MVC)**, **Model-View-Presenter (MVP)**, and **Model-View-ViewModel (MVVM)**, demonstrating their similarities, differences, and the contexts in which they shine. By understanding the strengths and weaknesses of each pattern, developers can make informed decisions when architecting their applications.

This chapter begins by exploring the principles of MVC, a pattern that has been widely adopted across various platforms, including web and mobile app development. We will delve into its three core components: the *Model*, responsible for business data; the *View*, responsible for the visual presentation of information to users; and the *Controller*, the intermediary between the Model and the View.

Next, we will shift our focus to MVP, a pattern that emerged as an evolution of MVC. We will examine how MVP addresses some of the limitations of MVC by introducing the Presenter, which orchestrates the exchange of data and user interactions between the Model and the View. We will analyze the **separation of concerns (SoC)** achieved in MVP and how it enables improved testability and maintainability.

Finally, we will explore MVVM, a pattern that became popular with data-binding frameworks. We will investigate how MVVM separates the concerns of the *Model*, *View*, and *ViewModel* and how data bindings facilitate the automatic synchronization of data between the View and the ViewModel. We will discuss the benefits of declarative programming and the increased SoC that MVVM offers.

We will thus cover the following topics in this chapter:

- MVC
- MVP
- MVVM
- Comparing MVC, MVP, and MVVM
- Beyond MVC, MVP, and MVVM

Technical requirements

You can find all the code files used in this chapter on GitHub: `https://github.com/` `PacktPublishing/Software-Architecture-with-Kotlin/tree/main/chapter-5`

MVC

The MVC pattern originated in the 1970s when the concepts of MVC were developed to structure code and separate concerns in the **graphical user interface** (**GUI**) of desktop applications.

In the late 1990s and early 2000s, web development became popular. MVC was adopted as part of web development frameworks; for example, **JavaServer Pages** (**JSP**), Ruby on Rails, ASP.NET, and so on.

The MVC pattern divides an application into three interconnected components: the Model, the View, and the Controller. Each component has distinct responsibilities and interacts with the others in a coordinated manner. This pattern promotes SoC and a clear division of responsibilities.

You may find various versions of interactions among the three components in different frameworks and languages. MVC represents the need to separate the Model, the View, and the Controller, and not as a prescription of how they work together.

The Model

The Model is the application's internal data, independent of the **user interface** (**UI**). Data is validated, manipulated, and transformed to other formats within the Model. It encapsulates the core behavior and business logic and can be shared across different Views.

The View

The View is responsible for presenting the UI to the end user. It displays the data from the Model and provides a mechanism to interact with users. The View is passive and reactive to users' actions. It only contains simple logic that is related to rendering data and responding to user input.

The Controller

The Controller is the intermediary coordinator between the Model, the View, and the user. It receives a request from the user and requests an update of the data in the Model. Once the Model accepts the request, the Controller updates the presentation in the View.

The Controller orchestrates the flow of data and the sequence of changes between the Model and the View. In other words, the Controller determines the application's behavior.

The collaboration

One version of the collaboration among the Model, the View, and the Controller is illustrated in the following diagram:

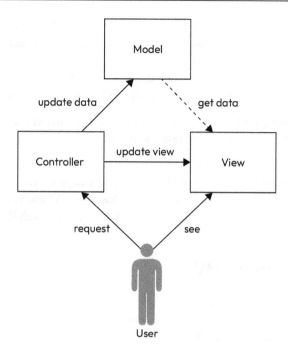

Figure 5.1 – The MVC pattern

The user sees the View and makes requests to the Controller. The Controller updates the data in the Model and then the presentation in the View, and finally, the user sees a visual response to its previous request to the Controller. The View can also be updated when the Model changes, with the use of callback functions.

> **Note**
>
> It is worth pointing out that the Model does not depend on the View or the Controller. On the contrary, the View depends on the Model. The Controller depends on both the View and the Model.

The benefits of MVC

The MVC pattern separates the concerns of data management (the Model), UI (the View), and user interaction (the Controller). As a result, it promotes modularity, code reusability, and testability.

The Model captures the application data and business logic, which can be reused among multiple UIs and user interactions. Multiple platforms, such as web browser interfaces and mobile app interfaces, can both depend on the Model as a module. A single update operation and a bulk update operation can reuse the same data structure and validation logic within the Model. The business logic in the Model can be tested in isolation without dependency on the View and the Controller.

In addition, modularizing the Model, the View, and the Controller enables each of them to be replaced without breaking or affecting other modules. If we were to rewrite the current UI, it would now be possible to write the next-generation UI as an independent module in parallel with the current UI, without the fear of breaking any existing functionality or degrading user experience. We could still maintain the current UI for one team while the new UI was being built by another team.

When the next-generation UI is launched, we can safely decommission the old UI module. This reduces a lot of dependencies and risks of releasing software.

On the other hand, it is not as usual to reuse the View and the Controller. As described in the previous diagram, the View depends on the Model, and the Controller depends on both the View and the Model. Reusing either of them brings the Model as the transitive dependency, locking down the Model to be used. Additionally, the Controller is usually tightly coupled with the View, making very little room for reuse.

A real-life example of MVC

We are going to apply MVC in building a frontend application for households to draft a contract for the exchange of service (the "contract") with their neighbors. We will use Android Studio and the Android **Software Development Kit (SDK)**.

The draft contract should contain basic information, such as each household's name and the services to be exchanged. The household uses a mobile application to create a draft contract record. The application as the View has only two screens, as shown here:

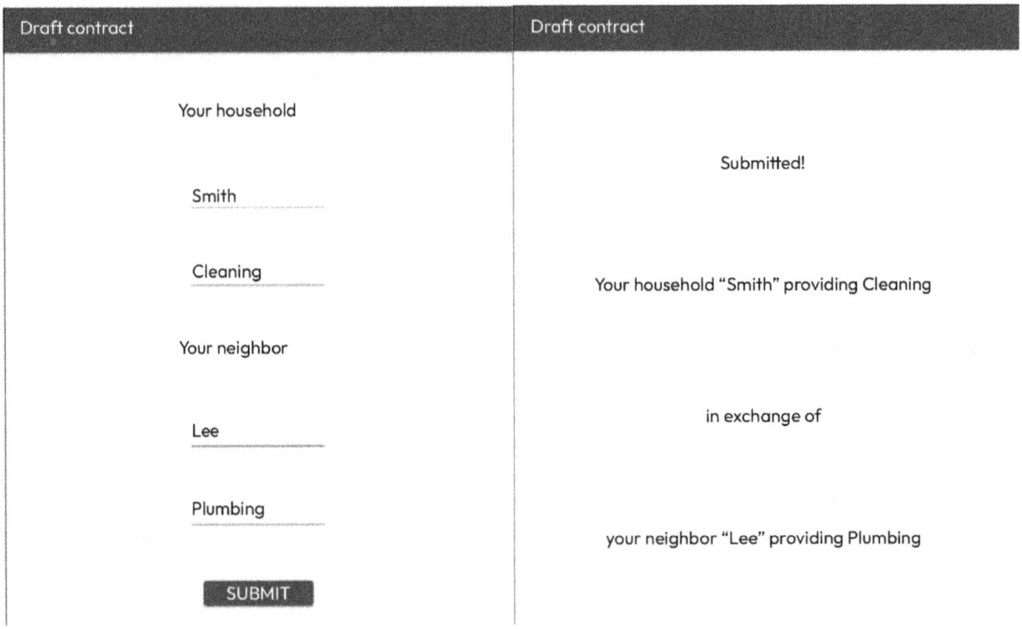

Draft contract	Draft contract
Your household	Submitted!
Smith	
Cleaning	Your household "Smith" providing Cleaning
Your neighbor	
Lee	in exchange of
Plumbing	
SUBMIT	your neighbor "Lee" providing Plumbing

Figure 5.2 – Sample mobile application for drafting a contract

The first screen allows the household to enter its name and the service it provides. In this case, it is the Smith household that provides a cleaning service. On the other hand, the household enters the neighbor's name and service in exchange. Specifically, here, it is the Lee household that provides a plumbing service.

The layout of the screen is defined by XML files as resources under the `/app/src/main/res/layout` project folder. For instance, the text field of **Your household** is declared as follows:

```xml
<EditText
    android:id="@+id/your_household_name_edit"
    android:layout_width="wrap_content"
    android:layout_height="wrap_content"
    android:layout_marginTop="25dp"
    android:ems="10"
    android:text="Name"
    app:layout_constraintTop_toBottomOf="@id/your_household_
header"
    app:layout_constraintLeft_toLeftOf="parent"
    app:layout_constraintRight_toRightOf="parent"
    app:layout_constraintBottom_toTopOf="@id/your_household_
service_edit" />
```

The XML block defines the View as an `EditText` component with an assigned ID, alignments, and dimensions. Copies (that is, display text) shown in the UI can be defined in a separate file and bound here using identifiers. This separates the concerns of copywriting and visual layouts.

View components in XML layouts can be bound to data sources in a declarative manner, using the Android Jetpack library. When the data changes in the Model, the View updates automatically without requiring manual updates in the code. This mechanism creates a more dynamic and responsive UI. The data binding can be expressed in the following XML:

```xml
<data>
    <variable
        name="household"
        type="com.example.Household" />
</data>
```

With the data defined, the View can be bound to the Model. In the following example, `TextView` displays the name of `Household`:

```xml
<TextView
    android:layout_width="wrap_content"
    android:layout_height="wrap_content"
    android:text="@{household.name}" />
```

When the **SUBMIT** button is clicked, the application navigates to the confirmation screen. On the screen, it acknowledges that the draft contract has been submitted, and the contract of exchanged service is shown to the user.

The Model should have two data classes. HouseholdInput captures the name and service provided by a household, and DraftContractInput has two HouseholdInput objects to form a contract. The two data classes are shown here:

```
data class DraftContractInput(
    val initiator: HouseholdInput,
    val neighbor: HouseholdInput
)
data class HouseholdInput(
    val householdName: String,
    val serviceProvided: String
)
```

There is also a sample repository class, ContractRepository, for handling the submission of draft contracts. The repository class is shown here:

```
class ContractRepository {
    fun submit(contract: DraftContractInput): Boolean {
        return true.also {
            println("Persisted contract: $contract")
        }
    }
}
```

The current implementation of the repository does not do anything but can be enhanced to validate and persist draft contracts.

The Controller interface in the MVC pattern is the one that coordinates between the View and the Model. In this example, an interface is defined for what the Controller can do:

```
interface Controller {
    fun submitContract(contract: DraftContractInput)
}
```

The MainActivity class implements the Controller interface and is a subclass of AppCompatActivity from the Android SDK. It sets up the content of the View, controls the screen navigation, and connects with the Model:

```
class MainActivity : AppCompatActivity(), Controller {
    private val contractRepository: ContractRepository =
ContractRepository()
    override fun onCreate(savedInstanceState: Bundle?) {
```

```
    super.onCreate(savedInstanceState)
    setContentView(R.layout.activity_main)
    val contractDraftFragment = ContractDraftFragment()
supportFragmentManager.beginTransaction().replace(R.id.fragment_
container, contractDraftFragment).commit()
    }
```

Up to this part of the MainActivity class, it creates a ContractRepository object from the Model. It also creates a ContractDraftFragment screen as the first application screen, as shown on the left in *Figure 5.2*. The submitContract function from the Controller interface invokes the function in the Model to submit the draft contract:

```
override fun submitContract(contract: DraftContractInput) {
    contractRepository.submit(contract)
     val bundle = Bundle()
    bundle.putString("yourHouseholdName", contract.initiator.
householdName)
    bundle.putString("yourHouseholdService", contract.initiator.
serviceProvided)
    bundle.putString("yourNeighborName", contract.neighbor.
householdName)
    bundle.putString("yourNeighborService", contract.neighbor.
serviceProvided)
    val confirmationFragment = ConfirmationFragment()
    confirmationFragment.arguments = bundle
    supportFragmentManager.beginTransaction().replace(R.
id.fragment_container, confirmationFragment).commit()
    }
```

Before the Controller navigates the View to the confirmation screen, it creates a Bundle object that contains the data submitted. The data is passed to ConfirmationFragment, which is the screen shown on the right in *Figure 5.2*. The **SUBMIT** button in ContractDraftFragment sends user actions to the Controller for draft contract submission. This is implemented in the onCreateView function of the ContractDraftFragment class:

```
class ContractDraftFragment : Fragment() {
    lateinit var controller: Controller
    lateinit var inflated: View

    override fun onCreateView(
        inflater: LayoutInflater, container: ViewGroup?,
        savedInstanceState: Bundle?
    ): View {
        inflated = inflater.inflate(R.layout.fragment_contract_draft,
container, false)
        controller = activity as Controller
```

After the View is inflated, a click listener can be set to the **SUBMIT** button. The text values from the `EditText` components are then extracted:

> **Basic elements in the Android SDK**
>
> The Android SDK provides a comprehensive set of tools and components for building Android applications. There are a few key elements that are used throughout this chapter. An Activity is a single screen with a UI, acting as an entry point for user interaction with the application. Fragments are modular sections of an Activity, and they can be reused across multiple Activities. Views are the basic building blocks for UIs, such as buttons, text fields, and images. Layouts are the declarative definition of the UI in XML format, which specifies how Views are arranged on the screen.

```
inflated.findViewById<Button>(R.id.submit_button)
    ?.setOnClickListener {
        controller.submitContract(
            DraftContractInput(
                initiator = HouseholdInput(
                    householdName = inflated.
findViewById<EditText>(R.id.your_household_name_edit).text.toString(),
                    serviceProvided = inflated.
findViewById<EditText>(R.id.your_household_service_edit).text.
toString(),
                ),
                neighbor = HouseholdInput(
                    householdName = inflated.
findViewById<EditText>(R.id.your_neighbor_name_edit).text.toString(),
                    serviceProvided = inflated.
findViewById<EditText>(R.id.your_neighbor_service_edit).text.
toString(),
                )
            )
        )
    }
    return inflated
}
}
```

A `DraftContractInput` object from the Model is created from the extracted values in the `EditText` components. The `DraftContractInput` object is then submitted to the `ContractRepository` class for further processing.

Finally, ContractDraftFragment retrieves the Bundle object passed from the previous screen. The View components are then set with the data from the Bundle object to display a confirmation screen with details of the draft contract:

```
class ConfirmationFragment : Fragment() {
    override fun onCreateView(
        inflater: LayoutInflater, container: ViewGroup?,
        savedInstanceState: Bundle?
    ): View? {
        val inflated = inflater.inflate(R.layout.fragment_
confirmation, container, false)


        val yourHouseholdName = arguments?.
getString("yourHouseholdName")
        val yourHouseholdService = arguments?.
getString("yourHouseholdService")
        val yourNeighborName = arguments?.
getString("yourNeighborName")
        val yourNeighborService = arguments?.
getString("yourNeighborService")
        inflated.findViewById<TextView>(R.id.your_household_summary).
text =
            "Your household \"$yourHouseholdName\" providing
${yourHouseholdService}"
        inflated.findViewById<TextView>(R.id.your_neighbor_summary).
text =
            "your neighbor \"$yourNeighborName\" providing
${yourNeighborService}"


        return inflated
    }
}
```

In this example, users first see the UI and fill in the text fields. Then, the users click the **SUBMIT** button. This user action invokes the Controller to update the View by navigating to a confirmation screen. The Controller also updates the Model by submitting a draft contract object to the repository. At the end, users see the confirmation screen.

It is worth pointing out that the code in the Model focuses merely on the business data and logic, and the View is solely responsible for rendering the UI. The Controller does all the coordination between the View and the Model, and this is how SoC is achieved in the MVC pattern.

Coming next, we are moving on to MVP, an architecture pattern that can be seen as evolving from MVC.

MVP

MVP can be considered a pattern evolving from the MVC pattern. MVP originated in the 1990s as a response to the limitations and challenges faced when applying MVC to desktop and web application development.

MVP is built upon the concepts of MVC. The View and the Model concepts are shared between the two patterns, but interactions between the View and the Model have significantly changed.

The major limitation of MVC is the tight coupling between the View and the Controller. It results in a limited ability to test the View and the Controller independently. Also, when the View is complex and has a lot of presentation logic, it becomes difficult to test and maintain.

In addition, any variation or extension to the current View inevitably requires a proportional change in the Controller as the Controller needs to understand all the variations and extensions that exist.

MVP promotes an even more decoupled relationship between the View and the Model by introducing the Presenter. The following diagram demonstrates the new relationships among the View, the Model, and the Presenter:

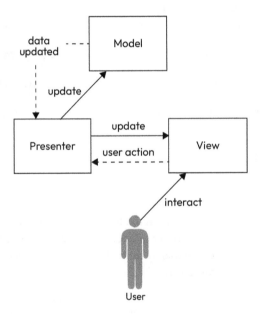

Figure 5.3 – The MVP pattern

As you can see, the user sees the View and interacts with the UI. The View then sends the user action to the Presenter. The Presenter updates the data in the Model. The Model calls back the Presenter when the data is updated. The Presenter then updates the View according to the data changed in the Model. Eventually, the user sees an updated UI based on the previous interaction.

Differences from MVC

The first noticeable difference between MVP and MVC is that the Model and the View do not interact. All messages come through the Presenter, and the Presenter depends on both the View and the Model. The View is self-contained and does not depend on either the Model or the Presenter.

The second difference is that the View can be completely passive in the sense that it is only responsible for rendering the UI as a response to the Presenter's request to update the View. However, the *Passive View* is considered an option for MVP. Passive View is a variant of MVP in which the View makes no decisions and contains no business logic.

If not passive, the View can contain certain presentation logic that does not affect the Model or the Presenter. Simple field validation such as data type and length is a typical example.

The third difference is that MVP typically enforces explicit communication with the View and the Model. The View informs the Presenter of user actions, and the Presenter then interprets and acts upon them. Defining explicit communication helps engineers understand and reason about the application's behaviors, as a result making the application easier to maintain.

The benefits of MVP

The further SoC among the View, the Model, and the Presenter brings about a few benefits on top of the MVC pattern.

The View under MVP can be independently tested, without the involvement of the Presenter. The explicit incoming messages to the View can be used as the input of test cases, and the UI is used for verification. On the other hand, user interactions can be the input of test cases, and the explicit outgoing message from the View is used for verification.

With MVP, it is now possible to have variants of View without any change in the Presenter. The variant of the View interprets messages from the Presenter differently. The variant might produce the same message to the Presenter from a slightly different user interaction. In this way, there is no need to change the Presenter to support a variant of the View. Nowadays, there are so many variations of UIs on different platforms, such as iOS applications, Android applications, web applications, and custom devices such as televisions. It is possible for these different Views to share the same Model and same Presenter while still giving users a unique experience that is tailored to the platform.

MVP standardizes messages explicitly sent to and received by the Presenter. It ensures there is no confusion and no room for deviation by different frameworks or implementations. It brings clarity to engineers and makes the application easy to understand.

A real-life example of MVP

We continue to use the same example we used for the MVC pattern. We are using the same real-life example used in MVP, where a household can draft a contract of exchanged services (the "contract") with another household.

Evolving from the MVC pattern, the View and the Model can be kept the same in MVP, but the ways of communication will change.

The `Controller` interface is renamed as `Presenter`, even though the declared function has not changed:

```
interface Presenter {
    fun submitContract(contract: DraftContractInput)
}
```

The Presenter has two-way communication with both the View and the Model. So, the first change would be to support a callback when the Model has changed:

```
typealias DraftContractSubmittedListener = (DraftContractInput) ->
Unit
```

The `DraftContractSubmittedListener` type alias acts as a callback interface when the draft contract is submitted to the Model. The `ContractRepository` class is enhanced to keep a `DraftContractSubmittedListener` object and will invoke the callback when a draft contract is submitted. The implementation of the repository class is shown here:

```
class ContractRepository {
    var onSubmitListener: DraftContractSubmittedListener? = null
    fun submit(contract: DraftContractInput): Boolean {
        return true.also {
            onSubmitListener?.invoke(contract)
        }.also {
            println("Persisted contract: $contract")
        }
    }
}
```

The callback function, when the model is updated, can be used to navigate to the confirmation screen with the submitted draft contract. This is the updated `submitContract` function in the `MainActivity` class:

```
override fun submitContract(contract: DraftContractInput) {
    contractRepository.onSubmitListener = {
```

```
            val confirmationFragment = ConfirmationFragment()
            confirmationFragment.lastSubmittedContract =
it              supportFragmentManager.beginTransaction().replace(R.
id.fragment_container, confirmationFragment).commit()
        }
        contractRepository.submit(contract)
    }
```

On the other hand, the ConfirmationFragment class is updated. The screen takes the values directly from the submitted draft contract that was just set from DraftContractSubmittedListener to MainActivity:

```
class ConfirmationFragment : Fragment() {
    lateinit var lastSubmittedContract: DraftContractInput
    override fun onCreateView(
        inflater: LayoutInflater, container: ViewGroup?,
        savedInstanceState: Bundle?
    ): View? {
        val inflated = inflater.inflate(R.layout.fragment_
confirmation, container, false)
        lastSubmittedContract?.also {
            inflated.findViewById<TextView>(R.id.your_household_
summary).text =
                "Your household \"${it.initiator.householdName}\"
providing ${it.initiator.serviceProvided}"
            inflated.findViewById<TextView>(R.id.your_
neighbor_summary).text =
                "your neighbor \"${it.neighbor.householdName}\"
providing ${it.neighbor.serviceProvided}"
        }
        return inflated
    }
}
```

The major difference between this MVP example and the MVC example is that the loading of the confirmation screen is triggered by the change in the Model, with the use of a callback function. In this way, all communications between the View and the Model are through the Presenter. It is now possible to test the View logic in the ConfirmationFragment class, the Model logic in the ContractRepository class, and the Presenter logic in the MainActivity class independently.

After MVP, we are going to delve into the MVVM pattern, which also aims to solve the same problem as MVC and MVP.

MVVM

MVVM was first introduced by John Gossman at Microsoft in 2005. It was created for UI development using the **Windows Presentation Foundation** (**WPF**) framework. Later it was adopted by other frameworks, such as the following:

- React

- Xamarin

- AngularJS

MVVM fundamentally retains the concepts of the Model and the View from the older models, MVC and MVP. However, it uses the View Model as an intermediary between the View and the Model. There is also a substantial preference for using declarative data binding to coding. The data-binding feature of MVVM supports the automatic synchronization between the View and the View Model.

The View Model

The View Model exposes data and commands that the view can bind to. The data binding allows an automatic two-way synchronization between the View and the View Model. In other words, updates from the View Model are reflected in the View automatically, and the View Model can react to user actions in the View. This reduces boilerplate code to manually synchronize the data between the View and the View Model and the code to update the View. The following diagram will throw more light on interactions among the View, the Model, and the View Model:

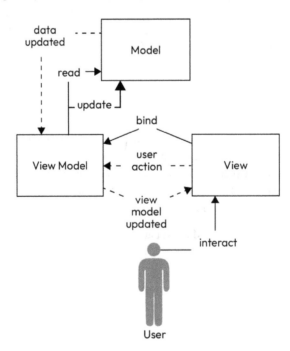

Figure 5.4 – The MVVM pattern

As you can see here, the View Model reads data from the Model, transforms it for presentation, and provides properties and functions for the View. The View receives the properties and function callback to render the UI.

A use case in which a user interacts with the View and ends up seeing changes in the View is demonstrated in *Figure 5.5*:

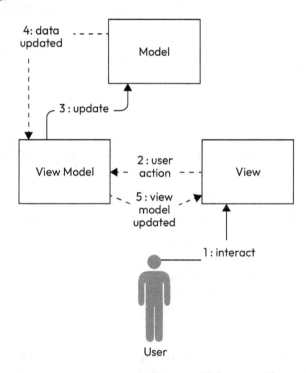

Figure 5.5 – User interacting and seeing changes in the View

When a user interacts with the View, the user actions are propagated to the View Model. The View Model executes commands to respond to the user actions, which typically involve updating the data in the Model. Once the data is updated in the Model, the View Model receives the data update and transforms it for presentation. Finally, the View receives the View Model changes and renders the UI as a response to the user actions.

The benefits of MVVM

MVVM separates the concerns of business logic even further from the presentation in the View. The View Model encapsulates presentation logic without needing to be concerned about how it is rendered visually. This implies the View Model can be tested in isolation, independent of specific details of the UI.

Properties and commands in the View Model can be shared while keeping the user experience consistent among multiple Views, such as web browsers, desktop applications, and mobile applications. Moreover, View changes can be made without updating the View Model. This promotes flexibility and extensibility to evolve the code base.

UI designers can better collaborate with frontend engineers. UI designers can focus on styling, layout, and visual components without the need to interfere with the business logic. This promotes working in parallel and improves productivity.

The automatic synchronization between the View and the View Model reduces boilerplate code to manually update the View when the View Model changes and vice versa.

A real-life example of MVVM

Continuing from the same example we used for the MVP pattern, the code base is going to evolve to the MVVM pattern. We are using the same real-life example from MVC and MVP, and the code base evolves from them using the Android SDK.

The View Model is introduced and named `DraftContractViewModel` to store transitional data before it is ready to become a draft contact:

```
class DraftContractViewModel : ViewModel() {
    var yourHouseholdName: String? = null
    var yourHouseholdService: String? = null
    var yourNeighborName: String? = null
    var yourNeighborService: String? = null
}
```

The `DraftContractViewModel` object is going to be shared among `Fragments` to keep building the data required for a draft contract. This is reflected in the mutable fields (known as `var` in Kotlin). Moreover, the View Model acts as a bridge between the View and the Model. The `toModel` function converts a View Model `DraftContractViewModel` object to the Model `DraftContractInput` object:

```
fun DraftContractViewModel.toModel(): DraftContractInput? =
    if (yourHouseholdName != null
        && yourHouseholdService != null
        && yourNeighborName != null
        && yourNeighborService != null
    ) {
        DraftContractInput(
            initiator = HouseholdInput(
                householdName = yourHouseholdName!!,
                serviceProvided = yourHouseholdService!!
            ),
            neighbor = HouseholdInput(
```

```
                        householdName = yourNeighborName!!,
                        serviceProvided = yourNeighborService!!
                )
            )
        } else {
            null
        }
```

Note that data integrity logic has been applied to the function to ensure that the Model object can only be created when all fields are present. This conversion logic can also be tested independently, as shown here:

```
@Test
fun `do not create model if the view model is empty`() {
    assertNull(DraftContractViewModel().toModel())
}
@Test
fun `create model when all fields are present`() {
    val viewModel = DraftContractViewModel().apply {
        yourHouseholdName = "Smith"
        yourHouseholdService = "Cleaning"
        yourNeighborName = "Lee"
        yourNeighborService = "Cooking"
    }
    val model = DraftContractInput(
        HouseholdInput("Smith", "Cleaning"),
        HouseholdInput("Lee", "Cooking")
    )
    assertEquals(model, viewModel.toModel())
}
```

This unit test is run by the **JUnit** framework. The first test creates a blank View Model object and then converts it to a Model object. Since none of the fields have values, the Model object cannot be created, and therefore it returns null. The second test creates a View Model object with all fields not null, and therefore it can be converted to a Model object.

The data between the View and the View Model is bound and synchronized automatically, using the following custom function:

```
fun EditText.bind(consume: (String) -> Unit) {
    consume(text.toString())
    addTextChangedListener {
        consume(it.toString())
    }
}
```

Initially, when the `EditText` View component is created, the default value is set to the View Model `DraftContractViewModel` object. Subsequently, any text change will trigger a callback to update the View Model. The data-binding process is kicked off in the `onCreate` function of the first screen, represented by the `ContractDraftFragment` class:

```
override fun onCreateView(
    inflater: LayoutInflater, container: ViewGroup?,
    savedInstanceState: Bundle?
): View {
    val inflated = inflater.inflate(R.layout.fragment_contract_
draft, container, false)
    val command = activity as Command
    val viewModel = ViewModelProvider(activity as
AppCompatActivity).get(DraftContractViewModel::class.java)
```

The View Model is looked up here, and the owner is set to be the activity so that it can be shared with the next screen. Then, a callback is registered upon clicking the **SUBMIT** button to submit the draft contract. Note that the `toModel` function is used to convert the View Model to the Model object:

```
inflated.findViewById<Button>(R.id.submit_button)
    ?.setOnClickListener {
        viewModel.toModel()?.let {
            command.submitContract(it)
        }
    }
```

The following code then binds the `EditText` View components with the View Model, field by field, using the `bind` function just mentioned previously:

```
inflated.findViewById<EditText>(R.id.your_household_name_edit)?.bind {
        viewModel.yourHouseholdName = it
    } inflated.findViewById<EditText>(R.id.your_household_service_
edit)?.bind {
        viewModel.yourHouseholdService = it
    } inflated.findViewById<EditText>(R.id.your_neighbor_name_
edit)?.bind {
        viewModel.yourNeighborName = it
    } inflated.findViewById<EditText>(R.id.your_neighbor_service_
edit)?.bind {
        viewModel.yourNeighborService = it
    }
    return inflated
}
```

The confirmation screen gets the submitted data from the View Model directly:

```
class ConfirmationFragment : Fragment() {
    override fun onCreateView(
```

```
        inflater: LayoutInflater, container: ViewGroup?,
        savedInstanceState: Bundle?
    ): View? {
        val inflated = inflater.inflate(R.layout.fragment_
confirmation, container, false)
        val viewModel = ViewModelProvider(activity as
AppCompatActivity).get(DraftContractViewModel::class.java)
```

The View Model is looked up here with the activity as the owner shared with the first screen. Then, the View gets the data from the same View Model object. There are now two screens sharing the same View Model object, but the Views are rendered differently:

```
inflated.findViewById<TextView>(R.id.your_household_summary).text =
        "Your household \"${viewModel.yourHouseholdName}\"
providing ${viewModel.yourHouseholdService}"
        inflated.findViewById<TextView>(R.id.your_neighbor_summary).
text =
        "your neighbor \"${viewModel.yourNeighborName}\" providing
${viewModel.yourNeighborService}"
        return inflated
    }
}
```

There are a few more potential features that can be added to this example. As the user types in the text fields, the callback function to synchronize the View Model keeps on being invoked. This makes it possible to provide real-time validation feedback to the user.

As the View Model is shared among multiple screens in the same activity, the View can be evolved into a series of screens as a wizard-style multi-step activity.

Also, if the Model is shared between two households in two copies of the application, the data of the draft contract can be synchronized in real time using a certain protocol such as a **peer-to-peer** (**P2P**) network. When the Model is updated externally from the network, the callback function for changes in the Model can populate the View Model and then update the View in real time.

Comparing MVC, MVP, and MVVM

The MVC, MVP, and MVVM patterns share the same concepts of the View and the Model. However, their relationships and ways of communication are different.

In MVC, one Controller has access to multiple Views and usually calls the functions of View directly. The View and the Model are tightly coupled. User inputs are handled by the Controller. Unit testing is limited to the Model on business logic only. Modifying the View or the Model would require changing the Controller as well. It is suitable for small projects only because the code footprint is the smallest.

In MVP, one Presenter manages at least one View. The View and the Model have no knowledge about the Presenter, but they communicate with the Presenter using callback functions. Also, the View and the Model are decoupled. User inputs are handled by the View, and then the View invokes the callback function provided by the Presenter. Unit testing can be done in the Model on business logic. The behaviors of callback functions from the Model and the View can also be tested. Modifying the View or the Model may not need to modify the Presenter if the callback function stays the same. It is suitable for small to more complex projects that require better testability of the Model and the View.

In MVVM, one View Model maps to one or many Views. The View and the Model are also decoupled, but even more separation of business logic from the View and communications are more event-driven and supported by the underlying frameworks. User inputs are handled by the View, and then the View invokes the callback function provided by the View Model. Unit testing can be done in the Model on business logic. The behaviors of callback functions from the Model, the View, and the View Model can also be tested.

The concerns are easier to separate, and the functions can be small enough to conform to the **single-responsibility principle (SRP)**. Modifying the View or the Model may not need to modify the View Model if the data binding has not changed. It is suitable for large and complex projects that may be deployed to multiple platforms and, therefore, multiple variants of the View and requires better isolation between the View and the Model.

The comparison is summarized in the following table:

MVC	MVP	MVVM
View and Model tightly coupled.	View and Model are decoupled.	View and Model are decoupled.
Controller depends on View and Model.	One Presenter manages at least one View via callback functions.	One VIewmodel manages at least one View via callback functions.
Controller handles user input.	View handles user input.	View handles user input.
Unit testing on Model only.	Unit testing on Model and View.	Unit testing on Model, View and Viewmodel.

Table 5.1 – Comparison of MVC, MVP, and MVVM

Beyond MVC, MVP, and MVVM

More architectural patterns have evolved from the three patterns we discussed previously. The in-depth comparison of these patterns is beyond this chapter, but they are worth mentioning:

- **Model-View-Intent (MVI)**: MVI emerged as a pattern influenced by MVC, MVP, and MVVM around the 2010s in the Android community. MVI has a unique focus on a unidirectional data flow to streamline state management. It also adopts reactive programming paradigms to asynchronously manage the unidirectional data flow, using libraries such as RxJava and RxJS. The interactions among them are shown in *Figure 5.6*:

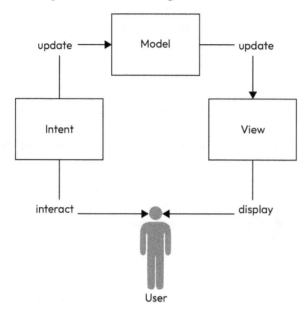

Figure 5.6 – MVI interaction

- **Atomic design**: Introduced by Brad Frost in his book *Atomic Design* in 2013, atomic design breaks down the UI into five levels:

  - **Atoms**: Elemental building blocks such as text fields

  - **Molecules**: Functional organization of atoms such as search bars

  - **Organisms**: Sectional organization of molecules such as navigation panels

  - **Templates**: Visual layout and organization of organisms that form a page

  - **Pages**: Business-aware and specific instances of pages with real content

- **Component-based**: Focus on separating functionalities into self-contained and reusable components. Each component encapsulates the behaviors, hides its lower-level details, and only exposes higher-level functions via interfaces. It goes together with design systems that contain a library of reusable components with well-defined behaviors. It aims at providing a consistent user experience and optimizing productivity during development. Each component is developed, tested, and deployed independently, which makes it easier to update applications.

- **Server-side rendering (SSR)**: SSR is primarily used in web development but can be extended to mobile and desktop applications. The content of a page is generated on the server instead of in the browser or on clients' devices. It aims at improving performance and response time by reducing loads in the browser or on clients' devices, which come in various computation powers. Optimization of data fetching can be done on the server side, and it reduces unnecessary traffic between client and server. It does, however, increase the server load for processing.

Summary

We began the chapter with the MVC pattern. We explored the Model, the View, and how the Controller interacts with them. We also illustrated the concepts with a real-life example of the drafting of a contract for the exchange of services among households. The UI of the drafting and confirmation screens was used in the example, with the Controller driving the navigation and submitting the draft contract.

Then, we bought in the MVP pattern by evolving from MVC. The Presenter was introduced to replace the Controller, and callback functions from the Model were added to the pattern to further isolate the View and the Model. Then, we came back to the same real-life example, and the original code base of MVC was modified to become MVP.

Afterward, we introduced the MVVM pattern by evolving from MVP. The View Model was added as an intermediary between the View and the Model. Data binding was supported to automatically synchronize data between the View and the View Model. We reused the same real-life example and refactored it to be an MVVM pattern. A custom bind function was introduced to bind values in View components to fields in the View Model. The View Model could be converted to the Model object upon submission. We discussed the potential enhancement provided by the MVVM pattern, such as real-time validation, distributed processing of the View, and multiple variants of the View.

We compared the three patterns from multiple perspectives. We discussed the relationship between the View and the Model and how coupled they were in each pattern. The ways of communication among the three patterns were then compared, as well as the ease of unit testing. We looked at the chain of modifications needed in each pattern. In the end, we covered which pattern was suitable according to the scale of the project.

Finally, we introduced a few architectural patterns in the frontend landscape that evolved from MVC, MVP, and MVVM.

In the next chapter, we will look into another set of architectural patterns and compare them: monoliths, micro-frontend, microservices, nanoservices, and serverless. They are applied in either frontend or backend systems, but they do share similar fundamental concepts that are worth a discussion.

6

Microservices, Serverless, and Microfrontends

In this chapter, we'll delve into the architectural styles of microservices, serverless, and microfrontends. They have revolutionized the way we design, develop, and deploy applications. They also empower organizations to build robust, flexible, and scalable systems. We'll explore the fundamentals, unique features, and tangible benefits of each approach. By the end, you'll have a comprehensive understanding of these architectures and their application in modern software engineering.

Our exploration begins with describing the traditional monolith, where the entire system is designed and developed as a single unit. Then, we'll discuss the challenges of this approach that are faced by many developers to bring about the need to break down this monolith into smaller and loosely coupled components.

After, we'll turn our attention to microservices architecture and examine how microservices solve the challenges of monoliths. We'll cover how a monolith can be transformed into microservices before discussing the benefits, challenges, and trade-offs that come with this distributed architectural style.

Next, we'll discuss how serverless computing helps developers focus on writing code without the concerns of infrastructure. We'll discuss the optimal use cases for serverless architectures and address the challenges associated with this paradigm.

Finally, we'll look at how a monolithic application can be transformed into microservices and microfrontends. We'll discuss how self-contained components benefit the developers and integrate with microservices and serverless backends.

We'll cover the following topics in this chapter:

- Monoliths
- Microservices
- Nanoservices

- Serverless
- Microfrontends

Technical requirements

You can find all the code files used in this chapter on GitHub: `https://github.com/ PacktPublishing/Software-Architecture-with-Kotlin/tree/main/chapter-6`

Monoliths

Monolith means *made of one stone*. In the context of software architecture, a monolith refers to a large system designed and developed as a single unit. In a monolithic architecture, there's typically a single code base, a unified database, and one deployable artifact.

Having a single code base means it usually relies on individual developers' efforts to keep the code tidy and clean. There's little room to enforce separation of concerns by design since all code is hosted in a single place. This often results in all the components, modules, and functionalities of the application being tightly coupled and interdependent.

A unified database, typically relational only, in a monolithic application is likely to produce a major – if not only one – schema that contains all the entities from all functionalities. Moreover, each entity table will contain all the columns that address all business concerns related to the entity. There may also be a spiderweb of foreign key constraints among tables. It often combines the concerns of a database used for transactions and reporting into one.

While monoliths have a wide range of code quality and database designs, they have one thing in common: there's one deployable artifact for the monolithic application, which contains the entire system. It's big and takes a long time to release. The release procedure usually requires all monolithic application instances to shut down first, after which infrastructure changes are made, the new deployable artifact replaces the old one, and the updated version of the application starts. Each release also often requires intensive pre-planning and coordination among teams to identify dependencies. The release plan can look like a Gantt chart or a project plan, as shown in *Figure 6.1*:

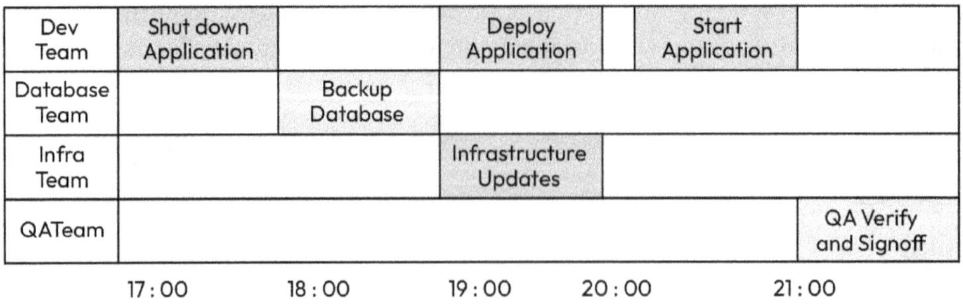

Dev Team	Shut down Application		Deploy Application		Start Application	
Database Team		Backup Database				
Infra Team			Infrastructure Updates			
QATeam						QA Verify and Signoff

17 : 00   18 : 00   19 : 00   20 : 00   21 : 00

Figure 6.1 – Release plan as a Gantt chart

In this release plan, the dev team shuts down the monolithic application first. Then, the database team backs up the database. Afterward, the dev team starts deploying the application, while the infrastructure team applies changes such as network or middleware upgrades. When this is finished, the dev team starts the application. Finally, the QA team verifies the environment and signs off the release. Some organizations may have a dedicated release team or operation team to formulate a playbook for each release and execute the plan as one team.

The release plan is visualized as a Gantt chart to show the dependencies among teams and show the timeline of the release from left to right.

Next, we'll cover the benefits and challenges of the monolithic approach as a background for the upcoming three architectural styles.

Benefits

Nowadays, few organizations would openly advocate monolithic architecture as an optimal style. However, there are still a few benefits that allow it to be considered a choice of architecture:

- **Simplicity**: Monolithic applications have the simplicity of one code base, one database, and one deployable artifact. Once the routines for build, deploy, and run are in place, developers can follow that one pattern that repeats over time. As we mentioned in *Chapter 2*, this is known as the **You aren't gonna need it (YAGNI)** principle. If this simplicity is all we need now, then it's not a bad idea to run with the monolithic approach initially.

- **Short time to market**: This situation typically resonates with developers if they work in a startup company, where time to market is the number one priority and nothing else matters. Sometimes, it's even a do-it-now-or-quit situation. It could also go well with experimental applications where sophisticated architecture may not be necessary.

- **Build first, optimize later**: Another benefit of monolithic architecture is situational. If the area of business is new and everyone is finding their paths on how to build the system as a product, then it's beneficial to delay any refactoring or optimization – that is, until everyone, including technical and non-technical stakeholders, has more experience with the subject matter and recognizes the need to break down the monolithic application. Also, it's better to understand the business ecosystem before trying to break it down by reasonable boundaries and which features naturally go together.

Monolith-first

This approach of making a conscious choice toward monolithic architecture is called **monolith-first**. This term was made popular by Martin Fowler in his engineering blog in 2015.

Challenges

While monolithic architecture has been widely used, it has some drawbacks. The tight coupling between components makes it difficult to update specific parts of the application independently. In other words, changing one part of the system would affect other parts unintentionally:

- **Slow development**: This makes any change bigger than it needs to be, and therefore increases the risk of release. Since every change is bigger, the probability of having code conflicts among engineers is significantly higher. Engineers would spend more time reviewing code and resolving code conflicts. More areas of testing are required to ensure the system is functional. Combined, these factors lead to slower development cycles and reduced flexibility.

- **Difficult to scale and tune performance**: Additionally, scaling resources in a monolith can be inefficient since the entire application needs to be replicated instead of individual components that require more resources being scaled. It's also harder to tune performance precisely since there could be other processes contending with the same resource, which affect the performance to be tuned intentionally.

- **Time-consuming test suite**: In a monolithic application, the different components and modules are tightly coupled, meaning that changes in one part of the application can have unintended consequences in other parts. Tests need to verify no unintended changes were made for business cases, leading to more complex test scenarios and a longer test execution time. The inter-dependencies also make it difficult to isolate and run tests independently, limiting the potential for parallel execution and shorter test execution times. Even a minor change in a monolithic application would need regression testing. This requires a comprehensive suite of test cases, which can be time-consuming.

- **Risky, long, and big releases**: Releasing a monolithic application usually takes a long time because the entire system is deployed as a unit. Even a minor change would result in the entire monolith having to be redeployed, which means it becomes harder to continuously deliver the system. Worse, it could end up accumulating more changes to release periodically since the monolith can't be deployed quickly and continuously. Engineers could be spending a long night aiming to release a monolith application, and these long and late hours may introduce more human errors due to fatigue.

    On the contrary, releasing a small application in a distributed system can be equally challenging. However, due to the smaller scope of change, it's possible to use modern strategies such as rolling releases, **blue-green releases**, or **canary releases**. These release strategies can be performed during business hours where most help is available, and thus reduce the risk of human errors.

- **Technology lock-in**: A monolithic application usually has a long lifespan. That means it may have chosen a technology stack a long time ago. Developers are faced with either upgrading the technology, which results in a substantial change in the code base or adopting a different technology in some parts of the codebase, which results in multiple tools doing the same job. This also means the space for experimenting with technology is severely limited.

- **Total system failure**: A failure in a monolithic application easily results in total system failure. Even the operational part may shut down since it's part of one monolith unit. It's harder to isolate and contain failures because there's no clear separation between components.

- **Team dependencies**: Lastly, multiple teams sharing one deployable artifact and probably one code base create a lot of dependencies. One team may have completed a feature that needs to be released as soon as possible, and the other team may still be working on a feature that isn't ready yet.

- **Slow time to market**: As they share one deployable artifact and one monolith, the first team may not be able to have their feature land on the market in time until other teams have completed theirs. This slow time to market could mean competitors may have taken opportunities and customers by the time the monolith is released. It hurts the business if the system is constantly catching up with competitors.

With that, we've set the context of the challenges that are faced by engineers when implementing monolithic applications. Next, we're going to look at architectural styles that aim to conquer these challenges.

Microservices

Before the term microservice architecture was coined, the concept of **service-oriented architecture (SOA)** became popular in the 2000s as an early response to the challenges posed by monolithic architectures.

SOA emphasizes encapsulating business functionality into independent services. Each service has a well-defined interface and communicates with other services. Standard protocols such as **Enterprise Service Bus (ESB)** are used for communication. The principles and concepts formalized in SOA to break down monoliths provided a basis for the future development of microservices.

In 2011, the term microservices was brought up in software architecture workshops as the participants increasingly became aware of the emergence of a new architecture. In 2012, the term microservices was officially decided. *James Lewis* and *Fred George* were the major initial contributors to this style.

Around the same time, companies such as *Netflix* and *Amazon* were also experimenting with similar architectural patterns. Netflix played a significant role in popularizing microservices through their adoption of the architecture for their scalable streaming platform. They shared their experiences and insights at various conferences and through blog posts, contributing to the growing interest and understanding of microservices.

Next, we're going to cover the key principles of microservices that shape their design and implementation.

Key principles

Primarily, a microservice should conform to the **single responsibility principle (SRP)** at the business capability or functionality level.

Let's consider the example we've used throughout this book about village households exchanging services with a contract. Functions such as record-keeping household information, negotiating the contract, exercising the contract, and notifying households are all microservice candidates.

A microservice should have a well-defined responsibility that handles a single concern or business domain. For this example, we can define each microservice like so:

- **Household service**: Masters the records of households

- **Contract service**: Maintains the workflow of contract negotiation from drafted to fully exercised

- **Notification service**: Sends proxy notification requests to email service providers

The details of how to break down a system into appropriate business domains will be discussed in depth in *Chapter 8*, where we'll cover **domain-driven development** (**DDD**). However, some architectural smells indicate whether microservices have well-defined responsibilities:

- Each microservice shouldn't be developed by more than one team of engineers. However, there could be exceptions, such as if responsibilities aren't delegated to the teams. This takes us back to *Chapter 1* when **Conway's law** was mentioned. It's recommended to re-organize the teams so that each team has well-defined responsibilities and those responsibilities don't overlap with other teams. The approach of re-organizing teams to aim for a better architecture is called the **Inverse Conway Maneuver**.

- A microservice shouldn't communicate too often with another to complete its feature. What's worse is if it invokes another microservice's endpoints iteratively. This is likely to indicate a "leak" of the service boundary. Perhaps the part that this microservice needs from another should be brought back and owned by the microservice.

- A microservice shouldn't depend on another microservice during a release. If a microservice is unavailable because other microservices are unavailable, this indicates a possible technical dependency.

- Two microservices having inter-dependency in terms of exchanging messages could indicate that responsibilities haven't been defined well enough. This is more of a problem if the communication is synchronous rather than asynchronous. If service A calls service B synchronously, when service B handles the call from service A, service B calls service A synchronously. This case would easily exhaust all threads in the request handler pool.

- Microservices shouldn't share code repositories, build processes, database schemas, and deployable artifacts with other microservices. Sharing them may hint at potential dependencies among microservices during build and release. The last thing you want is that your microservice can't be deployed until another microservice is deployed.

Having any of the symptoms discussed so far might suggest these microservices have emerged as **distributed monoliths**, which is worse than a traditional monolithic application.

Communication and integration

Microservices communicate with each other through well-defined interfaces, namely **application programming interfaces (APIs)**. The communication is either synchronous or asynchronous.

The synchronous and asynchronous communications that occur via APIs are specified by the popular **Open API** and **Async API** standards, respectively:

- Synchronous communication is often achieved by one microservice sending a request to another microservice and waiting for a response before continuing its execution. The APIs can be exposed as **Hypertext Transfer Protocol/Secure (HTTP/HTTPS)**, **Remote Procedure Call (RPC)**, **Simple Object Access Protocol (SOAP)**, and so on.

- Asynchronous communication usually involves messaging systems so that a microservice can send a message and immediately continue its execution. The other microservices receive the message when it's available.

Webhooks are an alternative and popular way to communicate among microservices asynchronously without the need for messaging systems. Instead of responding to a request, a microservice usually sends a message to another microservice via the HTTP/REST protocol but doesn't require a response to continue its execution. Webhooks usually require static configuration to be used with the target endpoints.

Considering the example of the four potential microservices, they could communicate in the following way:

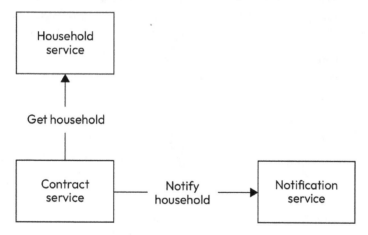

Figure 6.2 – An example of microservice communication

In the preceding diagram, **Contract service** needs to get household data from **Household service** to validate requests and manage their workflows. Then, **Contract service** sends requests to **Notification service** so that emails can be sent to households to inform them of any changes in their workflows.

Scalability and resilience

Microservice architecture provides inherent scalability due to its modular nature. Each microservice can be scaled independently based on its specific resource requirements.

In our example of microservices, the usage patterns can be hugely different. The following may apply:

- **Household service**: Low traffic as there's only a limited number of households
- **Contract service**: Most frequently used by users
- **Notification service**: Medium throughput of email requests but no strict latency requirements

Assuming this is a true reflection of its usage, we might need more instances of the **contract service** than any other service. Alternatively, other microservices can send asynchronous messages to request notifications, combined with queuing and batching mechanisms on the receiver side. Then, the **contract service** will be able to process a large volume of email requests in batches; other microservices don't need to wait to get a response from the **contract service** to continue their processes.

The **household service** is requested often in getting household data from the **contract service**. In other words, the availability of the **household service** has become more important than that of other services. However, we can also consider having a local cache of household data in the **contract service**. The **household service** would need to send asynchronous messages when household data is created, updated, and deleted. It can broadcast messages to all interested microservices, though the messages can be kept in a **last-value queue** messaging structure so that other microservices can copy the data to their local storage.

By combining these changes to address the concerns of scalability, performance, availability, and resilience, these services may communicate like so:

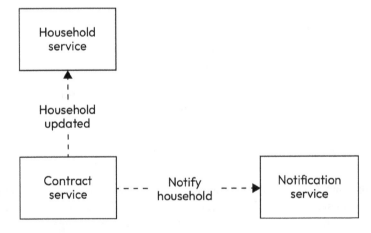

Figure 6.3 – Example of updated microservice communication

Note that there are no synchronous request-response messages in the system anymore. This implies that each microservice can operate on its own without other microservices being available, increasing the resilience of the system. For instance, if **Household service** is down, maintenance operations regarding household data are unavailable, but all other microservices are still operational as they use the last known household kept in their local storage.

However, it does rely more on messaging systems to provide features such as queuing, batching, and last-value queues. Messaging systems are typically configured and deployed as infrastructure so that they're more resilient than microservices.

Even with synchronous communication, there are techniques such as circuit breakers, bulkheads, and graceful degradation that can be employed to respond to failures gracefully.

Imagine that it was just a monolithic application of four modules. In that case, these concerns can't be addressed separately. Moreover, if the monolithic application is down, instead of having a partial system failure occur, we end up with a total system failure. No operation will be available.

Maintainability and technology choices

Each microservice should have a code repository. A microservice focuses on a single responsibility at the business capability level, so it's unlikely that a code change in one microservice would change something in another microservice. Moreover, keeping code changes small creates fewer chances of code conflicts among engineers, which also reduces the time required to review pull requests. The productivity of engineers increases as the code using the microservice style is more maintainable.

As each microservice has its own project, build script, and code repository, any choice that's made regarding the use of technology and libraries is confined within the project. When it comes to using a new library as a dependency or a newer version of the library, engineers can try it in one microservice to start with, learn and get familiar with it, prove it's working with one microservice, and then apply the proven approach to other microservices. A dedicated code repository for a microservice reduces many risks when experimenting with recent technologies. It also increases the chance of them being used in the system and keeps the system modern.

Testing and quality assurance

Testing microservices as black boxes has a smaller scope than testing a monolithic application. End-to-end test cases may involve a combination of behaviors from different modules.

However, in microservice architecture, these modules would have become microservices. With well-defined APIs, it's now possible to mock the behaviors of external interfaces so that the test case focuses on testing how it uses and responds to external APIs. This simplifies the test suite and each microservice focuses on testing its own behaviors instead. The exhaustive combination of behaviors from different microservices' communication can be inferred and thus remove the need for comprehensively testing all business cases via end-to-end testing.

Having said that, end-to-end testing may still be required to validate the overall communication among microservices while considering other factors such as URL routing, security controls, and API compatibility. Usually, end-to-end testing only contains critical business cases and focuses on overall system correctness.

As microservice communication using APIs is vital to ensure the overall system is functional, **contract testing** can be brought in to verify that these APIs are as per their specifications and that the microservices conform to them. This involves testing on both the consumer and provider sides of the APIs.

Consumers create contract tests based on their expectations, simulating the interactions with the microservice via APIs. These tests verify that the consumer's requirements are met. On the other hand, providers execute the consumer's contract tests against their implementation. These tests ensure that the provider meets the API's requirements and doesn't introduce any breaking changes.

These improvements allow engineers to verify the quality of the system faster and thus reduce the time to market of changes. We'll cover software testing in depth in *Chapter 13*.

Deployment and infrastructure

One of the key characteristics of monolithic applications is the single major deployable artifact. In contrast, one microservice should have its own deployable artifact. This allows us to implement the practice of **continuous integration and continuous deployment (CI/CD)** and, as a result, reduce or even eliminate downtime during release.

In our real-life example, and with the updated communications among microservices shown previously, each microservice can be released in isolation. Together with a rolling deployment procedure, it's possible to keep the system operating while the release is ongoing.

Moreover, each microservice can be deployed at its own cadence. There's no need to wait for other microservices to be deployed like in the days of monolithic applications. This encourages engineers to deploy microservices if they're ready to go, and thus speed up the time to market of software as products.

Microservice architecture often uses containerization technologies such as **Docker** and container orchestration platforms such as **Kubernetes**. Typically, building a microservice would generate its own Docker image, in which the dependencies and configurations are already set up. This results in consistent, repeatable, and predictable deployment, and each microservice has an isolated environment.

Kubernetes provides a declarative approach to managing how microservices are deployed. The desired state of each microservice is defined using Kubernetes manifest files and includes the Docker image to be used as a running microservice. The diverse needs of each microservice, as illustrated in our real-life example, can be realized by declaring the number of replicas and resource requirements in these manifest files.

The replicas setting defines the desirable number of instances of the **household service** that are running. Kubernetes' **Horizontal Pod Autoscalers** (**HPAs**) use this number to scale up and down based on resource utilization.

Kubernetes also provides mechanisms for microservices to discover and communicate with each other, such as **Domain Name System** (**DNS**) or environment variables.

Overall, these tools allow you to provision, scale, and manage the infrastructure needed to deploy and run microservices in an automated fashion.

Team organization

Microservice architecture goes hand in hand with the modern organization of teams. The system is broken down into microservices, and so should the teams.

The golden rule is that a microservice should be owned by one – and only one – team. This team is responsible and accountable for the full development cycle of the designated microservice.

The team should be given the autonomy to make small technical decisions within their scope while adhering to broader guidelines on the choice of technology to be used in the system.

Broader guidelines are there to maintain a certain degree of consistency among teams, such as the choice of commercial messaging, so that the firm reduces the complexity and cost of having too many technologies. Also, these guidelines provide agreed-upon principles and conventions to all teams, but each team has the power to decide how to execute and adhere to those guidelines.

The drawbacks of microservices

While microservices offer several benefits, such as modularity, maintainability, and testability, they also come with some drawbacks that must be considered:

- **Increased complexity**: Microservices architecture introduces a distributed system with more moving parts. Communication among microservices leads to additional complexity in development, testing, and deployment.

  Engineers will have to consider API versioning and compatibility. Introducing a breaking change in an API would break other microservices that stay in the older API versions. Maintaining a backward-compatible API or transitioning to a new major API version can be a challenge.

  Multiple microservices are used in the end-to-end test suite, which means these services need to be operational before the end-to-end test cases can be run. To make things worse, each microservice is usually managed by its own team, which means there are multiple streams of changes happening at the same time. There are more reasons to fail end-to-end tests now. It could be that one of the microservices failed to start, a change in one microservice ended up not being compatible with other microservices, and so on. It may end up that the engineering teams spend a lot of energy fixing the end-to-end tests.

Microservices architecture requires a more complex infrastructure, including service routing, load balancing, and container orchestration. This infrastructure as configuration can also act as a boilerplate as each microservice may have similar configurations but only differ in a few sections. The overhead of managing and maintaining this infrastructure can be significant, especially for smaller organizations or teams.

- **Network latency and overhead**: Breaking down a monolithic application into microservices implies local function invocations become remote. This can introduce latency and performance issues, especially if the services are geographically distributed.

  The overhead of network communication, including protocols, serialization, and deserialization, can impact the system's overall performance.

- **Distributed data management**: In a microservices architecture, data is often distributed across multiple microservices, which brings the challenges of keeping data manageable and consistent. Data could be split between two microservices, and there could be data that's represented differently in multiple microservices. Worse, there could be data among microservices that isn't consistent, so it's hard to understand the overall picture.

- **Monitoring and observability**: Tracing a business journey that travels through multiple microservices can be more challenging compared to monolithic applications. There are techniques to overcome this problem, but they require additional tooling and effort. These techniques will be covered in *Chapter 11*.

- **Fine-grained, infrequent, on-demand, or small tasks**: The overhead of microservices architecture could outweigh the benefits if you're running specific processes. For example, if a summary report of user activities needs to be exported as a file and uploaded to an SFTP folder monthly, it can hardly justify standing up a long-running microservice that's only used once per month. Similar situations apply to small tasks that are triggered upon request.

There's an alternative approach to microservices architecture when the scope is too small to justify the overhead. We'll discuss this in the next section.

Nanoservices

Nanoservices architecture, as the name suggests, takes the principles of microservices and makes them even more fine-grained. Microservices focus on breaking down monolithic applications into small, independent, and loosely coupled services, with one service for one business capability. Nanoservices take this concept even further by decomposing the system into extremely fine-grained, single-purpose components.

Nanoservices are designed to handle highly specific, autonomous, independent, and atomic functionalities. A nanoservice is often responsible for a single task or a tiny piece of logic within the overall system. Each nanoservice has a deployable artifact and can be deployed independently. Some of these nanoservices, when combined, can be seen as microservices.

Using the previous example regarding microservices, the **household service** can be broken down into several nanoservices:

1. Get a Household record by name.
2. Create or update a Household record.

These two nanoservices share the same database schema, while only one of them focuses on returning a Household record by name. The other nanoservice focuses on performing a create/update operation and sending asynchronous messages after a Household record is updated.

Benefits

Nanoservices have much smaller code bases, fewer dependencies, and less resource utilization (CPU, memory, and disk) compared to microservices. This reduced footprint results in simpler deployment and configurations. Scaling nanoservices is efficient as it only concerns the needs of one function.

Since nanoservices require less coordination and communication between each other, a nanoservice can be seen as a plumbing unit that only focuses on inputs, processes, and output.

The reduced complexity and overhead of nanoservices can make them particularly well-suited for resource-constrained environments, real-time systems, or scenarios where fault tolerance and rapid scaling are critical.

Drawbacks

Even though managing a nanoservice is easier than managing a microservice, a system that's been broken down into nanoservices has a significantly higher number of services to manage. This high number may outweigh the ease of managing one nanoservice.

The high number of nanoservices may bring significant network communication and collaboration challenges. The small resource footprint of one nanoservice may not translate well regarding overall resource consumption (CPU, memory, and disks).

Moreover, some nanoservices may share the same database schema for different operations. In our example of the read and update nanoservices for the **household service**, they share the same database schema. If the schema needs to evolve, there's additional complexity regarding how to apply the change in the database schema, and then the changes in both nanoservices. It's due to these fragmental concerns that some people would consider nanoservices architecture an anti-pattern.

Maintaining data consistency and coherence across a large number of highly autonomous nanoservices can be a significant challenge that requires careful design and coordination mechanisms. Imagine that there's one nanoservice for the create operation and another for the update operation; keeping the validation logic of the two nanoservices consistent can be a challenge.

Deciding between microservices and nanoservices

The decision of whether to have one microservice or multiple nanoservices is a balancing act on different overheads. In general, nanoservices work better if the function is simple and isolated. Any effort to coordinate with other nanoservices should be considered carefully.

In our previous example, the **notification service** has a simple objective compared to the other services. It merely translates an internal event into an email that contains an address and requests an email service provider to send the email. This is a suitable candidate to be a nanoservice as its task is simple. If we tweak the **notification service** so that it accepts email requests of a universal structure, then it can be an autonomous and independent nanoservice that doesn't depend on other services.

The overhead of managing a high number of nanoservices is still a concern to many engineers. However, the emergence of serverless architecture may have addressed this concern by having nanoservices managed by cloud providers. Next, we'll consider serverless architecture.

Serverless

Serverless architecture is a computing style in which engineers are no longer concerned with capacity planning, configuration, management, maintenance, resilience, scalability, physical servers, or virtual servers. There are still servers running but they're abstracted away.

Deploying web services used to be an expensive process. Physical server machines (the **bare-metal** aspect), network cables, and other accessories need to be purchased with the correct amount of storage, memory, and bandwidth. Operational engineers need to install and keep them on-site in a data center. Physical servers need to be set up correctly and connected to the network. Only then can web services be deployed to and hosted on these servers.

Bare-metal servers come with not only the initial cost of purchase but also ongoing costs such as electricity, renting from data centers, and visits by engineers to keep your server up and online every time. There are also security concerns as these physical machines are at risk of being damaged or stolen.

Most engineers aren't server specialists. Companies may need to either train their engineers to become system administrators, use hardware and network specialist contractors, or hire these specialist engineers to work with the application.

Every time the system needs to scale, it requires buying new machines or upgrading existing ones. They need to be configured so that they fit the other machines and be used by the application. Sometimes, purchasing and delivering the new machines takes time, so scaling doesn't happen when it's needed the most by the system.

Today, bare-metal servers are still the main choice for systems that require ultra-low latency and high-frequency processing, such as trading systems.

Serverless architecture aims to solve the issues from the days of bare-metal servers. Let's explore how.

The concepts of serverless architecture are deeply rooted in distributed computing. The history of evolution can be traced back to **grid computing**, in which computing tasks were distributed across a network of machines.

Serverless architecture wasn't popular in commercial systems until *Amazon* launched **Amazon Web Services (AWS)** in 2006. AWS provides a set of services for businesses to access computing resources over the internet (the **cloud**). Initially, AWS offered **Elastic Compute Cloud (EC2)** as virtual servers to run computation and **Simple Storage Service (S3)** as distributed file storage.

In 2010, *Microsoft* launched **Azure** and offered cloud services such as AWS, including virtual servers and storage. In 2011, *Google* launched **Google Cloud Platform (GCP)** to compete with Microsoft and Amazon when it came to cloud services. AWS, Azure, and GCP remain the three most popular cloud services nowadays, and cloud services are also provided by big companies such as *IBM*, *Oracle*, *Alibaba*, and *Tencent*. With the variety of cloud service offerings available, serverless architecture has come to fruition and is still evolving.

By using cloud services to run applications, the users are the **tenants** who subscribe to the service. Tenants rent and use the computing resources in the cloud on an on-demand basis, and hence the cost is arguably more flexible. Cloud services replace the need to procure and provision computer hardware and host it in a data center.

There are four major categories of serverless services provided by cloud service providers. Let's take a closer look.

Infrastructure-as-a-Service (IaaS)

IaaS offers computing resources in the cloud such as virtual servers, storage, and networking on an on-demand basis. It's like renting an empty space where tenants must configure everything in it.

Users are given an administrator account so that they can set up the infrastructure via a management console graphical interface, **command-line interface (CLI)**, or declarative configuration tools such as **Terraform**.

The following typical infrastructures are offered:

- **Virtual servers**: These are virtualized machines that can run anything set up by tenants. Tenants need to specify basic requirements such as CPU, RAM, disk spaces, and network addresses to reach the servers.

- **Secrets management**: There are various situations where we need to keep sensitive data as configuration for an application. This varies from encryption keys and API keys to foreign systems or credentials to access a database. With IaaS, these secrets can be managed separately and are injected into the runtime of the application that runs in, for example, virtual servers. As a result, these secrets can be viewed and managed by fewer people and be abstracted out of the code base. The cloud providers also offered advanced features such as key rotation and expiration for extra security.

- **Distributed file storage**: Cloud service providers offer scalable and durable storage services that can be accessed by applications. They allow tenants to store files of almost any size, and their storage scales as needed. They can replicate the files to multiple locations for redundancy and recovery purposes. They also support file versioning, so it's possible to retrieve previous versions of the same file object. Finally, they support fine-grained access control to the file and grant time-limited access to specific files for download purposes.

- **Databases**: Managed database services are a big category since there's a diverse range of choices. Most cloud providers offer relational and NoSQL databases, while some of them offer special types of databases, such as data warehouses. There's also a list of vendors and versions available that provides a smooth path for applications to move from bare metal to the cloud. They provide managed services that handle infrastructure provisioning, upgrades, scaling, replication, failover, and monitoring. Some of them provide advanced features such as data encryption for handling sensitive information.

- **Messaging**: Like databases, managed messaging services also have a big category of services per cloud provider. There are four main types of messaging available. The first type is a simple queuing service where a message is sent from a sender to a recipient. The second type is the **Publish/Subscribe (Pub/Sub)** pattern, where a message is published to a topic via a broker, and all subscribers to the topic receive the message. The third type is streaming, where messages are consumed as a continuous flow as they're sent. The last type is specialized messaging services, which target specific use cases such as emails and mobile application notifications.

  Cloud providers abstract away the complexity of setting up and managing the messaging infrastructure required. These managed services scale up and down on demand and take care of replication, security, and monitoring concerns.

In the next section, we'll discuss another big category of services that serve as a platform instead of infrastructure.

Platform-as-a-Service (PaaS)

PaaS provides engineers with a cloud platform so that they can develop, run, and manage applications without setting up the infrastructure themselves. Engineers still need to configure and manage their applications, runtimes, data, and services. The details of the configuration are abstracted away and specified in a declarative way. The cloud provider takes care of the lower-level concerns, such as hardware, operating systems, and network settings.

These services support specific programming languages and frameworks that enable engineers to focus on the application itself. The service handles the details of provisioning servers, load balancing, scaling, and monitoring.

Going further with this, if we don't want to build systems on a platform, perhaps we can simply use and integrate with the existing software available. This is the topic of the next section.

Software-as-a-Service (SaaS)

SaaS offers software that's ready to be used by end users or integrated with applications. This service involves tenants just using some software without having to code, manage environments, or even possess technical knowledge. Services in this category range from complete usable software solutions in the cloud and no-code application building to headless systems that can integrate with applications via APIs. In the latter case, tenants are still expected to run their applications via other means and set up a network connection to the SaaS service.

This category has the largest variety of software applications. Most companies would use at least one SaaS service, and a lot of companies aim to provide SaaS services in this open space.

Using SaaS gives us a holistic package of business functionalities. This is particularly popular when the business functionalities are necessities but not at the core of the organization.

Now that we've discussed bigger units, such as software, we're going to look at smaller units, which are functions in the serverless architecture.

Function-as-a-Service (FaaS)

FaaS allows engineers to write code and deploy it as a function, typically when reacting to events or triggers. These functions don't store states themselves, but they can make use of other resources, such as file storage and databases. Engineers don't need to manage any infrastructure. They're intended to be reusable functions so that higher-order functions can be built on top of other functions.

Cloud providers scale the runtime environment that's executing a function based on workload. They also charge based on the usage of the function, which is optimized for cost. Note that some of the services have restrictions, such as maximum execution time, memory usage, and the number of concurrent processes.

With these services, we can drop our functions as code into the cloud environment for execution. The cloud providers will do the rest for us.

With that, we've covered the four categories of cloud computing services that enable serverless architecture. Next, we're going to delve into how to build systems using these services. We'll discuss the benefits of these services and explain how to use them to create a modern, scalable, and easy-to-maintain system.

Benefits

The core value of serverless architecture is infrastructure concerns being abstracted and implemented by cloud providers. Here are the benefits that come with it:

- **Scalability**: Serverless architecture can automatically scale resources based on demand. When the application is under a heavy workload, the cloud provider dynamically allocates resources to handle the increased load and to ensure optimal performance. When the workload decreases or becomes idle, resources are scaled down, resulting in optimized cost and efficient resource utilization.

- **Cost efficiency**: Cloud providers offer a pay-per-use pricing model where tenants are billed by their actual usage. This pricing model optimizes costs and eliminates the need to purchase and maintain idle resources. This is attractive for organizations looking for cost-efficient solutions, particularly startups and small companies.

- **Time to market**: Since it's a lot quicker to spin up infrastructure to host applications, engineers can focus their time on developing business functions and specific functions. Plus, infrastructure settings now have a more declarative configuration than them having to work on the details of each infrastructure component. This results in a faster development and deployment cycle, the ability to continuously deploy changes, and a shorter time to market.

- **Adaptability and migration**: The range of available services allows engineers to host from big applications to small functions.

  A lot of companies migrate their systems from bare-metal monolithic applications to virtual servers in the cloud as the first step is to break them down into microservices and functions. This is more cost-efficient and quicker than breaking down monolithic applications first and moving to virtual servers afterward due to the comprehensive support cloud providers offer regarding infrastructure services.

  On the other side of the spectrum, there's a lot of FaaS support to just write a small function to perform a small task. The wide range of support from cloud providers concerning the size of the application makes it quite easy for engineers to adapt and migrate existing systems toward serverless architectures.

- **Diverse support for business domains**: Serverless architecture is suitable for event-driven and highly scalable systems. It's commonly used for building microservices, real-time processing systems, web and mobile backends, **Internet of Things** (**IoT**) applications, and more.

  There are many ready-to-use SaaS services that engineers could focus on in their business domains. For example, Amazon **Simple Email Service** (**SES**) can be used to send emails to customers, Azure Notification Hub can be used to send push notifications to mobile devices, and Google Cloud IAM can provide **multi-factor authentication** (**MFA**) and reCAPTCHA to verify users' identities.

However, it's important to note that serverless architecture might not be suitable for all use cases. Also, many services are provided by each cloud provider, so you need to err on the side of caution to ensure a suitable service is chosen to meet the requirements.

Cautions

While serverless architecture offers numerous benefits, there are important drawbacks to consider when adopting this approach:

- **Cold start latency**: FaaS functions are initiated on-demand, meaning that when a function is triggered for the first time or after a period of being idle, it might take a while to start up. This delay is known as a "cold start" and occurs while the cloud provider provisions the necessary resources on the fly.

If the function is triggered infrequently, which often causes cold starts, latency is increased for normal requests. If the application is expected to respond without noticeable delays, then PaaS or virtual servers should be used instead.

- **Vendor lock-in**: Cloud providers offer a wide range of services, while a lot of them provide proprietary APIs, frameworks, runtime environments, and even languages. While it's handy to have support from cloud providers in various areas, it's easy to rely too heavily on a specific cloud provider. This causes vendor lock-in, which makes it challenging to migrate to another provider.

  This creates barriers to migrating to another cloud provider or switching back to bare-metal infrastructure. While most cloud providers keep their pricing competitive, many companies find it crucial to have the ability to migrate if the situation arises. In response to this, some companies choose to use multi-cloud architecture with data synchronization processes between different cloud platforms.

- **Function granularity**: Decomposing an application into smaller functions appropriately is a key aspect of serverless architecture. However, breaking down functionality into excessively fine-grained FaaS functions can result in increased overhead due to the invocation and coordination of numerous functions, leading to release dependency, higher costs, higher latency, and more complex systems.

  Dividing applications and grouping functions so that they're the right size is the key factor for a scalable and cost-efficient system. We're going to explore this aspect in detail while considering our real-life example shortly.

- **State management**: FaaS functions are typically designed to be stateless, meaning they don't retain their memory of previous executions. When there's a chain of functions and triggers working together with data to share, it poses a challenge to how the state is shared across multiple function invocations. This pattern often involves other IaaS services, such as queues, databases, or in-memory caches. State management must be addressed carefully as it involves concerns such as concurrency, data housekeeping, and compatibility while evolving.

- **Monitoring and debugging**: Troubleshooting and monitoring serverless applications can be more complex than traditional architectures. When a business workflow is distributed among multiple functions and processes, it becomes challenging to diagnose, reproduce, and resolve issues. We should invest in observability tools such as log aggregation, monitoring, dashboards, and alerting. We also need to design the system so that it can handle errors gracefully.

- **Cost management**: While serverless architectures often optimize cost due to the pay-per-use model, it's essential to monitor and optimize resource consumption. Granular billing based on usage can lead to unexpected costs if the applications are designed inefficiently or experience unexpected spikes in traffic. This can be caused by inefficient system design or simply because the pattern of usage has changed over time. Adequate monitoring, performance testing, and optimization strategies need to be in place to control costs effectively. This is also an opportunity to discover system inefficiency so that the system can improve with new findings.

- **Long-running processes**: FaaS functions are typically execution time limits that are imposed by cloud providers. In other words, FaaS functions are meant to be small and executed quickly. If an operation requires significant processing time or must run continuously, it might be better to look for PaaS or IaaS alternatives, such as virtual servers. Careful consideration is needed to decide on the appropriate approach.

- **Security and compliance**: Serverless architectures introduce new security considerations. Ensuring secure function invocations, managing access controls, and protecting sensitive data within the serverless environment are critical. Compliance with regulations and industry standards should be thoroughly evaluated to ensure proper security measures are in place.

- **Non-functional requirements (NFRs)**: Even cloud providers offer a wide range of services that take away the concerns of infrastructure that are often parts of the NFRs. Our choice of serverless service needs to meet these requirements. Sometimes, it's hard to be in control of meeting these requirements since engineers can only configure the desired resources, and in the end, it's the platform that provisions the resources to meet the desired resources as configuration.

  In an extreme case, it might be justified to go back to bare-metal servers to have full control of the hardware and network that could fulfill the high-end NFRs.

By understanding and addressing these cautions, organizations can make informed decisions when adopting serverless architecture and mitigate potential risks associated with its implementation. Next, we're going to run through an exercise of adopting serverless architecture while utilizing the real-life example provided in this chapter.

Adopting serverless architectures in our real-life example

Consider the same real-life example that we used earlier in this chapter, where households exchange services with one another. Previously, we identified three potential microservices. Let's recapitulate what they are:

- **Household service**: Masters the records of households

- **Contract service**: Maintains the workflow of contract negotiation from drafted to fully exercised

- **Notification service**: Sends proxy notification requests to email service providers

Figure 6.4 shows how these four microservices communicate:

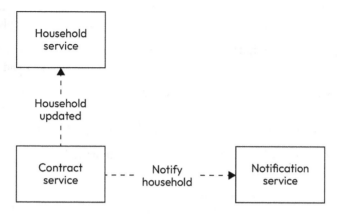

Figure 6.4 – Recap example of updated microservice communication

In this exercise, we'll assume that we want to have the system hosted in AWS. We need to decide which cloud service to use and what the desired setup is.

Function granularity and choosing the computing service

Previously, we mentioned we need to be cautious about function granularity as this will impact system efficiency and cost. We're going to review how these services can be executed and which computing service we might use.

The **household service** provides the classic **Create, Read, Update, and Delete (CRUD)** operations and connects to a relational database for persistent storage. These operations are highly cohesive as they cover the life cycle of households. They all assume the same database schema. Moreover, to ensure there's a way for the schema to evolve reliably, it seems reasonable to have the **household service** own its schema. This implies that incremental database migration tools such as **Flyway** can be used and that the incremental **Data Definition Language (DDL)** files should be hosted together with the source code that translates into the **Structured Query Language (SQL)** commands to perform the CRUD operations of households.

The incremental database migration runs as part of the service startup. The migration tool will check if the latest DDL file is of the same version as the version registered in the migration history records. If it's the same version, migration will finish as a **no operation (no-op)**; if the script version is higher than the recorded version, then the tool will run the incremental script until the version matches again. With this setup, any evolution in the database schema is released in one deployment action, with the schema changes and corresponding code changes going in a synchronized manner.

Moreover, there are three operations (Create, Update, and Delete) that would need an updated household event to be published. These operations would assume a specific message format. If the message format is going to change, it may affect all three operations. This also suggests they should be grouped as one deployable artifact to ensure smooth, reliable changes.

On the contrary, if the CRUD operations are separated into four FaaS functions or nanoservices, any change in data structure or message structure would require a coordinated release of these functions. This means function coupling, release dependency, downtime, and the risk of partial deployment failures.

Therefore, in this example, the **household service** is running as one microservice. The CRUD operations are exposed as RESTful services in the form of HTTP GET, PUT (create and update), and DELETE verbs.

The messaging technology in this example will be Kafka. We intend to publish events on a normal topic and a compacted topic. The normal topic is used to announce creation, updates, and soft deletion, while the compacted topic is used as a last-value queue to keep the last snapshot of the Household records.

The next consideration is about which serverless computing the **household service** should use. Here's an example of using AWS:

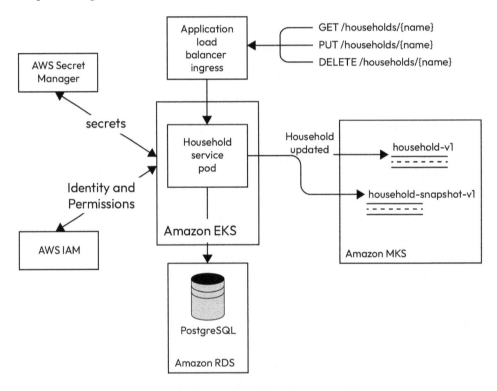

Figure 6.5 – The household service using AWS

We can use Amazon **Elastic Kubernetes Service (EKS)** to run the **household service**. This requires us to implement the following infrastructure setup:

- Specify the AWS region
- Create a **Virtual Private Cloud (VPC)** and subnet

- Create a role in AWS **Identity and Access Management (IAM)** for EKS to assume a role for the EKS cluster

- Define the EKS cluster that makes use of the VPC, subnet, and the IAM role

- Create a security group for the EKS cluster

- Attach the EKS cluster and EKS service policies to the IAM role

- Create an Amazon **Relational Database Service (RDS)** with PostgreSQL and its subnet

- Configure the Kubernetes provider

- Configure the Kubernetes namespace and config map

- Configure the Kubernetes secrets to be imported from AWS Secrets Manager, such as passwords

- Configure the ingress (incoming traffic route) and **Application Load Balancer (ALB)** so that the requests can reach the REST endpoints

- Configure Amazon **Managed Kafka Service (MSK)** on Kafka topics and security groups to allow an EKS pod to publish and consume messages

Given that the **household service** has the infrastructure set up, we can start a Kotlin project. There are many ready-to-go project creators available on the internet, including the following:

- Spring Boot

- Ktor

- HTTP4K

- Vert.x

These tools all create a skeleton project that can be built using their respective server frameworks. In this example, we're using Ktor as the server framework and REST endpoint routing. In Ktor, endpoint routing is defined like so:

```
routing {
    get("/households/{name}") {
    ...
    }
    put("/households/{name}") {
    ...
    }
    delete("/households/{name}") {
    ...
    }
}
```

We're using a declarative configuration as Kotlin code, and we're expected to define a payload format and set up corresponding serialization by using Ktor content negotiation.

The Kafka topics can be defined using Terraform, which provides a standard declarative format for specifying infrastructure. The normal topic will need to set a retention policy that determines how long the message should remain on the topic.

The compacted topic has a different setup. The message in the compacted topic should be retained for as long as possible. The newer message of the same key will replace the older one by compacting the logs. The cleanup policy of compacted topics should be set to "compact", with the retention period set to -1. Here's an example of how a compacted topic is specified in Terraform:

```
config {
    cleanup_policy = "compact"
    retention_bytes = -1
    retention_ms = -1
    . . .
}
```

The updated Household records are going to be sent to both topics. This is illustrated in the following code using the **Apache Kafka API**:

```
topicProducer.send(ProducerRecord(topic, household))
compactedTopicProducer.send(ProducerRecord(topic, key, household))
```

The message that's sent to the compacted topic contains a key to identify and remove older messages of the same key. In this instance, household names are used as keys.

The **contract service** provides controlled operations on the workflow regarding contract negotiation and contract exercise. It uses some form of persistent storage to keep a local copy of households and to maintain the state of the contract in its workflows. It uses a serverless computing service similar to that of the **household service**, as shown in *Figure 6.6*:

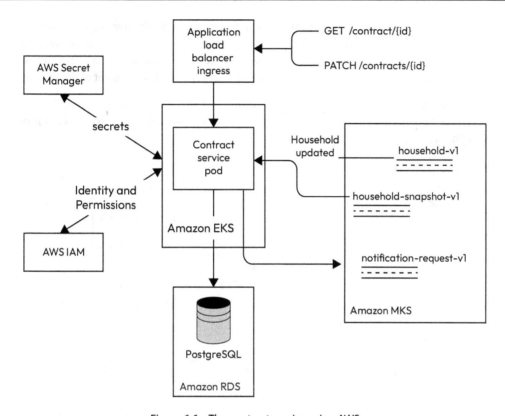

Figure 6.6 – The contract service using AWS

The **contract service** receives Household records from the topics published by the **household service**. Initially, it consumes all messages in the compacted topic to build its local cache of households and subsequently receives updates of Household records from the normal topic. It also sends notification requests to a topic to be consumed by the **notification service**.

In this setting, when a household is updated while the **contract service** is unavailable, the household updated event is published by the **household service** to the `household-v1` and `household-snapshot-v1` topics. The event in the queue is now waiting for the **contract service** to come back up. One instance of the **contract service** becomes available and takes this event for further processing.

The **contract service** uses the same AWS components as the **household service** in terms of IAM, Secrets Management, ALB, Kubernetes, and database services.

On the other hand, the **notification service** is simple in that it takes a notification request and proxies the request to an email service provider. There's no tight requirement to send emails instantly and it's OK to have the emails be sent a couple of minutes late. There's no need to maintain state either as the request message already contains the household email addresses and the content of the messages.

This is a suitable candidate for a FaaS service. While we can use AWS Lambda to meet the requirements, a nanoservice is an equally suitable choice. For this reason, the **notification service** is called **Email notifier** in physical deployment, as shown in *Figure 6.7*:

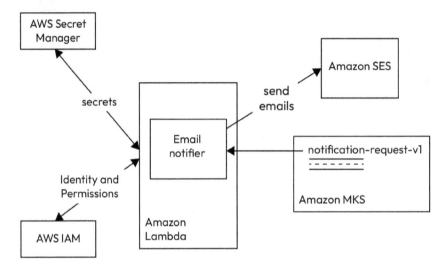

Figure 6.7 – The notification service using AWS

We can configure the function so that it's triggered by a new message in the Kafka topic. The function converts a request into email format and passes it to Amazon SES so that it can send the email.

The function must be configured to use a constant Kafka consumer group so that multiple instances of the same function don't consume the same message and effectively behave as a queue.

The function is stateless, and AWS provides all the means to connect to SQS and SES. There's no concern regarding a cold startup occurring as there's no tight latency requirement. The function also scales automatically based on traffic and is controlled by AWS. Similarly, this function uses IAM and Secrets Management to control accessible resources and secrets.

So far, we've covered the basic principles of serverless architecture, in conjunction with what's offered by the four major categories of services provided by major cloud providers. We've also discussed the benefits and cautions of applying serverless architecture. Finally, we ran an exercise in adopting serverless architecture for the real-life example specified in this chapter.

Next, we're going to briefly cover the microfrontend architecture, which works similarly to microservices in principle.

Microfrontends

The microfrontend architecture aims to enhance modularity, scalability, and autonomy by breaking down the UI into smaller, self-contained frontend modules.

The term *microfrontend* first appeared in 2016 under Thoughtworks Technology Radar with the recommendation of *Assess*. It's often compared to the concept of microservices on the backend. The microfrontend architecture promotes decomposing the frontend into independently deployable and maintainable units, each responsible for a specific part of the UI.

Same symptoms from the days of monolithic applications

A traditional monolithic frontend application has a single code base that handles the entire UI. Usually. There's more than one team of engineers working on it, which causes code conflicts, release dependency, slow build time, limited autonomy for each team, and challenges in scaling and maintaining large applications. This situation is the same regarding microservices, except this happens in the frontend.

The microfrontend architecture addresses these issues by enabling different teams to work independently on distinct parts of the UI, allowing them to choose their own technologies, frameworks, and release cycles.

Many small frontend modules as individual applications

In a microfrontend architecture, the UI is composed of multiple frontend modules. Each module is an application that can be developed, tested, deployed, and scaled independently. Like microservices, one frontend module should be owned by one – and only one – team, but as a common library.

Each module is a grouping of cohesive functionalities. Considering the real-life example provided in this chapter, there should be two frontend applications:

- The **household application**, which manages household account creation, updates, and deletion. Each household can manage its own account details via this application. This application primarily communicates with the **household service** in the backend.

- The **contract application**, which allows two households to progress from a draft contract to an agreement. It supports drafting a contract, similar to the screens we saw in *Chapter 5*. The two households that are involved can agree to the contract or amend it until both households agree with the details. It also tracks how the agreed-upon contract is exercised by the two households involved. Regarding the polymorphic nature of the different services that can be mentioned in the contract, as described in *Chapter 3*, there may be multiple screens for households to report the status of the services that are exercised based on the contract. This application primarily communicates with the **contract service** in the backend.

All these applications are bundled as self-contained artifacts that can be launched on their own, allowing separate teams to focus on their business domains.

However, there should be one more application that integrates with all other applications. This application doesn't contain business logic; instead, it's merely an over-delegation module that typically provides a menu for users to access other applications. This is the application that creates a unified UI at build time or runtime, depending on whether it's a web or mobile platform.

Overall, these frontend applications can be illustrated like so, together with the backend services they communicate with:

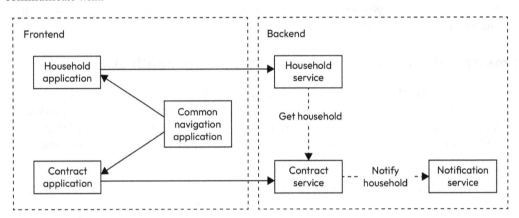

Figure 6.8 – The frontend and backend communication of the real-life example

In the preceding diagram, each frontend application has a primary microservice in the backend to communicate with. Each frontend application communicates with other frontend applications. Microservices also communicate with each other. The roles and responsibilities of each frontend application and each microservice are well-defined and clear.

This architecture enables each frontend application and its primary microservice to be owned by only one team. This is coherent with the idea of organizing teams by business function, as mentioned in *Chapter 1*.

Communication among frontend modules

Having communication and coordination among the frontend modules is critical in a microfrontend architecture. There are various techniques and patterns to facilitate this, such as asynchronous messaging, event-driven architectures, or shared state management.

In our example, a shared state managed by the collection of backend microservices is used to serve each frontend module.

These techniques enable seamless integration and collaboration between different modules while maintaining loose coupling and encapsulation. A well-integrated UI with a microfrontend architecture brings a connected and consistent user experience.

Design systems for consistent user experiences

Visualization is an essential element of any frontend application. While having smaller frontend applications autonomously run by their responsible teams, it's paramount to ensure the integration UI has a consistent look and feel. A design system provides the common UI components, such as buttons, checkboxes, text fields, and interaction styles, that align all frontend modules so that they behave the same way. In that sense, end users have a seamless experience with little learning required when navigating to another frontend module.

Benefits

The microfrontend architecture offers several benefits to engineering teams and organizations. By allowing teams to work autonomously, it promotes faster development cycles, easier maintenance, and the ability to adopt new technologies and frameworks without affecting the entire application. It results in higher productivity and quicker time to market. It also enables scalability by allowing individual modules to be scaled independently, providing flexibility in managing traffic and resources.

Furthermore, the microfrontend architecture advocates code reusability by reusing UI components brought from design systems that can be shared across multiple applications. This can lead to improved consistency, reduced duplication, reduced user learning, and increased productivity in frontend development.

Challenges

While the microfrontend architecture offers numerous advantages, it also introduces complexities and challenges such as module communication, versioning, and orchestration when integrating all frontend modules into one application. Successful implementation requires careful planning, design considerations, and selecting the appropriate tools and frameworks.

Variations among the web and other platforms

The web and other platforms have a slight difference when applying the microfrontend architecture. The web platform can achieve independent release as frontend modules are integrated primarily using hyperlinks.

Mobile and desktop applications are trickier because they need to generate a monolithic artifact for users to download and install. Releasing a frontend module would require regenerating the monolithic artifact and bumping the build versions. Some organizations might choose to release the application in a specific cadence to avoid excessive updates being required by the application.

Overall, the microfrontend architecture is a powerful paradigm that empowers engineering teams to create scalable, modular, and maintainable frontend applications by decomposing the frontend into smaller, independent modules. By embracing this architectural style, organizations can achieve greater flexibility, agility, and scalability in their frontend development processes.

An overall perspective

So far, we've discussed how monolithic applications evolve from a historical perspective. We've discussed that the monolithic architecture evolves into the SOA, where one big application is decomposed into chunks of smaller applications. Then, the era of microservice and microfrontend architectures begins as they're broken down into even smaller applications.

Finally, the serverless architecture emerges, which allows a single function to be executed as a unit in the cloud infrastructure. Meanwhile, it still supports bigger cloud applications and lets them run.

Putting them all together into one perspective, we can start to see how the sizes differ in each architecture:

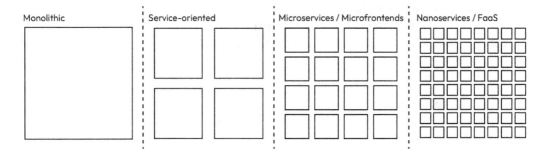

Figure 6.9 – A size comparison among covered architecture styles

It's worth noting that serverless architecture can adapt to all sizes. It can even adapt to monolithic applications, though usually, the first step is to break the monolithic application into smaller services. This is a typical example of *"First make the change easy, then make the easy change."*

> **Note**
>
> *"First make the change easy, then make the easy change"* is a quote attributed to Kent Beck, a pioneer of **Extreme Programming** (**XP**) and Agile methodologies.

Summary

In this chapter, we covered a few cases where monolithic architecture is justified. We discussed the basic principles of how to divide a monolithic application into microservices and nanoservices, as well as how to detect when the division isn't right. We used a real-life example to delve into the thought process of designing microservices and nanoservices.

Then, we introduced the serverless architecture and the most popular cloud providers. We covered the four major categories of cloud computing services (IaaS, PaaS, SaaS, and FaaS) and discussed the benefits and cautions when using serverless architecture. After, we conducted an exercise where we adopted serverless architecture and chose appropriate cloud computing services to meet the requirements.

Finally, we briefly covered the microfrontend architecture, where a monolithic frontend application is broken down into frontend applications. We used the same real-life example from before to illustrate the decomposition and how each frontend module communicates with the backend components. Finally, we covered the need for design systems to ensure a consistent user experience and briefly mentioned the benefits and challenges of using the microfrontend architecture.

In the next chapter, we're going to dive into the practice of separating concerns using selected methodologies to help drive us toward efficient, scalable, and maintainable applications.

7

Modular and Layered Architectures

The previous chapters have repeatedly mentioned the importance of appropriate modularization of the system and addressing concerns separately. In this chapter, we delve into four prominent architectural patterns that offer their approaches to separate concerns in layers, modularize code, and set up clean boundaries among modules.

All these patterns will be illustrated with the same real-life example to highlight the similarities and differences of these patterns.

By understanding these patterns with code examples in Kotlin, engineers can make informed choices to create loosely coupling and highly cohesive modules that are testable, flexible, and maintainable.

The following architectural patterns will be covered:

- Clean Architecture

- The hexagonal architecture

- **Functional core, imperative shell (FCIS)**

- The Connect pattern

At the end, these patterns will be briefly compared with one another. We will also explore the possibility of taking elements from each pattern to create a hybrid pattern to meet the requirements.

Technical requirements

You can find the code files used in this chapter on GitHub: `https://github.com/PacktPublishing/Software-Architecture-with-Kotlin/tree/main/chapter-7`

Clean Architecture

Clean Architecture is an architectural pattern that advocates organizing a software system into distinct layers, each with its own responsibilities and dependencies.

The term Clean Architecture was introduced by Robert Martin (known as *Uncle Bob*) in his book titled *Clean Architecture: A Craftsman's Guide to Software Structure and Design*, published in 2017. The foundation of this approach is built upon a few earlier architectural patterns:

- **The hexagonal architecture** (also known as **ports and adapters**) by Alistair Cockburn
- **Onion Architecture** by Jeffrey Palermo
- **Screaming Architecture** by Robert Martin
- **Data, context, and interaction (DCI)** by James Coplien and Trygve Reenskaug
- **Boundary-control-entity (BCE)** by Ivar Jacobson

Clean Architecture dissects a software system by numerous layers, where each layer is wrapped one on top of the other, like an onion. The **Dependency Rule** of Clean Architecture states that the outer layers always depend on the inner layers.

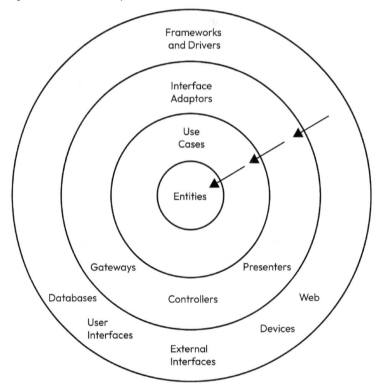

Figure 7.1 – Clean Architecture

Due to the Dependency Rule, any change in the outer layer does not affect the inner layer. On the contrary, any change in the inner layer may affect the outer layer.

Let us go through the layer from the innermost to the outermost, demonstrated by the real-life example we use throughout previous chapters—households in a village exchanging services with each other.

Entities

The **Entities layer** is the innermost layer, which depends on no other layer. This layer is designed to encapsulate business rules shared among applications.

It contains mostly data structures and functions only. It rarely depends on external libraries. The only libraries it depends on are most likely those that provide specialized data structures. This layer is also the least likely to change.

In our real-life example, there are a few candidates suitable to be hosted in the Entities layer. Household, Contract, Service, and subclasses of Service as Kotlin data classes belong to the Entities layer. Certain rules and policies can also reside in the Entities layer. Here are a few example rules.

Rule 1 – Household name must not be null and must have at least one member

This rule is enforced by the Kotlin non-null field syntax in data classes and the validation within the init function:

```kotlin
data class Household(
    val name: String,
    val members: List<String>
) {
    init {
        require(members.isNotEmpty()) { "Household must have at least
one member" }
    }
}
```

Rule 2 – Contract must be in one of the specified states

This rule is enforced by the Kotlin enumeration feature:

```kotlin
enum class ContractState {
    DRAFTED,
    UNDER_REVIEW,
    AGREED,
    REJECTED,
    PARTIALLY_EXERCISED,
    FULLY_EXERCISED,
```

```
        WITHDRAWN
}
```

Rule 3 – a Contract consists of two Household objects and a state

This rule is enforced by Kotlin data classes:

```kotlin
data class Party(
    val household: Household,
    val serviceProvided: String,
    val agreedAt: Instant? = null,
    val completedAt: Instant? = null
)
data class Contract(
    val partyA: Party,
    val partyB: Party,
    val contractState: ContractState
)
```

These classes are Pure Kotlin and can be shared among the four services we defined earlier in *Chapter 6*, namely *Household Service*, *Contract Service*, and *Notification Service*. Arguably, Household Service does not need a `Contract` class, and this may be a trade-off for most services to share entity classes but not all.

Use Cases

The **Use Cases layer** is one layer above the Entities layer. It is designed to encapsulate business rules within an application.

It contains use cases that make use of the data structures and functions in the Entities layer. Any change in this layer should not affect the Entities layer. This layer should also remain neutral to choices of frameworks and technologies, such as databases and messaging.

In our real-life example, we have a use case of a household drafting a contract with another household, using the Negotiation Service:

```kotlin
fun draftContract(
    householdA: Household,
    householdB: Household,
    serviceProvidedByHouseholdA: String,
    serviceProvidedByHouseholdB: String,
): Contract {
    require(householdA != householdB) { "Parties must be from
different households" }
    return Contract(Party(
        householdA,
        serviceProvidedByHouseholdA,
```

```
    ), Party(
        householdB,
        serviceProvidedByHouseholdB,
    ), ContractState.DRAFTED)
}
```

The `draftContract` function validates that the two households are not the same. If everything looks good, it creates a contract with both households and their services to be provided. In addition, it set the contract state to DRAFTED. This `draftContract` function in the Use Cases layer makes use of the `Household`, `Party`, `ContractState`, and `Contract` classes from the Entities layer.

There could be a bit of fluidity between the Entities layer and the Use Cases layer. If one feature in Entities is considered only relevant to one application, it can be moved to the Use Cases layer. Similarly, if there are duplicated logics in the Use Cases layer in different applications, they can be extracted into the Entities layer.

Interface Adapters

The Entities and Use Cases layers are considered internal models, where data structures are not exposed outside of the application. The **Interface Adapters layer** serves as the translation between the internal and the external models. Typical examples of external models are relational database tables, message payloads, HTTP request and response payloads, file formats, and visual representation in the **graphical user interface (GUI)**.

We already have a few examples of where the code should stay in the Interface Adapters layer:

- The peer-to-peer architectures covered in *Chapter 4* have illustrated the example code of conversion between a `Contract` object and a binary payload used for **User Datagram Protocol (UDP)** transmission.

- In the same chapter, there is a similar example, but the conversion is between a `Contract` object and a **JavaScript Object Notation (JSON)** payload that is defined by **OpenAPI** specifications, under the client-server architecture.

- The three frontend architectural styles covered in *Chapter 5*, MVC, MVP, and MVVM, would have the corresponding code in this layer, as they transform internal models to the view that is rendered as GUI.

If the application uses query languages, such as SQL, for relational databases, they should also stay in the Interface Adapters layer.

These external models and their corresponding conversion should not leak into other layers. The layer should not contain business logic either. The concern of internal models is separated from layers outside of the Interface Adapters layer, and the concern of external models is separated from layers inside of the Interface Adapters layer.

Frameworks and Drivers

The Frameworks and Drivers layer is one layer outside of the Interface Adapters layer. This is where external frameworks are added to make it an application. Typical examples are HTTP endpoint routing configurations, database connection details, Kubernetes configurations, and dependency management. Quite often, this layer contains configuration files more than source code.

This layer should never contain business use cases. It does not know any internal models and therefore no conversion from external models. This layer focuses on supporting configurations that turn code into an application executable in a runtime. It should address only non-functional requirements, such as startup time, or redundancy.

An example use case with Clean Architecture

Let us take a use case as an example of how different layers are used. A household is presented with a form to submit a draft contract, which is a web page in the Frameworks and Drivers layer.

The household then submits the form as JSON values and enters the controller in the Interface Adapters layer. The controller converts the form into a few internal objects, such as the objects of both `Household` and the services provided as strings. These internal objects are then passed to a `draftContract` function in the Use Cases layer:

```
fun draftContract(
    householdA: Household,
    householdB: Household,
    serviceProvidedByHouseholdA: String,
    serviceProvidedByHouseholdB: String,
): Contract
```

The function creates a `Contract` object, which comes from the Entities layer. The function passes a `Contract` object to the presenter in the Interface Adapters layer. The presenter converts the `Contract` object into a JSON value to be rendered by the web page in the Frameworks and Drivers layer. The whole journey is illustrated in *Figure 7.2*:

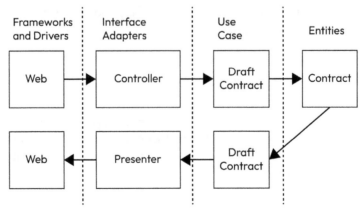

Figure 7.2 – Example use case of Clean Architecture

Benefits of Clean Architecture

The centerpiece of Clean Architecture is the Dependency Rule, not the four defined layers. With justifications, there could be variation in the layers, but the Dependency Rule should still apply.

Overall, concerns are separated in each layer in Clean Architecture. Each layer is dedicated to address specific concerns that no other layers do:

- **Entities layer**: Functional requirements shared among applications
- **Use Cases layer**: Functional requirements within an application
- **Interface Adapters layer**: Conversion between internal and external models
- **Frameworks and Drivers layer**: Non-functional requirements

With a clear separation of concerns, we now have the Entities layer and the Use Cases layer independent of the choices of frameworks and technologies. They have no knowledge about the external world. They are testable without **user interfaces (UIs)**, databases, messaging, files, or any external representation. It is computationally cheap to execute a test in these two layers, and therefore we can afford to run a comprehensive test suite without significant penalty on build times.

As the technology and framework choices only exist in the Interface Adapters layer and the Framework and Drivers layer, engineers can make changes to the framework in these layers, knowing that the functional logic in the Entities and Use Cases layers is intact. In addition, there could be test cases in these layers to ensure the correctness of internal-external model conversion, and the correctness of configuration of the framework in these layers.

Moreover, it enables a smooth transition of technology change. A new technology can be introduced and coexist with the old one. Engineers can commit incrementally to the changes required for the new technology. There can be toggles to switch between the new and old technology for testing purposes. Once the team is happy with the change, they can switch to the new technology and clean up the code afterward.

The hexagonal architecture is one of the architectural patterns that Clean Architecture is built upon. We are going to explore the hexagonal architecture in the next section.

Hexagonal architecture

The **hexagonal architecture**, also known as the **ports and adapters architecture**, aims to address the problem of coupling between the core business logic and external dependencies, such as databases, UIs, and external systems.

The hexagonal architecture was introduced by Alistair Cockburn in his paper, *Hexagonal Architecture*, published in 2005.

The two fundamental concepts of this architectural style are **ports** and **adapters**. Ports define the interactions between the internal and the external worlds, and adapters provide the implementation details of these interactions.

The concept of hexagonal architecture is visualized in *Figure 7.3* as a hexagon. It is worth noting that this architecture allows as many sides as possible, not limited to only six as the name *hexagon* suggests.

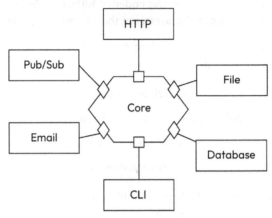

Figure 7.3 – An example of the hexagonal architecture

We will cover each element of the hexagonal architecture in the following sections.

The core

The core of the hexagonal architecture encapsulates the business logic of the application in a pure way, without involving any technology and framework. The core is often called "the Domain." The only exception may be a library that provides the data structure needed to support the business logic. The core does not depend on any adapter implementation.

The core contains data structures and functions that represent pure business logic. Taking the same real-life example we have for households exchanging service, we should have these elements in the core:

- **Data structures**: The `HouseHold`, `Party`, and `Contract` data classes; the `ContractState` enum class
- **Functions**: The `draftContract` function

Ports

Ports are the interfaces describing what the application can do. There are two types of ports in the hexagonal architecture:

- **Primary port**: Known as the driving port, this determines inputs required by the core to perform an operation
- **Secondary port**: Known as the driven port, this determines what outputs are produced by the core for the external world's consumption

The port interfaces should be defined by the needs of the core and not the external world. If we are writing a new application from scratch, we should start from the core and define port interfaces for what the core needs, even without any code in adapters.

In addition to the code we have in the core, we need to define port interfaces for the external world to use the core and consume the result produced by the core.

In the real-life example where a household intends to draft a contract, the core validates the request and produces a drafted contract. The core needs a repository to store the drafted contract.

We need a primary port to allow a contract to be drafted. The `ContractService` interface is exposed for external usage, but the implementation of the interface stays in the core:

```
interface ContractService {
    fun draftContract(
        householdA: Household,
        householdB: Household,
        serviceProvidedByHouseholdA: String,
        serviceProvidedByHouseholdB: String,
    ): Contract
}
```

We also need a secondary port to allow a draft contract to be persisted. The `ContractRepository` interface is implemented by adapters to provide the technical details of how a `Contract` object is saved:

```
interface ContractRepository {
    fun save(contract: Contract)
}
```

The implementation of the primary port interface, `ContractService`, validates the draft contract and creates a `Contract` object with a DRAFTED state. Then, the `Contract` object is passed to `ContractRepository` to be saved:

```
class ContractServiceImpl(
    private val contractRepository: ContractRepository,
) : ContractService {
    override fun draftContract(
        householdA: Household,
        householdB: Household,
        serviceProvidedByHouseholdA: String,
        serviceProvidedByHouseholdB: String,
    ): Contract =
        draftContract(
            householdA,
            householdB,
```

```
            serviceProvidedByHouseholdA,
            serviceProvidedByHouseholdB,
    ).also { contractRepository.save(it) }
}
```

The `ContractServiceImpl` class is a part of the core logic and stays in the core. It is able to implement business behaviors without specifying how `Contract` is saved. In other words, the core focuses on business rules and is free of the concerns of the choice of technology and frameworks.

Adapters

Adapters are responsible for translating external models to the internal models, which are defined in the core.

Adapters use the primary port as an entrance to the core and run business operations. An adapter is tied to at least one framework, and it has an external representation of the entities involved.

In the real-life example, the adapter can be a **Representational State Transfer (REST)** controller that exposes a POST endpoint to create a draft contract. The payload is a JSON value, represented by the `DraftContractRequest` class, which can be converted into a `Contract` object:

```
data class DraftContractRequest(
    val householdA: String,
    val householdB: String,
    val serviceProvidedByHouseholdA: String,
    val serviceProvidedByHouseholdB: String
)
```

Contract Service has locally cached `Household` objects, which can be looked up by household name from the `HouseholdRepository` repository:

```
interface HouseholdRepository {
    fun findByName(householdName: String): Household?
}
```

The function returns a `Household` object if the household of the given name is found. Otherwise, it returns a `null` value. The REST controller class, `ContractController`, is defined to accept HTTP requests to draft a contract. This controller uses Spring Boot as the framework to register URI mapping:

```
@RestController
@RequestMapping("/contracts/")
class ContractController(
    private val contractService: ContractService,
    private val householdRepository: HouseholdRepository,
) {
```

The controller is injected with the `ContractService` primary port to enter the core and draft a contract. It is also injected with the `HouseholdRepository` secondary port to look up `Household` objects for validation.

```
@PostMapping(
    value = ["draft"],
    consumes = [MediaType.APPLICATION_JSON_VALUE],
    produces = [MediaType.APPLICATION_JSON_VALUE],
)
```

The controller defines a mapping of `POST /contracts/draft` that accepts JSON value as input and as output.

```
fun draftContract(
    @RequestBody request: DraftContractRequest,
): ResponseEntity<ContractDto> {
    val householdA = householdRepository.findByName(request.
householdA) ?: return ResponseEntity(HttpStatus.NOT_FOUND)
    val householdB = householdRepository.findByName(request.
householdB) ?: return ResponseEntity(HttpStatus.NOT_FOUND)
```

The controller converts the `DraftContractRequest` request payload and validates that household names in the payload exist. If any household does not exist, a `404 (Not Found)` HTTP status is returned to the requester.

```
val contract =
    contractService.draftContract(
        householdA,
        householdB,
        request.serviceProvidedByHouseholdA,
        request.serviceProvidedByHouseholdB,
    )
```

The controller invokes the `draftContract` function in the `ContractNegotiationService` primary port, which validates the request and persists the draft contract in the repository.

```
    return ResponseEntity(contract.toDto(), HttpStatus.CREATED)
}
```

Finally, the operation has finished, and the controller returns a `201 (Created)` HTTP status back to the requester with the details of the draft contract. The response payload is represented by the `ContractDto` class:

```
data class ContractDto(
    val householdA: String,
    val householdB: String,
```

```
    val serviceProvidedByHouseholdA: String,
    val serviceProvidedByHouseholdB: String,
    val contractState: String,
)
```

There is a `toDto` function for the conversion from the internal model to the external model of the contract:

```
fun Contract.toDto(): ContractDto =
    ContractDto(
        partyA.household.name,
        partyB.household.name,
        this.partyA.serviceProvided,
        this.partyB.serviceProvided,
        this.contractState.name,
    )
```

The data was transformed and passed through the layers of the hexagonal architecture in this example, as demonstrated in *Figure 7.4*:

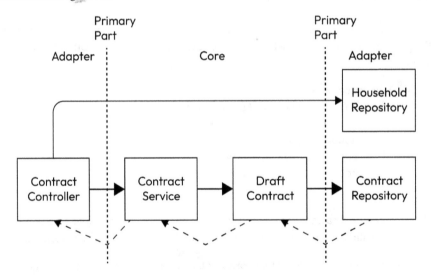

Figure 7.4 – Example use case of the hexagonal architecture

The request payload as JSON value is validated in the `ContractController` adapter with the help of a `HouseholdRepository` secondary port. Then, the payload is converted to the `Household` objects defined in the core. The core runs through the business process and uses a `ContractRepository` secondary port to persist a valid draft `Contract` object. Then, the result is populated to the `ContractController` adapter. Finally, the adapter converts the `Contract` object to a response payload.

Benefits of hexagonal architecture

Separating source code in the layers of the hexagonal architecture certainly makes the code base more complicated. It does bring a few benefits by separating the source code between the core and the adapter.

The core encapsulates pure business rules and the adapter contains all technology details. This separation makes it extremely easy to test the concerns of correctness and technology integration independently.

The core contains a comprehensive test suite that ensures the business rules are enforced as intended, without involving any technology.

On the other hand, the adapter contains test cases that verify the configuration of the chosen technology and frameworks work as intended, without mixing business rules.

An adapter is designed to be pulled and replaced by another adapter at any time. An adapter is specifically implemented for a chosen technology or framework, but the port has no knowledge about it. For example, if the request and response use messaging technology, such as queuing, then we can replace `ContractController` with a different adapter, such as `DraftContractRequestConsumer`.

The implementation of the secondary port as an adapter can also be replaced if needed. For example, we could have an implementation of a memory cache or relational database of `HouseholdRepository`. They can coexist and we can use configuration to decide which one is used at runtime. Each adapter can be tested in isolation.

This separation of concerns results in enabling engineers to conform to the **single responsibility principle** (**SRP**), in which the core has only one reason to change, and each adapter has only one reason to change.

Coming next, we are going to cover an architecture pattern that aims to solve this similar challenge, but in the functional style.

Functional core, imperative shell

FCIS emerged as an architectural pattern over time in the functional programming community. It is a design principle that advocates separating the immutable core business logic from the mutable aspects, such as persistent storage or external system integration. It aligns and encourages functional programming principles with the use of stateless functions and immutable data structures.

Stateless functions are sometimes called pure functions. They can be executed without causing side effects, in other words, for a given input, the function always produces the same output. Immutable data structures never change their content.

The FCIS principle has been influenced by various software development paradigms and architectural patterns. It shares similarities with the hexagonal architecture, which also promotes separating the core logic from the infrastructure concerns.

There are two major components in FCIS. The functional core contains stateless functions and immutable data structures that represent business logic and entities, respectively.

The imperative shell, on the other hand, is the layer outside of the functional core that interacts with the external world, such as database operations, messaging, or UIs. This layer is responsible for executing the imperative and mutable operations required by the system.

The FCIS architecture can be demonstrated in *Figure 7.5*:

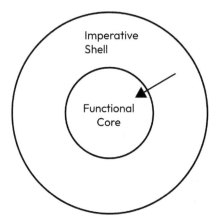

Figure 7.5 – FCIS

We are going to cover these two components of this architectural style here.

Functional core

The functional core focuses on the core business logic, which consists of stateless functions and immutable data structures only.

Using the same real-life example we have for households exchanging service, we should have these elements in the core:

- **Data structures**: The HouseHold, Party, and Contract data classes and the ContractState enum class
- **Functions**: The draftContract function

All data classes are immutable, and all functions are stateless in our example. They are tested in isolation by simply verifying the output of the function given the input.

However, the draftContract function would need a tweak from the implementation shown in the example from the Clean Architecture section, because we need to build up higher-order functions with potential errors found along the way.

To start with this approach, we need to define what errors we may encounter. We will start with defining the types of errors first:

```
enum class ErrorType {
    HOUSEHOLD_NOT_FOUND,
    SAME_HOUSEHOLD_IN_CONTRACT
}
```

We also need a wrapper data class for the error itself:

```
data class Error(
    val reason: String,
    val type: ErrorType
)
```

We need to be able to communicate that functions can return an expected result, but there is also a chance an error occurred. This new implementation of draftContract uses the Either class from **Arrow** library to express this outcome:

> **Arrow**
>
> **Arrow** (https://arrow-kt.io/) is a library for Kotlin. It aims to bring idiomatic functional programming constructs to Kotlin. It provides an alternative approach to handling null values using Option and result types for error handling using Either. It also provides various functional programming patterns, such as functors, monads, and applicatives. Arrow aims to improve code readability, maintainability, and robustness by enabling developers to express computations in a functional style, making it easier to manage complex data flows and side effects in Kotlin applications.

```
fun draftContract(
    householdA: Household,
    householdB: Household,
    serviceProvidedByHouseholdA: String,
    serviceProvidedByHouseholdB: String,
): Either<Error, Contract> =
```

The draftContract function returns an Either object in which the left type parameter is always the potential error, and the right type parameter is always the expected result:

```
    if (householdA.name == householdB.name) {
        Either.Left(
            Error("Parties must be from different households",
ErrorType.SAME_HOUSEHOLD_IN_CONTRACT),
        )
    }
```

The same validation ensures the contract does not have the same `Household` on both sides. However, instead of throwing an exception, the function returns the left side value, which is represented by the `Error` class just defined earlier on.

```
    else {
      Either.Right(
          Contract(
              partyA = Party(householdA,
serviceProvidedByHouseholdA),
              partyB = Party(householdB,
serviceProvidedByHouseholdB),
              contractState = ContractState.DRAFTED,
          ),
      )
  }
```

If everything is fine, the function returns the right side value, which is the `Contract` object itself.

Imperative shell

The imperative shell handles the necessary interactions with the outside world, providing the necessary integration points and adaptors.

In the real-life example, this includes the persistence of the `Contract` object and the REST endpoint controller that accepts HTTP `POST` requests to draft a contract.

Apart from the REST controller, there are two more imperative operations involved. The first one looks up a `Household` object by the name, and the second one persists a `Contract` object. We define them using `typealias` in this example:

```
typealias HouseholdLookup = (String) -> Household?
typealias ContractPersist = (Contract) -> Either<Error, Contract>
```

In addition to these two functions defined, we also need a function to ensure the household mentioned in the request exists:

```
fun DraftContractRequest.ensureHouseholdExist(
    householdLookup: HouseholdLookup
): Either<Error, Pair<Household, Household>> {
    val householdARecord = householdLookup(householdA)
    val householdBRecord = householdLookup(householdB)

    return if (householdARecord == null) {
        Either.Left(
            Error("Households not found: $householdA", ErrorType.
HOUSEHOLD_NOT_FOUND),
```

```
        )
    } else if (householdBRecord == null) {
        Either.Left(
            Error("Households not found: $householdB", ErrorType.
HOUSEHOLD_NOT_FOUND),
        )
    } else {
        Either.Right(
            householdARecord to householdBRecord,
        )
    }
}
```

The ensureHouseholdExist function makes use of HouseholdLookup to check if the two households mentioned in the DraftContractRequest request exist. If not, the left side of Either will be returned to report the household not found error. If both households exist, the household records are returned for further processing.

With this function defined, we can now inject them into the imperative controller implementation:

```
@RequestMapping("/contracts/")
class ContractControllerShell(
    private val householdLookup: HouseholdLookup,
    private val contractPersist: ContractPersist,
) {
    @PostMapping(
        value = ["draft"],
        consumes = [MediaType.APPLICATION_JSON_VALUE],
        produces = [MediaType.APPLICATION_JSON_VALUE],
    )
```

The draft function now takes full advantage of the Either class by collapsing the right type parameter with the flatMap function:

```
fun draft(
    @RequestBody draftContractRequest: DraftContractRequest,
): ResponseEntity<ContractDto> =
    draftContractRequest
        .ensureHouseholdExist(householdLookup)
        .flatMap { (householdA, householdB) ->
            draftContract(
                householdA,
                householdB,
                draftContractRequest.serviceProvidedByHouseholdA,
                draftContractRequest.serviceProvidedByHouseholdB,
```

```
                )
        }.flatMap { contractPersist(it) }
        .flatMap { Either.Right(it.toDto()) }
        .fold(
            { error -> ResponseEntity(error.type.toHttpStatus())
    },
            { contractDto -> ResponseEntity(contractDto,
HttpStatus.CREATED) },
            )
```

The flatMap functions chain the results of Either to return either the first error on the left or the final expected result on the right. The preceding code firstly checks and ensures that both households mentioned in the request exist. The next chained call gets the household records from the ensureHouseholdExist function and it passes all parameters to the draftContract function to validate business rules and return a Contract object of the DRAFTED state.

The next chained call receives the Contract object of the DRAFTED state and calls the ContractPersist function to persist this contract.

After the Contract record is persisted, it is transformed into a **data transfer object** (**DTO**) that will be exposed and returned to the HTTP client that initiated the request.

At the last part of the chained call, the fold function is invoked to differentiate the response back to the HTTP client. The success result as a Contract object, the right side, is converted to the ContractDto response payload by the toDto function. A 201 (Created) HTTP status is returned together with the response payload.

All the possible errors are collapsed onto the left side, and they are mapped to the HTTP status code, as shown here:

```
fun ErrorType.toHttpStatus(): HttpStatus = when (this) {
    ErrorType.HOUSEHOLD_NOT_FOUND -> HttpStatus.NOT_FOUND
    ErrorType.SAME_HOUSEHOLD_IN_CONTRACT -> HttpStatus.BAD_REQUEST
}
```

Benefits of functional core, imperative shell

FCIS separates the code into two parts.

The functional core is a purely functional area that only contains stateless functions and immutable data structures, which can be easily tested and reasoned about. There is no state management and no side effects. Each test is about verifying the output of the function given the input values.

The functional core is also free of technology choice. It makes the functional core focus on only business concerns. There is no need to change the code if we decide to use other technologies to receive requests and produce responses. This makes the core logic reliable, adaptable, and maintainable.

The only exception, as we shown in the example, is the use of the `Either` class brought from the Arrow library, to express that an operation can fail and return a different object.

This encourages engineers to organize the code to conform to the SRP in which each function has only one reason to change. We still need to organize our functions with the best practices to conform to SRP though. For example, each function needs to be small, reusable, stateless, and with one purpose only.

Separating the functional core from the imperative shell allows for easier evolution of the core logic without being tightly coupled to the external systems or implementation details. It also allows for greater flexibility and maintainability, leading to more robust and flexible software architectures.

The next architectural pattern we are going to cover focuses on adapting to a remote API call.

The Connect pattern

The Connect pattern was first introduced by David Denton in his technical article, *Smash your Adapter Monolith with the Connect pattern*, on the internet in 2011.

This pattern, however, has a different focus from the three architectural patterns previously discussed. It is specifically targeted at remote system integration. It aims to provide a testable and extensible approach to encapsulate remote API interactions.

The concept of the Connect pattern is illustrated in *Figure 7.6*:

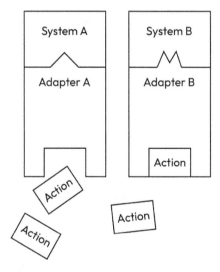

Figure 7.6 – The Connect pattern

An integration operation is abstracted as an Action. It understands how to generate a request and how to transform a response into an internal object. However, it does not know the connection details to the external system.

An adapter, on the other hand, is crafted to adapt to a specific system. It can establish a connection with an external system while delegating the actual request-response exchange to an Action.

Action

An **Action** is responsible for transforming requests from internal to external format and transforming responses from external to internal format. Using the same real-life example of the villagers exchanging services, there are some supporting functions that we need from the Household Service, and one of them is as simple as getting a household by the given household name.

The Action related to communicating with the Household Service is defined here:

```
interface HouseholdApiAction<R> {
    fun toRequest(): Request
    fun fromResponse(response: Response): R
}
```

There are only two simple functions. The `toRequest` function generates a request in an external format to communicate with Household Service. The `fromResponse` function transforms a response from Household Service to an internal object. The type variable, R, is specific to the given Action and can vary.

The Action to get a household name by the given household name is defined here:

```
val householdLens = Body.auto<Household>().toLens()
data class GetHousehold(
    val householdName: String,
) : HouseholdApiAction<Household> {
    override fun toRequest(): Request = Request(Method.GET, "/
households/$householdName")
    override fun fromResponse(response: Response): Household =
householdLens(response)
}
```

The GetHousehold class encapsulates the details needed to generate the HTTP request to Household Service. The response from Household Service is transformed to an internal data class, Household, using **HTTP4k Lens**. Please note that although this example makes use of the **HTTP4K** library, the Connect pattern itself is not restricted to this library. The internal Household data class is defined here:

```
data class Household(
    val name: String,
    val emailAddress: String,
)
```

So far, there are no connection details to Household Service, but this will be covered by the adapter.

Adapter

The adapter class provides a way to abstract away the connectivity details and mechanism to an external system. The Household API is defined here:

```
interface HouseholdApi {
    operator fun <R : Any> invoke(action: HouseholdApiAction<R>): R
    companion object
}
```

The HouseholdApi interface acts as a wrapper and handle for the invocation of the specific action. The companion object is defined as a placeholder for extension functions, which will be covered later. An HTTP implementation that communicates with a local Household Service is implemented as follows:

```
val token = "fakeToken"
fun HouseholdApi.Companion.Http(client: HttpHandler) =
    object : HouseholdApi {
        private val http =
  SetBaseUriFrom(Uri.of("http://localhost:9000"))
                .then(
                    Filter { next -> { next(it.header("Authorization",
"Bearer $token")) } },
                ).then(client)
        override fun <R : Any> invoke(action: HouseholdApiAction<R>) =
action.fromResponse(http(action.toRequest()))
    }
```

This Household API implementation is an anonymous inner class that sets the host of Household Service to localhost and sets the authorization bearer token. It assumes that all HouseholdAction would use the same connectivity settings.

Moreover, an extension function is defined to make the usage code tidier:

```
fun HouseholdApi.getHousehold(householdName: String) =
invoke(GetHousehold(householdName))
```

The code usage example is going to be covered in the following section.

Usage

With the Action and the adapter set up, the usage of the Household Service to get a household by the given name only requires three lines of code:

```
val app: HttpHandler =
    routes(
        "/households/{name}" bind GET to { request ->
```

```
            val householdName = request.path("name")!!.toString()
            Response(OK).with(householdLens of Household(name =
householdName, emailAddress = "same.address@domain.com"))
        },
    )
fun main() {
    val householdApi = HouseholdApi.Http(JavaHttpClient())
    val household: Household = householdApi.
getHousehold("Whittington")
    println(household)
}
```

The variable app is `HttpHandler`, which defines URI routings. Only a GET endpoint is defined in this example, together with a canned response back to the HTTP client.

In the `main` function, an HTTP client implementation is created to be fed to create an HTTP implementation of `HouseholdApi`. Then, the extension function is used to get a household with the name *Whittington*. Internally, a `GetHousehold` Action is created and passed into `HouseholdApi` and kicks off the API communication. However, from a usage point of view, an object of the internal `Household` data class is returned.

Test cases

One of the strengths of the Connect pattern is better testability. Each Action and API with the Household Service can be tested individually. This is the test case of getting a household from the Household API:

```
@Test
fun `Get the household from Household API`() {
    assertEquals(
        Response(OK)
            .contentType(ContentType.APPLICATION_JSON)
            .
body("{\"name\":\"Whittington\",\"emailAddress\":\"same.address@
domain.com\"}"),
        app(Request(GET, "/households/Whittington")),
    )
}
```

When there are more Actions, there will be more test cases, but each test case is isolated. In other words, the Actions and test cases scale without creating an interface with many functions.

Benefits

The major benefits of the Connect pattern are extensibility and testability. Given it is common to use multiple APIs of an external system, engineers often end up with one interface for the external system with many functions. With the Connect pattern, each API call is represented by an Action and thus breaks down the big interface into smaller pieces.

This pattern naturally conforms to the SRP as an Action represents only one API call. Moreover, each Action has its own dedicated test case, which is a lot simpler than testing an interface with many functions.

The adapter has abstracted away the concern of connectivity details to a remote system, so Action classes can focus on the message formats and interactions.

The use of Kotlin extension functions makes the code usage fluent, tidy, and small. A lot of details are hidden and encapsulated within the Action and adapter classes.

Although the example uses HTTP and Kotlin, the Connect pattern itself is not restricted to them.

This pattern is particularly useful in the usage of communicating with a monolithic application that exposes a lot of functions in one interface.

Coming next, we are going to briefly compare these architectural styles.

Comparisons of architectural styles

The first three architectural styles we discussed in this chapter have a great deal of similarities. They all aim to solve the same issues; the variations are in the approaches.

Meanwhile, the Connect pattern focuses on the testability and extensibility of remote system interactions.

Dependency on frameworks and technologies

Traditional architectures often tightly couple the business logic with specific frameworks, libraries, or technologies. This makes it difficult to switch or upgrade these components without making widespread changes throughout the code base.

Clean Architecture proposes the Entities layer for enterprise business rules and the Use Cases layer for application-specific business rules. Both are neutral to choices of frameworks and technologies.

The hexagonal architecture proposes the core as the centerpiece for business logic, also free of the choices of frameworks and technologies.

FCIS proposes the functional core for business logic, but with the use of stateless functions and immutable data structures.

The Connect pattern uses Action for the integration point of a single action and an adapter for the transport details of the interaction with the remote system.

Testability

In traditional architectures, testing the core business logic can be challenging due to dependencies on external systems, databases, or UI frameworks.

Testing a function coupled with a choice of technology typically requires a lot of setting up and tearing down of resources, and worse if there are asynchronous processes behind the scenes. This means it requires more effort from engineers to make the tests work, fewer tests can be written for the same amount of time, the test suite takes longer to run, and there could be flaky tests that fail occasionally due to some asynchronous processes involved. Any parallel executed tests can make the test suite even more flaky.

Clean Architecture offers dedicated layers for business logic only (the Entities and Use Cases layers), which can be tested in isolation without involving any choice of technology. The Interface Adapters layer focuses on internal and external model translation, which can be also tested independently. The configurations of the Frameworks & Driver layers can be tested without involving business rules.

The hexagonal architecture advocates the core as a technology-neutral area where unit tests can be easily written without the need for complex setups or mocking extensive external components. Each adapter can be tested individually and without involving any business logic.

FCIS suggests putting only business logic as stateless functions and immutable data structures in the functional core. This reduces testing of the functional core using a simple verification of the output result given by input. The imperative shell can also be tested easily by swapping the lower-order functions in the functional core, as a result, the immutable and the mutable parts of the systems can be tested separately.

The Connect pattern breaks down the large remote interface of a monolithic application into one Action per API call. This reduces a lot of overhead, excessive mocking, test double, or stubbing of the interface. The ability to test an API call in isolation improves testability and enables easy extension of the usage of a remote API.

Maintainability

Over time, applications tend to evolve and change, often requiring modifications to the core business logic or the choice of frameworks. In traditional architectures, making changes can be risky as these modifications may have unintended consequences throughout the system. Updating business logic may have intertwined with a deprecated library and eventually, both need to be changed.

Clean Architecture, the hexagonal architecture, and FCIS provide a clear separation between the core business logic and the surrounding infrastructure, making it easier to modify or extend the application without affecting the core business rules.

The Connect pattern is very lightweight and there is no overlapping among Actions. The connectivity and message interaction concerns are separated into adapter and Action classes, the maintenance of these classes is simple, and code changes are small.

Flexibility and adaptability

Applications often need to integrate with various external resources, such as files, databases, third-party services, or UIs. In traditional architectures, these integrations are deeply embedded within the application code, making it challenging to switch or modify these integrations.

Clean Architecture promotes the Interface Adapters and Frameworks and Drivers layers to contain external dependencies. This allows more flexibility and adaptability, as the business rules remain decoupled from specific technologies or protocols.

The hexagonal architecture promotes the use of ports and adapters, which act as interfaces and adapters between the core logic and the external systems. A different choice of framework results in a separate implementation of adapters but the port interfaces remain the same. Changing technology or a protocol is easy by swapping an implementation of the same interface.

FCIS uses the imperative shell layer to handle all the interactions with the external world. Any change in technology or protocol requires a change only in the imperative shell layer. With the high-level reuse of small functions, only a minor change is required to adapt to a new technology.

The Connect pattern allows engineers to implement a new adapter if it needs to integrate with a new remote system. If it needs to adapt to a new communication protocol, it is required to implement a new adapter and new Action, but there is no need to update the current code.

When to use which architectural style

Clean Architecture, the hexagonal architecture, and FCIS share a great deal of similarities that engineers may find hard to choose for their applications. The layers of these three architectural styles can be approximately mapped as follows:

Clean Architecture	Hexagonal Architecture	FCIS
Entities	Shared / Common libs	Shared / Common libs
Use Case	Core / Domain / Port	Core
Interface Adapters	Adapters	Shell
Frameworks and Drivers	Adapters	Shell

Table 7.1 – Approximate mapping among the three architectural styles

If we accept the opinion that the three styles can be loosely mapped, then the choice would become convention among engineers. The following are some opinions for reference but they are not strict rules:

- Engineers with more functional programming experience would prefer FCIS.

- Clean Architecture provides better support to monolithic applications or systems with a big source repository. Having said that, Clean Architecture can absolutely support smaller repositories or microservices.

- The hexagonal architecture fits microservice applications in terms of scope and scale.

There are also a lot of rooms to create a hybrid style. For instance, an application using the hexagonal architecture can borrow the concepts of FCIS, so all ports and adapters are basically functions using the Kotlin operator overload features:

```
class DummyContractPersist: ContractPersist {
    override fun invoke(p1: Contract): Either<Error, Contract> {
```

`ContractPersist` is a type alias we used in FCIS, and we can define a class that implements the type alias interface and provides the `invoke` function with operator override. So, in practice, callers can skip the `invoke` keyword and treat it as a function, like the following:

```
val persist = DummyContractPersist()
val result = persist(contract)
```

So, this concept can be extended to port interfaces, where they are only type aliases or interfaces with one function only.

The Connect pattern is an integration pattern that solves a different problem than the other three styles covered in this chapter. The Connect pattern can be used when there is a need to perform the same action in a business sense using external systems, but we want to decouple the technical integration details from the business logic.

In relation to the anemic domain model

The **anemic domain model** (ADM) is a controversial architectural style that some people classify as an anti-pattern, while others find it useful in certain circumstances. In the ADM, the core or Use Cases layer has mainly data structures and little to zero business behaviors.

The in-depth discussion on ADM is beyond the scope of this chapter, however, if a team has chosen to use ADM, then it is not advisable to combine it with Clean Architecture, the hexagonal architecture, or FCIS.

The main reason is that these architectures are designed to have business behaviors kept in the core or Use Cases layer; in other words, they are designed to work with the **rich domain model** (RDM) only. The application does not get any benefit from adopting the layers from Clean Architecture, the hexagonal architecture, or FCIS covered in this chapter.

> **Usage of ADM**
>
> Although ADM may be seen as an anti-pattern to some people, the lack of business behaviors may mean the application's goals are data processing and infrastructure plumbing only. For example, an ADM application may be responsible for ingesting a large file, splitting the data in the file into chunks, and processing each chunk in parallel. The application focuses on data manipulation and scalability, meanwhile, the processed data is read by other downstream applications that contain actual business behaviors related to the data. Another example could be an application that consumes the headers of external messages and forwards these messages to their corresponding internal topics for further processing.

Organizing source code as layers

There are two popular choices for organizing source code as layers. In Kotlin, the first approach is to put files into their belonging packages as layers.

In the real-life example we used, we could have the following packages in each architectural style:

- **Clean Architecture**:

  ```
  org.example.service.negotiation.entity
  org.example.service.negotiation.usecase
  org.example.service.negotiation.interface
  org.example.service.negotiation.framework
  org.example.service.negotiation.framework.rest
  ```

- **Hexagonal architecture**:

  ```
  org.example.service.negotiation.core
  org.example.service.negotiation.core.port
  org.example.service.negotiation.adapter
  org.example.service.negotiation.adapter.rest
  ```

- **FCIS**:

  ```
  org.example.service.negotiation.core
  org.example.service.negotiation.shell
  org.example.service.negotiation.shell.rest
  ```

Enforcing the layered architecture, where only the outer layer can use the inner layer and not the other way round, can easily be done using test cases and includes passing them as a part of a successful build.

This is an example of a test case that enforces the FCIS layer dependency, using **ArchUnit** as the test driver:

```
val classes = ClassFileImporter().importPackages("fcis")
@Test
fun `layer dependencies are_respected`() {
    layeredArchitecture()
        .consideringAllDependencies()
        .layer("Imperative Shell")
        .definedBy("fcis.shell..")
        .layer("Functional Core")
        .definedBy("fcis.core..")
        .whereLayer("Imperative Shell")
        .mayNotBeAccessedByAnyLayer()
        .whereLayer("Functional Core")
        .mayOnlyBeAccessedByLayers("Imperative Shell")
        .check(classes)
}
```

The second approach is the use of a source code module within a build framework, such as **Gradle** or **Maven**. We create multi-module projects for an application, and the outer modules declare dependencies on inner modules.

For example, the imperative shell of the Negotiation Service can have explicit dependencies declared in the Gradle Kotlin script of the imperative shell module.

```
implementation("com.example:service-negotiation-core")
```

It is important to note that this approach is more heavy-weighted than the package approach as it creates actual artifacts of inner layers.

The Connect pattern, however, is a modular but not layered architecture, so there is no need to enforce layer dependencies.

Summary

In this chapter, we discussed three architectural styles that aim to solve the same issues in traditional architectures where business logic and technology choices are tightly coupled. These three architectures were covered in depth: Clean Architecture, hexagonal architecture, and FCIS. We also discussed the Connect pattern, which focuses on breaking down large remote interfaces for integrating with remote systems.

We illustrated each architectural style using our real-life example and how each style is implemented in code.

We also compared the four architecture styles in terms of how they tackle the issues in traditional architecture. We briefly covered how code can be organized in a repository under layered architectures.

We mentioned that the core in the hexagonal architecture is sometimes named the *domain*. However, the term "domain" itself is worth a lengthy discussion. In the next chapter, we are going to cover the concepts surrounding the domain, with one common theme – **domain-driven development** (DDD).

8

Domain-Driven Design (DDD)

Engineers are often not the experts in business domains. Yet, they're responsible for building complex applications that represent real-world domains. Traditionally, software architectures often struggle to express the intricacies and subtlety of business domains effectively, leading to systems that are challenging to understand, maintain, and evolve. This is where **domain-driven design** (DDD) is brought into play.

In *Chapter 7*, we covered three architectural styles around the concept of having a dedicated layer to host business logic within an application. DDD aims to help engineers identify business behaviors that belong to the corresponding domain and the boundaries around it so that they can be implemented in the Core, Domain, or Use Case layer of an application.

This chapter explores the powerful software design approach of DDD, which centers around the business domain in the software design process. It focuses on capturing and expressing the core business concepts, rules, and behaviors.

First, we'll dive deep into the theoretical principles and practical implementation strategies of DDD, illustrated by real-life examples. Then, we'll explore how this approach can be used to build maintainable, scalable, and flexible software systems that align closely with business requirements.

By applying DDD, we can gain a better understanding of the domain and create a common language between domain experts and software developers.

We're going to cover the following topics in this chapter:

- Fundamentals of DDD
- Strategic and tactical designs in DDD
- Modeling activities in DDD

Technical requirements

You can find the code files used in this chapter on GitHub: `https://github.com/Packt Publishing/Software-Architecture-with-Kotlin/tree/main/chapter-8`

Fundamentals of DDD

The goal of DDD is to close the gap between the technical implementation of software and the business domain it serves. DDD heavily focuses on building software that accurately models the core concepts, business rules, and behaviors of the domain so that the software system is closely aligned with the needs of the business. This results in it being valuable, maintainable, flexible, and sustainable for the future.

DDD highlights the distinction between the problem space and the solution space:

- **Problem space:** The problem space is the reality of the business – that is, the current circumstances of the business operations

- **Solution space:** The solution space is the software system we have or will build to solve specific business cases in the problem space

The dominant part of the problem space is the **domain**, which represents specific business use cases and operations. The solution space provides a way to model the domain to solve the given business cases, hence the name **domain model**. This relationship is illustrated in *Figure 8.1*:

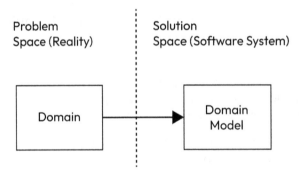

Figure 8.1 – Problem space and solution space

A domain model abstracts and selects certain elements in the domain so that a software system can be built upon it. The abstraction and selection result in the domain model is never 100% correct and complete. It is exactly what statistician *George Box* wrote in 1976 in a paper published in the *Journal of the American Statistical Association*:

"All models are wrong, but some are useful."

In DDD, domain models don't aim to be complete and accurate; instead, they aim to be useful in specific business contexts.

DDD encourages engineers to gain a deep understanding of the domain for which they're building software. There are domain experts who understand what software they need to get the job done. This is particularly true for the domains that originally used manual processes or paperwork to operate the business. Software systems are often seen as automation tools for business operations. Having a domain expert who operates the business brings a lot of value to engineers in building the corresponding software.

DDD comprises two design methodologies:

- **Strategic design**: This focuses on the overall structure and organization among multiple cohesive areas, named bounded contexts, within a larger business domain. It works toward a flexible and loose coupling system among bounded contexts by defining their collaborations.

- **Tactical design**: This refers to patterns, tools, and practices that make it simpler to build helpful domain models. We use tactical design when we have complex business logic to model or when complexity may be introduced in the future.

It's important to point out that DDD has nothing to do with what technology and frameworks are chosen. Modeling a business domain is purely the way a software system should be built, not which tools are used.

DDD – strategic design

It's recommended to start DDD with strategic design to establish the big picture before drilling down into the more granular tactical design. The very first step is known as **ubiquitous language**.

Ubiquitous language

Using a common language between engineers and domain experts is crucial to the success of software systems. Business domains often involve a lot of industry terms, specialized concepts, and subtle rules. However, not all of them can be applied to the scope of a software system. On the other hand, engineering involves a lot of technical terms, methodologies, and best practices, all of which are needed for the given software system.

Ubiquitous language is a term that was introduced by *Eric Evans* in his book *Domain-Driven Design: Tackling Complexity in the Heart of Software*, published in 2004. It serves as a common understanding and mental model of the domain that's shared between engineers and domain experts. It aims for a consistent, well-defined, and precise language to eliminate misunderstandings and ambiguities. It's a continuous, collaborative effort to build a common ground for effective and meaningful communication. Ubiquitous language is the common tongue between the domain and the domain model.

Ubiquitous language is also a form of documentation and the knowledge base of systems. Once established, new team members can understand the domain and the existing code base quickly. It also facilitates knowledge transfer among teams and stakeholders, thus promoting better collaboration and reducing the risk of information loss.

Ubiquitous language is the overlapping part between domain expert language and engineering language and implies a mutual understanding, as shown in *Figure 8.2*:

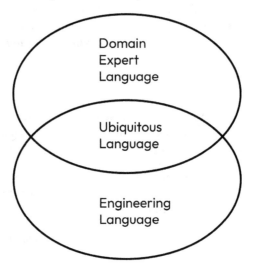

Figure 8.2 – Ubiquitous language in DDD

The benefits of ubiquitous language manifest themselves in various forms:

- **Glossary**: A glossary of terms and concepts and their definitions, available for everyone to read and learn about the business domain. Each term is reviewed and agreed upon by everyone involved in the development process. Ideally, there should be a process where changes can be submitted, reviewed, approved, and tracked in an auditable repository such as **GitHub**.

- **Documentation**: All documents related to the business domain should use the same terms and concepts that are defined in the glossary. These documents include user manuals, operation instructions, project plans, architectural design documents, diagrams, user stories, screen mockups, presentations, API documentation, and more. Any new term and concept should be added to the glossary.

- **Private large language modules (LLMs)**: The business domain knowledge, including terms, concepts, rules, and processes, can be used to train an LLM so that it can answer questions, complete text, generate dialog, and even become a part of the customer service bot. It does, however, require carefully crafting the input that's given to the model to generate the desired outputs or responses. This process is called **prompt engineering**, but it's beyond the scope of this book. OpenAI's documentation has a section on prompt engineering that provides practical guidance: `https://platform.openai.com/docs/guides/prompt-engineering`.

- **Source code**: The names of source files, functions, interfaces, classes, and even variables should use the same terms that have been defined in the glossary. Message payloads, database tables and fields, log messages, and error messages should also use these terms and concepts whenever applicable. These terms are used in every element in the code base. Seeing the same language everywhere related to the business domain for a software system is what we define as ubiquitous language.

Subdomains

A **subdomain** is a distinct area of the business domain that has its own set of concepts and business rules. The language that's used in a subdomain is part of ubiquitous language, and the corresponding concepts within the subdomain naturally form their own group.

Subdomains help break down the complexity of large domains into smaller, more manageable parts, allowing teams to focus on understanding and addressing the unique requirements and challenges of each subdomain. Subdomains belong to the problem space, and they may not always have a one-to-one mapping with a part of the system in the solution space.

Subdomains can be categorized into three groups:

- **Core domains**: Core domains are at the heart of business operations. Without them, there's no problem to solve, and there's no reason to build software systems. Core subdomains are the most critical part of an organization to differentiate them from competitors. They also have the most complex business cases.

- **Supporting subdomains**: Supporting subdomains provide peripheral tools and functionalities that complement and accelerate the core subdomains, but they aren't the primary area of expertise for the business. They're typically well-known capabilities where corresponding solutions can be found in the market or outsourced. They're still relevant to the business but don't provide significant competitive advantages.

- **Generic subdomains**: Generic subdomains refer to common problems that aren't specific to the business. Their corresponding solutions are off-the-shelf commercial products. They're essential for running business operations, but they don't directly contribute to the core value proposition of the business.

By identifying and modeling subdomains, DDD enables the development of cohesive, modular, and loosely coupled software systems. This leads us to an important concept in the solution space known as bounded contexts.

Bounded contexts

In *Chapter 6*, we mentioned the importance of identifying highly cohesive functions and grouping them as individual deployable artifacts so that we don't end up building a large monolithic application that's expensive to maintain, difficult to understand, and almost impossible to optimize. The system can be broken down into bounded contexts.

A **bounded context** is a concept in the solution space. It represents a cohesive area of the business domain. It has its own scope, responsibilities, and rules that don't overlap with other bounded contexts. A bounded context should have a clear purpose and a clear boundary. A well-defined bounded context gives a straightforward answer to whether a term or a rule belongs to the within or outside of the context. Within a bounded context, each building block has a specific semantic and purpose.

It takes away some parts of the complex business domain and turns them into a smaller and more manageable unit. Eventually, the sum of a sufficient collection of bound contexts is the overall domain model and thus eliminates the chance of it becoming a monolithic application.

A bounded context should represent one subdomain only, but a subdomain model might need a small portion of another subdomain model to function properly.

Also, a bounded context should have its own source code repository. It has its own data schema and data that are only shared with other bounded contexts via external representations defined in API documentation. It should also have dedicated deployable artifacts. They can be released independently without dependency on or affecting other bounded contexts. They should have their own release cadence.

A bounded context should be owned by one team only. The team has full autonomy in the choice of frameworks and development methodologies. In *Chapter 1*, we mentioned **Conway's law**, which states that an organization often produces software systems that mirror the internal structures of the organization. Instead of being constrained by the organization structure, teams should be re-structured based on the bounded contexts that are discovered during the DDD process.

Context mapping

Because bounded contexts break down a system, they need to collaborate for the system to function and achieve the overall goals. **Context mapping** is a technique that can be used to identify the relationships and interactions among bounded contexts.

Here are the common patterns in this relationship:

- **Partnership**: Two or more bounded contexts establish a collaborative relationship. This involves establishing close collaboration, shared understanding, and joint decision-making to address a specific business need. Even bounded contexts have their own goals, but their goals are connected to help solve a particular problem. So, they succeed and fail together:

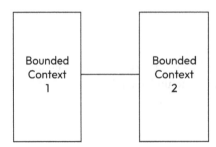

Figure 8.3 – Partnership

- **Shared kernel**: Two bounded contexts share a subset of their model or code. They might share the same data schema, a source code module, or compiled code as an artifact. However, it's considered an anti-pattern to share a data schema or raw source code between two bounded contexts. However, it's acceptable for two bounded contexts to depend on the same artifact that's treated as a shared library:

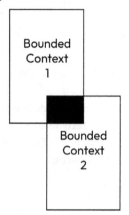

Figure 8.4 – Shared kernel

- **Customer-supplier**: The upstream bounded context supplies data, while the downstream bounded context consumes that data. The customer and the supplier collaborate and agree on the protocol of the data:

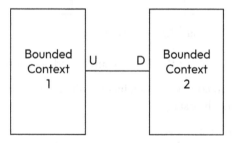

Figure 8.5 – Customer-supplier

- **Conformist**: The upstream bounded context supplies data and dictates the protocol of the data. The downstream bounded context conforms to the protocol and consumes that data. The upstream bounded context can be an external system or use an industry-standard protocol, making it unable to accommodate the downstream bounded context:

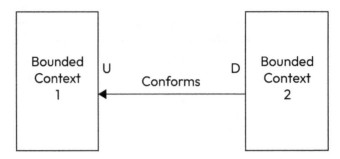

Figure 8.6 – Conformist

- **Anti-corruption layer**: The upstream bounded context supplies data and dominates the protocol of the data. The downstream bounded context, however, isn't willing to conform to the protocol. Instead, the downstream bounded context builds an anti-corruption layer to consume the data and translate it into the structure that it desires:

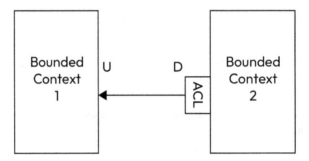

Figure 8.7 – Anti-corruption layer

There are several scenarios where the downstream bounded context decides not to conform:

- The upstream bounded context uses an inconvenient data protocol, making it difficult to integrate and consume the data

- The upstream bounded context is unreliable, changes often, or occasionally brings breaking changes that the downstream bounded context intends to minimize so that the impact of any issue brought by the upstream bounded context is diminished

- The data protocol used in the upstream bounded context brings conflicting or irrelevant data to the downstream bounded context

- The downstream bounded context reflects the core domain, which warrants reasons not to depend on a foreign data protocol

- **Separate ways**: There are no interactions between bounded contexts as they've decided to go separate ways. This can be due to integration being too expensive, unsustainable, or impossible. The following are some example scenarios where this has occurred:

  - The teams for each bounded context have a tough time collaborating and agreeing. This can be due to legacy systems being involved or just organizational politics. Instead of dragging on the long negotiation process, the bounded context finds it easier and quicker to replicate the logic in its own spaces.

  - The models between bounded contexts are too different for the conformist pattern to be used or too expensive for the anti-corruption layer pattern to be used compared to implementing tailored logic in its own bounded context. The upstream bounded context may only supply part of the data required by the downstream bounded context, while the downstream bounded context can replicate a part of the logic but create a complete model that's suitable for its specific purpose.

  - Often, it's in the generic subdomain where collaboration has little value compared to replicating the logic in the respective bounded contexts. It could be that certain libraries are used to generate data, hence why the cost of integration isn't justified.

- **Open-host service**: A bounded context defines and exposes a public API that other bounded contexts can use to extend its functionality. The public API is intentionally decoupled from the internal model so that both can be evolved independently. The internal model of the bounded context also remains private:

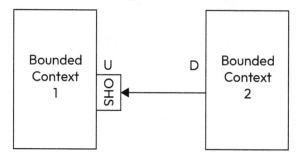

Figure 8.8 – Open-host service

- **Published language**: The published language focuses on establishing a shared language and glossary among bounded contexts. The published language doesn't intend to conform to its ubiquitous language, though there's no need to re-invent vocabulary if an appropriate term already exists in ubiquitous language.

Published language intends to expose a protocol that's convenient for consuming bounded contexts. It's expressed in an integration-oriented language that's usually not related to any programming language. Also, each bounded context should be able to translate between published language and corresponding internal models.

Published language ensures a consistent understanding of domain concepts and facilitates communication among bounded contexts.

Published language can be defined in many well-known formats, such as **OpenAPI**, **Avro**, **Protobuf**, fixed-length values, and comma-separated values.

Applying strategic design to a real-life example

So far, we've outlined the techniques and methods that are used in strategic design in DDD. Now, we're going to apply them to the same real-life example we've been using throughout this book.

Step 1 – synopsis of the business problem

Let's revisit the real-life example of households exchanging services. The team managed to find a senior lady who started to exchange services in the village. The team interviewed her, and their notes were captured. Here's the synopsis that was validated and clarified with her as the domain expert:

> *"We're a tight-knit community where villagers frequently exchange services to support each other. The village consists of various households, each with its unique skills, talents, and needs. The households recognized that by offering their services, they could help one another and create a stronger community.*
>
> *In this village, there were households specializing in different areas, such as carpentry, farming, cooking, and childcare. For instance, Mr. Whittington was a skilled carpenter who built and repaired furniture. When Mrs. Barker needed a new dining table, she approached Mr. Whittington to request his services.*
>
> *In return for Mr. Whittington's carpentry work, Mrs. Barker offered fresh produce from her farm to Mr. Carpenter's household throughout the year.*
>
> *Mrs. Barker drafted a contract to capture the details of the exchange, such as materials and dimensions of the table, what and how much fresh produce to provide, and a timeline. Mr. Whittington reviewed the contract and made a few adjustments. In the end, both Mr. Whittington and Mrs. Barker signed the contract.*
>
> *This arrangement helped Mr. Whittington and his family have a steady supply of nutritious food while allowing Mrs. Barker to enjoy beautifully crafted furniture in her home.*
>
> *These exchanges created the fabric of the village's social and economic ecosystem. They fostered trust, cooperation, and mutual support among households, creating a harmonious and resilient community."*

Through this interview, the team captured the essence of the household service exchanges in the village. The team now understands the motivations, interactions, and benefits involved in the process.

Step 2 – ubiquitous language

At this point, the domain expert and the team can start to develop a shared understanding of the domain by identifying the following concepts mentioned in domain storytelling:

- **Household**: A group of villagers who live together in the same place of residence.
- **Services**: The skills that a household specializes in and can be offered to another household.
- **Contract**: An agreement of the details of the services that have been exchanged between two households.
- **Draft contract**: A contract initiated by a household for another household to review.
- **Agreed contract**: A contract has its details mutually agreed upon and signed by the two households involved. An agreed contract is ready to be exercised.
- **Exercised contract**: A contract in which services performed by both households are completed, as per the details of each service.

This is the basis of the **ubiquitous language** in the form of a **glossary**. It's developed by both the domain expert and the team.

Step 3 – subdomains

Identifying subdomains is the next step of the DDD process. With the help of the glossary, the team has identified **Contract** as the core domain and **Household** as a supporting subdomain.

- **Contract** is the core domain as it's the heart of the business domain. Without it, there's no need to build a system. Household is an essential supporting subdomain so that the households involved in each contract can be identified.
- **Household** itself can't be a core domain because it's technically possible to solve the business problem with a Household subdomain. If households are merely names in each contract without capabilities to verify and identify them, there could be a cutdown version of the system that has no Household subdomain.

The team also recognized the need to notify households at several stages of a contract, such as when a contract is mutually agreed upon and ready to be exercised. Here, **notification** is also identified as a generic subdomain.

The core domain and the subdomains that have been identified are illustrated in *Figure 8.9*:

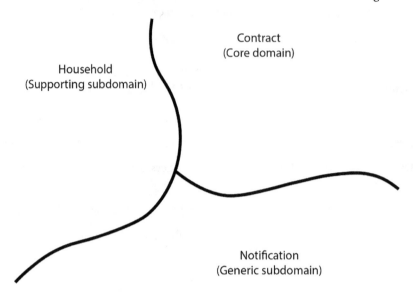

Figure 8.9 – Core domain and subdomains

Step 4 – bounded contexts

With the core domain and subdomains defined in the problem space, it's time to identify bounded contexts in the solution space. As mentioned previously, bounded contexts are defined by their scopes, responsibilities, and purposes.

The team understands that Contract is the core domain, and there are two workflows with contracts. The first one starts from a contract drafted until agreed. The second one starts from agreed until exercised. The team also understands that the only connecting point of these two workflows is an agreed contract.

There are team members who suggest one bounded context for the whole Contract core domain. There are also others suggesting one bounded context for the first journey and another one for the second.

The team decides that the first journey of a contract from drafted to exercised is a bounded context and names it **Contract Service**. This bounded context maintains the workflow of contract from drafted to agreed, and then to exercised. However, a contract must involve two different households and services provided by each household. As a result, **Contract Service** covers the major portion of the Contract domain and a small portion of the Household subdomain to validate a contract.

The supporting subdomain, Household, also needs a bounded context to support the classic **Create, Read, Update, and Delete (CRUD)** operations of households. The corresponding bounded context is named **Household Service**.

The solution intends to notify households involved in a contract when it's upon agreed or exercised. This generic subdomain, Notification, is covered by a bounded context named **Notification Service**.

Figure 8.10 demonstrates how the bounded contexts overlay the core domain and subdomains:

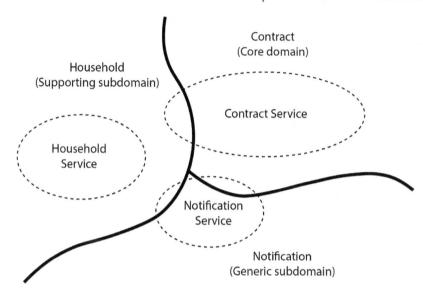

Figure 8.10 – Bounded contexts, core domain, and subdomains

Household Service is the only bounded context that's dedicated to its subdomain. Other bounded contexts have a major subdomain or core domain while also covering small portions of other subdomains so that they can function.

Step 5 – context mapping

The relationships among bounded contexts need to be defined via context mapping.

Household Service has no upstream dependencies, but **Contract Service** needs to receive household information to carry out their operations.

A household under Household Service contains information such as the household's name, contact email address, list of member names, residential address, and more. **Contract Service** only cares about the household name to validate a contract and the contact email address to be able to request a notification to be sent to a given household.

Since **Contract Service** represents the core domain, it's beneficial to avoid bringing in elements from other bounded contexts using an anti-corruption layer when communicating with **Household Service**.

Notification Service, as a generic bounded context, only needs to receive notification requests from a household and integrate with an email service provider to achieve its goal. It has a small portion of concepts that are supported by **Household Service** and **Contract Service**, but they dissolve into an email address, a title, and a body text. This is a customer-supplier relationship where **Notification Service** is the customer and other bounded contexts are suppliers.

The overall **context map** is shown in *Figure 8.11*:

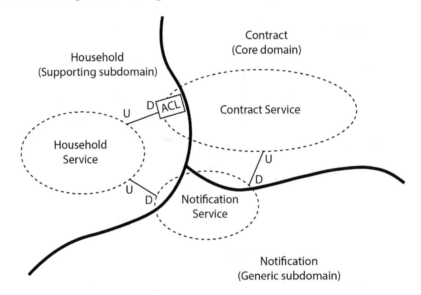

Figure 8.11 – Context mapping

The team and the domain expert have established ubiquitous language with a glossary as the output. They've also identified the core domain and subdomains. Finally, they've identified bounded contexts and the mapping among them.

The team now has a big picture of the whole household exchange service business model with strategic design in DDD. From now on, the team can focus on each of the bounded Contexts and their internal models.

DDD – tactical design

Tactical design focuses on the internal model and relationships within a bounded context. It aims to create a highly cohesive domain model that expresses the essential business concepts and aligns with the ubiquitous language that's used within the context.

Tactical design consists of several building blocks that provide a foundation for designing and building a bounded context within complex business domains:

- **Value objects**: These represent concepts without an identity. They're immutable and defined by their attributes rather than their identity. Value objects are used to model concepts considered as a unit. They're used for their attributes and can be shared and compared by value. The following `Address` class is a value object as it has no identity but encapsulates multiple fields that form an address:

```
data class Address(
    val line1: String,
    val line2: String? = null,
    val line3: String? = null,
    val postalCode: String,
    val city: String,
    val country: String
)
```

- **Entities**: Entities are objects that can be uniquely identified. They have a life cycle and can change over time. They represent concepts that are individually identifiable and meaningful within the domain. They maintain their state with their attributes and enforce business rules with corresponding behaviors. The `Household` class is an entity that's been identified by name:

```
data class Household(
    val name: String,
    val emailAddress: String
)
```

- **Aggregates**: In a bounded context, aggregates are clusters of related entities that are operated as a single unit to maintain transactional consistency and enforce business rules.

  The `Party` class is an aggregate because it contains the `Household` entity class:

```
data class Party(
    val household: Household,
    val serviceProvided: String,
    val agreedAt: Instant? = null,
    val completedAt: Instant? = null,
)
```

  The `Contract` class is an aggregate root as it's a top-level entrance to other aggregates, such as `Party`, and other entities, such as `Household`:

```
data class Contract(
    val partyA: Party,
```

```
        val partyB: Party,
        val contractState: ContractState,
    )
```

The entry point to read and modify the state of an aggregate is called an **aggregate root**. Aggregates take part in maintaining the integrity of the domain model and ensuring all related entities are linked together sensibly.

- **Domain services**: Domain services encapsulate domain behaviors that aren't tied to a specific entity or value object. They enforce collaboration among multiple objects. Domain services help maintain the cohesion and integrity of the domain model.

- **Repositories**: A repository stores and retrieves domain objects. It defines the possible storage and retrieval options for domain objects but abstracts away the actual storage implementation. A repository can be persistent, similar to databases or files. It can also be transient, similar to an in-memory cache. Persistence, availability, isolation levels, and underlying storage methods are the only implementation details. In other words, the **domain service** doesn't need to make technology choices for data storage.

- **Domain events**: Domain events represent things that have happened within a bounded context. They're all named in the past tense and are immutable.

Putting these building blocks together, the scope of tactical design in DDD can be illustrated like so:

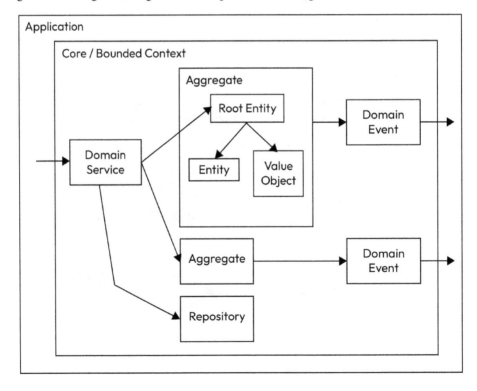

Figure 8.12 – Tactical design in DDD

Here, **Bounded Context** is the core of the application. Then, we have **Core**, which is the same concept that we covered in *Chapter 7* when we talked about layered architectures – it's a pure business concern area free of technology choices. This is also where all elements of tactical design are located.

The application transforms an external request into an internal request that **Domain Service** handles. The request is validated and handled by a set of business rules that are in **Domain Service** or the corresponding **Aggregate**. Then, **Domain Service** accesses **Aggregate** from the root **Entity** to access the underlying entities and other value objects. After, **Domain Service** uses **Repository** to persist and retrieve entities as part of the handling process.

Finally, **Domain Service** returns a response to the originator of the request. The application transforms the internal response into an external response. Meanwhile, domain events are produced due to request handling. These events are picked up by the application, transformed into external events, and published.

Applying tactical design to a real-life example

Previously, the team defined three bounded contexts during strategic design for the real-life example of households exchanging services. Here, the team will pick one bounded context and go through the tactical design exercise.

Step 1 – identify aggregates, entities, and value objects

The bounded context that's been chosen here is **Contract Service**, which represents the core domain of **Contract**. The goal of this bounded context is to maintain the life cycle of a contract from when it was first drafted to when it's mutually exercised. The team has identified an aggregate with the following structure:

```
data class Contract(
    val partyA: Party,
    val partyB: Party,
    val contractState: ContractState,
)
data class Party(
    val household: Household,
    val serviceProvided: String,
    val agreedAt: Instant? = null,
    val completedAt: Instant? = null,
)
enum class ContractState {
    DRAFTED,
    UNDER_REVIEW,
    AGREED,
    REJECTED,
    PARTIALLY_EXERCISED,
    FULLY_EXERCISED,
```

```
    WITHDRAWN,
}
data class Household(
    val name: String,
    val emailAddress: String
)
```

The **Contract** aggregate starts with the root **Contract** entity. The **Contract** entity is identified by an ID. The Contract entity contains two value objects of the same type: **Party**. The **Party** value object only holds the necessary fields to represent a party of a contract. The **Party** value object holds a **Household** entity.

The **Household** entity is local to **Contract Service** as it only contains a name and email address that are relevant to the bounded context. Here, **Household Service** supplies a full **Household** entity from the bounded context of **Household Service**. The foreign entity contains other fields such as residential address; these are ignored when the anti-corruption layer in **Contract Service** transforms the foreign entity into the local **Household** entity.

As a result, the local **Household** entity only contains a name and a contact email address. The local **Household** entity is identified by its name.

Step 2 – identify domain services, repositories, and domain events

Having defined the aggregate with the root, entities, and value objects underneath it, the team can identify the operations required by the bounded context to achieve its goal.

There are three major operations in this bounded context:

- A contract is drafted by a household
- A contract is agreed upon by all households involved
- A contract is exercised by all households involved

The corresponding timestamp should be set on the contract when these operations take place. The service should also notify the downstream bounded context using events.

Contract Service validates incoming requests such as whether the contract and the household exist, and whether the contract should change. If everything goes well, a timestamp is set against the corresponding service in the contract. If a contract has been drafted, agreed upon, or exercised, a corresponding domain event is published.

To support this operation, **Contract Service** needs to know both households. They are supplied by domain events published by upstream bounded contexts.

This bounded context consumes **Household Updated Event** published by **Household Service**. The **Household** entity is converted from this event and is stored in **Household Repository**.

The **Household** entity local to **Contract Service** is a trimmed down of the original **Household** entity in **Household Service**. **Contract Service** should only take the fields from **Household** that are relevant to the operations within its bounded context. Meanwhile, **Household Service** contains the full set of fields of **Household** relevant to the whole business domain.

These repositories serve as local caches, so **Contract Service** remains if other bounded contexts are unavailable.

The inside of the bounded context can be seen in *Figure 8.13*:

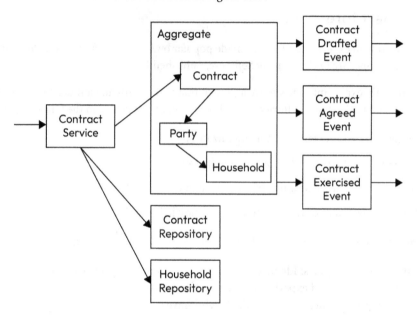

Figure 8.13 – Inside the bounded context – Contract Service

The domain expert and the team have run through both strategic and tactical designs for the real-life example. They've covered ubiquitous language, subdomains, bounded contexts, context mapping, aggregates, entities, value objects, domain services, domain events, and repositories. Through these exercises, the domain expert and the team have established a shared understanding of the business problems, and they now have a useful model that they can use as a foundation for building a software system.

There are a few formats of DDD workshops that any organization can consider bringing in to improve communication and collaboration among stakeholders and engineers. The next section will briefly introduce them and their formats.

Modeling activities for DDD

In our real-life example, we covered how the solution evolves and emerges from the input of the team and the domain expert. It's important to understand the actual modeling activities that are involved in DDD so that we can put them into practice.

There are a few popular modeling activities that drive the direction of the design from both the team and the domain expert.

Domain expert interview

The concept of a domain expert interview was made popular by *Eric Evans* in his book *Domain-Driven Design: Tackling Complexity in the Heart of Software*, published in 2003.

Performing a domain expert interview is an approach that you can use to gain deep insights into the business domain and understand its intricacies. It is particularly applicable in the following scenarios:

- The domain expert is external to the organization
- The domain expert has only limited time to be involved
- The organization starts a new line of business and brings in domain experts
- The team is new and doesn't have much prior knowledge of the domain

Here are some guidelines for conducting effective domain expert interviews in DDD:

- **Identify the right experts**: Identify individuals, both internally and externally, who possess in-depth knowledge and expertise in the specific domain. Look for subject matter experts, experienced practitioners, or individuals who have a deep understanding of the business processes and rules involved.

- **Prepare an interview plan**: State clear objectives of the interview. Develop an outline of each topic. Prepare a list of questions, preferably open-ended ones, to ask. Pay attention to potential pain points and areas of uncertainty.

- **Establish a comfortable environment**: Establish a collaborative atmosphere with the domain expert during the interview. Make them feel comfortable and valued. Clearly explain the interview's purpose and outline the topics to be covered. Emphasize that their opinions are critical for your project's success. Create an atmosphere where they feel free to share their knowledge and experiences.

- **Active listening**: During the interview, practice active listening. Pay close attention to the expert's verbal responses and non-verbal communication. Clarify their answers whenever necessary and ask follow-up questions to delve deeper into specific areas of interest. Show genuine interest in their insights and validate their contributions.

- **Capture notes**: Take thorough and detailed notes during the interview. Document important concepts, terms, processes, and examples that the expert shares. Record key details, such as business rules, decision-making criteria, and exceptions. Use visual aids, such as diagrams or sketches, to capture their explanations and mental models.

- **Validate and clarify information**: After the interview, review the notes that were taken and validate the information that's been gathered. Clarify with the domain expert or have follow-up discussions on ambiguity or uncertainty. It's important to ensure that the team has a clear and accurate understanding of the domain.

- **Share and validate your findings**: After the interview, share your findings with the domain expert and other stakeholders to validate your understanding. Actively seek their feedback and incorporate any corrections or additional insights they may provide. By incorporating their input, the domain model can be refined and improved, ensuring that the software system accurately reflects the intricacies and requirements of the business domain.

The domain expert interview is an iterative process. As the team understands more of the domain, new questions arise. Continuous collaboration and feedback with domain experts throughout the project can significantly contribute to the success of your DDD implementation.

Event storming

Event storming is a domain modeling technique that was developed by *Alberto Brandolini* in 2013. Event storming requires the team, domain experts, and other stakeholders to gather in the same place, ideally in person, and garner a mix of perspectives and knowledge about the domain.

An in-person event storming session requires a large whiteboard, many marker pens of assorted colors, and many stickies of many colors. Alternatively, online collaboration drawing tools that have the same elements can suffice.

Participants are expected to actively engage in every activity of the process. They're expected to move some stickies, erase lines, and draw some lines on the board simultaneously.

The session starts with outlining the scope of the session. It should focus on a specific business process or domain participants want to explore. This could also be a specific feature, a user journey, or a critical aspect of the domain.

Afterward, the session can be run in the following sequence. If necessary, participants can go back and correct any sticky notes as they learn more in later steps:

1. **Identify domain events**: Brainstorm and put a specific color stickie (for example, orange) for a domain event they've identified. A domain event should represent something significant that has happened in the domain, such as `Contract Agreed` or `Household Updated`.

2. **Arrange the events**: Once there's a collection of domain events, work on the domain events on the whiteboard. Group duplicated events, remove irrelevant events, or correct ambiguous events. Place the events in chronological order, creating a timeline from left to right. This helps visualize the flow of events and their sequence.

3. **Add actors and commands**: Identify the actors or entities involved in the events. These could be system components or human users. Capture actors as sticky notes but use a different color (for example, yellow). Place them above or below the relevant events.

   Identify any commands or actions that trigger the events and associate them with the respective events. Commands are the user's intent to do certain things. Commands or actions should use a new color (for example, blue) for stickies.

   Identify external systems that trigger the events. Use a dedicated color (for example, red) for the stickies.

4. **Explore policies and business rules**: Pay attention to policies, constraints, and business rules associated with the events. Capture them as separate sticky notes of a new color (for example, purple) and link them to the relevant events, commands, or actors. These rules help shape the behavior and interactions within the domain.

5. **Discuss and refine the model**: Facilitate discussions among the participants alongside the stickies for events, actors, commands, external systems, and policies. Encourage them to share their knowledge, insights, and questions related to events and their relationships. Refine the model by rearranging, adding, or removing stickies during the discussions.

6. **Identify aggregates and bounded contexts**: Look for patterns and events that often go together. This cluster of events may indicate potential aggregates. Identify bounded contexts, which are cohesive areas of the domain with well-defined purposes, boundaries, and language.

7. **Capture insights and next steps**: Capture any valuable insights, questions, or areas of uncertainty that arise. Make note of any follow-up actions or further investigations needed to refine the domain model.

Event storming is also an iterative process. Sometimes, it takes multiple sessions to fully explore and refine the domain model. Encourage collaboration, active participation, and idea sharing among the participants to gain a common understanding and drive the software system aligned with the business objectives.

Domain storytelling

Domain storytelling was introduced in 2019 by *Stefan Hofer* and *Henning Schwentner* in their book *Domain Storytelling: A Collaborative Approach to Domain-Driven Design*.

Domain storytelling is a collaborative and interactive approach to gaining a deeper understanding of a complex business domain. The team, domain experts, and other stakeholders come together, ideally in person, to develop stories that depict various aspects of the business domain.

Like event storming, an in-person domain storytelling session requires a large whiteboard, many marker pens, and many stickies. Again, online whiteboard collaboration tools that have the same elements can suffice.

Domain experts and stakeholders draw out a real-life business scenario by putting stickies on the whiteboard and connecting them with marker pens.

The domain story about drafting a contract may look like this:

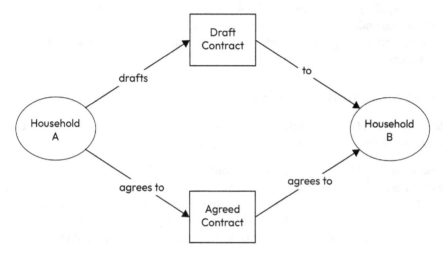

Figure 8.14 – A domain story about drafting a contract

These stories capture the context, challenges, interactions, and relationships within the domain. As the story is being told, everyone actively listens, asks questions, provides background information such as business rules, motivation, and pain points, or even picks up a pen and draws.

Participants may want to adopt a certain format, such as the **Business Process Modeling Notation** (**BPMN**) mentioned in *Chapter 2*, but this isn't mandatory. The essence of the exercise is communication and collaboration to align everyone on a shared understanding. Also, domain experts may not be familiar with the standard visual notions. Instead of having them struggle to get the right notions, participants should focus on getting the right information instead.

Participants should use this opportunity to clear up any ambiguous, unclear, and misused languages to aim for ubiquitous language.

The visual representation serves as a shared artifact that can be referred to and refined throughout the development process.

Domain storytelling helps bridge the gap between the team and domain experts by collaboratively working toward a shared language and understanding of the domain. It helps uncover hidden requirements, edge cases, and exceptional scenarios that may often be found in the middle or late stage of development. As a result, it reduces the cost of design modifications and lowers the risks of scope creep.

Additionally, domain storytelling provides a user-centric perspective to software systems by emphasizing the needs, goals, and experiences of the users within the stories. It aids the team and domain experts in identifying bounded contexts, aggregate roots, and domain entities, promoting a robust and accurate domain model.

Overall, domain storytelling serves as a powerful tool for domain exploration, analysis, and communication. It helps build a shared understanding of the domain, facilitates collaboration between stakeholders and the team, and supports building software systems that accurately reflect the intricacy and requirements of the business domain.

Comparing modeling activities

All modeling activities in DDD are iterative. They continuously refine and shape the software systems as participants understand more the subject matters, and as business evolves.

However, the dynamics of these three activities are different. In a domain expert interview, the team drives the interview by preparing the topics and questions. The domain experts primarily react to these materials, and the team actively listens and responds. In event storming, everyone works on all stickies on the board, guided by the knowledge shared among domain experts and stakeholders. Finally, in domain storytelling, it's the narrative of the domain experts and stakeholders but on a whiteboard, with the teams actively listening, reacting, and asking questions.

They're all good tools to use. Domain expert interviews are particularly useful if it's difficult to have the domain experts available. Event storming is useful if everyone has some knowledge and experience about the domain. It focuses on visualizing the flow of events in a timeline from left to right. Domain storytelling focuses on capturing domain knowledge with a narrative story. It doesn't require a timeline to be created from left to right and doesn't require all labels that event storming uses to be used.

Summary

In this chapter, we delved into two major design approaches in DDD. We covered the fundamental concepts of strategic design to get the bigger picture of the domain while providing a real-life example. Here, we covered concepts such as ubiquitous language, subdomains, bounded contexts, and context mapping.

Afterward, we explored tactical design by using a bounded context from the strategic design example. We showcased how to identify aggregates, entities, value objects, domain services, repositories, and domain events.

We also covered three popular modeling activities in DDD and discussed their agendas: the domain expert interview, event storming, and domain storytelling.

At this point, you should be able to plan and design an architecture with the DDD approach, using at least one of the modeling activities outlined.

In the next chapter, we're going to deep dive into some of the architectural patterns based on DDD, namely **Command and Query Responsibility Segregation (CQRS)** and **event sourcing**.

9

Event Sourcing and CQRS

The previous chapter, on **Domain-Driven Design (DDD)**, laid the foundation for us to dive into two powerful architectural patterns that answer to the demand for scalable, responsive, and maintainable applications: **Event Sourcing** and **Command-Query Responsibility Segregation (CQRS)**.

Firstly, we will explore the foundation of Event Sourcing. We will discuss how we can use Event Sourcing to model our domain, how to persist the state of your domain, and how to reconstruct the current state from the persisted events. We will explore the benefits of this approach.

Next, we will turn our attention to CQRS, examining how it separates the responsibilities of commands (write) and queries (read). We will discuss the key components of a CQRS architecture, including the command and query handlers, the domain model, and the event store. We will delve into the benefits of this separation.

As we delve deeper, we will examine the practical considerations of implementing CQRS and Event Sourcing together, including data modeling, event schema design, and handling eventual consistency. We will also discuss strategies for integrating these patterns into your existing software ecosystem, ensuring a seamless and scalable transition.

Through real-world examples and best practices, you will gain a comprehensive understanding of how CQRS and Event Sourcing can transform the way you approach software design and development. By the end of this chapter, you will be equipped with the knowledge and tools to harness the power of these patterns and unlock the full potential of your applications.

We will go through the main topics in the following order:

- Event Sourcing
- Command-Query Responsibility Segregation (CQRS)
- Combining CQRS and Event Sourcing

Technical requirements

You can find all the code files used in this chapter on GitHub: `https://github.com/PacktPublishing/Software-Architecture-with-Kotlin/tree/main/chapter-9`

Event Sourcing

Event Sourcing is a data management pattern, and its origin can be traced back to the 1990s, when engineers recognized the limitations of traditional data storage **Create, Read, Update, and Delete (CRUD)**, particularly in the context of building complex and event-driven systems.

Event Sourcing has its roots in the principles of **Domain-Driven Design (DDD)**, as covered in *Chapter 8*. DDD introduced the concept of an **Aggregate** as a fundamental building block of the domain model, and Aggregates usually need to be persisted in data storage.

The classic CRUD approach and its limitations

The classic CRUD approach is sufficient for capturing the latest snapshot of an Aggregate by CRUD operations, usually with the use of a relational database. There are, however, limitations to this approach:

- **History, auditability, and traceability**: While the CRUD approach can capture the current snapshot of an Aggregate, its ability to keep audit trails of all changes made to the Aggregate over time is limited.

  This is usually overcome by custom data persistence code to keep historical records, or with the assistance of database update triggers. This can make it challenging to track the history of changes, understand how the system reached a particular state, and comply with regulatory requirements.

- **Modeling complex domains**: CRUD-based systems work well with simple and straightforward data models, but they can struggle to effectively represent and manage the evolution of complex domain models over time.

  Traditionally, with the use of relational databases, a complex Aggregate object results in convoluted database schemas, complex data persistence operations, and difficulties in maintaining and evolving the system.

- **Event-driven capabilities**: The CRUD approach has no support for event-driven architectures, where the system needs to react to and propagate changes in a decoupled, scalable manner.

- **Concurrency and consistency**: CRUD-based systems often rely on traditional locking mechanisms to ensure data consistency, which often leads to performance bottlenecks in distributed, concurrent, and high-load environments.

  Maintaining strong consistency in the face of concurrent updates can be a significant challenge in CRUD systems.

- **Versioning and evolution**: Updating and evolving CRUD-based systems can be problematic, as changes to the data model or business logic may require complex migrations and data transformations.

  Versioning and handling historical data can also be more complicated in a CRUD-centric approach.

- **Analytics and reporting**: CRUD systems focus on the current snapshot of Aggregates, which can make it challenging to analyze, generate reports, or derive insights from the historical data of Aggregates.

In the face of these challenges, the idea of capturing the full history of Aggregate changes began to gain traction.

Events as first-class citizens

Event Sourcing aims to solve these challenges by making events first-class citizens. The term *event* here entails the same concept as the *event* in DDD mentioned in *Chapter 8*. An event captures the change in an aggregate, making it a key element in this framework.

Event Sourcing persists all the events of aggregates in an event store. There are no update or delete operations to an event because an event represents a change that has already happened to an aggregate. In other words, events are immutable and are stored as a journal in chronological order. Event stores are often not relational databases; they can be NoSQL databases or persistent queues.

In contrast to CRUD, in which the latest snapshot of an aggregate is a first-class citizen, Event Sourcing derives the latest snapshot of an aggregate by replaying the events from the aggregate from the first to the last event. As a result, the full history of an aggregate is preserved and no custom code is required to provide an audit trail of the aggregate.

Moreover, the history of an aggregate is captured as a linear timeline and naturally eliminates the challenge of keeping strong consistency with concurrent updates. There should be, however, version validation before a request to mutate an aggregate is accepted and eventually generates an event. This is to prevent the **Lost Update** problem, where concurrent updates of the same aggregate overwrite each other unknowingly.

Functional representations of Event Sourcing

The idea of representing the state of a system as a sequence of immutable events aligns well with the functional programming paradigm. Aggregates and events are immutable. Each change is performed by creating a new version of an aggregate from an event through stateless functions. This can be expressed through two basic functions written as Kotlin lambdas:

```
(CreatedEvent) -> Aggregate
(UpdatedEvent, Aggregate) -> Aggregate
```

The first function creates an initial aggregate. Subsequently, the update functions take the current version of the aggregate and create a new version.

An example of how a request is handled with Event Sourcing

Suppose there is a request to update an existing aggregate. The service that receives the request would need to get the latest version of the aggregate to validate the request. So, the service gets all the events for the aggregate from the event store.

All the events are replayed to recreate the latest snapshot of the aggregate. Assuming the request is all good, the service creates a new event. The service then plays this event on the current aggregate and creates an updated version of the aggregate.

The transaction is committed by appending the new event in the event store. The updated version of the aggregate can be used as a response to the original requester.

The whole interaction is illustrated as a sequence diagram, as shown in *Figure 9.1*:

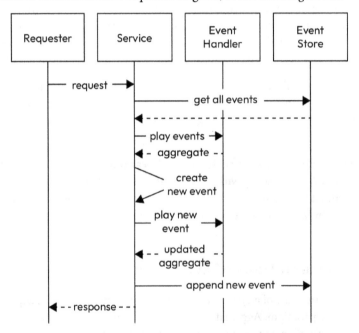

Figure 9.1 – An example of Event Sourcing

It is important to point out that the aggregate is not directly updated by the service. It is achieved by the handling of the new event. Also, the event store is responsible for distributing the new event to subscribers that are interested in these events.

Benefits of Event Sourcing

The benefits of Event Sourcing come from the persistence of full audit trails of an Aggregate:

- **Full audit trails with intents**: Not only are the full audit trails of an aggregate preserved, but also the intent of each change is captured. The name of each event of the aggregate ideally should come from the ubiquitous language so it becomes a business-aware and user-friendly history.

- **Time travel**: With the full history captured as a linear sequence of events, it is possible to travel back in time to construct a historical representation of the aggregate. It helps engineers to reproduce a scenario that happened in the past for investigation and troubleshooting purposes. It also enables users to see the historical aggregate as a feature.

- **Creation of read models**: Having multiple consumers of the same event of an Aggregate opens the door to multiple read models. Each read model consumes the same event but transforms it to meet its specific requirements. This approach provides diverse views tailored for particular business purposes.

Deciding whether Event Sourcing should be used

Choosing Event Sourcing as the way to store aggregates and their audit trails should not be taken lightly. It is a fundamental shift in how we reason about data, and it requires noticeable effort to make it work.

From the *YAGNI* principle we covered in *Chapter 1*, engineers should build the simplest things that work. When there is more than one solution, the simplest solution should be chosen.

> **A simple solution is different from an easy solution**
>
> Simple solutions are not complicated or are straightforward to reason about. Easy solutions require less effort to make. Take the example of capturing a new field. If we believe that the field should belong to a new entity, then creating a new entity that has the field is the most intuitive and straightforward approach. However, a new entity may mean adding new database tables, new validations, and new exposed APIs. On the other hand, if we attach the new field to an existing entity, we only need to enhance the existing entity, database table, and APIs. There is less effort involved in coding and testing, even though the field does not belong to the existing entity. This is an easy solution as less effort is required, but it is not simple because it is not intuitive and is instead confusing to see the field in an entity to which it does not belong.

An decision tree to determine if an aggregate should use Event Sourcing is shown in *Figure 9.2*:

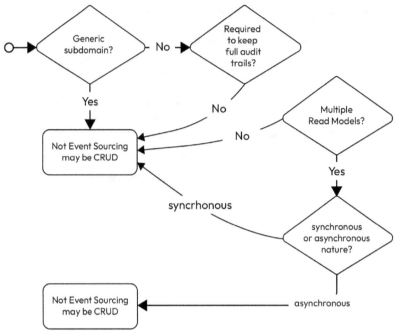

Figure 9.2 – A decision tree whether to use Event Sourcing

The most decisive factor is whether the aggregate being considered to use Event Sourcing belongs to a Generic subdomain or not. In *Chapter 8*, we identified Core domains, Supporting subdomains, and Generic subdomains. A Generic subdomain has a high likelihood of being fully replaced by off-the-shelf software products, which makes the benefits of using Event Sourcing not significant.

If the aggregate involved belongs to either a Core domain or a Supporting subdomain, the next step in the consideration is whether it is required to keep the full audit trails of the aggregate. Full audit trails can be used for regulatory reporting, replaying events to get a particular historical state of the aggregate, or performing time-series data analysis. It is a powerful feature of Event Sourcing, but not all aggregates need such power.

Another hint that helps when considering Event Sourcing is if there are multiple read models for the Aggregate. The definition of a read model here is the same as the read models that can be discovered during **Event Storming**, which was also covered in *Chapter 8*.

An aggregate that requires multiple read models can benefit from Event Sourcing. Each read model can consume the same event of the aggregate, but it transforms the data to its unique representation of the aggregate as a materialized view. Sometimes, a read model might even combine data from other aggregates or entities.

Event Sourcing uses events extensively for each change in an aggregate, and events are often processed asynchronously. If the operations for the aggregate are predominately synchronous, it imposes challenges in implementing Event Sourcing for the aggregate. There are techniques to synchronously process events to update aggregates, and the implementation has a cost.

It is important to reiterate that this is just an example decision tree. Each organization may have other factors in its decision-making. Sometimes, it may even make a different decision given the same question.

Usage of Event Sourcing with a real-life example

Let's revisit the real-life example of villagers exchanging services, with the three bounded contexts identified in *Chapter 8*:

- Core domains: **Contract Service**
- Supporting subdomain: **Household Service**
- Generic subdomain: **Notification Service**

Walking through the decision tree (see *Figure 9.2*) mentioned in the previous section, Notification Service, as a Generic subdomain, can be safely ruled out from using Event Sourcing.

Household as an aggregate in Household Service does not need to keep full audit trails because only the latest states of households are needed for business cases. The CRUD approach is sufficient.

Contract as an aggregate in Contract Service may need to keep full audit trails because disputes are likely to arise between households on the agreements in the contract.

There are also multiple read models involving contracts. The primary read model of a contract is the one that specifies the details of the contract between two households.

There can also be a unilateral read model for each household. It contains a list of services that the household should provide and to which household. There is another list of services that the household expects to receive and from which household.

In addition, there is potential read model that aims to highlight the most wanted services in the village and the most active households in exchanging services.

The negotiation process of a contract involves multiple rounds of amendments until both households agree. When a contract is drafted by one household, an email is sent to another household asynchronously. During the negotiation process, any change made by one household results in an email notification to the other household involved. There are also multiple messages between two households in providing the services as per the contract. This asynchronous nature of communication suggests that a contract is a suitable candidate for using Event Sourcing in the Contract Service.

In this example, we are going to focus on using Event Sourcing to capture the full history of the aggregate contract in Contract Service.

Let's revisit the aggregate contract as a data class:

```
data class Contract(
    val id: UUID,
    val draftedAt: Instant,
    val updatedAt: Instant? = null,
    val version: Int,
    val partyA: Party,
    val partyB: Party,
)
data class Party(
    val householdName: String,
    val serviceProvided: String,
    val agreedAt: Instant? = null
)
```

The Contract data class contains an id field, which uniquely identifies this aggregate. There is also a field named version, which is a monotonic increasing integer that shows how many events have been played for this aggregate.

The basic construct of a ContractEvent should have the unique identifier of the aggregate and the time when the event happened:

```
interface ContractEvent {
    val contractId: UUID
    val targetVersion: Int
    val time: Instant
}
```

It also has a target version, which is the version of the aggregate after the event is applied.

In this example, we are using a simple in-memory event store. It has two basic functions. The append function adds a new event at the tail of the sequence by the aggregate ID, and the get function returns a chronological sequence of events given the aggregate ID:

```
class EventStore<KEY, AGGREGATE> {
    private val aggregatesByKey = mutableMapOf<KEY, List<AGGREGATE>>()
    fun append(id: KEY, payload: AGGREGATE) {
        aggregatesByKey.merge(id, listOf(payload)) { t1, t2 -> t1 + t2
    }
    }
    fun get(id: KEY): List<AGGREGATE>? = aggregatesByKey[id]
}
```

If this is a real system, reputable event store middleware should be used to make it durable, highly available, and resilient.

The creation of the aggregate contract starts with a household that has drafted a contract, and it should contain all the information required to create the first version of the aggregate:

```
data class ContractDraftedEvent(
    override val contractId: UUID,
    override val targetVersion: Int = 0,
    override val time: Instant,
    val draftedByHousehold: String,
    val counterpartyHousehold: String,
    val serviceProvided: String,
    val serviceReceived: String,
) : ContractEvent
```

The Contract Drafted Event class should provide a function to create the aggregate. It is a simple function that puts the values into the appropriate structure:

```
fun ContractDraftedEvent.play(): Contract = Contract(
    id = contractId,
    draftedAt = time,
    version = targetVersion,
    partyA = Party(
        householdName = draftedByHousehold,
        serviceProvided = serviceProvided
    ),
    partyB = Party(
        householdName = counterpartyHousehold,
        serviceProvided = serviceReceived
    )
)
```

Any subsequent event must take a parameter of the current version of the aggregate to generate a new version. For instance, an event that captures when a household amends and agrees to a drafted contract could look like this:

```
data class ContractAmendedEvent(
    override val contractId: UUID,
    override val targetVersion: Int,
    override val time: Instant,
    val amendedByHousehold: String,
    val serviceProvidedUpdate: String?,
    val serviceReceivedUpdate: String?,
) : ContractEvent
data class ContractAgreedEvent(
    override val contractId: UUID,
    override val targetVersion: Int,
```

```
        override val time: Instant,
        val agreedByHousehold: String,
) : ContractEvent
```

Note that this event does not necessarily follow the data structure of the aggregate. The key point is to keep the event lean and simple. So, this event only mentions one household, and it relies on the corresponding play function to apply the change correctly. Note that the play function takes a parameter of the current aggregate:

```
fun ContractAmendedEvent.play(current: Contract): Contract {
    validate(current, amendedByHousehold)
    return if (amendedByHousehold == current.partyA.householdName) {
        current.copy(
            version = targetVersion,
            updatedAt = time,
            partyA = current.partyA.copy(
                serviceProvided = serviceProvidedUpdate ?: current.
partyA.serviceProvided
            ),
            partyB = current.partyB.copy(
                serviceProvided = serviceReceivedUpdate ?: current.
partyB.serviceProvided
            )
        )
    } else {
        current.copy(
            version = targetVersion,
            updatedAt = time,
            partyA = current.partyA.copy(
                serviceProvided = serviceReceivedUpdate ?: current.
partyA.serviceProvided
            ),
            partyB = current.partyB.copy(
                serviceProvided = serviceProvidedUpdate ?: current.
partyB.serviceProvided
            )
        )
    }
}
fun ContractAgreedEvent.play(current: Contract): Contract {
    validate(current, agreedByHousehold)
    return if (agreedByHousehold == current.partyA.householdName) {
        current.copy(
            version = targetVersion,
            updatedAt = time,
```

```
            partyA = current.partyA.copy(agreedAt = time),
        )
    } else {
        current.copy(
            version = targetVersion,
            updatedAt = time,
            partyB = current.partyB.copy(agreedAt = time)
        )
    }
}
```

You will notice there is a `validate` function, which is important for ensuring data integrity:

```
fun <T : ContractEvent> T.validate(current: Contract,
expectedHouseholdName: String): T {
    require(contractId == current.id) {
        "Aggregate ID mismatch - expected: $contractId, was ${current.
id}"
    }
    require(targetVersion == current.version + 1) {
        "Unexpected version - expected: ${targetVersion - 1}, was
${current.version}"
    }
    require(
        expectedHouseholdName == current.partyA.householdName ||
            expectedHouseholdName == current.partyB.householdName
    ) {
        "Unexpected household - expected: ${expectedHouseholdName},
was ${
            listOf(current.partyA.householdName, current.partyB.
householdName)
        }"
    }
    return this
}
```

This `validate` function asserts that the event refers to the aggregate in the parameter. Then, it asserts that the current aggregate is one version lower than the target version of the event. Finally, it asserts that the involved household is mentioned in the aggregate contract.

There should be an iterative function that takes a list of Contract Events and eventually returns a Contract object:

```
fun List<ContractEvent>.play(): Contract? {
    if (isEmpty()) return null
    var current: Contract = (first() as ContractDraftedEvent).play()
```

```
    var index = 1
    while (index < size) {
        val event = get(index++)
        current = when (event) {
            is ContractAmendedEvent -> event.play(current)
            is ContractAgreedEvent -> event.play((current))
            else -> throw IllegalArgumentException("Unsupported
event")
        }
    }
    return current
}
```

The function uses a List of contract events as the receiver. The return type is nullable in the case of an empty list. It assumes the first event is ContractCreatedEvent, which sets up the initial snapshot of the Contract. It loops from the second event to the last, generates a new version of the Contract, sets it as current to pass to the next event, and at the end returns the Contract object. An example of its usage is as follows. A list of events of the same aggregate is ordered and is played sequentially:

```
val contractId = UUID.randomUUID()
val eventStore = EventStore<UUID, ContractEvent>()
val createdEvent = ContractDraftedEvent(
    contractId = contractId,
    time = Instant.now(),
    draftedByHousehold = "HouseholdA",
    counterpartyHousehold = "HouseholdB",
    serviceProvided = "Cleaning",
    serviceReceived = "Babysitting"
)
val amendedEvent = ContractAmendedEvent(
    contractId = contractId,
    targetVersion = 1,
    time = Instant.now(),
    amendedByHousehold = "HouseholdB",
    serviceReceivedUpdate = "Dish washing",
    serviceProvidedUpdate = null
)
val agreedEventByHouseholdA = ContractAgreedEvent(
    contractId = contractId,
    targetVersion = 2,
    time = Instant.now(),
    agreedByHousehold = "HouseholdA"
)
```

```
val agreedEventByHouseholdB = ContractAgreedEvent(
    contractId = contractId,
    targetVersion = 3,
    time = Instant.now(),
    agreedByHousehold = "HouseholdB"
)
listOf(
    createdEvent,
    amendedEvent,
    agreedEventByHouseholdA,
    agreedEventByHouseholdB
).forEach { eventStore.append(contractId, it) }
val aggregate = eventStore.get(contractId)?.play()
println("Aggregate is of version: ${aggregate?.version}")
```

The code does not directly update the aggregate. Instead, it creates a few events and lets them play through. Eventually, the version should be 3 because the first version is 0. The following should be printed to the console when the previous code is executed:

```
Aggregate is of version: 3
```

This example illustrates a simple form of Event Sourcing where each event generates a new version of the aggregate. These events should be persisted to an event store as permanent storage and be received by subscribers so other read models can be built upon.

In complex systems, processing an event could produce a list of events as reactions, and that would require a recursive function to walk through the processing. It may also require grouping related events as one transaction due to the chained reactions.

Although the example here is simple, there are many ways Event Sourcing can go wrong. We are going to discuss some best practices that should be considered in the implementation.

Event Sourcing best practices

Event Sourcing is a different way to reason about an aggregate in a domain from the classic CRUD approach. It only works if we design and architect our system with the mindset of events being first-class citizens. Otherwise, it could become an anti-pattern and undo all the benefits that it brings. Here are some of the fundamental best practices.

Randomization and idempotence

It is important that replaying the same sequence of events for an aggregate generates the same snapshot of the aggregate every time. In other words, the processing of events must be idempotent. There are two major factors that could violate this behavior: time and randomization.

If the event processing contains logic that makes use of the time the event is processed, then it will generate different results depending on the time of processing. For example, the following `expire` variable would have different Boolean values based on the system clock:

```
val expire = If (event.time < System.currentMillis()) true else false
```

Any information related to the system clock should be stamped on the event instead. In this way, the result has been determined and will not change over time. Any time-based trigger or schedule job should obtain the system time and have the value captured in the events.

Any randomization at the time of event processing will also generate different outcomes for each iteration. Values generated from randomization should be captured in the event payload, and there is no randomization involved in the event processing. If identifiers must be generated during the processing, they can be unique values within the scope of the event. Externally, they are used together with the event identifiers as composite keys. Here is an example:

```
val externalValueId = "${event.id}-${event.value.id}"
```

The value inside the event can be identified externally by concatenation of the event ID and the value ID inside the event, delimited by a hyphen.

Event design

An event should have one and only one aggregate. Mixing multiple aggregates, whether they are of the same or different types, results in unnecessary coupling between aggregates. The coupling created by mixed aggregates in one event makes it difficult to scale events and their topics.

There could be business cases where multiple aggregates are affected. In this scenario, multiple events should be created as a result, and each event describes what happened to each aggregate.

Each event should capture the intent of the change in an aggregate. For example, `ContractCreatedEvent` is a bad name because it does not describe why the aggregate contract is created. A better name would be in line with ubiquitous language, such as `ContractDraftedEvent`.

Event topologies

Events are published for subscribers to receive and can be logically grouped as **topics**. A topic here is not to be mistaken for the topic in traditional pub-sub messaging, in which messages are no longer in a topic once all subscribers acknowledge receipt. In Event Sourcing, events are meant to be kept permanently as an append-only and sequential log of events. For example, a Kafka topic with an infinite retention period can be used to keep events, and each topic represents a logical grouping of events.

All events of one aggregate should only go to one topic only. This is to simplify creating and reading the linear history of an aggregate.

Spreading the events of an aggregate to multiple topics imposes difficulties in recreating the full history of an aggregate. It is also more difficult to scale performance and increase throughput, which are separate concerns from the event design.

Event schema compatibility

As Event Sourcing intends to keep all historical events, it is important that all events are backward compatible; in other words, old events can still be read and processed when the event schema evolves.

Maintaining backward compatibility is a big topic in itself. There are many things that can keep or break backward compatibility. Here are some examples:

- **Keep**:

  - Adding an optional field

  - Adding more enum values to a type

  - Reducing the constraints of a field

- **Break**:

  - Adding a mandatory field

  - Renaming a field

  - Changing the data type of a field

  - Removing a field

  - Increasing the constraints of a field

In the context of Event Sourcing, a backward-compatible event schema ensures that the system can always read the full history of an aggregate to re-create the latest snapshot of the aggregate.

Forward and full compatibility

Forward compatibility means that an old consumer can read and process events of a new schema. A fully compatible schema means it is both backward and forward compatible.

Performance and Memento

While the current version of an aggregate can always be derived from all the events of that aggregate from the beginning of time, it is not always ideal to have to play these events if a current snapshot is requested.

A performance optimization is to persist the latest version of the aggregate as a derived record. This pattern is called **Memento**. The usage of this pattern can be justified if current snapshots are frequently requested.

In the case of using events to recover the latest state of an aggregate, it may also be justified to use the Memento pattern. The reason for this is that the number of events will keep growing, and therefore the total time to replay all events will become longer and longer. Applying the Memento pattern changes the total time used for recovery versus number of events from linear to constant for a given aggregate.

Migration from CRUD

Migrating an aggregate from CRUD to Event Sourcing is interesting in that usually, CRUD does not have full audit trails to allow a complete history to be rebuilt as events. Instead, the latest snapshots of aggregates are treated as the first versions, and then subsequent events are persisted.

In this case, something like `ContractMigratedEvent` would be the first event.

Moreover, the mutation of an aggregate will be done through the playing of events, not a direct update to the aggregate. As a result, any code that directly updates the aggregate will need to be deprecated.

We have covered the basics of Event Sourcing with a real-life example and source code. There is another architectural pattern that works with Event Sourcing and is also based on DDD. We are going to cover this pattern now.

Command-Query Responsibility Segregation (CQRS)

The origin of CQRS can be traced back to another design pattern called **Command Query Separation (CQS)**. CQS is the core concept that defines two types of operations handled in a system: a command that executes a task, and a query that returns information, and there should never be one function that does both jobs.

The term CQS was created by Bertrand Meyer in his book *Object-Oriented Software Construction* in 1988. He created it as part of his work on the Eiffel programming language.

CQRS takes the defining principle of CQS and extends it to specific objects within a system, one retrieving data and one modifying data. CQRS is a broader architectural pattern, and CQS is the general principle of behavior.

The term CQRS was coined by Greg Young in 2010. Since then, CQRS has gained traction, and various frameworks and libraries have been developed to support the pattern's implementation in popular languages such as Java and .NET.

There are four basic elements in CQRS: **aggregate**, **query**, **command**, and **event**.

Aggregate

Aggregate in CQRS has the same meaning as in Event Sourcing and DDD. It is an aggregated entity that represents the current state of the domain model. The aggregate contains a basket of other entities and value objects to represent a domain concept as defined in ubiquitous language.

Query

A query is a request from clients to retrieve a representation of the state of the domain model. Handling queries is a read-only operation and does not change the state of any aggregate. However, queries may be targeted to a certain read model related to an aggregate.

Command

A command is a request from clients intending to change the state of an aggregate in the domain model. The intention is handled to determine whether the state should be changed and how. A command may only contain the necessary information for the change, and not the whole aggregate in the request.

Event

An event is a confirmed and immutable change of the state of an aggregate. An event can be created because of a command, or because of the handling of another event. This is the same as the concept of events in DDD and Event Sourcing.

How CQRS breaks down CRUD

CQRS has broken down the classic CRUD into many small queries, commands, and events. Each of them carries a precise meaning of what is happening, to the point that it matches the ubiquitous language.

Take the real-life example of the negotiation process of a service contract between two households. Both households can amend the contract and eventually agree to it.

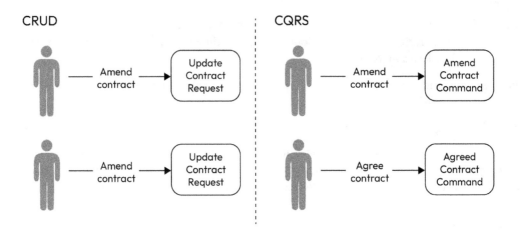

Figure 9.3 – CRUD versus CQRS – update versus command

In CRUD style, both amendments to and agreement of a contract result in a request to update the contract, and the difference is the content of the contract. In CQRS style, amendments and agreements have dedicated commands to capture not only what needs to be updated, but also the intent and business context of the update.

The CQRS style results in the amendment and agreement operations being separated. This leads to a cleaner and more modular design. The separation also allows independent scaling and the optimization of commands.

On the query side, as shown in the following figure, households A and B can get the contract between them by using a CRUD read request, and the responses will be the same for both households. However, the CQRS query allows multiple read models, and in this case, it can return a custom read model depending on which household makes the query.

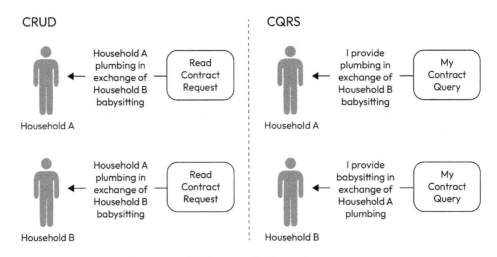

Figure 9.4 – CRUD versus CQRS – read versus query

The CQRS style can build a materialized view for each household as a read model by consuming the events produced when a command is accepted. In CRUD style, these custom views are typically implemented using SQL commands and the custom views do not materialize.

A materialized read model can scale independently without concerns for commands. For example, if the read-write ratio of the aggregate contract heavily tilts towards reading, then it is sensible to consider materializing the corresponding read model in a separate data store infrastructure, so the writing is not affected even under a heavy load of query operations.

As read models are materialized by consuming events via asynchronous messaging, changes in the aggregates may not be immediately reflected in the read models but will eventually be synchronized.

It is important to point out that handling commands does need some existing information for validation, integrity checks, and concurrency control. These read operations are necessary for handling commands, but not for serving requests.

When should CQRS be considered?

Like Event Sourcing, CQRS should be considered when a couple of prerequisites are met and there are legitimate problems that can be solved by CQRS. CQRS is a paradigm shift in how we reason about a system, and significant effort is required to implement it correctly. Applying CQRS to the wrong system increases the complexity with no benefits.

CQRS is an architectural pattern built upon DDD. If the current system has no concept of DDD, bounded contexts, or aggregates, then it is a non-starter. Even if the system includes bounded contexts, using CQRS may not be necessary for generic subdomains due to their limited complexity. CQRS is most likely beneficial only for core domains, where the domain itself is complex enough to warrant its use.

There are, however, a few signs that CQRS can be considered in the domain:

- Multiple actors working on the same aggregate. This usually means not all actors are concerned with everything in an aggregate. Some actors may work on a part of an aggregate but not all of it.

- Multiple use cases of updating the aggregate. There are specific use cases in which only a part of the aggregate should be updated.

- Multiple views of the same aggregate. There are alternate views of the same aggregate, and sometimes there may even be a view combining multiple entities that deviate from the aggregate.

- Imbalanced read-write ratio. If either read or write operations are significantly more frequent than the other, read and write would need to be scaled differently as their needs are different.

Benefits and costs of CQRS

CQRS separates the concerns of read (query) and write (command) operations so their requirements can be met in isolation. This leads to smaller code footprints per function or per class, but there will be more functions or classes due to the separation.

This separation drives the code toward the **Single Responsibility Principle (SRP)**, as mentioned in *Chapter 2*, where there should be one and only one reason to change a class. Each use case for each actor has its own class, either as a query or as a command.

The separation of queries and commands enables independent performance optimization, resulting in improved system performance and scalability overall. For example, queries can be optimized for faster execution due to the dedicated read models, and commands can be optimized for high throughput and consistency. However, this also results in more moving parts in the system and thus increases its complexity.

Queries and commands are broken down into their own functions or classes. This means that extending functionality is unlikely to need to change existing queries and commands, and therefore it is easier than in CRUD, where there is a big repository class that contains all the CRUD operations.

Dedicated queries and commands for each business case eliminate the need for clients to deal with unrelated fields and details about an aggregate, or to create a CRUD-style update or read request. This is in line with the **Interface Segregation Principle (ISP)**, as mentioned in *Chapter 2*, where a client is not forced to depend on fields and functions it does not use.

Supporting multiple read models using CRUD is challenging. It often requires complicated SQL statements to join relevant data together. Moreover, it is difficult to optimize performance as different read models have different needs. Quite often, compromises are made so that different read models have reasonably acceptable performance.

Using CQRS, read models are materialized by consuming the events of aggregates. They have their own storage so they can scale and optimize performance that is unique to the non-functional requirements. This comes at the cost of the replication of data in various forms, and more storage is needed to keep these read models. Also, each read model requires its own code to transform the event and persist data that's relevant to its data structure.

You may recognize the synergy between CQRS and Event Sourcing at this point. We are going to illustrate how they work together with a concrete example.

Combining CQRS and Event Sourcing

CQRS and Event Sourcing are complementary patterns that work well together in building robust, scalable, and maintainable distributed systems.

The **command handler** in the CQRS architecture is responsible for validating write requests. If a command is valid, an event is persisted to an event store, which is the core of the Event Sourcing pattern. An example of how the CQRS command and Event Sourcing integrate is shown in *Figure 9.5*:

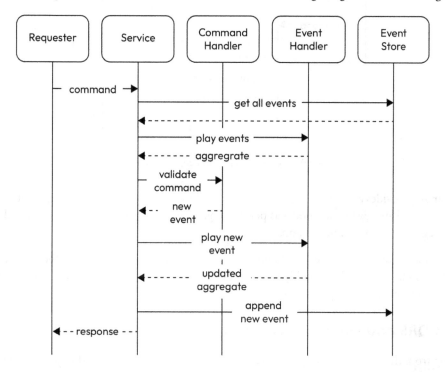

Figure 9.5 – CQRS command and Event Sourcing

The **service** receives a command from the **requester**. The **service** requires the current state of the aggregate, which is rebuilt by replaying events retrieved from the **Event Store**. The **command** passes the validation, so a new event is generated. The new event is played on the aggregate to generate a new state. The new event is appended to the **Event Store** and the updated aggregate is returned to the **requester**.

Event Sourcing answered the question from CQRS of how to update an aggregate and inform subscribers of the changes to an aggregate. CQRS answered the question from Event Sourcing of how an event was created.

The query, in turn, rebuilds the current state of the application by replaying the events stored in the event store. Also, multiple read models are rebuilt by transforming the event payloads to build their unique data structures. An example of how CQRS query and Event Sourcing integrate is shown in *Figure 9.6*:

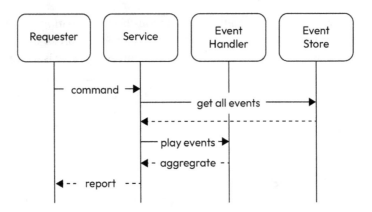

Figure 9.6 – CQRS query and Event Sourcing

Event Sourcing provides a way for a CQRS query to rebuild a snapshot of a given aggregate. It enables the query to build any given read model as per the request. It also permits building a historical view of the aggregate from a given timestamp.

This separation of concerns between the command and query models, combined with the event-driven nature of Event Sourcing, allows highly scalable, flexible, and maintainable systems that can easily adapt to changing business requirements.

Using CQRS and Event Sourcing together

Extending from the previous example of Event Sourcing, adding CQRS would require a couple of command and query classes to be created. We will need a class to capture the query of the current state of a contract among households and a class to capture the command for drafting a contract. The corresponding code is shown here:

```
data class CurrentContractQuery(
    val contractId: UUID
)
data class DraftContractCommand(
    val draftedByHousehold: String,
    val counterpartyHousehold: String,
    val serviceProvided: String,
    val serviceReceived: String,
)
data class AgreeContractCommand(
    val contractId: UUID,
    val agreedByHousehold: String,
)
```

You will find these command classes look quite like the event classes. The differences are as follows:

- The command that creates the aggregate does not contain the aggregate ID
- The command does not contain the aggregate version or the timestamp

This is because the aggregate ID, version, and timestamp are populated when handling the commands. In this example, command handling is not idempotent. It uses randomization for aggregate IDs and a system clock to stamp timestamps.

There could be various implementations that supply random values and system timestamps to make command handling idempotent. Both approaches can be justified if they are consistent and well understood.

In this example, the handling of every command has two potential outcomes. A successful outcome creates an event, and this event needs to be persisted. A failure outcome will inform the callers of the cause, and no event will be created. It is necessary to have a class to encapsulate the information for a failure outcome:

```
data class Failure<T>(
    val request: T,
    val message: String? = null,
    val error: Throwable? = null
)
```

The Failure class contains the original request, an optional message, and an optional Throwable object.

Each query and command requires a handler. Taking advantage of the EventStore class in the example of Event Sourcing, the query handler is straightforward with the use of Kotlin extensions and the event store as a parameter:

```
fun CurrentContractQuery.handle(
    eventStore: EventStore<UUID, ContractEvent>
): Contract? = eventStore.get(contractId)?.play()
```

The query handler simply gets all the events for the given contractId and then plays all events to re-create the latest version of Contract as the return value.

The command handler has two main styles: creating and updating. The handler for the creation command generates a random **Universally unique identifier (UUID)** and the timestamp. These fields are captured in the creation event:

```
fun DraftContractCommand.handle(
    eventStore: EventStore<UUID, ContractEvent>,
    onSuccess: (ContractDraftedEvent) -> Unit,
    onFailure: (Failure<DraftContractCommand>) -> Unit
) {
```

```
    if (draftedByHousehold == counterpartyHousehold) {
        onFailure(Failure(this, "Same household is not allowed:
$draftedByHousehold"))
    } else {
        ContractDraftedEvent(
            contractId = UUID.randomUUID(),
            time = Instant.now(),
            draftedByHousehold = draftedByHousehold,
            counterpartyHousehold = counterpartyHousehold,
            serviceReceived = serviceReceived,
            serviceProvided = serviceProvided
        ).also{
            eventStore.append(it.contractId, it)
        }.also(onSuccess)
    }
}
```

The command handler requires two callback functions, one for success and one for failure. Only one of the callback functions is invoked during the execution. If the command fails validation (in this case, when the same household is used for the draft contract), no event is created and the failure callback function is invoked. Otherwise, an event is created to capture the randomized contract ID, the time of the event, and the rest of the fields. The event is persisted to the event store. The event is then passed to the success callback function.

The handler for the update command requires validation of whether the aggregate exists, and whether the same aggregate ID is retained. The rest of the implementation is the handler for the create command:

```
fun AgreeContractCommand.handle(
    eventStore: EventStore<UUID, ContractEvent>,
    onSuccess: (ContractAgreedEvent) -> Unit,
    onFailure: (Failure<AgreeContractCommand>) -> Unit) {
    validate(
        eventStore = eventStore,
        contractId = contractId,
        householdName = agreedByHousehold,
        onSuccess = { contract ->
            ContractAgreedEvent(
                contractId = contractId,
                targetVersion = contract.version + 1,
                time = Instant.now(),
                agreedByHousehold
            ).also { eventStore.append(contractId, it)
            }.also(onSuccess)
        },
```

```
        onFailure = { onFailure(it)}
    )
}
```

There is a `validate` function that is meant to be shared with other update command handlers:

```
fun <T> T.validate(
    eventStore: EventStore<UUID, ContractEvent>,
    contractId: UUID,
    householdName: String,
    onSuccess: (Contract) -> Unit,
    onFailure: (Failure<T>) -> Unit) {
    val events = eventStore.get(contractId)
    if (events == null) {
        onFailure(Failure(this, "Contract not found: $contractId"))
    } else {
        val contract = events.play()
        if (contract == null) {
            onFailure(Failure(this, "Failed to reconstruct Contract:
$contractId"))
        } else if (contractId != contract.id) {
            onFailure(Failure(this, "Contract ID mismatched. Expected:
$contractId, was: ${contract.id}"))
        } else if (householdName != contract.partyA.householdName
            && householdName != contract.partyB.householdName) {
            onFailure(Failure(this, "Household not found in contract:
$householdName"))
        } else {
            onSuccess(contract)
        }
    }
}
```

The success callback function will have the `Contract` passed in because the latest version of the aggregate has been found and re-created. The failure callback function will have the `Failure` object passed in for delegation.

Finally, when using this example of CQRS and Event Sourcing, the client only needs to create a command and pass it in the event store to start with. Then, the extension `handle` function is invoked:

```
    var contractId: UUID? = null
    val eventStore = EventStore<UUID, ContractEvent>()
    DraftContractCommand(
        draftedByHousehold = "HouseholdA",
        counterpartyHousehold = "HouseholdB",
```

```
            serviceProvided = "Cleaning",
            serviceReceived = "Babysitting"
        ).handle(
            eventStore = eventStore,
            onSuccess = { contractId = it.contractId
                println("Contract drafted: $contractId") },
            onFailure = { "Failed to draft contract: $it"}
        )
        AmendContractCommand(
            contractId = contractId!!,
            amendedByHousehold = "HouseholdB",
            serviceReceivedUpdate = "Dish washing",
            serviceProvidedUpdate = null
        ).handle(eventStore = eventStore,
            onSuccess = { println("Contract amended: $contractId") },
            onFailure = { println("Failed to amend contract:
    $contractId")}
        )
```

The success callback function captures `contractId` for future updates. To update the aggregate, an update command needs to be created and the contract ID needs to be specified. Afterwards, the `handle` extension function is invoked:

```
        AgreeContractCommand(
            contractId = contractId!!,
            agreedByHousehold = "HouseholdA"
        ).handle(eventStore = eventStore,
            onSuccess = { println("Contract agreed: $contractId") },
            onFailure = { println("Failed to amend contract:
    $contractId")}
        )
        AgreeContractCommand(
            contractId = contractId!!,
            agreedByHousehold = "HouseholdB"
        ).handle(eventStore = eventStore,
            onSuccess = { println("Contract agreed: $contractId") },
            onFailure = { println("Failed to amend contract:
    $contractId")}
        )
```

After all these updates, we can query the latest Contract and see if all these updates have accumulated. A query is created with the captured contract ID. The handle extension function is invoked, and the event store is passed in:

```
    val aggregate = CurrentContractQuery(contractId!!).
handle(eventStore)
    println("Aggregate is of version: ${aggregate?.version}")
```

Because the event store keeps on capturing events as commands are handled, it already has the full history of the aggregate. This is the console output you get after executing all the commands and queries:

```
Contract drafted: 3a25642c-fc9b-4024-b862-daf10fc645a6
Contract amended: 3a25642c-fc9b-4024-b862-daf10fc645a6
Contract agreed: 3a25642c-fc9b-4024-b862-daf10fc645a6
Contract agreed: 3a25642c-fc9b-4024-b862-daf10fc645a6
Aggregate is of version: 3
```

This example has illustrated the powerful combination of CQRS and Event Sourcing at work. They complement each other and work together seamlessly. It has also demonstrated that each command and query has its own class and functions. This breaks down the traditional CRUD approach, where there are usually repository classes that contain all four types of operations in a big file.

Outbox pattern

It is worth pointing out that in real systems, there is a trend to also apply the **Outbox** pattern to manage the delivery of events in a reliable and fault-tolerant manner. This is implemented by having an outbox of messages in persistent storage, such as a relational database table.

There is a separate process that reads the unsent outbox messages and delivers them to the target destinations. If a message is delivered, the corresponding record is considered sent and will be deleted.

If the event store is unavailable, this delivery process will retry delivery automatically until the event store is operational again. The delivery process can also scale independently and potentially deliver messages to different destinations in parallel.

A similar pattern to the Outbox pattern is the **Change Data Capture (CDC)** pattern. CDC detects changes to records by database triggers, transaction logs, or change trackers and creates an event. The created event eventually goes into the event stream or topic. While events are created before the Outbox process, events are retrospectively created in CDC. That means that CDC is less intuitive in capturing the intent of the event.

Traditional relational databases provide strong consistency and transactional guarantees. This means we can have one transaction for normal database operations and event delivery as database records for either Outbox or CDC, achieving the all-or-none transactional behavior.

By storing the Outbox messages in relational databases, the reliability, fault tolerance, consistency, and scalability of event sending are also improved.

Popular frameworks and infrastructure for CQRS and Event Sourcing

CQRS and Event Sourcing are architecture concepts that do not rely on a particular technology or framework. They are also agnostic to programming languages. However, there are frameworks and infrastructure that aim to support CQRS or Event Sourcing.

- CQRS / Event Sourcing frameworks:
  - Axon framework (`https://www.axoniq.io/products/axon-framework`)
  - Akka (`https://akka.io/`)
- Event stores:
  - EventStore (`https://www.eventstore.com/`)
  - Apache Cassandra (`https://cassandra.apache.org/`)
  - MongoDB (`https://www.mongodb.com/`)
- Messaging infrastructure:
  - RabbitMQ streams (`https://www.rabbitmq.com/docs/streams`)
  - Apache Kafka (`https://kafka.apache.org/`)

It is important to mention that using these tools does not automatically make CQRS or Event Sourcing work in your system. Your current framework and infrastructure may already be ready for these architecture styles, as long as the team implements the system using the semantics of CQRS and Event Sourcing.

Summary

We began by covering the classic CRUD architecture and its limitations. Then, we introduced Event Sourcing as an alternative approach to managing data and explored its history. We delved into how a team can decide whether Event Sourcing should be considered in their systems.

We used the real-life example of villagers exchanging services to demonstrate how Event Sourcing can be implemented. We also briefly laid out a plan for how a CRUD system can migrate to Event Sourcing.

Afterward, we moved to the topic of CQRS architecture. We discussed using commands as write operations and queries as read operations. We mentioned the basic constructs of CQRS and how they relate to the DDD and Event Sourcing architectures. We saw a side-by-side comparison of CRUD and CQRS in breaking down multiple update operations.

We then discussed using both CQRS and Event Sourcing. We described how these two architectures complement each other with the extension of the real-life example.

Lastly, we briefly covered using the Outbox pattern with CQRS and Event Sourcing.

In the next chapter, we are going to discuss the idempotence, replication, and recovery aspects of distributed systems.

10
Idempotency, Replication, and Recovery Models

Distributed systems are very common in modern software architectures. The challenges of ensuring data consistency, fault tolerance, and availability become critical. This chapter is going to cover three key concepts that help address these challenges:

- Idempotency
- Replication
- Recovery models

Idempotency is a fundamental non-functional system property that ensures operations can be executed safely and repeatedly without causing unintended side effects. In a distributed system, network failures and system crashes are common. Idempotency is essential for maintaining data integrity and consistency. By designing operations to be idempotent, engineers can build more resilient and fault-tolerant systems that can recover from partial failures without compromising the overall system state.

Replication, on the other hand, is a technique that's used to improve the availability and durability of data in distributed systems. By maintaining multiple copies of data across different nodes, replication provides redundancy and helps ensure that the system can continue to operate even if one or more nodes fail. However, replication introduces its own set of challenges, such as ensuring consistency between replicas and efficiently managing the replication process.

Finally, **recovery models** define the strategies and mechanisms that are used to restore the state of a distributed system after a failure or disruption. These models can range from simple backup-and-restore approaches to more sophisticated techniques. Choosing the right recovery model is crucial for building resilient distributed systems that can weather unexpected events and maintain high levels of availability and responsiveness.

In this chapter, we'll explore each of these topics in greater depth, discussing their underlying principles, trade-offs, and best practices for applying them in real-world distributed applications. After this chapter, you should be able to implement idempotency, replication, and recovery models at a level suitable for your system.

Technical requirements

You can find the code files used in this chapter on GitHub: `https://github.com/PacktPublishing/Software-Architecture-with-Kotlin/tree/main/chapter-10`

Idempotency

Idempotency is a concept in software engineering that refers to the non-functional property of operations that can be performed multiple times while still having the same effect as performing it only once. In other words, an idempotent operation can be safely repeated without side effects. Let's cover a short scenario where idempotency is required.

A use case where idempotency is required

Imagine that we're building an online banking application. A key capability is **Transfer Funds**, in which a user transfers money from one account to another. This capability is a fundamental yet critical part of the system, and it needs to be implemented in a way that ensures the integrity and reliability of the user's financial transactions.

If the **Transfer Funds** operation isn't idempotent, then the user could accidentally click the **Transfer** button multiple times, and the system would execute the transfer operation multiple times, resulting in an unintended debit from the source account and a corresponding credit to the destination account.

Most mature user interfaces can avoid this situation by blocking the button once it's pushed until a response is received. However, there are also API integrations that require idempotency.

This result isn't intended by the user, and it has multiple consequences. First, if the user has insufficient funds from the second and subsequent transfer, the user will have overdraft funds and be subject to interest charges. Second, these incidents trigger user complaints and can result in the potential involvement of financial regulatory bodies. Not only the user experience but also the unintended side effect results in reputational damage to the bank.

To prevent these issues, the **Transfer Funds** operation should be designed to be idempotent. This means that no matter how many times the user clicks the **Transfer Funds** button, the system will only execute the transfer once, ensuring that the final state of the accounts is correct and matches the user's intent.

Key aspects of idempotency

Idempotency is an important concept in software development, particularly in the context of distributed systems, APIs, and data processing pipelines. Here are some key aspects of idempotency:

- **Constant outcomes**: An idempotent operation always produces the same result, regardless of how many times it's executed. If an operation isn't idempotent, each subsequent execution might produce a different outcome.

- **Error handling and retries**: Idempotency helps in handling errors and retries gracefully. If an operation fails, the system can safely retry the operation without causing unintended side effects.

- **Data consistency**: Idempotent operations ensure data consistency by preventing accidental data modifications or duplications, which can occur when retrying non-idempotent operations.

- **Scalability and reliability**: Idempotency is crucial in distributed systems, where multiple instances of an application may be processing the same request concurrently. Idempotent operations allow the system to scale and handle failures without compromising data integrity.

Let's cover a few practical scenarios where idempotency can be applied.

Scenario 1 – evolutionary database migration script

Evolutionary databases aim to create database systems that can evolve and adapt to changes over time. They aren't defined by static and rigid models. The database schema is defined by incremental changes that build the target schema.

Consider Flyway, an open source database migration tool. The incremental changes are specified by SQL scripts:

```
V1_create_new_tables.sql
V2_add_new_columns.sql
```

For simplicity's sake, let's assume that the V1 script only contains the following statement for creating a table:

```
CREATE TABLE HOUSEHOLD (
id UUID primary key,
name text not null
);
```

The CREATE SQL statement will create a new table called HOUSEHOLD if it doesn't already exist. Otherwise, an error will be reported and the V1 script will fail. In other words, it isn't idempotent, and repeated executions don't have the same outcome. Here's an idempotent version of the script:

```
CREATE TABLE IF NOT EXISTS HOUSEHOLD (
id UUID primary key,
name text not null
);
```

The IF NOT EXIST syntax ensures the table is created if it doesn't exist, or nothing is performed if the table already exists. The outcome is the same in either case, which is that the HOUSEHOLD table exists in the database.

The execution of the V2 script will add a new column to this table as a non-null column. Some database vendors support clever SQL statements that create a non-null column and populate values in the same statement. For the sake of this argument, let's assume that this isn't supported. We've resorted to the classic approach of adding a nullable column, populating the value, and then setting the column to non-null. Like the modified V1 script, we can make it idempotent:

```
ALTER TABLE IF EXISTS HOUSEHOLD ADD COLUMN deleted boolean;
UPDATE HOUSEHOLD SET deleted = false;
ALTER TABLE IF EXISTS HOUSEHOLD ALTER COLUMN IF EXISTS deleted SET NOT
NULL;
COMMIT;
```

The IF EXISTS syntax ensures that the table or columns will be altered if they exist, or nothing is performed if they don't. The outcome is the same and therefore it's idempotent. The classic guideline would have suggested that the **Data Definition Language** (**DDL**) should be separated from the **Data Manipulation Language** (**DML**), in which ALTER TABLE is DDL and UPDATE is DML. This was suggested because DDL is immediately committed while DML requires an explicit commit. However, with idempotency, this is no longer an issue as each statement can be repeated to produce the same outcome.

Scenario 2 – create/update operations

Using the real-life example of villagers exchanging services, there's a business case to ensure households are kept in the system record. However, the household users don't know if the household has already been persisted.

A CRUD-based system may define create and update as two independent operations. These operations are well-suited as users want the household records to persist regardless of whether they exist. There could have been a network outage, so users may not know if their previous requests were successful.

In other words, users want an operation that can be repeated and yet generate the same outcome. They need an idempotent operation to ensure the household records have been stored, despite whether they already exist.

This operation is often referred to as **upsert**, which means **update or insert**. The key characteristics of an upsert operation are as follows:

1. **Idempotent**: It can be executed repeatedly with the same outcome. If the record already exists, the record is updated; if the record doesn't exist, the record is created.

2. **Atomic**: The operation is executed in a transaction of serialized isolation. This means the operation was either completed or it didn't happen.

3. **Option 1 – pessimistic**: The pessimistic approach would check if the record already exists or not to determine whether it's an update or a create operation.

4. **Option 2 – optimistic**: The optimistic approach would assume the record either exists or not and perform an update or create operation, respectively. If the update operation hasn't found the record, it switches to the create operation. Alternatively, if the create operation fails due to a unique constraint violation, it switches to the update operation.

Here's an example of the upsert operation for a household in an SQL statement. It's implementing the optimistic approach:

```
INSERT INTO HOUSEHOLD (id, name, email) VALUES ('d0275532-1a0a-
4787-a079-b1292ad4aadf', 'Whittington', 'info@ whittington'.
com') ON DUPLICATE KEY UPDATE name = 'Whittington', email = 'info@
whittington'.com';
```

This SQL statement attempts to insert a new household record. If the record doesn't exist, a new row is inserted. If the execution hits a duplicate key violation, it becomes an update operation to name and email.

If this operation is exposed as an external API – that is, as a REST endpoint – the contract can be expressed in the following ways:

1. GET: Multiple invocations of the GET endpoint shall return the same result, given the system state remains unchanged.

2. PUT: The PUT endpoint implies creating a new resource or replacing a representation of the household with the request payload.

3. DELETE: The DELETE endpoint intends to remove the resource, regardless of whether it already exists. If the resource isn't found, then it should return a successful **Hypertext Transfer Protocol (HTTP)** status code.

The HTTP method itself doesn't bring idempotency. For example, if the response payload of the GET endpoint contains the current time or random values, then multiple invocations don't return the same result, and therefore it's not idempotent.

The POST and PATCH endpoints aren't defined as idempotent. The POST endpoint in REST architecture implies the request to create a resource and assumes the resource was absent. The PATCH endpoint assumes the resource already exists so that the resource can be partially updated.

HTTP methods

HTTP defines a few methods to categorize the request to perform an action on a resource. The GET method is a read-only operation that returns data from the server. The POST method creates resources in a server. The PUT method replaces or creates a resource. The PATCH method partially updates an existing resource. The DELETE method removes a resource from the server. The HEAD method returns the header of the resource without the body content. The OPTIONS method describes the options to communicate with the specific resource. Finally, the TRACE method is a diagnosis operation that echoes the final receipt of the request to provide information for troubleshooting.

Scenario 3 – processing events in sequence

Something that consumes events from a stream or a topic usually takes an event one at a time and processes them sequentially. If the sequence of events that's processed is important, then there's a need to gracefully process events in the face of duplication and out of sequence.

There are two levels where an event sequence could be compromised. The first level is the transport level, where the offset of the last consumed event is reset to older events due to network issues, partition changes, or consumer group changes. The second level is the application level and is where the publisher has sent older events.

Application-level deduplication at the consumer level could handle event sequences being compromised at the transport or application level. However, that would require publishers to provide sequential information on each event. This could be a sequence number on the event or a timestamp where an event occurred.

The consumer can maintain the last processed sequence number or timestamp per publisher. If the consumer receives an event where the sequence number is lower than the last to be processed, or where the timestamp is older than the last to be processed, then the consumer skips this event until a newer event is received.

Here's an example implementation of an event listener that prevents older events from being processed:

```
class HouseholdEventListener {
    var lastProcessedTime: Instant? = null
    @KafkaListener(
        topics = ["\${household-v1-topic}"],
        clientIdPrefix = "\${client-id}",
        groupId = "\${group-id}",
        containerFactory = "kafkaListenerContainerFactory",
        properties = ["auto.offset.reset=earliest"]
    )
    fun onMessage(
        @Payload(required = false) event: HouseholdEvent?,
        @Header(name = "kafka_eventTime", required = true) key:
String,
    ) {
        if (lastProcessedTime != null && event?.time?.
isBefore(lastProcessedTime) == true) {
            log.warn { "Skipping event with time ${event.time} because
it is before the last processed time $lastProcessedTime" }
            return
        }
        // some processing logic here
        lastProcessedTime = event?.time
    }
}
```

Here, `HouseholdEventListener` keeps the timestamp of the last processed event. The incoming events from Kafka have a header field, `kafka_eventTime`, that's provided by the publisher. The value is when the event occurred, not when the event was published.

The first event process wouldn't perform any timestamp check. Subsequently, the listener would skip processing if the event timestamp from the header is earlier than the last processed timestamp. This indicates that the incoming event is old and can be skipped.

If the event isn't skipped and has finished processing, the last processed timestamp is updated, and the event is acknowledged by the Kafka broker. The listener is now ready to consume another event.

In a production system, the last processed time should be persisted in the database and be in the same transaction where business processing takes place. The last processed time should be restored when the listener starts. This would allow the listener to resume its consumption of events after a restart.

This implementation illustrates how a consumer can detect an older event with the help of the publisher. The older event isn't processed, and the consumer can keep the last processed timestamp as an offset to verify the next event.

To extend to this example, the timestamp of the last processed event can be persisted in a database so that the value is restored after a restart.

Scenario 4 – the multiple bounded context saga

A **saga** is a pattern in **domain-driven design (DDD)** that involves distributed transactions. The challenge is to maintain data consistency across multiple bounded contexts.

Let's use our bank transfer example, where we need idempotent operations to ensure the fund is only transferred once and only once. The banking phone application intends to send a request to the backend service.

However, there are multiple backend services involved in this operation. First, there's **Transfer Service**, which validates the request.

Once validated, it needs to reserve the amount in the withdrawing account until the transfer has been completed. This is done by another service called **Account Service**.

Account Service orchestrates reserving funds by moving funds from a customer account to the corporate account. Later, it orchestrates adding funds by moving funds from the corporate account to a customer account. This is done by communicating with the legacy **Core Banking System**.

Once the funds have been reserved, **Transfer Service** can request the second part of the transfer by moving the funds from the corporate account to the customer account. The request is handled by **Account Service**, which communicates with the legacy **Core Banking System** to transfer the funds. Once this has been acknowledged and completed by **Core Banking System**, **Account Service** returns the result to **Transfer Service** and thus completes the transfer.

This interaction is demonstrated in *Figure 10.1*:

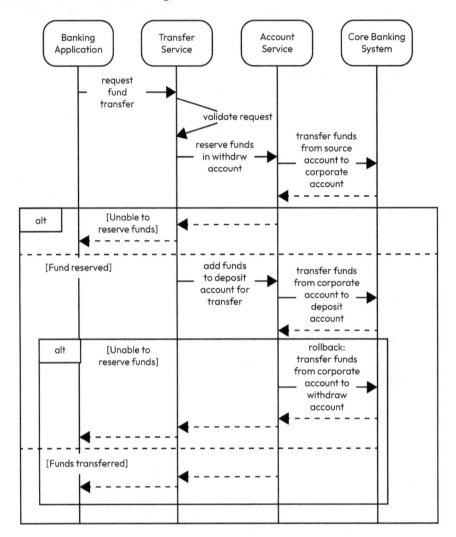

Figure 10.1 – Example sequence for a bank transfer

Making the whole transfer operation idempotent is complex because transactions are distributed among services. Moreover, we need a way to identify that the user only wants the transfer funds once, despite multiple attempts from the banking application.

Often, some parts of the system are legacy systems that may not be enhanced so easily. In this case, let's assume **Core Banking System** can't take the idempotency key in the request.

Let's explore how each component involved in this process can work toward idempotency.

Banking application

The first step should be the banking application generating an **idempotency key**, which can identify multiple attempts belonging to the same user intent. Ideally, the idempotency key should be carried to all services involved.

Transfer Service

Transfer Service can cache these idempotency keys for a certain period. Within that period, the same idempotency keys are treated as duplicated requests.

To avoid consistency issues under concurrent requests, many systems use explicit locks to ensure the requests of the same idempotency keys are processed only one at a time, across multiple instances.

The service can decide to skip the remaining interactions with other services and return the response that was sent previously to the banking service. This approach is OK if we are sure the remaining services have acknowledged completion of the request.

If, for example, there was a timeout when **Transfer Service** communicated with **Account Service**, then it may be sensible to repeat the interaction with **Account Service**. This allows the operation to be repaired and continue until completion. This approach also assumes that **Account Service** can handle duplicated requests in an idempotent manner.

Account Service

In this operation, **Account Service** provides two functionalities: reserve funds and add funds. To be able to identify duplicate requests, the idempotency keys should be persisted alongside the records related to holding and moving funds.

When **Account Service** handles the requests of reserving or adding funds, it must check whether duplicate requests already exist by using the idempotency keys. If they do, **Account Service** returns the response from the records, as if it had been processed this time.

If the reserve fund request is rejected by **Core Banking System** due to insufficient funds, **Account Service** needs to roll back the operation by reversing the fund back to the withdrawal account.

Like **Transfer Service**, there should be some form of explicit locking to ensure only one request for a given idempotency key is processed at a time across multiple instances.

Core Banking System

Core Banking System is a legacy system that doesn't support idempotency. It isn't able to take idempotency keys or process them. Since **Account Service** is the service that communicates with **Core Banking System**, **Account Service** should persist the response from **Core Banking System** together with the corresponding idempotency key.

If the record of the response already exists with the idempotency key, **Account Service** skips communication with **Core Banking System** and uses the previously persisted response from **Core Banking System** to complete the process.

This is getting complex as there could be a timed-out request for **Core Banking System**. **Account Service** doesn't know whether **Core Banking System** has processed the transfer or not. **Account Service** would need to query the recent transaction history to identify the previous request to **Core Banking System**, either success or failure, to recover and resume the transfer operation. Otherwise, retrying may still result in an inconsistent state.

Sometimes, this recovery may even involve manual correction, which is error-prone. You can see when a process can't be idempotent as it becomes substantially more complex, inefficient, and expensive.

With that, we've run through four scenarios where idempotency is required, and we've explored multiple approaches for these scenarios. Now, let's delve into a concept related to idempotency – replication.

Replication

Replication serves as a safeguard against potential failures, allowing the system to maintain continuity of service even when individual components malfunction or become unavailable.

This aspect of replication has a close relationship with recovery, which will be covered later in this chapter. In short, some replication techniques can prevent system downtime, which requires recovery. Also, some replication techniques enable and enhance recovery processes.

Another aspect of replication is that it can improve system performance by distributing load to multiple nodes, as well as by allowing the system to scale based on traffic.

The copy of the data or running instances is usually called a *replica*. There are many areas where replication is applicable. Let's take a look.

Data redundancy

Multiple replicas are distributed across different nodes or servers. If one node fails, the data can still be accessed from the replicated copies on other nodes. It also prevents data loss if some nodes become permanently unavailable.

This redundancy ensures that the overall system can continue to function, even if some nodes or components are unavailable.

This can apply to relational databases, NoSQL databases, durable message brokers, distributed object caches, and nodes in **peer-to-peer** (**P2P**) networks.

Service redundancy

Having the running service instances of the system distributed and replicated brings a few key benefits.

First, requests can be routed to the most available and responsive replica, reducing the risk of overloading a single node and improving overall system performance. This load balancing helps maintain availability by preventing bottlenecks and ensuring that the system can handle increased traffic or workloads.

Second, it enables the system to scale out by adding more replicas or instances as demand increases. This horizontal scalability allows the system to handle higher loads and maintain availability as the number of requests or resources required grows.

Moreover, if a primary node becomes unavailable, the system can automatically failover to a secondary or backup replica, ensuring a seamless transition.

The secondary replica can take over the workload, maintaining service continuity and high availability.

Replication also facilitates faster recovery as the system can restore services by promoting a healthy replica to become the new primary.

It's also common for data and services to be replicated across multiple geographical locations and data centers. This practice can improve availability in the event of regional failures or disasters. If one data center or region experiences an outage, the system can continue to operate using the replicas in other locations, ensuring that the service remains available to users.

CAP theorem

Let's look at a couple of replication and recovery models that we should discuss. They cater to various levels of consistency, availability performance, and scalability non-functional requirements.

According to the **CAP theorem**, also known as **Brewer's theorem**, it's impossible for a distributed system to provide all three of the following non-functional properties simultaneously:

- **Consistency (C)**: All nodes in the system have the same data at the same time. Consistency ensures that the data is always in a valid state

- **Availability (A)**: Every request receives a non-error response, but there's no guarantee that it contains the most recent data

- **Partition tolerance (P)**: The system continues to operate despite arbitrary message loss or failure of part of the system

The theorem states that when communication between nodes fails, a distributed system can only satisfy two of the three properties (C, A, or P) at the same time. This is known as the **CAP trade-off**.

> **The history of the CAP theorem**
>
> The CAP theorem was proposed by Eric Brewer in 2000 during the Symposium on **Principles of Distributed Computing** (**PODC**). The theorem was later proved by Seth Gilbert and Nancy Lynch of Massachusetts Institute of Technology in 2002, in their paper *Brewer's Conjecture and the Feasibility of Consistent, Available, Partition-Tolerant Web Services*.

The three possible choices are as follows:

- **Consistency and partition tolerance (CP)**: The system sacrifices availability to uphold strong consistency in the face of a network partition. This is common in traditional database systems, such as relational databases.

- **Availability and partition tolerance (AP)**: The system remains available but forgoes maintaining consistency during network failure. This is common in NoSQL databases.

- **Consistency and availability (CA)**: The system offers both consistency and availability, but this is only possible in a fully connected system with no network partitions. In practice, it rarely happens, and the system must choose between consistency and availability.

Although there are three combinations, the choice is more fluid and situational. For example, a system may be initially AP, but as more nodes fail, it may fall back to a single node running with CA.

The CAP theorem is a concept that helps developers understand the trade-offs they need to make when designing a distributed system. It's an important consideration when you're choosing the appropriate data storage and processing solutions for a particular application.

When exploring these models, it's important to understand and discover the non-functional properties your system should aim for. Not all models are suitable for all systems. It's about finding the most suitable models based on your needs and anticipated scenarios.

Model 1 – primary-secondary

The **primary-secondary** (also known as **single-leader**) replication has a **Primary** node (the "leader") that handles all write operations and replicates data changes to the **Secondary** nodes (the "followers"). Single-leader replication is demonstrated in *Figure 10.2*:

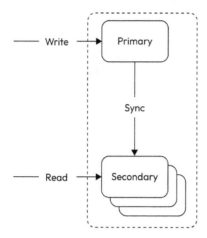

Figure 10.2 – Primary-secondary replication

Read and write operations

The **Primary** node is responsible for all write operations. Whether the **Primary** or **Secondary** nodes should serve read operations has a profound impact on system quality attributes such as consistency, throughput, availability, and resilience.

If the **Primary** node serves all read operations, then the **Secondary** nodes can be either cold backup or hot standby. Cold backup implies the **Secondary** nodes aren't running but the data files are being replicated. Hot standby implies the **Secondary** nodes are up but not serving any request.

This setup provides strong consistency, but serving both read and write operations means the **Primary** node takes all the load. This increases resource consumption and makes it more challenging to achieve high performance. Moreover, if the **Primary** node fails, it may take some time for the cold backup to start up and cause an outage. The hot standby would have better availability as the **Secondary** nodes are already running, but all read requests to the failed primary node are still impacted. This will cause a "blip" until one of the **Secondary** nodes becomes the **Primary** node.

If **Secondary** nodes serve read requests, the throughput of read operations is increased. More nodes are available to handle read requests. If some of the **Secondary** nodes fail, others can continue to operate. This approach comes with the trade-off of potential inconsistency issues. Imagine if one of the **Secondary** nodes failed to connect to the **Primary** node; this **Secondary** node would have outdated data but still performs a read operation and provides outdated data, something that's inconsistent with other nodes.

Replication

When you're replicating data changes from the **Primary** node to **Secondary** nodes, you have two options: synchronous or asynchronous replication. An example sequence diagram of the synchronization process is shown in *Figure 10.3*:

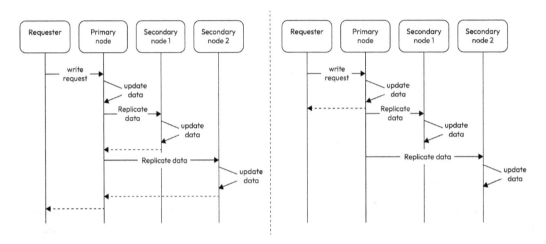

Figure 10.3 – Primary-secondary synchronization – synchronous (left)/asynchronous (right)

This diagram is split vertically into two approaches. On the left-hand side, we have synchronous replication. Here, a write request is sent to the primary node. The primary node updates the data in its local storage but doesn't commit the transaction. Then, it sends the data change to all secondary nodes.

This is a blocking and synchronous process where the primary node waits for responses from all secondary nodes. If all responses are successful, then the primary node commits the transaction and flushes the changes to local storage. Finally, a response is returned to the original requester. The synchronized approach maintains strong data consistency across all nodes at the cost of higher latency due to synchronous communication between the primary and secondary nodes.

On the right-hand side, after the primary node completes the write request, the data change is committed to local storage, and the response is returned to the requester. The data changes are synchronized in the background without blocking. This is either done as a scheduled background process or as an event that's published to the secondary nodes. This approach has reduced latency as replication isn't required to return a response. However, it introduces scenarios where data could be inconsistent.

If the communication between the primary and some secondary nodes fails, some of the secondary nodes will have the latest data and some won't. Meanwhile, all secondary nodes serve read operations that return different versions of the same data.

The risk of inconsistency can be mitigated by stamping the data with a version number or timestamp. Any outdated data can be spotted and then skipped.

The requester can also have a sticky connection with the secondary nodes serving read requests. The data that's returned to the requester will change in tandem with the secondary node. This provides some level of reliability that a request won't get one version of the data, and then get an older version.

Failover

If the primary node fails, one of the secondary nodes needs to become the primary node. The new primary node can be determined by the round-robin rule, or a potentially more complex leader election algorithm.

If data is replicated asynchronously, losing a primary node may result in losing the latest data. This happens if the primary node has updated its local storage and returned the result, but then fails before it can notify secondary nodes.

It's even worse if the failed primary node gets backed up but loses the connection to some of the secondary nodes. Here, a new primary node may have been assigned. We now have a split-brain situation where there are two primary nodes, and secondary nodes are fragmented. This usually requires manual intervention to shut down one of the primary nodes and reconnect all secondary nodes to the one primary node.

Primary-secondary replications are commonly used in highly available databases and message brokers.

Model 2 – partitioned and distributed

Partitioned and distributed (known as **multi-leader**) replication distributes data management into partitions. It allows multiple nodes to serve requests at the same time. These nodes replicate the changes to the other nodes, enabling higher write throughput and availability.

It's typically used when data and services are replicated across multiple geographical locations, often in different data centers or cloud regions. This provides availability and resilience against regional failures or disasters. This is illustrated in *Figure 10.4*:

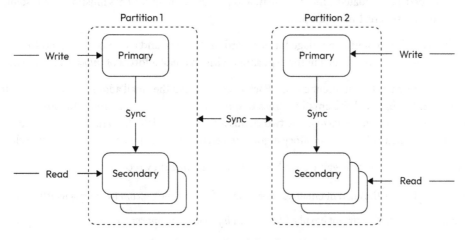

Figure 10.4 – Partitioned and distributed replication

Requests are geographically partitioned so that users of a given region can access the corresponding services in that region. Within this region, this partitioned and distributed replication can behave exactly like primary-secondary replication, where primary nodes serve write requests and secondary nodes serve read requests.

Across regions, an additional synchronization process occurs so that the data in one region is copied to another. Some data is fully partitioned and regional, which means that all requests for the data are served within the designated region in normal circumstances. Some data is shared and may need to be fully replicated. This introduces the need to resolve conflicts if it's updated in both regions.

This setup is more complex compared to primary-secondary replication. However, it can be justified if there are non-functional requirements such as the following:

- Serve requests coming from multiple geographic regions
- Recover in the face of total data center failure
- Decouple from a particular cloud provider architecturally and operationally
- Support offline operations
- Support collaborative update operations

On the other hand, it will become difficult to uphold strong consistency if the same data across multiple regions can't be updated at the same time.

If a data center has failed, requests for the corresponding partition should be routed to the running data center. Data that hasn't been replicated in the running data center would be lost. In this situation, clients may need to roll back to the last replicated state.

Resolving write conflicts and avoiding lost updates

Partitioned and distributed replication requires some mechanisms to resolve write conflicts in which the same piece of data is updated simultaneously, and perhaps differently. Let's illustrate the resolution of write conflicts with a real-life example.

Imagine that each household in a village has a record of its name and a contact email address. The *Whittington* household has a record in the repository with an email address of *info@whittington.com*.

This record is exposed to two different clients. Each client has read the email address, *info@whittington.com*. One client has updated the email address to *query@whittington.com*, while the other one has updated it to *contact@whittington.com*. The two clients attempt to update the value in the repository by providing their updated ones. The repository is going to receive the write requests from these two clients.

Both clients determine the new value based on the current value they receive:

- **Client A**: Update the current email address from *info@whittington.com* to *query@whittington.com*
- **Client B**: Update the current email address from *info@whittington.com* to *contact@whittington.com*

If Client A requests an update earlier than Client B does, then the process of updating the email address to *query@whittington.com* would be lost. This is because Client B almost immediately overwrote the value with *contact@whittington.com* without knowing Client A had also requested an update. This problem is called the **lost update** problem.

This problem is typically solved by having a version number or timestamp on the data. If an incoming request update is identified as older than the one in the system record, then it's safe to skip the update. Having a monotonic increasing version number is a preferred method compared to timestamps due to the risk that the system clock on each machine can be different.

We can model this situation with the following data class:

```
data class Household(
    val version: Int,
    val name: String,
    val email: String,
)
```

Here, the Household class has a version field as an integer. This will be used for comparison during the update operation. There's also a repository class for Household to handle the update request. Here's the scenario simulated in code:

```
fun main() {
    val repo = HouseholdRepository()
    val name = "Whittington"
    val email1 = "info@whittington.com"
    val email2a = "query@whittington.com"
    val email2b = "contact@whittington.com"
    val household1 = Household(0, name, email1)
```

First, a household record is created as a version, after which there are two updates based on it:

```
    repo.create(name) { household1 }
    repo.update(name) { household1.copy(version = 1, email = email2a)}
    repo.update(name) { household1.copy(version = 1, email = email2b)}
    repo.get(name)?.also {
        println("${it.version}, ${it.email}")
    }
}
```

In this situation, we would expect the second update to be skipped because it was based on version zero. The second update would require refreshing the household record to version one and computing the potential update.

A version check should be in place in the repository to prevent the lost update problem. Here's an example implementation:

```
class HouseholdRepository {
    private val values: ConcurrentMap<String, Household> =
ConcurrentHashMap()
```

The `HouseholdRepository` class holds a `ConcurrentMap` interface that uses the household name as the key. The `create` function makes use of the atomic `putIfAbsent` function to ensure the value won't be overwritten by mistake:

```
fun create(
    key: String,
    callback: () -> Household
): Household {
    val household = callback()
    val result = values.putIfAbsent(key, household)
    return result ?: household
}
```

The `update` function checks that the updated value must be one version higher than the existing value by using the atomic `computeIfPresent` function:

```
fun update(
    key: String,
    callback: (Household) -> Household
): Household? = values.computeIfPresent(key) { _, existing ->
    callback(existing).let { updated ->
        if (updated.version == existing.version + 1) {
            updated
        } else {
            existing
        }
    }
}
```

For completeness, there's also a `get` function so that we can get what's kept in the map after the run:

```
fun get(key: String): Household? = values[key]
}
```

The output of the program is as follows:

```
1, query@whittington.com
```

This means the second update is skipped.

Model 3 – quorum-based replication

Quorum-based (also known as **leaderless**) **replication** requires nodes to agree on the state of the data before committing a write operation. This ensures consistency and availability, even if some nodes have failed.

The key difference of quorum-based replication is the lack of a primary node, a leader, or a central coordinator. Instead, the data is decentralized and distributed among the nodes in the cluster:

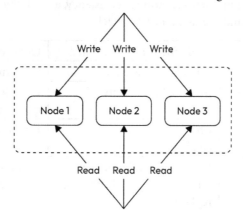

Figure 10.5 – Quorum-based replication

A write operation is only considered successful if it's acknowledged by the majority (quorum) of the participating nodes in the system. This quorum requirement ensures that a write is only committed if it's been replicated to enough nodes, making the system resilient to individual node failures.

The quorum size is typically set to at least more than half of the total nodes, ensuring that even if some fail, the system can still make progress and maintain a consistent state. The data that's synchronized among the nodes is versioned for a couple of reasons:

- The data synchronization process needs to identify an older version of the data, as well as increment the version to indicate an update
- Clients can read the version to understand whether the data that's received is outdated

For example, in a five-node cluster, a quorum size of three would be required for a write operation to succeed. This way, the system can tolerate the failure of up to two nodes without compromising data consistency.

Since all the nodes have the same state, there's no actual failover mechanism. Instead, each request would need to be able to remove duplicated or older responses. This can be done if the data is versioned.

Quorum-based replication is commonly used in distributed databases, key-value stores, P2P networks, blockchains, and coordination services, where maintaining strong consistency and availability in the face of node failures is of utmost importance.

Comparing the three replication models

Choosing the appropriate replication mode in a database or data system depends on several factors, including non-functional requirements regarding consistency, availability, performance, and fault tolerance. Here's a summary and use case for each model:

Primary-Secondary	Partitioned and Distributed	Quorum-Based
Strong consistency	Eventual consistency	Configurable consistency
Simple and easy to maintain	Increased complexity	Complex quorum maintenance
Low tolerance for data loss	Challenges in conflict resolution	Fault tolerance
Performance is limited by the capacity of the leader and replication lag	Performance is limited by the capacity of the leader and replication lag	Additional latency to achieve consensus for each change Higher resource usage
Less available	Highly available; load balancer options are available	Depends on the number of nodes available
Single point of failure	No single point of failure	No single point of failure
Suitable for traditional databases and systems that read more often than write (for example, content management systems)	Suitable for systems spread across different regions and collaborative applications	Suitable for distributed data stores and critical systems that aren't latency-sensitive

The failover mechanism is part of the recovery process, but it focuses on shifting the workload to other running nodes. Recovery also covers bringing up nodes that weren't running. These approaches will be covered in the next section.

Recovery

The recovery process of a system heavily relies on accessible data replicas, except stateless systems. This implies that the recovery approach heavily relies on the replication approach.

Snapshots and checkpoints

The most common approach for recovery is to have a snapshot of the last known system state. Periodically saving the state of the distributed system is known as **checkpointing**.

In the event of a failure, the system can be rolled back to the last known good checkpoint to restore the system to a consistent state. Data that didn't persist in the snapshot will be lost. The amount of data loss would depend on how often the snapshots are taken.

Change logs

A system state can also be restored by replaying the change logs of all operations and transactions within the distributed system.

It's common to recover distributed systems using a combination of checkpoints and change logs. This is similar to the event sourcing recovery method mentioned in *Chapter 9*, where an aggregate is stored by replaying all related events.

This approach helps recover from failures by replaying the missed or lost operations.

Re-route and re-balance

After a node is brought up, it needs to create or join a network of nodes. Requests may need to be re-routed and partitions may need to be re-balanced.

This may also trigger the election of a new primary node. Consensus protocols such as **Raft** (https://raft.github.io/) and **Paxos** (https://www.microsoft.com/en-us/research/publication/part-time-parliament/) may be used to coordinate the actions of the other nodes, ensuring the system remains operational even when individual nodes fail.

Case study – Raft leader election

To demonstrate the details of recovery, we're going to walk through a simplified **Raft** leader election process, as demonstrated in *Figure 10.5*:

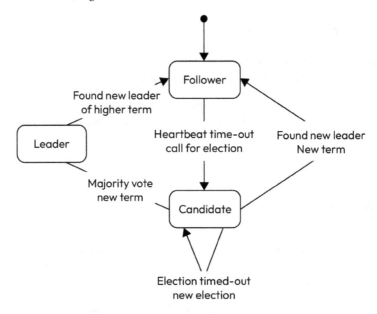

Figure 10.6 – Node state transition in Raft leader election

Raft uses primary-secondary replication in which the primary node replicates data changes to all secondary nodes. The primary node keeps an integer called **Terms**; this number increments for each election. Each request that's received by the primary node is stamped by Terms.

The primary node broadcasts heartbeat messages to all secondary nodes. They're like pulses to keep announcing that the primary node has been up.

When a secondary node hasn't received heartbeat messages over the configured time, it becomes a candidate and calls other secondary nodes to vote for itself.

Other secondary nodes can either accept or reject their votes. When a candidate has been accepted by receiving the most votes, they become the primary node, and others revert to followers.

This mechanism happens concurrently and means there will be conflicts to resolve:

- **Conflicting elections**: Conflicting elections can happen if the timed-out configurations for heartbeat messages are the same among all secondary nodes. This can be avoided by randomizing the timed-out configuration in each node. Moreover, if there are ties of conflicting elections, all elections are called off, after which another election can be called.

- **Multiple leaders**: If a part of the network is disconnected from another, we can end up with a split-brain situation, where each inter-connected portion starts its own election. Since the majority should be more than half of the total number of nodes, only one part can reach majority votes and elect a leader.

  If the original leader is in the smaller part of the split network, there will be multiple leaders when the whole network has recovered. At this point, the value *Terms* can be used to make the original leader step down because the new leader will have a higher term value than the original.

- **Outdated candidates**: Some secondary nodes could be behind others in replication but would still call for an election and put themselves as candidates. If one of them became the primary node, its outdated data became the source of truth, and some updates could be lost.

To avoid this situation, the secondary nodes will reject candidates whose Terms are lower than other candidates, and whose data isn't up to date. A candidate who has outdated data can be spotted by the number of items in the change log.

Summary

In this chapter, we covered three topics: idempotency, replication, and recovery. First, we discussed four scenarios where idempotency is useful and how it can be achieved with reference implementation.

Then, we briefly mentioned how to replicate data and services. We brought up the CAP theorem, in which trade-offs need to be considered for each system. We also delved into three models of replication, namely primary-secondary, partitioned and distributed, and quorum-based.

Finally, we covered some common mechanisms of recovery, outlining how a newly launched node can become operational in the context of distributed systems.

In the next chapter, we'll cover the audit and monitoring aspects of a distributed system.

11

Auditing
and Monitoring Models

This chapter is dedicated to covering the auditing and monitoring aspects of software systems. Implementing a robust auditing and monitoring strategy is key for an organization to improve the overall reliability, security, and performance of its systems while also gaining valuable insights to support data-driven decision-making and continuous improvement.

This is particularly crucial for distributed systems, where the increased complexity and inter-dependencies introduce additional challenges compared to traditional monolithic applications.

In this chapter, we'll explore the following topics:

- The importance of auditing and monitoring
- The challenges of distributed system auditing and monitoring
- Key aspects of auditing and monitoring
- Basic elements of meaningful audit trails

By the end of this chapter, you'll have a solid understanding of how to establish robust auditing and monitoring capabilities for your systems, enabling you to proactively identify and resolve issues, ensure compliance, and maintain overall system health.

Technical requirements

You can find the code files used in this chapter on GitHub: `https://github.com/Packt Publishing/Software-Architecture-with-Kotlin/tree/main/chapter-11`

The importance of auditing and monitoring

Auditing and monitoring are two distinct but closely related concepts that are critical for the effective management and oversight of a system.

Auditing

Auditing is the systematic approach of reviewing, examining, and verifying the various aspects of a system to ensure its compliance, security, and overall integrity. Auditing covers the following key areas:

- **Compliance**: Inspecting the system's conformity to relevant laws, regulations from authority, industry standards, and company policies.

- **Security**: Assessing the system's security infrastructure, policies, and procedures. This includes vulnerability assessments, penetration testing, data protection mechanisms, and access controls.

- **Change management**: Reviewing the processes and documentation associated with system changes and updates.

- **Incident management**: Examining the effectiveness of responses to the system incident and disaster recovery procedures.

- **Performance**: Evaluating the efficiency of the system's operations, resource utilization, and overall performance.

The auditing process typically involves collecting and analyzing various system logs, configuration files, user activities, documentation, and other relevant data to identify potential issues, vulnerabilities, and areas for improvement.

The auditing process is typically done at regular intervals. It's common for organizations to have quarterly, semi-quarterly, and annual audits. The cadence is usually determined by factors such as the regulatory requirements, the system's complexity, criticality, risk profile, and the organization's overall risk management strategy.

A system of higher risk would suggest a more frequent auditing cadence, and some organizations may even exercise a continuous auditing process.

An ad hoc auditing process may be required in the face of certain events, such as a significant system change, security incident, major industry change, or regulatory update.

Monitoring

Monitoring, on the other hand, involves continuously observing and tracking a system's operational state, performance, and behaviors. The following are some monitoring activities:

- **Real-time monitoring**: Continuously collecting and analyzing system metrics, such as system availability, resource utilization, network traffic, and error rates, to detect and respond to issues promptly

- **Anomaly detection**: Identifying unusual or unexpected system behavior that may indicate potential problems or security threats

- **Trend analysis**: Examining historical data to identify patterns, trends, and changes in the system's performance and usage over time

- **Alerting and notifications**: Triggering alerts and notifications when predefined thresholds or conditions are met, enabling proactive issue resolution

- **Dashboards and reporting**: Providing visual representations of system health, performance, and key metrics to support data-driven decision-making

Monitoring typically involves deploying various monitoring middleware components, agents, and frameworks that collect, aggregate, and analyze data from different components of the system.

Why are auditing and monitoring important?

Auditing and monitoring are critical for the effective management and operation of any system. Here are some of the key reasons why auditing and monitoring are so important:

- **Ensuring reliability and availability**: Proactive monitoring helps identify and address issues before they escalate into system failures or downtime. Real-time alerts and incident management enable rapid response and resolution of problems, minimizing the impact on end users. Comprehensive audit trails provide the necessary information to troubleshoot the root causes of system failures, improving the system's reliability and availability.

- **Maintaining security and compliance**: Audit logs and data monitoring can be used to detect and investigate security breaches, unauthorized access attempts, and other malicious activities. Compliance regulations often mandate the implementation of robust audit and monitoring capabilities to ensure the integrity and confidentiality of sensitive data and systems. Audit reports and monitoring dashboards can demonstrate an organization's adherence to compliance requirements, reducing the risk of penalties and reputational damage.

- **Optimizing performance and efficiency**: Monitoring system metrics and resource utilization can help with identifying bottlenecks, optimizing resource allocation, and improving overall system performance. Audit data can provide insights into usage patterns, workload trends, and areas for potential optimization.

- **Enabling data-driven decision-making**: Auditing and monitoring data can be leveraged to identify patterns and generate valuable business intelligence, supporting strategic planning and decision-making. Detailed reports and visualizations can provide stakeholders with a comprehensive understanding of the system's health, performance, and overall status. Historical data and trend analysis can help with predicting future resource requirements, planning for capacity expansions, and identifying opportunities for process improvements.

- **Facilitating troubleshooting and root cause analysis:** Comprehensive audit trails and monitoring data can help engineers and support teams quickly identify the root causes of problems, reducing the time required for issue resolution. Detailed event logs and contextual information can aid in reconstructing system behaviors and recreating problematic scenarios. Auditing and monitoring data can be used to validate the effectiveness of implemented fixes and ensure that issues don't recur.

By investing in robust audit and monitoring capabilities, organizations can ensure the reliability, security, and optimization of their distributed systems, ultimately delivering better experiences for their end users and stakeholders.

Auditing, monitoring, and measuring systems

"You can't improve what you don't measure" is a statement from the management consultant and writer *Peter Drucker*.

Without measurement, the organization could fall into the following scenarios:

- **Opinion-based decision-making:** Without quantitative evidence, people can only express opinions they have little ground to base on. This leads to ineffective communication among stakeholders and engineers and a fragmented understanding of the problem.

- **Hit-and-miss improvement:** Any attempt to improve the system features or quality attributes becomes hit and miss. Some of them may work, and some of them may not, due to the lack of understanding of the problem. Even worse, there is little way to objectively reflect the effect of the improvement. The organization would then carry on the opinion-based decision-making in a vicious cycle.

On the contrary, measuring the system via monitoring benefits the organization in the following ways:

- **Establishing baselines:** Measuring the current state of a system, whether it's performance metrics, security integrity, or compliance conformity, provides the necessary baseline against which future improvements can be assessed and compared.

- **Identifying opportunities:** Measurement and monitoring data can uncover problems, bottlenecks, or inefficiencies within a system that may not be apparent without quantifiable evidence.

- **Tracking progress:** Once improvements or changes are implemented, continuous measurement and monitoring allow organizations to track the impact and effectiveness of those changes, ensuring that they make a positive impact and that desired outcomes are being achieved. If not, the organizations can decide to pivot from the original changes to avoid further deterioration.

- **Informed decision-making**: Reliable data and metrics enable data-driven decision-making, allowing organizations to prioritize and allocate resources more effectively toward the areas that will yield the greatest improvements. This is also an antidote to opinion-based decision-making. Quantitative evidence is one of the best ways to align people's understanding and to effectively drive consensus on the improvement required.

- **Continuous optimization**: By establishing a culture of measurement and monitoring, organizations can continuously identify new opportunities for improvement, creating a cycle of ongoing optimization and refinement.

When are auditing and monitoring not necessary?

There are a few exceptions where auditing and monitoring may not be necessary.

If the system is extremely simple, with very few components and minimal dependencies, the need for comprehensive audit and monitoring may be reduced.

In experimental, low fidelity, or proof-of-concept systems, where the primary focus is on validating a specific concept, hypothesis, or functionality, the investment in audit and monitoring may not be a top priority. However, if the system turns out to be a viable ongoing business later, it's worth investing more in auditing and monitoring.

Systems that are used for testing, personal experimentation, or other low-impact use cases may not warrant the same level of auditing and monitoring as mission-critical production systems.

Note that some systems or organizations may not be subject to strict regulatory or compliance requirements that mandate comprehensive audit and monitoring capabilities.

Also, some systems are isolated and even disconnected from the internet. If they have strict control access, it may be less critical to have extensive audits and monitoring.

If the system is designed to be temporary or short-lived, with a well-defined lifespan, the investment in comprehensive audit and monitoring may not be justified. This applies to one-off data processing tasks or systems with a predetermined sunset date.

The combination of auditing and monitoring provides a comprehensive approach to managing the integrity, security, and performance of a system, especially in complex distributed environments. Audit findings can help inform and enhance monitoring strategies while monitoring data can provide valuable inputs for the audit process. It's most beneficial if auditing and monitoring go hand in hand for any organization.

Implementing auditing and monitoring isn't trivial in modern systems, where they're usually distributed to multiple components. We're going to discover these challenges in the next section.

The challenges of distributed system auditing and monitoring

Distributed systems pose several unique challenges that make their auditing and monitoring more complex than traditional monolithic architectures:

- **Distributed data sources**: In a distributed system, the relevant data and logs are scattered across multiple nodes, services, and communication channels. Collecting, aggregating, and correlating this information is a crucial but challenging task.

- **Dynamic infrastructure**: Distributed systems often involve highly dynamic infrastructure, with nodes and services being added, removed, or scaled on demand. Keeping track of the constantly evolving topology and resource utilization is essential for effective monitoring.

- **Interdependencies and cascading failures**: The intricate interdependencies between components in a distributed system can lead to cascading failures, where a failure in one part of the system triggers issues in other areas. Identifying and tracing these complex relationships is crucial for root cause analysis and recovery.

- **A mixture of various technologies**: Distributed systems often incorporate a diverse set of technologies, including various programming languages, data stores, and middleware components. Developing a unified approach to auditing and monitoring that can handle this heterogeneity is a significant challenge.

- **Real-time responsiveness**: Distributed systems are often expected to provide real-time responsiveness, requiring auditing and monitoring solutions to process and analyze data at high speeds without introducing significant latency or performance overhead.

- **Compliance and regulatory requirements**: Many industries and organizations have strict compliance regulations that mandate comprehensive audit trails and monitoring capabilities. Ensuring that the distributed system meets these requirements is a critical responsibility.

To overcome these challenges, we'll explore the key aspects of auditing and monitoring with concrete examples.

Capturing the appropriate data

To address these challenges and establish effective auditing and monitoring practices for distributed systems, we need to capture the most appropriate, basic building blocks.

Audit trails

The following are essential fields that are typically captured in audit trails:

- **Timestamp**: The date and time when the event occurred. It's important to have a universal time zone for all audit trails. **Coordinated Universal Time (UTC)** is a sensible choice as it's atomic and doesn't tie to any time zone. There's no daylight saving or clock change complication. It can easily be converted into any local time zone. It's also a global standard for timekeeping. This is valuable information for correlating different actions that happened around the same time to reflect a pattern.

- **User IDs**: The identifier of the user who performed or was affected by the action. The user's identity must be tokenized and not contain any PII. This is often regulated by local laws and regulations, particularly on data protection and privacy. Therefore, using a tokenized user ID reduces most of the legal hassle of exposing user details. Accessing user information by user ID is restricted to only authorized individuals and local authorities.

- **Event or action type**: The type of event or action that's been performed (for example, login, logout, data access, or data modification).

- **Details of the action performed**: The specific details of the action, which are usually the input parameters for the action. Different actions usually have different structures of data. Please note that the details may contain sensitive information that needs to be protected. The protection techniques for sensitive information will be covered in *Chapter 14*.

- **Resource accessed**: The resource involved in the action that's been performed. It's typically linked to an aggregate, an entity, or a value object. Often, it involves multiple of them.

- **Outcome**: The result or consequence of the action. It's worth noting that success and failure outcomes are equally important in terms of capturing audit trails. For success, it's essential to capture what will happen next. For failure, any error message or invocation stack trace should be included. Also, it's important to capture any side effects so that further investigation can be performed on them.

- **Session ID**: The identifier of the session during which the event occurred. Having the session ID helps any correlation investigation figure out what other actions may have been performed in the same session.

- **Application ID**: The identifier of the application where the event occurred. This information helps engineers pinpoint where an issue may have occurred so that the situation can be improved.

Monitoring data

The data that's captured for monitoring can look remarkably similar to audit trails. However, monitoring has a unique focus on metrics, availability, and the non-functional properties of a system. Here are the essential fields:

- **Timestamp**: The date and time of the event. Most of the modern systems use UTC over other time zones.

- **System metrics**: CPU usage, memory usage, disk I/O, network traffic, messaging infrastructure, databases, and caches.

- **Application metrics**: The number of API calls, background job executions, response times, request rates, and error rates.

- **Service health**: Status of services (for example, up, down, or degraded).

- **Performance metrics**: The latency and throughput of operations.

- **Logs**: Application logs and system logs.

- **Alerts**: Notifications under predefined criteria.

- **User activities or business metrics**: General user activity patterns, not specific actions. This usually covers business-related patterns, such as "how many new users have signed up in the last 2 hours" or "how many transactions were created in the last 30 minutes."

Application log messages

Application-level log messages are generated by code written by engineers with the aid of logging frameworks. Therefore, the quality of the log messages depends on engineers.

Each organization should define its conventions and best practices for logging messages. Several aspects need standardization.

Logging levels

Organizing logging messages by hierarchical levels provides perspectives of the system at multiple levels of abstraction. It's like a map of the system that can be zoomed in and out. Additionally, it defines the level of responses required for what happens in the system. Typically, there are six levels:

1. **TRACE**: The most detailed and fine-grained level of information. The message is very verbose and full of technical data that can be referenced to the source code. TRACE logging is usually only turned on in local development environments and exceptionally for troubleshooting critical problems in higher environments

2. **DEBUG**: Less verbose than the trace level, the DEBUG log message provides information that may be needed for diagnosing and troubleshooting issues. The debug level is usually switched off in production environments but switched on in lower environments for testing purposes.

3. **INFO**: A standard-level log message that announces the change in application state or that something has happened. In the context of the real-life example we previously used for villagers, an info log message could be an announcement of a new household record being created, together with some essential information such as household name. INFO log messages intend to capture only the result of successful cases, and they require no corrective action. This is also the lowest level of log messages to be shown in a production environment.

4. **WARN**: An unexpected situation has happened in the application. There may be a problem within this instance in the process, but the application can continue to work. For example, there may be a request to delete a household that didn't exist. It could indicate a data-consistent issue for that household record, but the application can carry on handling other requests. A WARN log message may require investigation by engineers, but not as an emergency.

5. **ERROR**: One or more functionalities can't be completed. This isn't a single instance of a failure but a consistent failure of a part of the system. The system has degraded, and corrective actions may be required to recover the failed functionality.

6. **FATAL**: A fundamental error in the crucial functionality no longer works. An example would be losing connection to a database so that none of the persistence functions can be completed. An urgent corrective action or even manual intervention is required to recover the situation.

Log message formats

Having a consistent format in log messages helps engineers to quickly triage and identify issues. A good log message should contain a timestamp, the name of the logger, the log level, the thread name, the class name where the message was logged, and the message itself.

Luckily, most of this information is provided by the logging framework. However, engineers will still need to code the content of the logging message.

A good log message should have the following characteristics:

1. **Concise**: The message should be short and ideally in one sentence.

2. **Mindful use of tenses**: Two major tenses should be used. The past tense is used to describe what happened. Continuous tense is used for logging processes that are still running and should be concluded with a log message announcing the process has been completed.

3. **Key information**: The message should contain the essential IDs so that engineers who read the message can troubleshoot the related issue. Engineers who wrote the log message can read the content from the console and run a drill troubleshooting session.

4. **Incite an action**: Engineers can act on the log message, either as an investigation or confirmation of the outcome of a process as this would be valuable.

5. **Consistent style**: A consistent style promotes easier understanding and faster response to a log message.

Logging frameworks

Despite that different components may use different technologies and languages, the same logging framework should be used whenever possible. This would reduce the inconsistencies of log messages in the system, and thus reduce the cognitive load of engineers using the log messages for troubleshooting purposes.

Structured versus unstructured logging

An **unstructured log** message is a plain string with some formatting, as shown here:

```
09:50:22.261 [main] INFO  o.e.household.HouseholdRepository - Created
a new household 'Whittington'
```

Given that the format is consistent, it isn't too bad and can be read by humans. However, when it comes to log aggregation, alert triggering, and analysis, it's hard to extract the exact information accurately and consistently.

Structured logging, however, promotes well-defined fields and structures so that data can easily be extracted. The previous plain unstructured text log message can be expressed as a JSON object:

```
{
    "@timestamp": "2024-08-20T09:50:22.261878+01:00",
    "@version": "1",
    "message": "Created a new household 'Whittington'",
    "logger_name":
    "org.example.household.HouseholdRepository",
    "thread_name": "main",
    "level": "INFO",
    "level_value": 20000,
    "householdName": "Whittington"
}
```

Structured logging allows for custom fields that provide even more value to the log messages for further monitoring and analysis. This feature is powered by most logging frameworks.

The preceding logging message is supported by the **Kotlin Logging** framework (https://github.com/oshai/kotlin-logging), which wraps the **Simple Logging Facade for Java (SLF4J)** framework (https://www.slf4j.org/). Underneath, it uses the **Logback** framework (https://logback.qos.ch/) to configure how the log message is appended to the destination, such as the system output console. In addition, the **Logstash Logback Encoder** (`https://github.com/logfellow/logstash-logback-encoder`) is used to format the JSON-structured log message. The dependency looks like this in a Gradle Kotlin DSL file – that is, `build.gradlde.kts`:

```
implementation("io.github.oshai:kotlin-logging-jvm:7.0.0")
implementation("org.slf4j:slf4j-api:2.0.16")
implementation("ch.qos.logback:logback-classic:1.5.7")
implementation("net.logstash.logback:logstash-logback-
encoder:8.0")
```

In the Logback configuration file, `logback.xml`, the Logstash encoder is used to format log messages as JSON strings:

```
<appender name="structuredAppender" class="ch.qos.logback.core.
ConsoleAppender">
    <encoder class="net.logstash.logback.encoder.LogstashEncoder">
    </encoder>
</appender>
<root level="debug">
    <appender-ref ref="structuredAppender" />
</root>
```

Then, `structuredAppender` is attached to the root as a log appender. The code to log a structured message is as follows:

```
log.atInfo {
    message = "Created a new household '$householdName'"
    payload = mapOf(
        "householdName" to householdName
    )
}
```

Apart from the main message, the `payload` field supports custom fields in key-value pair format.

It should be emphasized that the log message content is created in a Lambda expression, not as parameters. It's optimal because the logging framework can choose not to execute the Lambda expression if this message has a lower log level than the configuration.

On the contrary, values that are passed in the log function as parameters are evaluated before the logging framework decides to use them. This may have a performance impact if we were to log very detailed information in a low log level such as TRACE.

Contextual logging, or Mapped Diagnostic Context (MDC)

Contextual logging, also known as **Mapper Diagnostic Context** (MDC), aims to group or correlate log messages with the use of IDs (for example user ID, request ID, session ID, and so on). It highlights the fact that these log messages belong to the wider business context or process. This helps engineers identify and diagnose issues by going through a small set of log messages under the same context.

This contextual data can also be used for monitoring and alerting. For example, it's possible to monitor user activities by session ID to understand actions that are also performed together in a session.

Contextual logging can also cut through layers of abstraction in the log messages. There might be logging in the service layer, and the repository layer can be grouped by the contextual data.

Contextual logging is also compatible with structured logging. Contextual data is added as custom fields to the log messages within the scope so that these log messages can be grouped and analyzed.

Extending from the example provided for structured logging, Kotlin Logging provides a `withLoggingContext` function to facilitate MDC:

```kotlin
withLoggingContext("session" to sessionId) {
    log.atInfo {
        message = "Created a new household '$householdName'"
        payload = mapOf(
            "householdName" to householdName
        )
    }
}
```

The `withLoggingContext` function accepts multiple key-value pairs as the contextual data. In this example, `session` is added as the contextual data. The Lambda expression that follows defines the scope of the context, so all the function invocations in the Lambda expression will automatically have the contextual data added as custom fields to the structured log messages.

Optionally, the contextual data can be surfaced in the content of log messages by adding the contextual field in the log format:

```xml
<appender name="plainTextWithMdc" class="ch.qos.logback.core.
ConsoleAppender">
    <encoder>
        <pattern>%d{HH:mm:ss.SSS} [%thread] %-5level %logger{36}
MDC=%X{session} - %msg%n</pattern>
    </encoder>
</appender>
```

As a result, the JSON string log message is enhanced with contextual data:

```json
{
    "@timestamp": "2024-08-20T09:50:22.261878+01:00",
    "@version": "1",
    "message": "Created a new household 'Whittington'",
    "logger_name": "org.example.household.HouseholdRepository",
    "thread_name": "main",
    "level": "INFO",
    "level_value": 20000,
    "session": "57fa4035-0390-406c-9f2b-7dfcfc131d5a",
```

```
    "householdName": "Whittington"
}
```

The `session` field is automatically added to all messages that are logged inside the scope by the `withLoggingContext` function. This approach also separates the concern of logging contextual data from the main application logic. This contextual data doesn't need to be passed into any function that's invoked inside the scope.

There are wider scopes on how to centralize and aggregate data for monitoring and auditing purposes. We're going to cover these next.

Centralizing and aggregating data

Previously, we discussed the challenges of auditing and monitoring distributed systems, one of which is the data that's scattered across multiple places. It's common to have a business process perceived as a unit but executed in multiple services and devices in distributed systems.

In this scenario, the auditing and monitoring data only makes sense when we can aggregate it into a centralized place for consolidation and analysis.

Centralized audit trail aggregation

Let's revisit the real-life example of villagers exchanging services and imagine that we need to aggregate auditing and monitoring data from numerous services. There are three services: **Household service**, **Contract service**, and **Notification service**. The need to aggregate audit trails would warrant a new generic subdomain service that collects all events that happened in other services. The new service, **Audit service**, and its interactions with other services are depicted in *Figure 11.1*:

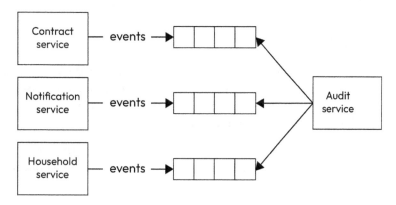

Figure 11.1 – An example of Audit service interactions

Audit service consumes all events generated by the four other services. It's responsible for understanding these events, transforming them into standard data structures, and persisting them into permanent storage for queries in the future.

This interaction pattern doesn't require other services to know the existence of **Audit service**, reducing coupling or dependencies. Other services may need to change code just to inform consumers of what's happened in their domain but without the burden of auditing requirements.

> **Alternative approach**
>
> The alternative approach would be to have other services imperatively inform **Audit service**, usually by calling a **REST endpoint**. This would make other services depend on **Audit service**. It's also more complex for synchronous REST communication to provide the same reliability guarantees compared to asynchronous events. Now, all other services are aware of auditing requirements, which is considered a leak in the bounded context of auditing. So, this isn't a recommended approach.

Audit data structure unification

The downside of this approach is that **Audit service** must know the schema of all auditable events of all services. There are a lot of dependencies to manage in **Audit service**.

There's a workaround for this problem. If the system can be aligned to adopt a standard envelope of all events, then the auditing fields are defined at the envelope level, while domain-specific fields are defined at the content level.

Having said that, it's still essential to capture the domain-specific fields as part of the audit trail. These fields can be stored in their native formats without transformation. This transformation will only be needed when retrieving the data.

Linking related audit trails using IDs

The ability to link related audit trails is paramount in reporting a complete business journey. This is typically implemented by generating a **correlation ID** for the entry point service or any other component that the distributed system needs to associate with related audit events. The events may not necessarily be part of the same request or transaction.

Correlation IDs are useful for troubleshooting and understanding the relationships between different components in a distributed system within a business journey, even if they're not directly part of the same request flow.

Discoverability of event topics

In a large distributed system, having to keep track of new event topics to be consumed by **Audit service** could be an exhausting effort. Ideally, **Audit service** should be able to discover and dynamically consume event topics. There are several ways to achieve this:

1. Use service discovery mechanisms, such as service registries or service meshes, to discover the available event topics or event streams.

2. Use a centralized event catalog, which can be in the form of a standalone service, or just a resource such as a last-value queue that can be accessed by **Audit service**.

3. Use messaging brokers. Some (for example, RabbitMQ and Kafka) provide APIs to discover event topics.

4. Use configuration management tools such as Spring Cloud Config or Kubernetes as they provide APIs that can be used to look up event topics.

Once event topics have been looked up dynamically, as well as the standard envelope, **Audit service** can automatically consume and persist events in a dedicated database for audit reporting.

Example of an audit trail event

Combining all the key aspects of audit trails that we discussed previously, we can come up with an example of the audit trail as a Kotlin data class. The most important element of an audit trail is the actor involved in the event:

```
data class Actor(
    val id: UUID,
    val type: String,
    val involvement: String,
)
```

The `Actor` class uses a UUID as the tokenized identifier. While it typically represents a human user, it can sometimes be a scheduled trigger or an external system that kicks off a business journey. The type of actors (for example, user, external system, or scheduler) is captured by the `type` field. The involvement of the actor is captured by the `involvement` field – for example, "executed by," "on behalf of," and so on.

They use the `String` type in contrast to enumeration for two reasons:

- Adding a new enum value isn't backward compatible
- Removing an existing enum value isn't forward compatible

Having it as a plain string ensures it can always be parsed to construct a full audit trail from the beginning of time, knowing that changes in values might be introduced in the future.

Another important element is the resources involved:

```
data class Resource (
    val id: UUID,
    val type: String,
    val applicationId: String,
    val version: Int? = null
)
```

Each resource is identified by a UUID, but it can just be a plain string. The resource also comes up as a type field, which can be the name of an aggregate, entity, or value object (for example, "household," "contract," and so on). It's also useful to capture to which application the resource belongs. This information is captured as application ID (for example, "household service"). If the resource is versioned, then that's also captured.

From these two data classes, the event envelope data class can be defined as follows:

```
data class EventEnvelope<E>(
    val id: UUID,
    val sessionId: UUID? = null,
    val correlationId: UUID? = null,
    val happenedAt: Instant,
    val action: String,
    val outcome: String,
    val actor: Actor,
    val otherActors: Set<Actor>? = null,
    val resource: Resource,
    val otherResources: Set<Resource>? = null,
    val content: E,
    val diffs: List<Difference>? = null,
)
```

It starts with an event ID as a UUID type and unique identifier. The session ID is captured to correlate activities that happened in the same login session. There's a correlation ID that links multiple business activities together. The timestamp of the event is captured as the happenedAt field. The action field captures what initiates the business journey, while the outcome field captures the result as the event occurs.

The envelope uses the Actor class in two ways: it initiates the business journey and sets other actors that are involved in this event. A null set is treated the same as an empty set. The Resource class follows the same pattern in that there's a main resource and other resources.

The content of the event makes use of the generic E type as there will be many forms of events under the envelope.

Finally, there's a generic list of differences between the main resources before and after the event. A Kotlin data class can be expressed as a JSON object, and there are open source libraries that can generate a list in JSON Patch format given two JSON objects. Then, the list of differences can be represented by a data class – that is, `Difference`:

```
data class Difference(
    val op: String,
    val path: String,
    val fromValue: Any? = null,
    val toValue: Any? = null
)
```

This class has four fields. The `op` field represents the data operation types such as "add," "replace," or "delete."

The `path` field is the path of the field as if it were a JSON object – for example, */party/0/householdName*. The values that are changed before and after the event are captured as `fromValue` and `toValue`, respectively.

This audit trail envelope is just one example, and each organization should have an envelope that suits its needs. Next, we'll turn our attention to monitoring data collection and aggregation.

Monitoring data collection and aggregation

Monitoring tools use a hugely different approach to collect their data. They use multiple methods to collect data from various sources, such as the following:

- **Agents or daemons**: Small software components called agents are installed on the systems being monitored. These agents collect data and send it to a central monitoring server.

- **System-level metrics**: These agents can collect various metrics, such as CPU usage, memory usage, disk I/O, network traffic, and more.

- **Application-level metrics**: Applications can log messages in the format so that they can be accounted for as a metric, or applications can submit the metric numbers directly to the monitoring tool. For example, a Kotlin/JVM application can use **Java Management Extensions (JMX)** to expose resource usage, application data, configuration, and performance metrics. JMX can be accessed as **Managed Beans (MBeans)** and can also be integrated with third-party monitoring tools for visualization and alert purposes.

- **Log file collection**: These agents can listen to the system standard output and system error output. These agents can also tail the log files and send them to the monitoring data source. The log messages can also be directly submitted to a data source, such as Elastic Store, for aggregation purposes.

- **Agentless**: By using standard network protocols, it's possible to collect monitoring data, particularly network monitoring data, without installing an agent. For example, **Window Management Instrumentation** (**WMI**) provides an operating system interface where notifications and device-related information from the nodes are enabled. Another example is an extra node in a multicast UDP network that captures network metrics to be sent to the monitoring tool.

- **API integration**: Some monitoring middleware software uses direct API integrations with services, applications, and cloud platforms. It can go both ways: either the node being monitored provides an API to expose monitoring data, such as Spring Actuator, or the monitoring tool provides an API for nodes to submit monitoring data.

- **Performance measurement**: The performance of certain processes can be measured, and the technique depends on the scope:

  - Full process measurement can be performed by aspect-oriented techniques where the times when the process starts and ends are captured by wrapping the function so that its full duration can be measured.

  - In Kotlin, partial process measurement can be performed by built-in functions. There's one function for millisecond precision (`measureTimeMillis`) and another for nanosecond precision (`measureNanoTime`):

    ```
    val elapsedInMillis = measureTimeMillis { someProcess() }

    val elapsedInNanos = measureNanoTime { someProcess() }
    ```

- **Trace IDs and span IDs**: A **trace ID** is a unique identifier that represents an end-to-end business process or request as it flows through a distributed system. It's used to group all the individual spans (see the following paragraph) that are part of the distributed transaction or request. Trace IDs allow us to understand the complete journey of a request as it moves across multiple services, components, and systems.

  A **span ID** is a unique identifier for a single operation or unit of work within a distributed transaction or request. Spans represent individual steps or operations that are performed as part of a larger trace, such as an HTTP request, a database query, or a function call. Spans are hierarchical and can be nested within a trace to represent the different components, services, or processes involved in handling a single request. The relationship between trace IDs and span IDs is shown in *Figure 11.2*:

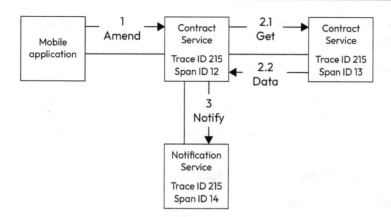

Figure 11.2 – Trace IDs and span IDs in a real-world example

Here, one request is coming from the mobile application through **Contract Service** to amend a contract, while **Trace ID 215** and **Span ID 12** are assigned to this request. **Contract Service** requests household information from **Household Service** while processing the request. This means that **Household Service** is involved in processing this request, as indicated by **Trace ID 215** but a different span value – that is, **Span ID 13**. **Contract Service** notifies **Notification Service** to send emails to the affected households, so **Notification Service** is also involved in this request, using the same trace – that is, **Trace ID 215** – but a new span – that is, **Span ID 14**.

With many third-party monitoring tools on the market (for example, **Elastic Slack (ELK)**, Splunk, Datadog, Kibana, Prometheus, Grafana, New Relic, Jaeger, and others) and various methods in collecting data, it's recommended to avoid the vendor lock-in issue. It may become too expensive to consider other monitoring tools if the system is integrated with the monitoring tools using proprietary methods.

OpenTelemetry (OTel)

OpenTelemetry (OTel) is a community-driven open source framework that aims to standardize the way we collect, process, and export observability data from applications. It provides a set of APIs, libraries, agents, and instrumentation tools that can support various programming languages and frameworks. This interoperability makes it possible to trace and monitor applications that use different technologies, and we can monitor the system holistically.

Moreover, it's cheaper to migrate from one monitoring tool to another given they all use OTel as a standard, and thus we aren't locked into using only one vendor.

Setting up OTel begins with using its libraries. This is shown in the following code, which uses the Gradle Kotlin DSL:

```
implementation("io.opentelemetry:opentelemetry-api:1.43.0")
implementation("io.opentelemetry:opentelemetry-sdk:1.43.0")
implementation("io.opentelemetry:opentelemetry-exporter-
otlp:1.43.0")
implementation("io.opentelemetry:opentelemetry-extension-
annotations:1.18.0")
```

The next step is to configure the `tracer` and `span` processors:

```
val tracer: Tracer = run {
    val oltpEndpont = "http://localhost:8123"
    val otlpExporter = OtlpGrpcSpanExporter.builder()
        .setEndpoint(oltpEndpont)
        .build()
    val spanProcessor = SimpleSpanProcessor.create(otlpExporter)
    val tracerProvider = SdkTracerProvider.builder()
        .addSpanProcessor(spanProcessor)
        .build()
    OpenTelemetrySdk.builder()
        .setTracerProvider(tracerProvider)
        .buildAndRegisterGlobal()
    GlobalOpenTelemetry.getTracer("example-tracer")
}
```

The preceding code defines an endpoint to export telemetric data to an **OpenTelemetric Protocol (OTLP)** server. A simple span processor is also defined. Finally, a `Tracer` object is created to be used in the traceable process. Let's look at how this object is used in starting and ending a span:

```
fun main() {
    val span: Span = tracer
        .spanBuilder("process data")
        .startSpan()
        .apply { setAttribute("data.source", "memory") }
    try {
        println("process finished")
    } catch (e: Exception) {
        span.recordException(e)
    } finally {
        span.end()
    }
}
```

This example `main()` function starts a span with a custom attribute added to provide contextual information. If the process succeeds, the span is acknowledged and ended. Otherwise, the span records the exception that has been captured.

It's important to note that the monitoring APIs are designed to not throw errors that would otherwise interfere with the actual process. In this example, the code will run even if the OTLP server can't be reached.

This data will be exported to a monitoring tool for further usage, something we're going to cover in the next section.

Metrics, visualization, and dashboards

Since monitoring data is centralized and aggregated, a monitoring tool can start using this data for many purposes. For example, heartbeat messages and regular health checks of applications provide an uptime ratio per application as a metric. This metric can be visualized in a dashboard that operators and engineers can observe.

We must create intuitive visualizations and dashboards that provide a clear, at-a-glance understanding of the distributed system's health, performance, and overall status.

The metrics that are measured and visualized on dashboards can be grouped into two categories.

- **Service-level metrics**: Known as **service-level indicators** (**SLIs**), these metrics measure the reliability, availability, latency, and performance of a system at the service level. It focuses on the **Quality of Service** (**QoS**) provided to users and external systems.

  Apart from the common metrics, such as CPU utilization, network latency, memory used, and disk space utilization, metrics that are part of the **service-level objective** (**SLO**) and **service-level agreement** (**SLA**) should be highlighted in the dashboard. These are sensitive metrics that could affect customer satisfaction, relationships with external entities, and the reputation of the organization.

  A typical service-level metric is the response time to a frequently used feature. Application response time is likely part of the SLO or SLA and should be measured and visualized continuously.

SLA versus SLO versus SLI

A SLA is a formal contract between a service provider and a customer that defines the expected level of service, including the specific performance metrics that are guaranteed and penalties for not meeting the agreement.

A SLO is a specific and measurable goal that defines the target level of the service. It sets the performance standards that the service provider aims to achieve.

A SLI is a metric that's used to measure the performance of a service, in particular against SLOs. It provides the data needed to determine whether the SLOs are being met.

- **Business-level metrics**: Business-level metrics focus on patterns and usage that should bring awareness to the business. For example, an e-commerce system would be interested in monitoring how many new users have signed up in the system.

Business-level metrics are often compared against the defined **key performance indicators (KPIs)**, which are used to demonstrate how effectively an organization achieves its **objectives and key results (OKRs)**.

The **objective** part of OKR is a qualitative and visionary goal that may not be measurable. However, the **key results** are measurable and usually set up regularly.

In this example of users signing up for the e-commerce system, the objective can be to "*sign up as many active purchasing users as possible.*" This objective can be translated into the following key results:

I.   Sign up 30% of new users in the **third quarter (Q3)**

II.   Ensure 80% of new users stay active in the last 30 days in Q3

III. Ensure 50% of new users purchase at least one item in the system in the last 30 days in Q3

These key results are missions within the boundary of time. They're measurable goals that aim to inspire bold goals.

On the other hand, KPIs continuously measure performance. To support the aforementioned OKRs, the following KPIs need to be measured:

I.   The number of users signed up in the last 3 months (that is, new users)

II.   The number of new users that logged in to the system in the last 30 days

III. The number of new users who bought at least one item in the last 30 days

The number can be collected and aggregated from either application log messages or from persistent databases directly.

An example of comprehensive metrics – DORA

Measuring metrics can be an anti-pattern if there's a way to game the numbers but not improve anything. For example, if the metrics are only about service uptime, then it's possible to have 100% uptime for services that can't perform any operation other than answering health checks.

It's important to have a comprehensive suite of metrics to close this loophole. If multiple metrics measure various aspects of the subject, gaming one metric would skew the others and therefore be impossible to hide. In this section, we're going to run through an example of comprehensive metrics and how they avoid cheating.

DevOps Research and Assessment (**DORA**) metrics are a set of KPIs to ensure the effectiveness and efficiency of software development and delivery processes. These metrics help organizations understand their DevOps performance and identify areas for improvement. The four primary DORA metrics are as follows:

- **Deployment frequency**: How often a production release has succeeded. A higher frequency indicates a higher velocity and responsive development process.

- **Lead time for changes**: The time taken between committing code to production. Shorter lead times represent a more efficient development pipeline.

- **Change failure rate**: The percentage of deployments that cause a failure in production. Lower rates indicate more stable and reliable releases.

- **Mean time to recovery** (**MTTR**): The average time taken to recover from a failure in production. Faster recovery times indicate better incident response and resilience.

Any attempt to game one of these metrics would be detected by another. For instance, if development skips running tests, the lead time for change will decrease, but the change failure rate will increase due to lack of testing.

The DORA team has also developed **SPACE** metrics, which provide a holistic perspective of engineering productivity in addition to software delivery efficiency. Let's see what SPACE stands for:

- **Satisfaction**: This is a quantitative and qualitative measurement of how satisfied engineers are with their work, work-life balance, and tools

- **Performance**: This specifies the quality, effectiveness, and impact of the software that's been delivered

- **Activity**: The volume of activities that have contributed to the completion of work – for example, the number of commits and pull requests

- **Communication and collaboration**: This involves evaluating the effectiveness of team meetings, cross-team cooperation, and collaborative tools

- **Efficiency**: This measures how time, effort, and tools are effectively utilized for desired outcomes, delivery, and waste reduction

SPACE metrics are designed to cover many angles of team productivity, as well as to avoid any metric from being manipulated by having other metrics detect it. For instance, having excessive meetings might have boosted the volume of activity, but the lack of effectiveness will be caught by evaluating communication and collaboration.

DORA and SPACE are complementary and can be measured at the same time to provide an all-rounded insight into the health of the team and its delivery of software products.

Good metrics should come as a comprehensive suite to provide a greater perspective of the organization's performance.

Automated alerting and incident management

Having a visual dashboard that shows metrics is nice, but when it comes to detecting system faults and raising alerts, an organization can't rely on human eyes. There should be automated alerts and a well-defined workflow of incident management so that the organization can recover the system as quickly as possible.

We must establish mechanisms for real-time alerting and incident management so that we can rapidly respond and resolve problems that arise in the distributed system.

Monitoring tools allow the organization to trigger alerts under various conditions:

1. Resource utilization is too high (for example, more than 90% CPU usage over 10 minutes)

2. The given metric has exceeded the threshold (for example, there were more than 20 HTTP responses with status code 400 in the last 5 minutes)

3. When security threats or anomalies are detected, such as unauthorized access attempts

4. A bespoke error log pattern is detected (for example, an error log message such as "Unable to authorize payment" has been detected)

The workflow for incident management varies in every organization. Some organizations have dedicated round-the-clock support teams that respond to incidents, while others have engineers to act as support persons on a rotational basis. Additionally, some organizations have three levels of escalation in case a major incident can't be solved immediately.

There are no golden incident management procedures, but there are principles of incident management that should be considered.

- **Establish and document the incident management workflow**: The workflow needs to be defined and documented so that the people involved in incident management have a process to follow.

- **Implement communication channels**: It's recommended to have a dedicated instant messaging channel for each incident so that you have relevant and focused collaboration among people. Emails and phone calls should be used for notification purposes because they don't have a well-structured conversation format. Other people joining later in the investigation process will find it difficult to follow.

   Moreover, the instant messaging channel has built-in timestamps and participant identifications, which are useful for compiling the communication section of an incident report.

- **Document the journey for each incident**: It's important to document each incident to capture the findings of the problem, the troubleshooting journey, the resolution of the problem, and the communication during the incident. This is useful for internal improvement, audit, and regulatory requirements. The incident report should also be standardized to allow for comparisons and further analysis.

- **Conduct follow-up meetings**: There are three other known names for this type of meeting: **after-action review (AAR)**, post-mortem, and autopsy meeting. The purpose of this meeting is to review and replay the incident, identify what was learned from this incident, and discuss preventative measures and any potential improvements (processes, communication, tooling, and so on).

The action items from this meeting are prioritized in the backlog of the responsible teams and are linked to the incident to motivate the change.

An example workflow for incident management is shown in *Figure 11.3*:

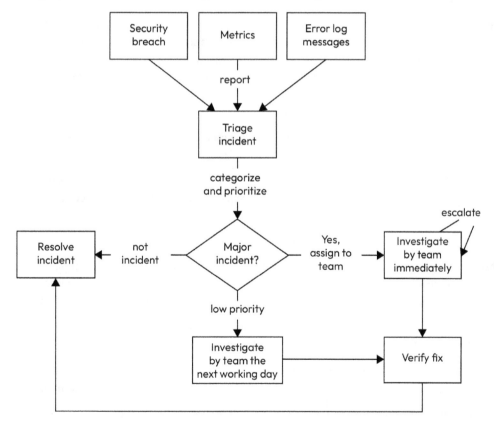

Figure 11.3 – An example workflow for incident management

In this diagram, multiple sources can report an incident that occurred. The support person is informed by the incident management tool via email, phone, instant message, or a phone application. The support person triages the incident by finding the answers to the following questions:

1. Is it an actual incident or just a false alarm?
2. Which business area is impacted?
3. Who's impacted by this incident?
4. How severely is the business area impacted?
5. Which team is responsible for the impacted business area?
6. Does it need to be fixed immediately?

If the incident turns out to be a false alarm, the incident is resolved. If it's an actual incident but doesn't require an immediate fix, then the incident will be picked up by the responsible team the next working day.

If the incident is major or substantial, then a second-level support person from the responsible team is involved to start the investigation immediately. During this stage, the investigation could escalate, depending on the progress of the investigation. Sometimes, another team needs to be involved, or a big decision needs to be made by upper management. Once the fix has been applied and verified, the incident is resolved.

If the system is mission-critical, it's worth considering an enterprise incident management system that supports escalation policies, rotational support management, communication channels, automatic reporting, and backlog ticket integration.

Improvements in incident management are often made after an incident has occurred. It's important for an organization to continuously learn and improve its incident management process.

Summary

In this chapter, we walked through the importance of auditing and monitoring. We emphasized the importance of measuring systems to avoid organizations going into the vicious cycle of opinion-based decision-making. A few exceptions of not needing auditing and monitoring were mentioned.

We also identified a few challenges when auditing and monitoring distributed systems. After highlighting the challenges we faced, we started to cover the key aspects of auditing and monitoring.

The data that's captured for auditing and monitoring is different. A sample of the audit trail was demonstrated by Kotlin code so that we could cover the various types of data available for monitoring.

Next, the best practices for application-level logging were demonstrated through the use of sample code and a few logging frameworks. The techniques of structured logging and contextual logging were covered.

Afterward, we moved on to the aspect of centralizing and aggregating auditing and monitoring data. The approach of the standard envelope and discoverable topics for audit trails were presented. We also mentioned multiple approaches for collecting monitoring data.

Then, we identified two levels of metrics: the service level and the business level. We covered how a qualitative goal can be translated into quantitative measurable metrics and used **DORA** metrics as an example of a comprehensive suite of metrics to prevent the gaming of metrics.

Finally, we discussed the aspects of automated alerting and incident management. We presented a sample workflow of incident management to illustrate the importance of appropriate tooling, effective communication, and documentation.

The next chapter will cover the performance and scalability aspects of software systems.

12

Performance and Scalability

Software systems grow with business and changing environments manifested in higher complexity, more diverse user demands, and heavier workloads. The ability to maintain high performance and scale under growth becomes critical. Performance refers to how quickly a system can process and respond to requests, while scalability describes a system's capacity to handle a higher volume of traffic and usage over time.

Poor performance can lead to frustrating user experiences, lost productivity, and even complete system failures. And systems that can't scale to meet rising demands will quickly become overwhelmed and unusable. Therefore, ensuring optimal performance and scalability is a key challenge for any software engineering project.

In this chapter, we'll explore the core concepts and principles of performance engineering and scalable system design. We'll discuss common performance bottlenecks and mitigation strategies, review techniques for load testing and benchmarking, and cover architectural patterns and design choices that enable horizontal and vertical scalability.

By the end of this chapter, you'll have a solid understanding of how to build highly performant, scalable systems that can withstand the pressure of real-world demands.

We're going to cover the following topics in this chapter:

- Dimensions of performance and scalability
- Optimize performance now or later?
- Performance test planning
- Executing a performance test
- Micro-benchmarking
- Strategies for performance improvement
- Ultra-low latency systems

Technical requirements

You can find all the code files used in this chapter on GitHub: `https://github.com/PacktPublishing/Software-Architecture-with-Kotlin/tree/main/chapter-12`

Dimensions of performance and scalability

Performance is the efficiency of a system in executing tasks and responding to requests. It's measured by various metrics:

- **Latency**: The time taken for the system to respond to a request.

- **Throughput**: The number of requests processed in a given time frame.

- **Resource utilization**: The percentage of resources (for example CPU, memory, network, files, and so on) used during operations.

- **Concurrent users**: The number of users effectively served by the system simultaneously without degradation in performance.

- **Page load time**: The total time taken for a screen to fully load, including all assets (images, videos, scripts, and so on)

- **Queue size**: The number of requests waiting to be processed by the server

- **Time to first byte** (**TTFB**): The time that elapsed from when the client initiated a request to the client receiving the first byte from the server.

- **Cache hit ratio**: The percentage of requests served from the cache versus those from the slower secondary data source. A higher ratio indicates more efficient caching.

- **Error rate**: The percentage of requests resulting in errors (for example, HTTP error statuses). High error rates indicate problems with the application or infrastructure.

Scalability is the capacity of a system to handle increased load without degrading performance. It indicates how well a system can grow and adapt to an increase in user traffic and data volume. Scalability can be categorized into two types:

- **Vertical scaling**: Adding more resources (for example, CPU or RAM) to a single node to increase its capacity. This is also known as **scale up**.

- **Horizontal scaling**: Adding more nodes to distribute the load and improve capacity in a distributed system. This is also known as **scale out**.

Scalability is also the capacity of a system to downsize when the load is reduced. Scaling down is usually concerned with the flexible use of resources and cost savings. It's still an important aspect of scalability, but the focus is usually on scaling up and scaling out.

Scalability can be measured by the following metrics:

- **Scalability ratio**: The ratio of the increase in performance to the increase in resources such as the number of servers

- **Time to scale**: The time taken between adding resources to extra resources becoming operational in the system

These metrics are useful in measuring how a change in the system may affect performance and scalability. Without them, it's difficult to decide whether performance should be optimized or not. We're going to discuss this decision in depth in the next section.

Optimize performance now or later?

Engineers and architects often face the question of whether performance should be optimized now or later. This happens from the early stages of system design to already established production systems.

We all know optimizing performance is crucial, but whether to prioritize it from day one isn't a simple binary question.

You may have heard of someone who said *"Premature optimization is the root of evil."* The statement itself is theatrical, but there are some merits in it.

You may also have heard a quote saying, *"Make it work, make it right, make it fast."* This was coined by software engineer *Kent Beck*.

So, what would be the consequences if a system is optimized prematurely, or if we reverse the order to "make it fast" too early?

Spending too much time on performance improvements before understanding user behaviors and requirements can lead to wasted effort. Moreover, it creates an unnecessarily complex architecture that hinders the team's productivity. The team may have to simplify the over-engineered system, which also requires effort. In that sense, the team is punished twice for improving performance too early.

Considerations for optimizing performance and scalability

There are several factors to consider regarding whether the system should be optimized for performance and scalability:

- **Core features completeness**: If the core features of a system are still being developed, then it's often more important to focus on delivering core features and functionality initially. This is the first step: *"Make it work."*

  In addition, we must ensure the system behaves as expected as per functional requirements. Correctness should always come before performance. This is the second step: *"Make it right."*

- **Performance metrics**: Before optimizing performance or improving scalability, it's paramount to have current performance metrics as a baseline. A performance baseline provides insights into the current system bottlenecks that help the team prioritize which area should be improved first.

  A performance benchmark enables empirical and objective comparison of whether a change has resulted in better or worse performance, or whether an attempt to improve performance has achieved its goals.

- **Non-functional requirements**: Non-functional requirements are a useful source of guidance on whether the system needs to be optimized now. Non-functional requirements for performance can be driven by regulatory constraints, external system integration conformance, or principles of user experiences.

- **Critical use cases, user experiences, and competitors**: If the application is expected to handle high traffic from the beginning (for example, product launch events, training, or marketing campaigns), then early optimization is essential. If the application's performance directly impacts user satisfaction, it's important to address performance concerns early to avoid negative feedback. The current performance metrics of competitors also indicate how much the application's performance should be optimized.

- **Scalability needs**: If rapid growth or scaling needs are anticipated for an application, implementing good performance practices from the beginning will save time and effort later.

Best practices for performance

Even if it may not be the right time to optimize performance, there are some best practices to at least not make performance worse:

- **Measure first**: Measure the current performance metrics, ideally all operations, but as a bottom line, measure the core features and most frequent operations.

- **Implement basic optimization**: Basic performance best practices such as efficient database queries in the early stage of development.

- **Plan for scalability**: Plan and have scalability in mind when designing system architecture to allow for easier optimization later without major refactoring. Sometimes, it's about not putting restrictions that would limit scalability.

While it isn't always necessary to optimize performance on day one, incorporating basic performance considerations into your development process can lead to better long-term results. Focus on delivering value first, then iterate on performance as the application evolves. Let's go through an example of performance measurement to understand this better.

An example of basic performance measurement

Here's a basic example of an operation to be measured:

```
fun sampleOperation() {
    Thread.sleep(1)
}
```

The goal of this example is to find out the following aspects:

- **Throughput**: How many operations can be performed in a second

- **Latency**: How long it takes to finish an operation on average

A small function, `measureTotalTimeElapsed`, must be defined to measure the total time elapsed for all iterations of the operation:

```
fun measureTotalTimeElapsed(
    iterations: Int,
    operation: (Int) -> Unit,
): Long =
    measureTimeMillis {
        repeat(iterations, operation)
    }
```

This function uses the `measureTimeMillis` Kotlin function from Standard Library to capture the time spent in repeating the operation.

Finally, this is the `main` function to launch the test:

```
fun main() {
    val iterations = 1_000
    val operationTime = measureTotalTimeElapsed(iterations) {
sampleOperation() }
    println("Total time elapsed: ${operationTime / 1000.0} second")
    println("Throughput: ${iterations / (operationTime / 1000.0)}
operations per second")
    println("Latency (average): ${operationTime / iterations} ms")
}
```

This function defines the operation to be executed 1,000 times. After invoking the `measureTotalTimeElapsed` function with the Lambda expression that runs the `sampleOperation` function, the total time elapsed in milliseconds is returned. Then, the throughput is calculated as the number of iterations divided by the total elapsed time in seconds. The average latency is calculated as the inverse reciprocal of throughput – the total time elapsed divided by the number of iterations.

This is a sample output from running the test:

```
Total time elapsed: 1.264 second
Throughput: 791.1392405063291 operations per second
Latency (average): 1 ms
```

Since the sample function, `sampleOperation`, only makes the thread sleep for 1 millisecond, the average latency is 1 millisecond, as expected. The throughput in this run is close to 800, but it varies in every run.

Kotlin Standard Library provides a few functions for time measurement:

- Return time elapsed in milliseconds (used in this example): `measureTimeMillis`

- Return time elapsed in nanoseconds: `measureNanoTime`

- Return time elapsed as `Duration`: `measureTime`
- Return time elapsed and the value returned from the Lambda expression: `measureTimedValue`

For real-life performance critical systems, this is certainly not enough. Due to this, in the next section, we'll cover the main types of performance tests.

Performance tests

Performance tests are a category of test that evaluates the speed, responsiveness, and stability of a system under a given workload. In this section, we'll look at the main types of performance tests.

Load testing

Load tests aim to assess the behaviors of a system under expected load conditions, such as a configured number of concurrent requests. The goal is to identify bottlenecks in application or infrastructure where performance may degrade under load. It ensures the system can handle anticipated traffic without performance degradation.

Stress testing

Stress tests aim to evaluate the system's performance under extreme load conditions beyond its normal operational capacity. They also help us determine the breaking point of the system and how it fails under stress, so proactive monitoring and alerts can be deployed for precautions.

Endurance testing (soak testing)

Endurance tests, known as soak tests, focus on the stability and performance of a system over an extended period. This extended period is used to identify issues that accumulate or emerge over time, such as memory leaks, resource exhaustion, or performance degradation.

Spike testing

Spike tests introduce a sudden increase in load (the "spike") so that we can observe how the system reacts in this situation. The result illustrates how the system can handle abrupt changes in traffic without failure.

Volume and latency testing

Volume tests evaluate the system's performance with a large volume of data. Latency tests measure the time delay between a request and the corresponding response. They usually measure metrics such as throughput and latency to ensure the application can meet **service-level agreements (SLAs)** or **service-level objectives (SLOs)**.

Scalability testing

Scalability tests aim to determine how well the system can scale up or down in response to increasing or decreasing loads. It measures the performance of the system as resources are added or removed.

Configuration testing

Configuration tests aim to identify the optimal configuration for performance. They involve running performance tests under different configurations, including hardware, software, and the network.

Planning a performance test

Although there are different types of performance tests, planning and executing performance tests are similar. The difference is in the details of each step. In this section, we'll explore the journey of planning and executing a performance test.

Planning

In the planning phase, first, the objectives of the test should be defined. This means we must define the information we want to get out of the tests – for example, can a household record be created within 50 milliseconds? Can the system handle 5,000 concurrent requests without degradation? These objectives are the primary drives to plan and execute a performance test. They also determine which type of performance tests can be used.

Then, business scenarios for performance tests should be defined. Usually, the objectives would have given a great hint at which scenarios would be used, but it's worth exploring the details of the steps involved in each scenario and formalizing them as a blueprint of the test script.

The last part of planning is to specify the load levels to run, including the number of users and the duration of the test. Sometimes, it isn't so clear which level to run, especially if we want to find the breaking point of the system. This is OK initially since performance tests are meant to run iteratively.

Preparation and development

Once there's an initial plan, the performance test can be prepared and developed. These activities can happen in parallel.

The test script is the core of the test execution. The test needs to be automated to achieve consistent results. This involves a big decision on which tool to use. Here's a list of commonly used tools:

- **Apache JMeter** (`https://jmeter.apache.org/`): Open source, free, GUI support, distributed testing, plugin support, and Java-based
- **LoadRunner by OpenText** (`https://www.opentext.com/`): Commercial licenses, GUI, integration with CI/CD tools, analytics and reporting support, and support for Java

- **Gatling** (`https://docs.gatling.io/`): Open source, commercial licenses with additional features, and scripts can be written in Kotlin

- **K6** (`https://k6.io/`): Open source, subscription-based for cloud features, and can integrate with CI/CD scripts written in **JavaScript (JS)**

- **Locust** (`https://locust.io/`): Open source, GUI support, distributed testing, and scripts written in Python

- **BlazeMeter** (`https://www.blazemeter.com/`): Free with limited features, commercial licenses, cloud-based, GUI support, real-time reporting and analytics, integrated with CI/CD, and supports JMeter scripts

These tools provide comprehensive features such as organizing test scripts, managing multiple test configurations, metrics measurement, analytics, and reporting. You also have the option to build your own drivers of performance tests. This is applicable if your tests are simple and there are sufficient metric measurements without external tools.

Appropriate metric measurement needs to be set up according to what the test script requires. The metrics can be measured by the testing tools, or by the monitoring tools already embedded in the system, as discussed previously in *Chapter 11*. Any missing metrics need to be set up before executing the tests.

Meanwhile, a test environment needs to be set up for execution. Ideally, the environment should be comparable to the actual production environment where the system runs. If that's too expensive, an environment of a smaller scale can be used to project expected performance, with a degree of inaccuracy in mind.

The test environment should be an isolated sandbox that does nothing but the performance tests. It can be a challenge for some organizations to replicate a production-like environment for performance testing. Replicating an environment with data alone may already be a challenge for some organizations. In addition, the environment needs to have the necessary data to run the test scenarios.

Sometimes, the system has integration with third-party systems. In this case, the external integration would need to be stubbed out with simulators.

Execution and iteration

Once we have the test scripts, test environments, and corresponding metrics set up, we're ready to execute the performance test. It's vital to allow an iterative feedback loop where tests can run multiple times, and there could be changes between each test. Within each iteration, the same operation should be executed numerous times so that we have enough data points to perform analysis.

The tests should be run twice at a minimum, where the initial run identifies a bottleneck, then a change is made with the intent to eliminate the bottleneck, and finally, another run proves the bottleneck no longer exists, as indicated by metrics.

Realistically, another bottleneck will emerge after the biggest one is eliminated. The performance landscape will change for every change that's made to improve performance. The iteration can end when the objectives are completed, or a new problem may be discovered during the process.

The iterative execution of a performance test can be seen in *Figure 12.1*:

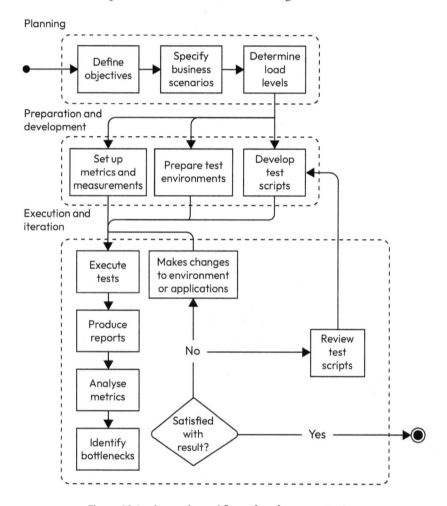

Figure 12.1 – A sample workflow of performance testing

In each run, the test is executed by running the test script. The test script usually starts with warm-up operations. For example, if we're going to send 10,000 requests 100 times, the first 10 times can be treated as a warm-up, so the metrics aren't considered.

Warming up allows the system to reach a stable state before actual performance measurements are taken. Processing initial requests triggers the cache so that it populates with frequently accessed data.

It also allows the system to allocate resources such as thread, memory, and database connections effectively. Other transient factors such as just-in-time compilation, garbage collection, and resource contention can be reduced by warming up the system.

After running the test, a report should be generated from the metric data that's been collected. The report should be constructed in a format that allows iterations to be compared. The raw data is then analyzed to produce statistical figures such as the following:

- The mean and median percentiles of the response time
- Average and peak throughputs; increase in throughput divided by the increase in resource which indicates scaling efficiency
- The overall error rate and error rates by types
- Average and maximum latency
- The number of concurrent users being handled without degradation
- The time for which the load was maintained

From these numbers, some bottlenecks may be identified. Some figures can be below the non-functional requirements, SLAs, or SLOs. Some figures can stand out as particularly slow compared to others. These bottlenecks drive the changes required to improve overall performance.

Especially in early iterations, deficiencies in the test scripts may be identified. It isn't uncommon to realize the test script itself isn't efficient and causes slowness in the system. The test script may have unnecessary loops or complex logic that slows down the script's execution time. The test script may have an artificial wait time between requests, which as a result limits the throughput. Other factors, such as error handling, synchronous operations, resource contention, and network performance, can also skew the result of performance tests. These findings lead to the test script being reviewed and updated for future runs.

After changes are made, the performance tests should be executed again to examine whether the target performance statistical figures have improved, and at the same, to ensure the changes don't deteriorate system performance in other areas.

This repetitive exercise carries on until we're satisfied with the results. There are several possibilities where the iteration should stop:

- The test objectives have been completed – for example, we've detected the maximum number of requests the system can handle without performance degradation
- The performance metrics have fulfilled the non-functional requirements, SLAs, or SLOs
- The time spent on performance testing has exceeded the original time-boxed duration

Performance testing is meant to be a recurring exercise. A successful and satisfactory performance test only supports the assumption that the system is capable of handling requests within the configuration and parameters in the test scripts. The system usage pattern is constantly changing due to business growth and new features being introduced over time.

Benefits of performance testing

Performance testing provides insights into how the system performs under pre-configured loads. It indicates how we can optimize the system to provide a fast and reliable user experience, even under heavy load. It helps stakeholders understand system limits and make informed decisions about scaling and infrastructure. It also identifies potential issues before they impact users, reducing the risk of downtime or service degradation.

Performance tests are essential for ensuring that applications meet user expectations and maintain stability under varying conditions. By conducting different types of performance tests, organizations can identify and address potential issues, optimize performance, and enhance overall user satisfaction.

Next, we'll consider a technique that's used iteratively to measure a function's performance. This technique is called micro-benchmarking.

Micro-benchmarking

While performance testing focuses on system-level performance, micro-benchmarking is a performance measurement of a small and isolated piece of code at the function level. Micro-benchmarking is usually applicable to the following areas:

- The algorithm that sits in the core of the whole system – for example, a search algorithm for an internet search engine

- The function that's used most frequently by end users

- The function that's exposed as an API to external systems

- The code path that's mission-critical and performance-sensitive

- When comparing the implementations of a function, an algorithm, or a code change

Kotlin benchmarking (`https://github.com/Kotlin/kotlinx-benchmark`) is the most popular tool for running benchmarks for Kotlin code. It wraps the classic **Java Microbenchmark Harness (JMH)** framework, and it supports Kotlin through **Java Virtual Machine (JVM)**, JS, Native, and even **Web Assembly (WASM)**.

Setting up micro-benchmarking with a Gradle Kotlin DSL script

It's simple to set up benchmarking with a Gradle Kotlin DSL script. For example, for JVM, we need the following plugins:

```
plugins {
    id("org.jetbrains.kotlinx.benchmark") version "0.4.11"
    kotlin("plugin.allopen") version "2.0.20"
}
```

The first plugin is for Kotlin micro-benchmarking, while the second plugin is used to open the final Kotlin classes for instrumentation. Now, we need to make sure the plugins and dependencies can be looked up from repositories:

```
repositories {
    mavenCentral()
    gradlePluginPortal()
}
```

Next, a code dependency on Kotlin micro-benchmarking needs to be declared:

```
implementation("org.jetbrains.kotlinx:kotlinx-benchmark-runtime:0.4.11")
```

Then, we need to configure the allOpen plugin so that it only opens Kotlin classes with the State annotation:

```
allOpen {
    annotation("org.openjdk.jmh.annotations.State")
}
```

The final part of the setup is setting up micro-benchmarking itself:

```
benchmark {
    targets {
        register("main")
    }
    configurations {
        named("main") {
        }
    }
}
```

The configuration is called main and has been chosen to run. It's possible to configure the number of warmup iterations, the number of iterations to be measured, and the length of how long each iteration should last. However, an annotation-based configuration has been used in this example.

The micro-benchmarking test

The actual benchmark runner code is annotated so that it can be picked by the runner for execution with a specific configuration. Please note that this test should be placed in the `main` source folder (not the `test` source folder) so that it can be picked up by the plugin:

```
@State(Scope.Benchmark)
@Fork(1)
@Warmup(iterations = 10)
@Measurement(iterations = 20, time = 1, timeUnit = TimeUnit.
MILLISECONDS)
class MicrobenchmarkingTest {
    private var data = emptyList<UUID>()
    @Setup
    fun setUp() {
        data = (1..2).map { UUID.randomUUID() }
    }
    @Benchmark
    fun combineUUIDBenchmark(): UUID = data.reduce { one, two -> one +
two }
    private operator fun UUID.plus(another: UUID): UUID {
        val mostSignificant = mostSignificantBits xor another.
mostSignificantBits
        val leastSignficant = leastSignificantBits xor another.
leastSignificantBits
        return UUID(mostSignificant, leastSignficant)
    }
}
```

This micro-benchmarking test evaluates the performance of the function that combines two **Universally Unique Identifiers (UUIDs)**. The `State` annotation triggers the `allOpen` plugin to open this class for instrumentation. Then, the `Fork` annotation defines how many threads are used for execution. Other annotations specify the number of iterations for warmup, execution, and the duration of each iteration.

For example, the `setup` annotation function is used to create the data required to run the test, while the `combineUUIDBenchmark` function, which has the `Benchmark` annotation, is the major function to be measured.

Micro-benchmarking runner

To run micro-benchmarking, we can use the following Gradle command:

```
./gradlew benchmark
```

The summary of the result is printed to the console, while the detailed report is generated under the `/build/reports/benchmarks/main` folder:

```
Success: 109349297.194 ±(99.9%) 15493649.408 ops/s [Average]
  (min, avg, max) = (55205844.260, 109349297.194, 132224154.121),
stdev = 17842509.699
  CI (99.9%): [93855647.787, 124842946.602] (assumes normal
distribution)
```

The format of micro-benchmarking is designed to compare runs. Improvements can be made between runs, and the next run should demonstrate whether the changes have made a difference.

Micro-benchmarking is a valuable subset of performance testing that focuses on code implementation. By understanding the performance characteristics of isolated functions, engineers can make targeted optimizations. In contrast, performance testing takes a holistic approach to assess how well the entire system performs under various conditions. Both practices are essential for delivering high-performance systems.

There's another tool that measures and analyzes the performance of an application, but visually with graphical user interfaces. This tool is called the application profiler, and we're going to cover it in the next section.

Application profiling

Profiling works by monitoring and analyzing the performance of an application at runtime. Profilers instrument code and intercept calls to collect performance measurements, such as elapsed time and the number of invocations. It can generate the stack trace of the application to visualize relationships between functions.

The profiler tool also monitors memory allocation and deallocation, analyzes the heap dump, and identifies potential memory leaks.

At the same time, the profiler tool measures CPU cycles that have been consumed by various parts of the code and identifies computing-intensive functions. The profiler tool also monitors the usage of other resources, such as file operations, network activities, and interactions, among threads to provide a comprehensive view of resource utilization.

The profiler tool comes with detailed reports that are visualized in the user interface to assist engineers in pinpointing the areas that require optimization.

However, running an application with the profiler significantly slows down performance due to invasive instrumentation and measurement. The metric data that's captured should be treated as a magnification of the actual runtime and be used to find areas that are slow, inefficient, or resource-consuming.

There are several popular profiler tools available for Kotlin engineers:

- **YourKit Java Profiler** (https://www.yourkit.com/java/profiler/)
- **VisualVM** (https://visualvm.github.io/startupprofiler.html)

- **IntelliJ IDEA Profiler** (`https://www.jetbrains.com/pages/intellij-idea-profiler/`)

- **JProfiler** (`https://www.ej-technologies.com/jprofiler`)

- **Async Profiler** (`https://github.com/async-profiler/async-profiler`)

- **Java Mission Control** (`https://www.oracle.com/java/technologies/jdk-mission-control.html`)

Application profilers should be used to analyze performance-critical operations. They don't usually run in production environments due to instrumentation being slowed down significantly. It's common to run profilers in a lower environment with inputs simulating the production environment.

Next, we're going to cover a few performance improvement strategies.

Strategies for performance improvement

Improving the performance of a system often requires a diverse approach that addresses various aspects. No silver bullet magically boosts performance. However, some common strategies help engineers navigate the problem to meet the non-functional requirements.

Testing, testing, testing

Performance tests should be conducted continuously and repetitively. When there's a perceived performance issue, it's unlikely to know the root cause without running performance tests. Instead of blindly applying "performance fixes," engineers should execute performance tests to understand the problem first.

Performance tests should be treated as both troubleshooting and discovery tools. There are always bottlenecks in the system that surprise engineers.

Avoiding expensive operations

More often than not, performance issues are caused by a mismatch between the nature of the operations and the actual implementation. In other words, resources are used in unnecessary areas that would use excessive resources and computation power. If excessive resources are spent on expensive operations, then there will be performance issues.

Let's consider an example scenario that demonstrates performance optimization by avoiding expensive operations.

Scenario – iteration on expensive operations

Imagine that there's a function that's expensive to execute. This expense is high for several reasons:

- It's a remote synchronous call to another application

- It's computationally expensive and/or resource-hungry

- It involves files, databases, messaging, networks, or other resources

- It may be blocked until a result comes back

We know the following function isn't expensive, but let's pretend it is for the sake of discussion:

```
fun someExpensiveOp(n: Int): Int = n
```

On top of this function, we'd like to run some filtering, mapping, and selection:

```
val result = listOf(1, 7, 3, 23, 63).filter {
    println("filter:$it"); it > 3
}.map {
    println("expensive:$it"); someExpensiveOp(it)
}.take(2)
println(result)
```

First, this piece of code filters to take only numbers greater than 3. Then, it invokes the `expensive` function and gets a new number. At the end, only the first two numbers are selected. The `println` function is called to show which value is evaluated in the `filter`, map, or `take` function.

Executing this piece of code produces the following console output:

```
filter:1
filter:7
filter:3
filter:23
filter:63
expensive:7
expensive:23
expensive:63
[7, 23]
```

All five numbers are evaluated if they're greater than 3. The numbers 7, 23, and 63 are greater than 3, so they're passed to the `expensive` operation. Finally, only the first two numbers from the expensive operation are returned.

The expensive operation for the third number isn't necessary because only the first two numbers are selected at the end. In addition, it could have found the first two numbers during filtering and stopped checking the rest of the values.

Optimized with the `asSequence` function from Kotlin Standard Library, the code looks as follows:

```
val result = listOf(1, 7, 3, 23, 63)
    .asSequence().filter {
        println("filter:$it"); it > 3
    }.map {
```

```
            println("expensive:$it"); someExpensiveOp(it)
        }.take(2)
    println(result)
```

However, executing the preceding code prints the following to the console:

```
kotlin.sequences.TakeSequence@246b179d
```

No filtering, no expensive operation, or selection was run. This is because the `asSequence` function doesn't build the list until there's a terminal function. Let's update the code:

```
    println(result.toList())
```

Now, the execution prints the following to the console:

```
filter:1
filter:7
expensive:7
filter:3
filter:23
expensive:23
[7, 23]
```

The sequence operation understands it only takes the first two numbers, so it looks for the first two numbers greater than 3 and stops there. The number 63 wasn't even processed. The first number greater than 3 was 7, so 7 was passed to the `expensive` operation. The second number greater than 3 was 23, so 23 was also passed to the `expensive` operation. This implementation has saved one `expensive` operation compared to the previous one.

An example of a performance improvement journey

The households in the village have decided to run a survey to rate each household's services. A vote consists of a rating from 1 to 3:

- **1**: Good

- **2**: Average

- **3**: Poor

A household can vote for all other households, but only one vote can be made per household. Households are given 1 day to submit all the votes. Let's also assume one household provides only one service.

Each household has a "score," which is the sum of the rank numbers of all votes to that household. The household that has the highest score becomes the household that provides the best service in the village.

So, if there are *n* households in the village, the maximum number of votes will be n x (n- 1). We need a system that calculates the score of all households being voted for, and that records all votes as audit records. The system also needs to display non-final scores for each household when voting is in progress.

A simplistic architecture of this voting system may look as follows:

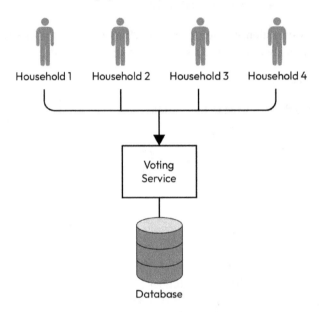

Figure 12.2 – Simulated survey architecture v0.1

All households submit their votes to be validated by **Voting Service**. The service validates the following aspects:

- All households involved are valid

- A household can't vote for itself

- A household can only vote for another household once

- The vote has a valid rank

Since the voting happens in one day for the village, there's a need for the system to respond quickly (**latency**) so that it can process many votes within a certain period (**throughput**) and support a vast number of households (**scalability**).

The system expects many concurrent requests to **Voting Service** at a time, and that could cause a spike.

It's possible to scale up the service vertically by adding more resources (CPU, memory, and so on). However, there are physical limitations regarding the number of CPU sockets or the maximum RAM it can support. Adding more resources also leads to diminishing returns, in which performance doesn't improve proportionally due to other bottlenecks. The only running instance is also the single point of failure that if this instance fails, the entire system becomes unavailable.

Alternatively, the system can scale out horizontally if we add more instances of the service. A **load balancer** can be deployed to distribute load across multiple instances of the service, preventing any single instance from becoming a bottleneck. This significantly increases throughput by enabling parallel processing.

The load balancer has some knowledge of the load of each instance, so it can route the next request to the instance with the least load. This allows us to add more instances to handle increased loads. With that, the architecture has changed, as shown in *Figure 12.3*:

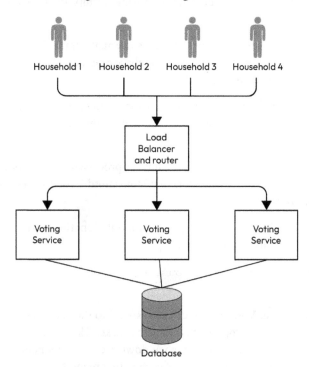

Figure 12.3 – Simulated survey architecture v0.2

Now, **Voting Service** has two stateful validation rules. The first is that the households involved must be valid. The second is that each household can only vote for other households once.

The household records are frequently accessed, and they can be queried in the database remotely. **Caching** all household records in each service instance is a sensible strategy to speed up validation.

Enforcing the rule that one household can only vote for another household would benefit from caching. If we cache a list of households that a given household has voted for (the *x-voted-by-y-list*), then we can enforce this business rule. However, there's a complication if any instance can handle any household because it implies sharing the list.

There are two options we can consider. The first option is that we can use a distributed in-memory database such as Redis so the *x-voted-by-y-lists* can be shared, at the cost of having a distributed in-memory database and potential resource contention.

The second option is to configure the load balancer so that it supports sticky routing. Requests from one household always go to the one responsible instance. Each instance knows its assignment and can locally cache the *x-voted-by-y-lists* from the database during startup. The local cache is also updated as it processes incoming requests.

At this point, the bottleneck has shifted to the database since all the traffic is eventually funneled into it and each request can only be responded to after database operations have finished. This impacts the latency of the response to each voting request.

The score needs to be calculated for each household being voted in. This is an accumulated number that leaves little room for parallel processing. Each validated vote also needs to be kept as an audit record in the database.

However, votes validated by **Voting Service** can be further processed asynchronously. Each vote can be partitioned by the household being voted for, so if **Household 1** votes for **Household 2**, the vote goes to the "bucket" for **Household 2**.

Resolve a household to a bucket can be as simple as a modulo function, that is, the remainder of a hash number divided by the number of buckets:

```
Bucket number = (hash number of household name) mod (number of
buckets)
```

Each bucket is an event stream. **Voting Service** can respond to the voting request after an event is published to the corresponding event topic representing the bucket. The vote counting, score calculation, and vote persistence metrics will be processed when downstream components consume the event. This change will significantly reduce the latency of each voting request.

The updated architecture looks like this:

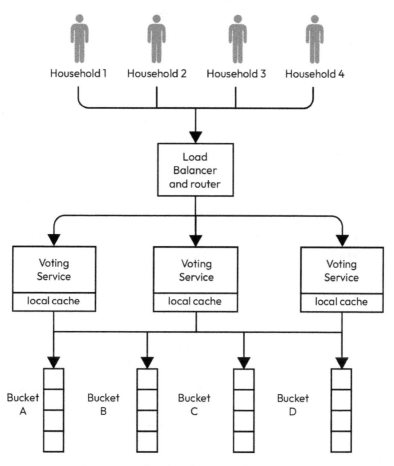

Figure 12.4 – Simulated survey architecture v0.3

This approach has a limitation: the number of buckets that are fixed at runtime. Events are already routed to the bucket, and we need to maintain the bucket assignment to calculate the score correctly.

The downstream operations require persisting the result in the database eventually, and we want to avoid overloading the database. Let's examine the data to be persisted:

- **Score for each household**: One accumulative number per household; historical numbers don't matter

- **Vote audit record**: Each record needs to be kept, and each record is independent of each other

The score numbers and vote audit records are different in their natures, so it makes sense for them to be processed differently. It's better to keep this temporary data in a transient local cache to reduce database load but persist the values periodically.

Here, we can introduce two components:

- The first one, **Vote Counter**, consumes the event stream for its one assigned bucket and calculates scores for its responsible households. It doesn't update the score records in the database immediately. Instead, it flushes the latest scores to the database with a fixed schedule – for example, every 10 minutes. This mechanism "soaks" the spike of votes and turns it into regular updates.

  There are multiple instances of **Vote Counter**, and there should be at least two instances consuming one bucket to provide availability. Each score record should consist of a household name, the number of votes, the score, and a timestamp. There should be de-duplication rules that only persist newer records and skip the old ones.

- The second component, **Vote Journalist**, consumes a batch of events at a time and flushes the update into the database in one transaction. If the transaction fails, the events in the batch aren't acknowledged and will be processed again later. **Vote Journalist** instances of the same bucket should be configured so that only one instance receives the batch of events. The batching processing significantly increases the throughput of vote audit record persistence. However, it would require performance testing to discover the optimal batch size that can scale with the number of votes and still be processed within the memory limits of the process.

With all these performance concerns considered, we have the final 1.0 architecture, as shown in *Figure 12.5*:

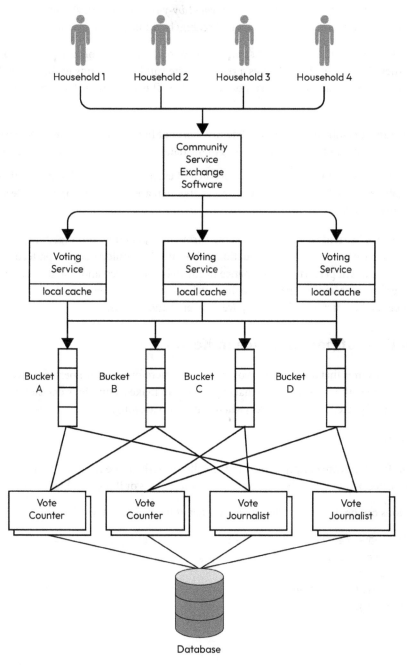

Figure 12.5 – Simulated survey architecture v1.0

In this architecture, we've optimized the process of load balancing the incoming requests to multiple instances of **Voting Service** for validation. This increases the throughput and scalability. Then, we introduced local caching of households and the *x-voted-by-y-lists* in each service instance to speed up the validation process. It also supports horizontal scaling by adding more instances.

After, we created a few buckets of event streams for each one responsible for several households exclusively. After **Voting Service** validates a request to be valid, it responds to the original request and publishes an event stream to the corresponding bucket. This reduces the latency for the response to the voting request:

- **Vote Counter** is introduced to calculate the scores of households that have been assigned to the given bucket. It sends the latest scores to the database periodically and soaks up the spike.

- **Vote Journalist** is introduced to receive a batch of events at a time and to persist them to the database in one transaction. Batch processing increases the throughput of vote audit record persistence.

In this example, we learned how to optimize the throughput, latency, and scalability of a system. Performance improvements are highly situational. We simply shouldn't copy a pattern to another system and believe it will perform. Performance needs to be measured and tested. A change is only considered a performance improvement when the metrics prove it. However, some known best practices of performance can be improved, something we'll cover in the next section.

Best practices of performance in Kotlin

Kotlin has a few features that aim to reduce overhead and therefore improve performance. However, these features come with justifications so that engineers can make a conscious decision when to use them. They aren't expected to be used everywhere without reasoning.

In-line functions

In-line Kotlin functions are simply copied to the caller to reduce the need to invoke the function itself. This is particularly useful if there's a deep stack of functions or if there's a higher-order function.

In-line functions can be declared by adding a modifier at the function level, like so:

```kotlin
inline fun <T> measureTime(block: () -> T): T {
    val start = System.nanoTime()
    val result = block()
    val timeTaken = System.nanoTime() - start
    return result.also { println("taken: $timeTaken") }
}
```

The use of immutable and mutable data structures

Immutable data eliminates the need for locking in multi-thread environments. In Kotlin, List, Set, and Map collections work with immutable data.

However, if we're building a bigger object, such as a string, it's advisable to use mutable collections or the StringBuilder class to avoid unnecessary object creation that could trigger garbage collection in Kotlin/JVM.

The use of coroutines for asynchronous operations

Kotlin's coroutine library enables the program to invoke asynchronous operations so that the thread isn't blocked and can perform other operations while waiting for the asynchronous result to come back. It enables better resource management and quicker response in applications.

For example, imagine that there are two time-consuming functions:

```
suspend fun task1(): Int {
    delay(1000)
    println("Task 1 completed")
    return 42
}
suspend fun task2(): Int {
    delay(1500) // Simulate a 1.5-second delay
    println("Task 2 completed")
    return 58
}
```

These two functions have the suspend modifier to indicate they can be paused and resumed without blocking the thread. The main function that uses these two suspend functions is shown here:

```
fun main() =
    runBlocking {
        val result1 = async { task1() }
        val result2 = async { task2() }
        val combinedResult = result1.await() + result2.await()
        println("Combined Result: $combinedResult")
    }
```

The runBlocking function starts a coroutine that blocks the current thread until its execution is complete. Within this block, there are two async functions to invoke the two time-consuming suspend functions. The async function returns a Deferred object on which we invoke the await function to block until the result returns. The two numbers that are returned by the respective time-consuming functions are added and the sum is printed to the console.

Note that Kotlin code written with the best practices of performance in mind would still need to be measured. Empirical results are the only proof.

Next, we're going to briefly mention ultra-low latency systems and how they push performance and scalability to the extreme.

Ultra-low latency systems

Ultra-low latency systems operate in the microsecond or nanosecond magnitude. They run in an environment where low response time is critical and even essential. They can be seen in financial trading, telecommunications, gaming, and industrial automation.

These systems aim to achieve the lowest possible latency, highest efficiency, high predictability, and high concurrency regarding processing. They involve all aspects of a system to reduce response time, such as network optimization, hardware acceleration, load balancing, and efficient algorithms.

These systems are usually written in system-level programming languages such as C++ and Rust. However, there are a few ultra-low latency systems written in Kotlin or Java that operate in the microsecond magnitude.

The low latency systems in Kotlin or Java employ several technical designs that aren't as common:

- Reuse objects, avoid object creation, and avoid garbage collection.

- Use specific JVM vendors for better performance.

- Avoid the use of third-party libraries to reduce overhead and ensure you have full control over performance.

- Use the **Disruptor pattern** as it provides a large ring buffer for inter-thread lock-free communication and memory barriers for data visibility in a thread.

- Use a single-thread model for each JVM process to reduce context switching, lock contention, and the need for synchronous and concurrency processing.

- Write code or design systems that are aware of and optimized for the underlying hardware and network infrastructure they run on. This is also called **mechanical sympathy**.

Ultra-low latency systems have the justification that they can break a few design principles (for example, immutable objects) in exchange for higher performance. They are exceptional cases due to the demanding need for low latency, high throughput, and quick response time. When developing these systems, performance tests are critical and should be part of the normal development activities.

Developing ultra-low latency systems is a specialized topic whose content is beyond the scope of this chapter. However, there are a few pieces of reading material that you may find useful:

- *Mechanical empathy*, by Martin Thompson (`https://mechanical-sympathy.blogspot.com/`)

- *LMAX Disruptor* (`https://lmax-exchange.github.io/disruptor/`)

- *Simple Binary Encoding* (`https://github.com/real-logic/simple-binary-encoding`)

- *Aeron messaging* (`https://github.com/real-logic/aeron`)

Summary

In this chapter, we covered different dimensions of performance and scalability and mentioned a few essential metrics that measure how well a system performs and scales. We emphasized the importance of performance tests, several types of performance tests, and how to plan one. We also provided an example of micro-benchmarking in Kotlin before discussing the use of a profiler to achieve better performance.

Then, we delved into some strategies for performance improvement. We considered a scenario where only necessary expensive operations were executed. We also looked at an example of a journey of performance improvement for a system in a real-life situation. This allowed us to consider a few best practices regarding performance in Kotlin through code examples.

Finally, we briefly introduced ultra-low latency systems and where they can be used.

In the next chapter, we're going to discuss the topic of software testing.

13
Testing

Software testing serves as a critical part of the software development life cycle, acting as a safeguard against defects and enhancing the overall quality of software products. Certification from **Quality Assurance (QA)** is often used as the indicator of whether the software product is ready to go live.

This chapter delves into the fundamental principles of software testing, exploring its significance, methodologies, and best practices.

We will discuss the role of QA and software testers in the industry. We will summarize the understanding of the role and how it might mean something different to different people.

We will explore several types of software testing and the testing pyramid. Additionally, we will discuss automated testing practices, which have gained popularity for their ability to enhance efficiency and ensure consistent test coverage.

We will also run an exercise of strict **Test-Driven Development (TDD)** using Kotest to gain insights into this methodology.

This chapter aims to provide a comprehensive overview of software testing, equipping you with the knowledge and tools necessary to implement effective testing strategies. This chapter will empower you to contribute to the creation of high-quality software that meets user expectations and stands the test of time. We are going to cover the following topics in the chapter:

- The role of QA and its involvement in software development
- The testing pyramid
- TDD with an exercise
- BDD
- Live testing, A/B testing, and segmentation

Technical requirements

You can find all the code files used in this chapter on GitHub:

https://github.com/PacktPublishing/Software-Architecture-with-Kotlin/tree/main/chapter-13

The role of QA and software testers

The primary goals of software testing are as follows:

- To identify and rectify defects before a product reaches the end user
- To ensure the software product behaviors meet the functional specifications or business expectations

It is essential even for a startup company or the first product launch by a new company.

The role of QA or software tester can be confusing and is often misunderstood. Like software architect as a role, QA is not necessarily a job title, though you might have seen these titles in the job market:

- QA
- QA tester
- QA engineer
- Quality engineer
- Software tester
- Test engineer
- Automation tester
- **Software Development Engineer in Test (SDET)**

Different organizations may have different interpretations or expectations for each title. In this chapter, we use the term QA to represent an engineer who is responsible for software quality.

The role of a QA is illustrated in *Figure 13.1*:

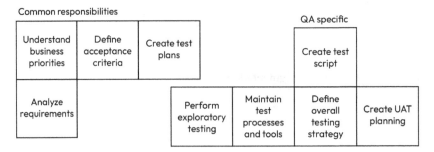

Figure 13.1 – The role of QA

It is important to emphasize that QA should be a full-time engagement embedded in the team organized by business functions, as described in *Chapter 1*. QAs, just like other engineers, are involved in understanding business priorities, requirement analysis, test plan creation, and acceptance criteria definitions.

However, from this point onward, QAs have a different focus than the engineers who develop the software for the business. QAs focus on overall testing strategies, test script creation, test processes and tools, **User Acceptance Test (UAT)** planning, and exploratory testing.

The objectives of QAs are like those of the engineers who develop the software. They both want the software to have complete features that are good enough to meet business expectations. QAs do have a different focus and approaches to achieving the objectives though – by ensuring the software is developed to a high standard as required.

To code or not to code?

The question of whether a QA should code often lacks clarity. QAs should leverage all available tools and resources to meet software quality standards. Coding can be essential for creating specific test scripts or enhancing tools. Ultimately, the debate about whether QAs should code is somewhat misguided; for many situations, writing code is a necessary part of their role.

Job titles for QA in the industry tend to include the term *engineers* (e.g., QA engineers) when the organization expects the QA person to write code.

Software quality is everyone's responsibility

It seems obvious to say that software quality is everyone's responsibility, but it may not be so clear to some organizations. Software quality is best assured when it is embedded in the software development process from the beginning to the end.

That includes all the activities during the software development process, starting from clear business priorities to well-written code, and eventually business user signoff and software launch. This involves every member of the team, not just QAs.

QA is the role that ensures software quality is taken care of every step of the way, so the outcome is a high-quality and well-tested software product.

With increasing complexity in software systems and the growing demand for robust applications, effective testing strategies are essential. By adopting a systematic approach to testing, organizations can mitigate risks, reduce costs associated with post-release defects, and foster user trust.

By fostering an environment that prioritizes QA, organizations can not only improve product outcomes but also enhance team collaboration and communication.

QA's involvement in the software development life cycle

The team, including QAs, understands business priorities collectively. Then the team analyzes the requirements together and creates a couple of user stories. Each user story represents a unit of work and is a part of the bigger business feature, but each story also brings some value to the business.

A user story needs to be refined to have a set of acceptance criteria that decides whether the story has satisfied the expectations of stakeholders. Every acceptance criterion should be concise and testable.

> ### The convention of acceptance criteria
>
> An acceptance criterion can follow a popular structure of **given-when-then**. *Given* provides the initial context of the state of the system before the action is performed. *When* is the action performed given the context. *Then* is the expected outcome because of the action performed. An example of an acceptance criterion in given-when-then structure is as follows: *"Given that a household does not exist in the system, when the household creates an account in the system, then the corresponding household record is created."*

From the acceptance criteria, engineers start their technical design on how to make a change to satisfy the conditions. Meanwhile, QAs start creating a test plan on how to verify that the change has satisfied the conditions.

The test plan should be cascaded into actual test scripts. Test scripts are detailed executable scripts describing how the software is tested. It includes setting up the data (the *given*), executing the actions (the *when*), and verifying the results (the *then*). The test scripts can be in any format, such as a document of the steps, an automation script, or even an independently executed program. The content of the testing is more important than the format.

In addition to scripted testing, QAs perform exploratory testing, which emphasizes the testers' autonomy and creativity. QAs can explore the application freely, learning about it while actively testing it. Often, QAs find inconsistent system behaviors, loopholes, or hidden defects that cannot be discovered with fixed scripts. Exploratory tests are often time-boxed. There will also be a document on the findings, bugs discovered, unusual behaviors, and areas that require further investigation. These documents are often hosted in an **issue tracking system** such as JIRA, Asana, Trello, GitHub Issues, and so on.

QAs are also involved in planning UATs where business testers (stakeholders and potentially real users) are involved. QAs help shape the testing process and are the ones to respond to queries by business testers. This is also an opportunity for QAs to confirm that the requirements are fully captured and to identify any features missed in the scope.

Apart from business delivery-focused testing activities, QAs are also responsible for having an overall testing strategy to align with other teams and share best practices. QAs are also responsible for maintaining test processes and tools. Quite often, QAs enhance existing test frameworks and maintain the end-to-end test suite.

Up next, we are going to concentrate on the testing methodology, starting with the testing pyramid.

Testing pyramid

The testing pyramid is a conceptual framework in which various levels of tests in software development emerge as a hierarchical structure. This concept was made popular by Martin Fowler in 2009 in his *The Testing Pyramid* article. The testing pyramid is illustrated in *Figure 13.2*:

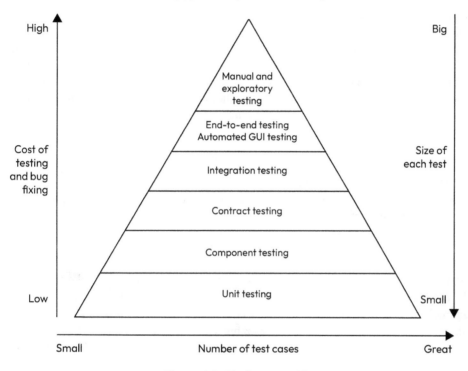

Figure 13.2 – Testing pyramid

In this section, we'll explore all the levels of the testing pyramid.

Unit testing

The bottom level of the pyramid is unit testing. Unit tests are the foundation of the testing pyramid. They focus on the smallest building blocks that can be tested in isolation. They often test the behaviors of functions, and they are executed as a part of the local project build.

Unit tests are comparatively easy to write and execute due to their small size and scope. Unit tests can be run inside the **Integrated Development Environment** (**IDE**), which provides the quickest feedback loop. Bugs can be found and reported by unit tests within minutes – if not seconds.

It is common for the local project build to fail if any unit tests are unsuccessful. Integrating automated unit tests into the build process helps identify bugs early in development. Testing and fixing bugs is most cost-effective during unit testing because the bugs are smaller in size, require less effort to address, and provide quicker feedback compared to other testing stages. Additionally, a system typically has more unit tests than any other type of test, as unit tests target the smallest components, resulting in a larger quantity compared to larger tests.

> **Unit tests should be meaningful**
>
> While unit tests are the smallest building blocks that can be tested, there are a few cases where a function is too small to be tested. If engineers struggle to explain what the test aims to verify, it is likely that the function is too small to be tested. A private function usually does not require a unit test, but a function that's called by other packages (i.e., a public function) should have a unit test. Functions extracted merely to avoid duplicated code are unlikely to form a meaning that requires testing. To summarize, unit tests should be meaningful.

Here is an example of a unit test in Kotlin powered by the Kotest framework:

```
class FindBiggestNumberKtTest : FunSpec({
    test("Find the biggest out of positive numbers") {
        findBiggestNumber(listOf(17, 18, 6)) shouldBe 18
    }
})
```

The Kotest framework provides many test templates as specifications. FunSpec is the one used in the example. The test cases are passed in as lambda expressions. The test function takes the test name as an argument. A lambda expression under the scope of TestScope is passed in for the actual test. This unit test targets the findBiggestNumber function, which is given a list of integers: 17, 18, and 6. The shouldBe infix function mimics the natural English language and validates whether the expected result is 18.

Parameterized testing

You might question whether one test case is not enough to thoroughly test this function. The Kotest framework supports parameterized testing as follows:

```
class FindBiggestNumberParameterizedTest : FunSpec({
    context("Find the biggest out of positive numbers") {
        withData(
            emptyList<Int>() to null,
            listOf(8) to 8,
            listOf(99, 8) to 99,
            listOf(17, 18, 6) to 18,
            listOf(944, 0, 633) to 944,
```

```
            listOf(0, -32, 76) to 76,
            listOf(-11, -32, -102) to -11,
            listOf(-25, -57, 0) to 0,
            listOf(
                Integer.MAX_VALUE + 1,
                Integer.MAX_VALUE,
                0,
                Int.MIN_VALUE,
                -Int.MIN_VALUE - 1,
                -Int.MAX_VALUE,
                Int.MIN_VALUE - 1
            ) to Integer.MAX_VALUE,
        ) { (allNumbers, expectedMax) ->
            findBiggestNumber(allNumbers) shouldBe expectedMax
        }
    }
})
```

For a function that takes a list of integers and returns the maximum number, there are many cases we can think of:

- Empty lists

- Lists of one integer

- Lists of two integers

- All positive integers

- All negative integers

- A mixture of zero, positive, and negative integers

- Maximum, minimum, maximum plus one, minimum minus one, and the negation of these integers

With parameterized testing, it is possible to test them all with code footprints smaller than if we had to duplicate them into separate test cases.

At this point, you might want to see the source code of the function being tested, to ensure that you have covered all cases, but do you need to? There is no right or wrong answer here because it represents two methods of software testing: **blackbox testing** and **whitebox testing**. Please note that these two testing styles are applicable to all levels of testing in the pyramid.

Before we discuss these two testing styles in detail, let us reveal the implementation:

```
fun findBiggestNumber(numbers: List<Int>): Int? = numbers.maxOrNull()
```

It is a very simple implementation and uses the built-in `maxOrNull` Kotlin function to find the maximum number in the list or null for an empty list.

Blackbox testing

Blackbox testing evaluates the functionality being tested without any knowledge of the internal code or structure. Testers focus merely on the inputs, expected outputs, and alleged functionality provided (known as the *contract*).

Whitebox testing

Whitebox testing goes in the opposite direction. It involves examining the internal implementation of the functionality being tested. Testers have knowledge of the code and internal logic, allowing them to design test cases based on the implementation details.

Comparing blackbox and whitebox testing

Blackbox testing focuses on the results and functionalities that would affect user experience. Not depending on implementation also enables testers to discover any discrepancies between actual and expected behaviors, revealing requirements that may not have been thoroughly defined. It may, however, miss some code branches in the test suite, which potentially hinders complete code coverage. Organizations that have independent QA teams, separated from the development teams, typically use blackbox testing as their default approach.

Whitebox testing enables comprehensive testing of internal logic, leading to the discovery of hidden bugs or vulnerabilities under specific circumstances. Knowing the code also helps testers identify security vulnerabilities and optimization opportunities that would help meet the non-functional requirements. Knowing the code also brings bias in test cases to unknowingly omit test cases that can comprehensively cover external behaviors and user experience.

There are also human factors in play between the two styles. Once a tester has seen the internal implementation, it is difficult to pretend not to have seen it before and to write bias-free blackbox tests.

Both test styles have their merits and disadvantages. Due to the human factor mentioned, it is recommended to start writing blackbox tests without knowing the implementation first and to focus on testing the external behaviors. Afterward, check the implementation to write whitebox test cases and focus on code branches and non-functional requirements.

This will lead to a topic called TDD, which will be covered later in this chapter.

Component testing

Known as **module testing**, component testing is one level above unit testing in the pyramid. It focuses on testing the higher-order behaviors of self-contained modules. Component focuses on the behaviors emerging from the interactions of several units of code.

Component tests are also included as part of the local project build. So, if a component test has failed, the local project build fails. It is also often executed from IDE to provide a quick feedback loop.

However, component tests are bigger and require more effort to write. Each test usually involves setting a combination of states before the test. The test itself often involves multiple steps, and there are usually multiple places to verify the results. If there is a problem found, it is not immediately obvious where the problem is, and it would require some time to troubleshoot and debug. So, the cost of testing and fixing bugs is higher than unit testing.

One of the examples of component testing can be found in applications that use modular and layered architecture, as mentioned in *Chapter 7*. For example, if we use the **hexagonal architecture**, component testing can be conducted at the core layer to verify the pure business logic without coupling technology choices. This is particularly useful if the bounded context of the application belongs to the Core domain, as mentioned in *Chapter 8*.

The core layer of the Core domain is often perceived as the "crown jewel" of the entire system. It serves as the heartbeat around which everything else revolves. It makes the case to use component testing to ensure the central pure business behaviors are intact in every change made in the system.

Component testing the core layer of the Core domain with blackbox testing first would become the **Behavior-Driven Development (BDD)** approach, which will be discussed later in this chapter.

Mocking external resources

When writing component tests, it is almost inevitable to encounter situations when the code tries to integrate with external resources such as queues, files, databases, or other applications. These integration points put a burden on the testers to prepare the context and increase the effort of writing the test.

Mocking enables testers to isolate the component being tested from external dependencies. There are a few common mocking scenarios:

- Verify whether the component has interacted with the external dependencies as expected, such as checking whether the correct API with expected parameters was called

- Enable the component test to run without needing external dependencies to be available, for example, the database

- Verify whether the component can handle the failures of external dependencies as expected

- Maintain states that allow testing different conditions, such as returning different values based on the context of the tests

Here is an example of component testing with mocking, also using Kotest:

```
class ExerciseExecutorTest : BehaviorSpec({
    Given("Today is sunny") {
        val exerciseLog = mockk<ExerciseLog>()
```

```
val executor = ExerciseExecutor(exerciseLog)
every { exerciseLog.record(any(), any()) } returns Unit
val weather = Weather.SUNNY
When("doing an exercise") {
    val now = Instant.now()
    Then("running in the park") {
        executor.doExercise(weather, now) shouldBe Exercise.
RunInThePark
    }
    And("the exercise is logged") {
        verify { exerciseLog.record(Exercise.RunInThePark,
now) }
    }
}
}
})
```

Firstly, this component test uses the `BehaviorSpec` from Kotest that follows the given-when-then format. It also matches the test pattern of **Arrange, Act, Assert (3A)**.

> **The 3A test pattern**
>
> The 3A test pattern can be used in a unit test. It helps engineers and testers to organize tests by dividing them into three distinct sections. As a result, test scripts are easier to read, understand, reason, and maintain. *Arrange* is the initialization of preconditions and input data for the test. *Act* is the execution of the behaviors being tested. *Assert* is the verification of the actual outcome against the expected result.

Secondly, there is an external `ExerciseLog` dependency, which may involve persisting data in files or databases:

```
interface ExerciseLog {
    fun record(time: Instant, exercise: Exercise)
}
```

The function record accepts an `Exercise` object and the corresponding time when the exercise was done:

```
enum class Weather {
    SUNNY,
    RAINY,
    CLOUDY,
    STORMY,
}
```

As the focus of the test is the logic of `ExerciseExecutor`, not `ExerciseLog`, we use the mockk function from the **Mockk** library to create a mock object that implements the `ExerciseLog` interface. We set up the mock object to accept the invocation of the `record` function with any parameters and to return a `Unit`.

The primary validation is that when the weather is sunny, the function returns `RunInThePark`, as defined by this sealed class:

```
sealed class Exercise {
    data object RunInThePark: Exercise()
    data object GoToGym: Exercise()
}
```

The second validation is that `ExerciseExecutor` has passed the correct parameters to `ExerciseLog` to record this exercise. Here is the full implementation of `ExerciseExecutor`:

```
class ExerciseExecutor(
    private val log: ExerciseLog
) {
    fun doExercise(
        weather: Weather,
        time: Instant
    ): Exercise {
        val exercise = when (weather) {
            Weather.SUNNY, Weather.CLOUDY -> Exercise.RunInThePark
            Weather.STORMY, Weather.RAINY -> Exercise.GoToGym
        }
        log.record(time, exercise)
        return exercise
    }
}
```

Mocks are one of the five types of **test doubles** used in software testing. Here is the full list:

- **Mocks**: These are pre-programmed with expectations of how they should be used. They are used to verify whether the specific functions are invoked with the expected parameters

- **Stubs**: These provide pre-defined responses to functions but do not verify interactions.

- **Spies**: Spies log the parameters used and count the function calls. The actual function is still invoked.

- **Fakes**: These allow for a simplified implementation of the external dependencies for testing purposes.

- **Dummies**: A dummy is a simple object used just to satisfy parameter requirements without needing to implement any behavior.

Contract testing

Contract testing focuses on the interaction between API producers and consumers. It only aims at the communication protocol and the message content. It should not be used for business case testing because we already have component testing covering it in the lower level of the testing pyramid.

There are two types of contract testing:

- **Consumer testing**: This focuses on the service that makes requests to another service. It defines the expectations of the interactions it will have with the producer, typically through a contract. It also verifies that the consumer service can handle all documented responses to the requests made. Consumer contract testing uses stubs or fakes to set up the target service to communicate with.

- **Producer testing**: This focuses on the service that provides the functionality or data requested by another service. It aims to assert that the producer has fulfilled the API contract and met the expectations of its consumers. Producer tests may involve running the actual service, which makes it seem as though it should be higher up in the testing pyramid. It is also possible that producer testing mocks the business logic to produce the message and response defined in the contract. Producer testing is often used to ensure that updates and changes to contracts are backward compatible.

It is, however, important to have contract tests focus on the communication and message content only. For example, the **OpenAPI** specification document mentioned in *Chapter 4* is a good target for writing contract tests. The contract tests ensure that both consumers and producers behave as specified in the openapi.yaml file. This leads to more reliable and maintainable systems, especially in microservices architectures.

Integration testing

Integration testing focuses on the interactions between different components or modules of the application. It is one level up from contract testing in the pyramid as integration tests do not use stubs or fakes. They identify issues when integrating various parts of the system and verify the parts work together as intended. Integration testing is also a part of the local project build.

Integration testing usually involves databases, file systems, external services, or APIs. The following are the common types of integration testing:

- **API integration testing**: Use the exposed APIs to interact with the application for the given use case and to verify the result from the response.

- **Database integration testing**: Confirm that data is correctly processed in the database. This is typically related to **Create, Read, Update, Delete (CRUD)** operations.

- **File system integration testing**: Verify that the application can read from or write to files correctly, and verify the file reflects the result of the operations in the test.

- **Middleware or external service integration testing**: Verify that the integration of middleware or external service connectivity is correctly configured, as well as that the application and middleware or external service can communicate as intended.

Integration tests are bigger than component and unit tests due to the required configuration and preparation. Integration tests are also more complex to write and reason about. Integration tests might involve various combinations of configurations, for instance, supporting multiple pluggable databases or message providers, while the business functionality remains the same.

Some tests may become uncertain due to how external resources or external services behave, especially if there is asynchronous processing external to the application.

Referring to component testing, if component testing focuses on the Core layer of a hexagonal architecture application, then integration testing focuses on the adapter layer.

Extending the exercise code example, we are going to write an integration test for an implementation of the `ExerciseLog` interface that appends a line to a file for each invocation. Each line starts with a local date-time using UTC, separated by a colon, and ends with the name of the exercise, as shown here:

```
2024-09-30T18:39:03.353250: GoToGym
```

An integration test can be written as follows:

```
class ExerciseExecutorIntegrationTest : StringSpec({
    "Gym when cloudy and run in the park when rainy as recorded in
file log" {
        val file = File.createTempFile("Exer", "cise")
            .apply { deleteOnExit() }
        val exec = ExerciseExecutor(ExerciseFileLog(file))
        val now = Instant.now()
        val fourHoursLater = now.plus(4, HOURS)
        val utc = ZoneId.of("UTC")
        exec.doExercise(RAINY, now)
        exec.doExercise(CLOUDY, fourHoursLater)
        FileReader(file).readLines() shouldBe listOf(
"${now.atZone(utc).toLocalDateTime()}: GoToGym",
"${fourHoursLater.atZone(utc).toLocalDateTime()}: RunInThePark",
            )
        }
})
```

The test starts by creating a temporary file that will be deleted on exit. Then a list of two exercise entries is passed into the `ExerciseFileLog` object. The verification starts by reading the file line by line and asserts that each line contains the expected content.

The `ExerciseFileLog` class itself is straightforward:

```kotlin
class ExerciseFileLog(
    private val file: File,
) : ExerciseLog {
    val utc = ZoneId.of("UTC")
    override fun record(
        time: Instant,
        exercise: Exercise,
    ) {
        try {
            val utcDateTime = time.atZone(utc).toLocalDateTime()
            val text = "$utcDateTime: $exercise\n"
            file.appendText(text)
        } catch (e: IOException) {
            println("error writing to the file: $file")
        }
    }
}
```

Test scripts should mostly be integration tests in the supporting and generic subdomain applications, as discussed in *Chapter 8*. This is because these subdomains usually do not contain a lot of business logic, or the combination of business cases is simple enough to be covered by integration tests.

End-to-end and automated GUI testing

So far, all the tests we have discussed have focused on either a single backend service or a specific group of software components. The next level is end-to-end automated testing, which includes graphical user interface (GUI) testing and contract testing. This type of testing evaluates system behavior across multiple services horizontally and across various tiers vertically. Additionally, it becomes more transparent to business stakeholders.

End-to-end and automated GUI testing focuses on a user journey that covers multiple services or components in the system. For example, an end-to-end test could involve creating two household records, and then having one household draft a contract with another household. Both households would then negotiate to reach an agreed contract, and finally, each of them would exercise the contract for the service described in the contract.

End-to-end testing uses APIs for communication with various parts of the system, while automated GUI testing simulates human interaction with the system.

Some systems have a suite of public APIs for integration with external **Software-as-a-Service (SaaS)** platforms (as discussed in *Chapter 6*). In this case, end-to-end testing should ensure that the user journey can be fulfilled by calling the exposed public APIs. The testing of this public API integration, known as headless integration, is as important as visual GUI testing.

The test script for one user journey is complex and fragile. It requires multiple services to be operational in an environment, which implies stable infrastructure as well. It is not practical to test all the variations of user journeys, as the test suite takes a long time to finish.

Tests at this level typically only cover the most crucial and user-facing features. They also usually only cover successful cases. The tests are run periodically, or on demand. If an error is found during the test, it would take a longer time to troubleshoot, and sometimes it could be caused by stability issues in the environment instead of actual bugs.

Manual and exploratory testing

Manual and exploratory testing is the highest level in the pyramid. It is not automated, so it is up to the QAs to manually run through the cases. This level of testing is the most time-consuming and laborious.

If a manual can be automated, QAs will aim to automate it as soon as possible to reduce the cost. There are a few cases where manual testing is necessary:

- **Usability testing**: Evaluating user experience requires subjective analysis, involving elements such as visual layout, design, and overall satisfaction.

- **Short-lived features**: Investment in automating tests may not be justified for short-lived features.

- **Context-heavy testing**: Some tests heavily depend on complex workflows, interactions, or context understanding. Automating these tests to be reliable could outweigh the effort of testing them manually.

- **Security testing**: Many security assessments, such as penetration testing, rely on the security expertise of humans to identify vulnerabilities that automated tests may not catch. Some tests require a quick pivot of the next step decided by security experts; these are difficult to automate.

Manual and exploratory testing is often executed on an ad hoc basis; however, some organizations allow QAs to timebox exploratory testing to discover hidden defects and usability issues.

Benefits of the testing pyramid

The testing pyramid serves as a guiding principle for structuring a testing strategy in software development. As testing and bug fixing become more expensive going up each level, it is natural to prioritize unit tests, followed by component tests, all the way up to manual tests, so the team can achieve a more efficient and cost-effective QA process.

By putting test cases at their appropriate level in the pyramid, the team not only enhances the overall quality of the software but also allows for a quick iterative feedback loop that incrementally improves software development practices.

So far, all the test case examples in this chapter have only used Kotest. However, there are a few other frameworks that can be considered as well:

- Atrium: `https://github.com/robstoll/atrium`

- Kluent: `https://markusamshove.github.io/Kluent/`

- Spek: `https://spekframework.github.io/spek/docs/latest/`

Up next, we are going to discuss the TDD approach.

TDD

TDD has a history dating back to the 1970s, when the idea of "test-first" programming was discussed. It was not popular until TDD became a part of **Extreme Programming** (**XP**), which was introduced by Kent Beck in the 1990s.

> **XP**
>
> XP is an agile software development methodology that aims to deliver high-quality software, meet evolving user requirements, and reduce risks due to uncertainties in the process. It has five core values — *communication, simplicity, feedback, courage,* and *respect.* It emphasizes short iterative development cycles and close collaboration between developers and stakeholders, encouraging frequent feedback to adapt to changing requirements. The key practices of XP include pair programming, TDD, continuous integration, and frequent releases of small and incremental changes.

In 2002, Beck published the book *Test-Driven-Development: By Example*, which provided detailed guidance on the TDD process and has since significantly influenced a lot of engineering practices, even today. TDD has even become a must-have interview coding practice in some organizations.

TDD uses a simple workflow of writing tests and production code, as shown in *Figure 13.3*:

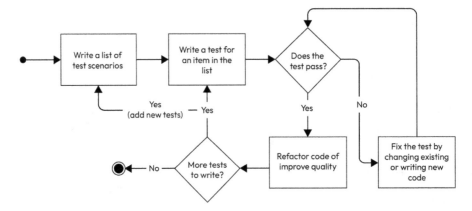

Figure 13.3 – TDD workflow

The first step of TDD is to write a list of test scenarios. Test scenarios are written in business language that does not involve technical implementation. It describes what the expected behavior of the application is under certain conditions, without knowing how the application achieves it.

A test scenario is picked from the list, and we start writing the test. This part is interesting because the test case code usually does not compile due to requiring an enhancement of current APIs or a new API. This is normal because API contracts should be derived from the needs of the user, not the provider. Designing an API from users' perspectives naturally conforms to the **Interface Segregation Principle (ISP)**, which we discussed in *Chapter 2*. The test case should set up the preconditions, attempt to execute the steps, and verify the result.

At this moment, you are left with a test case that either does not pass (**red**) or does not even compile. The next step is to change the code so that the test passes (**green**). It is important to ensure that all other tests pass too. This is exactly what the influential advocator of TDD, Kent Beck, suggested when he said *"fake it till you make it"*.

The test will now pass, but you might not be unsatisfied because the code can be optimized or organized better. This is your opportunity to improve quality by refactoring the code while ensuring all tests continue to pass. That is why TDD has another name: **red-green-refactor**.

There may be more test scenarios that need test cases written, or we may discover missed test scenarios. Nonetheless, the cycle repeats until there are no more test cases to write.

An exercise on TDD

The essence of TDD is best experienced in practice. So, we are going to run through a small exercise on TDD.

The team is asked to develop a feature to allow users to create a household record in the system. There is no code written for this feature.

Step 1 – write a list of test scenarios

The first step for TDD is to write a list of test scenarios. QAs and engineers should ask stakeholders a lot of questions and turn these answers into test scenarios. Here are some examples:

- What are the attributes of a household record? The answer would be a surname and email address.
- Can two different households have the same surname? No, this is a small village where all households have distinct surnames.
- Can a household have no surname? No.

This is the first draft list of test scenarios from the answers:

- Fail to create a household with an empty surname

- Successfully create a household

- Fail to create a household if the surname already exists

Now we can pick the first test scenario and write a test case.

Step 2 – write a test case

We want to assert that creating a household record with an empty surname results in failure. Again, we are using Kotest framework's `StringSpec` as the testing style:

```
class HouseholdServiceTest : StringSpec({
        "fail to create household of empty surname" {
            val service = HouseholdService()
            service.createHousehold(Household(surname = "")) shouldBe
    Failure(
                "Surname must be non-empty"
            )
        }
    })
```

This test case creates a `HouseholdService` object and then invokes the `createHousehold` function with a `Household` object with an empty surname. The test expects the function to return a `Failure` object that provides an appropriate reason for the failure.

Obviously, the code does not compile. The `HouseholdService` and `Failure` classes are dreamed up by the test case. They do not exist. However, writing this test case requires us to consider how the API should be built and what the user's expectations are.

Step 3 – make tests pass

Your IDE should indicate compilation errors for the non-existing classes and functions. Hopefully, your IDE should have a "quick fix" function that creates classes for you. It is recommended to let the IDE first create all classes, then functions, so the IDE has the context to generate functions with new classes. These classes are empty and may look like this:

```
class Failure(reason: String) { }
class Household(surname: String) { }
class HouseholdService {
    fun createHousehold(household: Household): Failure {
        TODO("Not yet implemented")
    }
}
```

We are ready to run the test. It has failed with this message:

```
kotlin.NotImplementedError: An operation is not implemented: Not yet
implemented.
```

This is a good start. The test runs and it is red (i.e., it has failed). Now try to *make it green* with the *simplest possible implementation*.

Hardcoding the function to return the expected `Failure` object would be the simplest option, wouldn't it? Most engineers would feel the urge to fix everything and make the classes reasonable. However, the goal here is to write the least amount of code to make the test pass. Here are the changes:

```
data class Failure(val reason: String)
class Household(surname: String) { }
class HouseholdService {
    fun createHousehold(household: Household) = Failure("Surname must
be non-empty")
}
```

The `Failure` class has changed to a `data` class so that the test case gets the reason for verification. The `createHousehold` function now returns a hardcoded `Failure` object just to pass the test. The `Household` class has not changed.

At this point, this is only a hack implementation. However, it will evolve with more test cases. Let us pick the next test scenario.

Step 2 again – a new test case

The next test scenario is the successful creation of a household record. The surname of the household is no longer empty, and the test expects `HouseholdService` to respond with a successful result that contains the created `Household` record. See the code of the test case here:

```
"successfully create a household" {
    val service = HouseholdService()
    val household = Household(surname = Arb.string(minSize =
3).next())
    service.createHousehold(household) shouldBe Success(household)
}
```

The test case uses the Arb class from the Kotest property module (`io.kotest:kotest-property`) to generate a random surname for the `Household` object. The test case uses a randomly generated string with a minimum size of three as the surname.

Again, the test case does not compile. The `Success` class does not exist, and the `createHousehold` function does not return such a type.

Step 3 again – make all tests pass

Aiming to have two test cases pass is going to drive the code's development. This is quite literally development driven by tests. We can use the IDE feature to generate the Success class. It is also easy enough to write one ourselves:

```
data class Success(val household: Household)
```

The compilation error is resolved. We need to run *all* the tests during the TDD cycle. This is to ensure that we do not break existing tests. Test results show that the first test still passes, but the second test fails with the following message:

```
Expected :Success(household=example.tdd.step2_2.Household@1f958876)
Actual   :Failure(reason=Surname must be non-empty)
```

We need the createHousehold function to return a Success object for successful creation or a Failure object for failure. The simplest approach is the use of Kotlin's sealed class. Engineers may use other constructs, such as the following:

- Result4k<Household, String> from the **Result4K** library (https://github.com/fork-handles/forkhandles/tree/trunk/result4k), where the left parameter is the type for success response, and the right parameter indicates the failure message as String

- Either<String, Household> from the **Arrow** library (https://arrow-kt.io/), where the left parameter indicates the failure message as String, and the right parameter is the type for the success response

The sealed class approach would look like this:

```
sealed class Result {
    data class Success(val household: Household): Result()
    data class Failure(val reason: String): Result()
}
```

The createHousehold function needs to evolve to handle both test cases. Doing so would require removing the previous hack implementation and implementing actual validation logic. The Household class is changed to a data class so the function can access the surname to perform the validation:

```
data class Household(val surname: String)
```

The function has changed the return type to Result. A simple validation is also added to ensure that only non-blank surnames are accepted:

```
fun createHousehold(household: Household): Result =
    if (household.surname.isNotBlank()) {
        Success(household)
```

```
        } else {
            Failure("Surname must be non-empty")
        }
```

Now all tests have passed. However, the use of the IsNotBlank function might get you thinking that non-empty strings filled with spaces or tabs should have resulted in failure, but these cases are not tested.

Step 4 – refactor code

We want to enhance the first test case by parameterizing several blank strings, as well as mixing whitespaces, tabs, and new-line characters. The DescribeSpec in Kotest supports this type of parameterization better, so the test class is changed to inherit from DescribeSpec. This change also affects test case number two, and all test names are updated accordingly:

```
class HouseholdServiceTest : DescribeSpec({
    val blankStrings = listOf("", " ", "\t", "\n", "   ", " \t", " \t \n
")
    describe("household creation") {
        blankStrings.forEach { blankString ->
            it("ensures surname is not blank") {
                val service = HouseholdService()
                service.createHousehold(Household(surname = blankString))
shouldBe Failure("Surname must be non-empty")
            }
        }
        it("succeeds with non-blank surname") {
            val service = HouseholdService()
            val household = Household(surname = Arb.string(minSize =
3).next())
            service.createHousehold(household)  shouldBe  Success(household)
        }
    }
})
```

Now we have a parameterized setting for the first test, covering multiple combinations of blank strings. We are now satisfied enough to repeat the process.

Additional steps

If this exercise goes further and picks up the next test scenario, "fail to create a household if the surname already exists," then it involves keeping a created household record somewhere to provide a stateful validation if a household already exists. To drive a persistent implementation, such as saving the household record, we need to add test scenarios such as "retrieve a household record created by another household service instance." In a way, it encourages us to write better and more test scenarios as well.

Moreover, as we suggest making all tests pass with the simplest possible implementation, we end up with the simplest but complete implementation, which fulfills both the **Keep it simple, stupid! (KISS)** and **You aren't gonna need it (YAGNI)** principles, as discussed in *Chapter 2*.

The KISS principle

The KISS principle is a design philosophy emphasizing simplicity in both design and implementation. It was first seen in the American newspaper *Minnesota Star Tribune* in 1938. The KISS acronym was coined by lead military engineer Kelly Johnson. The KISS principle advocates that systems should be as straightforward as possible, avoiding unnecessary complexity. Simplicity enhances maintainability, reduces the likelihood of errors, and improves user experience.

TDD is meant to be practiced as a short and iterative process, as illustrated by the TDD exercise steps explained earlier. Together with the simplest possible implementation during the process, TDD can produce simple implementations that are naturally 100% covered by tests.

TDD is particularly useful if QAs and engineers are learning features as they go because TDD encourages learning and improving both test cases and implementation via short iterations.

However, for well-established systems, a strict TDD approach may not be as effective. The APIs may already be there and there could be only one line of code that's updated for the behavior change. It may just be simpler to update existing tests to assert the new behavior and make them fail than to update the implementation to make all tests pass. There may not be a need to start from nothing.

Coming next, we are going to discuss a sibling of TDD – BDD.

BDD

BDD evolved from TDD with the goal of addressing some of the limitations of TDD, such as test case classes filled with technical syntax that non-technical stakeholders would find difficult to read.

The concept of BDD was introduced by Dan North in 2003 during the discussions on improvement collaboration between technical and non-technical team members. This is also the year when he started the development of the **JBehave** framework as a replacement for the **JUnit** framework, emphasizing behaviors rather than tests.

The **Gherkin** language was created in the year after that, as a domain-specific language that is close to the natural English language. The language aims to bring non-technical stakeholders closer to technical team members.

The test scenario we have worked on during the TDD exercise can be expressed in the Gherkin language as follows:

```
Feature: Household creation
  Scenario: Creation of households with non-empty surnames
```

```
Given the household surname is non-empty
When the user requests to create the household
Then the household is created
```

Gherkin uses a simple structured syntax to define test scenarios. The primary keywords include the following:

- **Feature**: A feature of the application
- **Scenario**: A specific situation or example
- **Given**: Conditions before the test starts
- **When**: Action or event that triggers behavior
- **Then**: Expected outcome
- **And/But**: Add additional steps, conditions, or expected outcome

A test scenario written in the Gherkin language needs to be translated into programming languages to be executed. **Cucumber** (`https://github.com/cucumber`) is the first major tool for BDD, and it was developed around 2005. It can translate test scenarios in Gherkin language to test scripts into multiple programming languages, such as Ruby, Rust, Java, Go, JavaScript, and Kotlin.

Specification by Example (SBE)

BDD has a close relationship with **Specification by Example (SBE)**. The term SBE was made popular by *Gojko Adzic* in his book *Specification by Example*, which was published in 2011.

SBE advocates using concrete examples in real-world scenarios to clarify specifications and to communicate with non-technical stakeholders. This has influenced the conventional format of user stories as follows: *"As a [user], I want to [feature], so that [business values]"*. This ensures clear and testable specifications based on real examples.

A user story is further expanded to have acceptance criteria to determine whether the feature is completed to the user's satisfaction. These acceptance criteria are reflected in the test scenarios, possibly in the Gherkin language as a BDD practice.

Adopting SBE and BDD has several implications. The test scenarios are written in Gherkin language and the vocabulary used should align with Ubiquitous Language, as discussed in *Chapter 8*. Secondly, human-readable test scenarios strongly suggest blackbox testing as the major approach.

Finally, many teams using Agile methodologies would even use SBE and BDD to improve their requirement gathering and testing processes. In a way, the concrete examples from SBE and test scenarios from BDD become the de facto agreement with non-technical stakeholders on the understanding of the feature.

BDD adoption in Kotlin

BDD is still actively adopted by many teams nowadays. Many Kotlin engineers are still using Cucumber as their BDD tool. However, there are reasons why some teams make a conscious decision not to use the Gherkin language to define test scenarios.

The Kotlin language is concise and less verbose than its predecessor, Java. Kotlin provides a lot of innate syntactic support and syntactic sugar to simplify the code for better readability.

With modern testing frameworks such as Kotest, Spek (`https://www.spekframework.org`), and Kluent (`https://github.com/MarkusAmshove/Kluent`), it is possible to have readable Kotlin-based test scripts that mimic the Gherkin format for test scenarios to a good extent.

It diminishes the need to introduce a translation layer, which can sometimes introduce bugs during testing. It is also a balanced act between the benefits of reading test scenarios and the cost of translating Gherkin test scripts to Kotlin.

However, having BDD and SBE in mind in the agile development process is always beneficial, as it elicits meaningful conversations with non-technical stakeholders in the endeavor of understanding user requirements.

There are a few types of testing that are conducted in production environments. There are justifications for why they need to run in customer-facing environments, and we are going to explore the reasons behind them.

Live testing, A/B testing, and segmentation

Live tests are no replacement for other types of tests conducted in lower environments. Each type of live testing serves a unique purpose in that it can only be executed in a live environment.

Post-release testing

Some systems integrate with external systems that do not provide a lower environment for testing. Engineers would normally mitigate this risk by having a simulator running in lower environments. The simulator is a fake component that runs simplified logic just to act like the target external system. Engineers rely on documentation or information from the third-party company to implement the simulator.

This approach is not ideal, but it is better than having nothing to detect defects in lower environments. Several risks come with this approach:

- The simulator logic needs to closely follow the steps of external system changes. Otherwise, it creates a time gap of discrepancies.

- The external system may release its changes without informing the team, resulting in malfunctioning of the system and requiring hotfixes.

- Engineers must ensure that the simulator never runs in production environments to create false data. Data damage and remediation come at a huge cost.

- Having all safety measures in place, the external system may simply be unavailable after release. Thus, the system is only partially operational.

Regardless of whether there is a test environment for external system integration, some mission-critical systems, such as financial trading systems, would perform a "test trade" with a minimal amount to ensure that the crucial features are operational and the corresponding data is correct.

A/B testing and segmentation

Some tests are run in production for a longer period for reasons other than QA. A/B testing and segmentation are executed to discover needs and opportunities in the market.

Some organizations would segment their users into at least two groups. The segmentation can be done in the following ways:

- A stateless algorithm

- User data, such as demographics or preferences

- Signed up voluntarily by users

- Random and sticky assignments

- Manually assigned to small groups

Each group has a different user experience, and metrics are in place to measure business metrics such as page landing counts, purchase statistics, and customer satisfaction. This is a typical segmentation setup:

- **Control group**: The original experience; the baseline for comparisons

- **Variant groups**: The modified experiences

By conducting A/B testing, the organization can gather useful information about users and the market. The data collected provides a quantitative perspective on which user experiences lead to a better outcome. This provides insights on real-user behaviors using empirical evidence, and it fosters a culture of hypothesis testing and data-driven decision-making.

Some A/B tests could run only for a limited time just to collect enough data for analysis, while some could run for a very long time for continuous improvements. Some organizations would even run multiple A/B tests at the same time, but this comes at the cost of exponential complexity when performing statistical analysis.

Summary

In this chapter, we discussed the role and involvement of QA in the software development cycle. We covered the testing pyramid in depth, explored each layer with code examples, and mentioned some of the techniques used in test scripts such as blackbox and whitebox testing, mocking, and parameterized testing.

We explored the concepts of TDD. We ran through an exercise of TDD with small and frequent iterations, using real-life examples.

We discussed BDD, a close relative of TDD. We elaborated on its history and how it evolved from TDD. We also introduced SBE, which works closely with BDD practices. Finally, we briefly discussed the modern adoption of BDD in Kotlin.

We also briefly introduced some types and examples of testing that are executed in live environments and the reasons behind them.

The next chapter will cover an important aspect of software systems – security.

14

Security

This chapter covers the fundamental principles and practices associated with system security, with a focus on the aspects that affect software architecture and the everyday life of engineers.

It begins by defining key concepts such as **confidentiality**, **integrity**, and **availability** (the **CIA** triad), which form the backbone of security strategies. The chapter outlines several types of threats, including malware, phishing, and insider attacks, highlighting the need for comprehensive risk assessment and management.

Next, it explores various aspects of authentication and how it affects the engineering design of software features, such as **multi-factor authentication** (**MFA**). Then, we will discuss how to use access control to ensure that only authorized users can access certain resources.

Additionally, the chapter addresses compliance with legal and regulatory requirements, such as the **General Data Protection Regulation** (**GDPR**) and the **Health Insurance Portability and Accountability Act** (**HIPAA**), and it shapes security practices. Moreover, we will explore some ways we can handle confidential data in the system.

We will delve into how network security shapes software architecture, such as security layers, encryption, and secure API designs that protect the system from malicious attacks.

Finally, we will run an exercise of threat modeling with a real-life example.

We are going to cover the following topics:

- Authentication
- Authorization
- Handling sensitive data
- Network security
- DevSecOps and threat modeling

Technical requirements

You can find all the code files used in this chapter on GitHub: `https://github.com/PacktPublishing/Software-Architecture-with-Kotlin/tree/main/chapter-14`

The importance of security in software architecture

System security refers to the processes, measures, and practices implemented to protect information systems from unauthorized access, misuse, damage, or disruption. It includes a wide range of mechanisms aimed at safeguarding the confidentiality, integrity, and availability of data and resources within a system.

System security consists of multiple dimensions, including hardware, software, policies, and human factors, to create resistance against malicious threats and vulnerabilities.

Software systems often handle sensitive information. Sensitive data can be grouped into several categories:

- **Personally identifiable information (PII)**: Full names, dates of birth, addresses, telephone numbers, and personal email addresses
- **Personal information**: Health insurance policies, medical test results, treatment records, prescriptions, education certificates, transcripts, university grades, and student identification numbers
- **Authentication credentials**: Passwords, PINs, security questions and answers, and fingerprints
- **Financial information**: Bank account details, credit card numbers, tax returns, financial statements, and income information
- **Confidential business information**: Client lists, business plans, trade secrets, and internal communications
- **Legal documents**: Contracts, litigation documents, and settlement agreements
- **Intellectual property**: Copyrights, patents, trademarks, source code, user activity history, system data, and proprietary algorithms
- **Government and national security information**: Government contracts, intelligence reports, and classified documents

Ensuring security in software architecture shields sensitive data from unauthorized access, breaches, and leaks, maintaining confidentiality and privacy.

Security measures protect the integrity of data throughout its life cycle, free from unauthorized modifications. This can guarantee that users receive accurate and reliable information, which is important for decision-making and trust.

A secure software architecture is designed to withstand vicious attacks and ensure that services are available to legitimate users. This is critical for maintaining business continuity, building a positive reputation, fostering satisfaction and trust among users, and providing competitive advantages.

Many industries are subject to regulations regarding data protection and privacy, such as GDPR in the European Union and HIPAA in the United States. Software architecture compliant with these regulations protects organizations from legal penalties and reputational damage.

Security should be part of the early phase of software architecture design. The design process involves identifying potential threats and vulnerabilities. Proactively addressing security risks reduces the chance of security incidents from day one. It is also more cost-effective to implement security measures early than after a breach happens. The financial losses related to legal fees, remediations, and loss of business can be massive.

Security threats are constantly evolving, and a well-designed software architecture is flexible to incorporate new security technologies and practices. This adaptability and extensibility are essential for staying ahead of potential vulnerabilities and maintaining a robust security posture.

Security-focused architecture encourages the integration of secure coding practices into the software development cycle, such as **DevSecOps**. This cultural shift enhances overall security awareness within development teams.

A secure system is supported by logging, monitoring, and alerting mechanisms that facilitate quick detection and response to security incidents, as discussed in *Chapter 11*. This is essential for reducing damage and recovering from breaches effectively.

By prioritizing security from the beginning, organizations can build resilient systems that not only defend against current threats but also adapt to future challenges, fostering trust and enhancing their overall business success. One of the most discussed foundations of security is the CIA triad, which we are going to cover next.

The CIA triad

The **CIA triad** is a foundational model in information security that outlines the three core principles of information security: **confidentiality**, **integrity**, and **availability**. It was initially mentioned in *Computer Security Technology Planning Study*, known as *The Anderson Report*, in 1972, authored by a team led by William Anderson. The concept was then discussed in the book, *Computer Security A Practitioner's Approach* in the 1980s by Frederick Cohen. The term *CIA triad* was coined later by Steve Lipner around 1986. The CIA triad was popularized by Willis Ware in 1993 from his study distributed by the US think tank, **Research and Development Corporation (RAND)**. Since then, it has gained popularity in the cybersecurity landscape.

The CIA triad is shown in *Figure 14.1*:

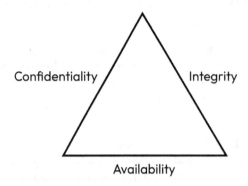

Figure 14.1 – The CIA triad

We will briefly introduce each principle in the following sections.

Confidentiality

Confidentiality ensures that sensitive information is only accessible to authorized individuals or systems. This includes keeping data away from bad actors with malicious intent. Individuals within an organization are also subject to limits on data access.

Common methods to maintain confidentiality include the following:

- **Authentication**: Confirm the identity of a user, device, or system. The primary goal is to ensure that an entity trying to access a system is who they claim to be.

- **Authorization**: Grant or deny an authenticated identity to specific resources, actions, or data within a system.

- **Encryption**: Convert readable data into encoded data to prevent unauthorized access. Even if unauthorized individuals have obtained encrypted data, they need to also have the keys and know the decryption algorithm to unlock the data.

- **Redaction**: Retain functionality and usability without exposing sensitive information.

Some of these methods will be used and discussed in the sections ahead.

Integrity

Integrity refers to the accuracy and consistency of data throughout its life cycle. This principle ensures that information is not altered or tampered with by unauthorized users and that it remains accurate, trustworthy, and reliable.

Common techniques to ensure integrity include the following:

- **Checksums and hash functions**: A fixed-length string calculated from the data by an algorithm. Checksums or hash values usually come with the data itself. Any tampering with the data would produce a checksum (or hash value) different from the original checksum, so it is detected by the system as corrupted data.

- **Digital signatures**: A document is signed by a hash value generated by a private key from the sender. The recipient receives the document together with the digital signature. The recipient computes the hash value of the document using the same algorithm. The recipient decrypts the digital signature using the sender's public key and retrieves the original hash value. Two hash values being identical confirms that the document has not been modified. The sender's private and public keys form a pair, whereas the private key is only known to the sender and the public key is available to anyone.

- **Versioning control**: Version control systems maintain a complete audit trail and history of changes made to a document. If errors or corruptions are detected, the document can be reverted to a previous version.

Availability

Availability ensures that information and resources are accessible to authorized users when needed. This principle focuses on maintaining system functionality and minimizing downtime due to attacks, failures, or other disruptions.

Strategies to enhance availability include the following:

- **Redundancy**: Avoid a single point of failure by having extra components and alternative paths to ensure continued operations and data integrity in the event of failure.

- **Load balancing**: Distribute incoming traffic across multiple servers to ensure incoming requests are served.

- **Regular backups**: Maintain copies of the database, file storage, and messaging store across multiple servers or locations to ensure data availability and to recover from data issues.

- **Disaster recovery planning and drills**: Outline specific steps to take during a disaster to bring the system back up and make it operational. Periodically run disaster recovery drills to verify the plan and identify gaps. Establish clear communication channels to keep engineers and stakeholders informed during a disaster.

Importance of the CIA triad

The CIA triad serves as a guiding framework for organizations to develop and implement effective security policies and practices. These three principles help organizations create a comprehensive approach to information security and protect the business from various threats and vulnerabilities.

We are going to go deeper into selected subjects that are based on the CIA triad.

Authentication

Authentication is the process of verifying the identity of a user or a device before granting access to resources. This is the first step of establishing trust between two parties. An oversimplified authentication process looks like *Figure 14.2*:

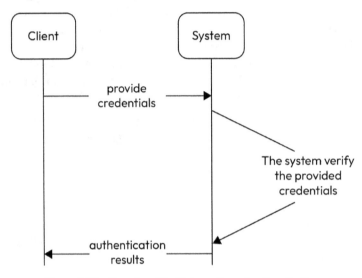

Figure 14.2 – Oversimplified interaction of authentication

The client (a user, a device, or a system) initiates the authentication with the target system, and it provides credentials to claim who it is. The system receives the credentials and starts the verification process. The system acknowledges a positive result if it can identify the client, otherwise, a rejection is sent back to the entity.

This interaction is merely conceptual as actual authentication has a lot of aspects to consider. Firstly, the transport layer needs to be secured to ensure there is no eavesdropping, also known as **man-in-the-middle (MitM)** attacks.

> MitM attack
>
> A MitM attack is a cyberattack where an attacker secretly intercepts and relays communication between two parties. The attacker eavesdrops and captures communication potentially containing sensitive information. The attack might alter the messages exchanged or record them for further malicious intents, such as identity theft and financial fraud. MitM attacks can occur in various forms, such as intercepting unencrypted Wi-Fi traffic, exploiting vulnerabilities in secure communications, or tricking users into connecting to malicious networks. The attack threatens the confidentiality and integrity of communication among individuals and organizations.

Transport Layer Security (TLS)

Transport Layer Security (**TLS**) plays a significant role in securing communications over networks, as a defense against threats, such as MitM, we have just mentioned.

TLS evolved from its predecessor, **Secure Sockets Layer** (**SSL**). SSL was first developed by Netscape in 1994, as a protocol aimed to provide secure communications over the internet. It was never published due to security flaws. Subsequently, SSL 2.0 and SSL 3.0 were released, but they still faced vulnerabilities that led to the need for further development.

TLS was first released in 1999. It was based on SSL 3.0 but it addressed the weaknesses of SSL and it provided better support for modern cryptographic algorithms. Subsequent versions of TLS have brought significant improvements in security and performance. TLS is widely used in various ways to secure communications on the internet, such as secure web browsing, email content encryption, secure messaging, **virtual private networks** (**VPNs**), and secure inter-system communications.

TLS requires the client and server to exchange a few rounds of messages to establish a secure transport communication. TLS is built on top of **Transmission Control Protocol** (**TCP**). The first few steps are the messages exchanged to establish a TCP connection. Afterward, there are a few exchanges of messages to establish a TLS communication:

1. **Client hello**: The client initiates TLS by sending to the server a message specifying supported TLS versions, cipher suites (known as encryption algorithms), and a random number generated by the client.

2. **Server hello**: The server responds with its chosen TLS version and cipher suite, and a random number generated by the server.

3. **Server certificate**: The server sends its TLS certificate containing the server's public key and is signed by a trusted **certificate authority** (**CA**). Certain cipher suites require the server to include additional key exchange parameters.

CA

A CA is a trusted entity that issues digital certificates to verify the identity of individuals, organizations, or devices within a secure communication framework. CAs play a crucial role in **public key infrastructure** (**PKI**) by binding public keys to the identities of their owners, enabling secure protocols, such as TLS/SSL, for encrypted communication. They conduct identity verification before issuing certificates, maintain a chain of trust through root and intermediate certificates, and manage certificate revocation to ensure ongoing security. By providing this trust foundation, CAs enable users to confidently communicate and transact over the internet.

---

4. **Server hello done**: The server acknowledges finishing its part of the handshake.

5. **Client key exchange**: The client generates a pre-master secret, which is a random string without meaningful data, encrypts it with the server's public key received from the server certificate, and sends it to the server.

6. **Session keys creation**: Both the client and server use the pre-master secret along with the previously exchanged random numbers to generate session keys. These keys will be used for encrypting the data during the session.

7. **Finished messages**: The client and server exchange `Finished` messages, indicating that the handshake is complete and that they will now start using the session keys for secure communication.

The interaction is shown in *Figure 14.3*:

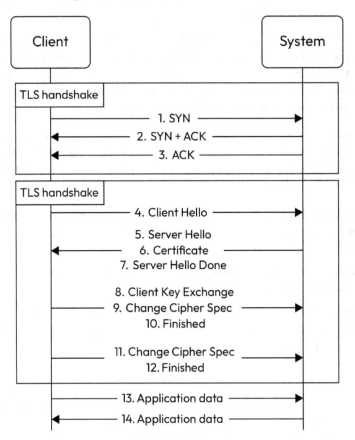

Figure 14.3 – TLS handshaking

During the TLS handshake, both the client and server independently generate session keys that are unique to that session only. Any replay of messages outside the session is not valid and will be detected. The session key never exists in messages exchanged.

Also, if a MitM attacker wants to decrypt the content of application data, it needs the symmetric session key. The session key is formed by random numbers generated by both sides and the pre-master secret. The pre-master secret can only be decrypted by the server's private key, which is never exposed in any message exchanged. In other words, the MitM attackers cannot read the encrypted application data.

In addition, each message exchanged contains a sequence number. Any out-of-order message will be detected and not processed further. Each message also contains a **Message Authentication Code** (**MAC**) that acts like a checksum to confirm whether the data has been altered in transit.

TLS uses digital certificates issued by trusted CAs to authenticate the server's identity. This prevents MitM attacks, where an attacker impersonates the server. In the case of mutual TLS, the client can also present a certificate to prove its identity, further enhancing security.

At this point, we have confidence that we have secure transport between the clients and the server. However, we still need to verify the identity of the client to authorize resources and actions allowed. We are going to discuss further how to authenticate the client in the next section.

Multi-factor authentication (MFA)

Simple authentication requires only one such piece of evidence (known as a factor), typically a password. This approach has several weaknesses that make it inadequate for securing sensitive information:

- **Weak passwords**: Easily guessed by attackers
- **Phishing**: Attackers trick users into revealing their passwords (e.g., fake landing page)
- **Password reuse**: If one password is compromised, attackers can access other services using the same password
- **Brute force**: Automated tools can keep guessing the one password
- **Social engineering**: Manipulate users into sharing passwords
- **No user verification**: Password verification only checks whether the provided credentials are the same as the ones in the record, instead of verifying that the person attempting to gain access is the actual user

MFA aims to harden the authentication process by verifying multiple factors, further validating that the user is who they claim to be. These factors are categorized into three groups:

- **Knowledge factor**: Passwords, security questions and answers, PINs, or IDs
- **Possession factor**: Smartphones, hardware tokens, authentication applications, and one-time passcodes
- **Biometric factor**: Fingerprints, faces, and voices

At a minimum, MFA requires at least two factors from distinct categories. It is less likely for attackers to get a hold of multiple factors from a target user, and thus it reduces the risk of unauthorized access. Moreover, some industries, such as banking, have regulatory requirements to enforce the use of MFA to protect sensitive data.

It is worth pointing out that MFA does not necessarily require TLS, but using TLS for MFA is strongly recommended to ensure there is no eavesdropping and interception during the MFA process, especially when transmitting sensitive information, such as biometric data and passwords.

Implications of MFA to software architecture

The prevalence of MFA in everyday life, such as online banking and e-commerce, has influenced modern software architecture. There is a strong need for dedicated services to focus on authentication and decouple from business logic. This is due to the high complexity of the authentication process and the sensitivity of the data it handles. It is better to have a service specialized in authentication that keeps sensitive data within its bounded context to reduce risks.

Together with the rise of serverless cloud computing, as discussed in *Chapter 6*, every organization that runs its services in the cloud must choose one of the following:

- The **identity providers** (**IdPs**) native to the cloud providers (e.g., Active Directory for Azure, Google Identity for GCP, Cognito for AWS)

- Platform independent IdPs, such as Okta, Auth0, and Duo Security

- Write its own **identity and access management** (**IAM**) service, optionally as a proxy to other IdPs

- No authentication required

It is exceedingly rare these days to see systems skipping authentication. There are a few cases, such as public websites, anonymous surveys, and low-risk functions, such as calculators, that may not require authentication.

It may be justified to build an IAM service tailored to an organization's needs. Unless the organization itself specializes in security solutions, IAM services belong to the generic subdomain, as discussed in *Chapter 8*. Most third-party IdPs provide the sufficient authentication capabilities required by an organization. If there is any organization-specific justification, it is recommended to build an IAM service to act as a proxy for a third-party IdP. If the third-party IdPs provide new features that are currently custom-built, this approach minimizes the impact of feature migration.

A sample interaction of MFA

Given a user wants to log on to a system to request an operation from an application on a smart device, the messages exchange may look like *Figure 14.4*:

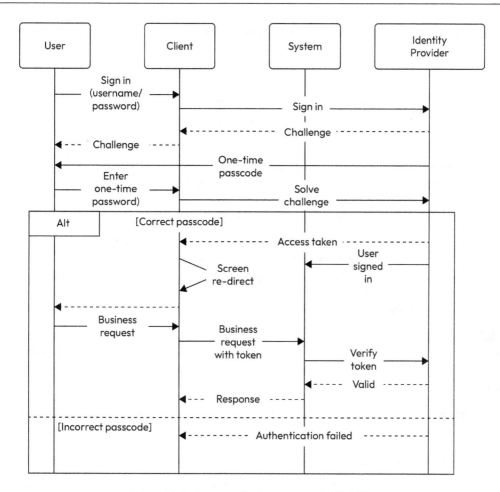

Figure 14.4 – A sample business request with MFA

This is just a sample interaction because the communication varies with different IdPs and different factors involved in authentication. In this sample, the IdPs provide a white-label page themed for the organization.

> **White label page**
>
> A **white label page** is a customizable web page or application that can be re-branded and used by different organizations. The screen is themed for the target organization and the original organization's branding is hidden. It is a common feature for a SaaS product to allow seamless integration with any organization while maintaining a consistent user experience.

The user signs in and provides the username and password, using HTTPS over TLS. The username and password are joined by a colon as a string:

```
username:password
```

The string is then encoded in Base64 and is passed to the HTTP header as a part of the **HTTP basic authentication**. Since it is HTTPS, the header is also encrypted. The sign-in request is equivalent to the following command:

```
curl -i http://api.example.com/api/sign-in \
  -H "Authorization: Basic dXNlcm5hbWU6cGFzc3dvcmQ="
```

This data forms the knowledge factor of the authentication.

The IdP confirms that the username and password do exist and match, but then it issues a challenge to the client to enter a **one-time passcode (OTP)**. The OTP is then sent to the user's phone number via **Short Message Service (SMS)**. The user who possesses the phone receives the OTP and enters the passcode. The passcode is sent from the client to the IdP to solve the challenge. This is the possession factor of the authentication.

The IdP verifies whether the OTP is correct or not. If it is incorrect, the IdP responds to the client and reveals that the authentication has failed. If it is correct, the IdP generates a **JSON Web Token (JWT)** as an access token and sends it to the client as a response. Soon after, the IdP also informs the server that a user is successfully authenticated via a webhook.

A **JWT** is an encrypted JSON string used to carry claims about the roles and permissions of the user. It consists of three parts:

- **Header**: The type of the token as "JWT" and the algorithm used to encrypt the token.

- **Payload**: Registered claims, such as issuer, audience, expiration time, and ID. Also contains public claims, such as application user roles, and private claims for information to be shared only between parties using the token.

- **Signature**: The proof that the sender is who it claims to be and the whole JSON string has not been modified.

The authentication success response also triggers a screen redirect to the landing screen for the user to start making business requests.

The authenticated user makes a business request. The client sends the request to the server with the access token attached to the HTTP header as a `Bearer` token:

```
curl -i http://api.example.com/api/business-request \
  -H "Authorization: Bearer mytoken123"
```

The server receives from the client the request along with the `Bearer` token. The server verifies with the IdP whether the token is valid. The IdP confirms that the token is valid, so the server processes the request and responds to the client.

The client can continue to use the `Bearer` token for other operations, without further authentication, until the session ends. The IdP is in control of the validity of the token throughout the session. The token can also be refreshed upon request to the IdP.

The token exchange and refresh flows are a part of the industry standard protocol for authorization, **OAuth** (`https://oauth.net/2/`).

OAuth

OAuth is an authorization framework that enables third-party applications to obtain limited access to resources without exposing credentials. Users are granted access to their data from one service to another service through various grant types, such as authorization code, implicit, and client credentials. The user submits authentication requests to an authorization server, which then issues access tokens for accessing protected resources on a resource server. OAuth emphasizes flexibility and is widely adopted for secure delegated access in modern applications.

This sample interaction also allows the `Bearer` token to be used for authentication of other systems that use the same IdP. As the user has already been authenticated by the IdP, other systems using the same IdP can verify the identity of the user in the same way. This mechanism enables the **single-sign-on (SSO)** experience where a user only needs to be authenticated once to access a basket of applications and systems that share the same IdP.

Step-up authentication

Sometimes, the authenticated user is asked to perform additional verification beyond their initial authentication. This additional step is called **step-up authentication**.

Step-up authentication typically applies to deliberately chosen situations when they involve accessing sensitive information or high-risk actions, such as updating passwords, making a bank transfer, or moving the account data to an unfamiliar device.

Step-up authentication can also be dynamically applied based on the context of the access requests, such as a new geographic location, new device, new bank account, and so on.

The simplest approach to step-up authentication is to repeat the same MFA process under TLS communication. Some companies would deliberately add more challenges, such as CAPTCHA or biometric verifications.

By implementing step-up authentication, organizations can significantly reduce the risk of unauthorized access while maintaining a seamless user experience for lower-risk activities.

We go to great lengths to get to the point where the system has verified the identity of an entity entering the system. Now that the entity has signed in the system the next question is this: What can the entity access and execute in the system? We are going to explore this in the next section.

Authorization

Authorization determines what resources a user or entity is allowed to access and what actions they can perform. After a user is authenticated, it is authorized to only interact with data and features explicitly granted rights. This restricts sensitive information to only individuals the system knows and maintains the integrity of systems.

Authorization conforms to the **principle of least privilege (PoLP)**, known as the **principle of minimal privilege (PoMP)** or the **principle of least authority (PoLA)**. PoLP states that a user, entity, or system should have only the essential permissions to operate its functions. This minimizes risks and limits potential damage from accidents or malicious actions that we might not have anticipated or known.

In addition, knowingly granting permissions for specific resources and actions improves accountability and compliance with security policies. Staying with the knowns promotes a safer sense of security.

As we have briefly mentioned, authorization has two elements: data and actions. They are different concepts in authorization and can be managed differently:

- **Data entitlement**: Whether the user is entitled to access specific data or resources
- **Permission**: Which actions the user is allowed to perform on a resource or data

For example, a user is entitled to see their own user account. A user in the Administrator role is entitled to see other users' accounts. However, the user must be granted permission to read user accounts to start with. A user is granted write permission to update their own user account. A user in the Administrator role, however, may not have the write permission to update other users' accounts.

There are four typical approaches to implementing authorization:

- **Role-based access control (RBAC)**
- **Attribute-based access control (ABAC)**
- **Access control lists (ACLs)**
- **Policy-based access control (PBAC)**

We are going to perform a deep dive into them.

Role-based access control (RBAC)

An RBAC approach has users assigned to roles, and each role has specific permissions assigned to it. Users are granted permissions based on the assigned roles within the organization. This is illustrated in *Figure 14.5*:

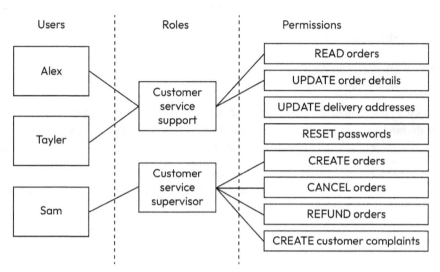

Figure 14.5 – An example of RBAC

In the preceding RBAC configuration, Alex and Taylor are assigned the role of *Customer service support*, which is granted permissions to perform basic-level actions, such as updating a customer's order. More advanced actions, such as refunding an order, can only be executed by a person such as Sam with the *Customer service supervisor* role.

RBAC is commonly used in companies in which different job functions require various levels of access. It is more efficient than assigning permissions to users individually. It is also efficient in situations such as when an employee takes a holiday and another employee temporarily takes over the duty, or a new employee requires the same level of access as their teammates.

Access control lists (ACLs)

An ACL grants a list of users or groups of users to have access to a specific resource and defines which actions are allowed. This approach is suitable for granting permissions to resources that can be precisely specified, such as the following:

- **Filesystems**: Folders, read/write actions, and filenames
- **HTTP paths**: **Uniform Resource Identifiers** (**URIs**) and HTTP methods

- **Networking**: IP addresses, ports, and transport layer protocols
- **Database**: Schemas, tables, and actions

Some of the ACLs also support wildcard matches for more flexible configuration. This approach is suitable for managing the entitlement of resources at a fine-grained level.

Policy-based access control (PBAC)

PBAC grants permissions based on pre-defined policies that consider various criteria, such as user roles, attributes, and context.

These policies are pre-defined, but they support parameters. They are usually managed by GUI tools or set up as declarative configurations. The authorization tool itself may be custom-built, but the maintenance of policies does not require code change.

The policies can be fine-grained and highly configurable. They can also be changed at runtime without deployment or restart. They are useful in dynamic environments where access needs to adapt based on real-time conditions or compliance requirements.

PBAC is effective for compliance regulatory requirements because well-defined policies can be treated as a technical implementation of compliance policies.

Attribute-based access control (ABAC)

ABAC grants permissions to attributes associated with users, resources, and the environment. It provides the most flexible way to control permissions that can be sensitive to the context such as time and geographic locations.

For example, a completed customer order can only be updated by a customer service supervisor, but an open order can be updated by both customer service support and supervisor.

This approach is suitable for complex environments where access decisions depend on multiple, often dynamic, factors, such as user attributes (e.g., department, clearance level), resource attributes (e.g., sensitivity), time of access request, environment configurations, and so on. The control can be as granular as it needs to be.

Due to its high flexibility, ABAC is often written as code instead of configuration. Some of these ABAC policies may even involve the concept of permission inheritance, at either the user level or resource level. The implementation can easily become complex.

Writing ABAC in code also brings the challenges of testing and maintenance. It is possible that a bug in ABAC code leads to leaks of resources to unauthorized persons.

Impacts of authorization on software architecture

There are several dimensions of how authorization impacts software architecture. Microservices, nanoservices, and FaaS (as discussed in *Chapter 6*) themselves require access to infrastructure resources, such as databases and filesystems.

If they are often run under cloud providers, RBAC and ALCs can be used in defining and restricting what resources which component is allowed to access, and which actions are allowed. More than often, organizations would use the cloud-native IdP to manage infrastructure permissions and data entitlements used by applications.

As we mentioned when discussing PoLP, an application should be granted exactly sufficient permissions and data entitlements to perform its operations, but no more.

If there is a need to grant write access to a specific resource (e.g., database schema) to more than one bounded context, then it can be a smell of unclear or leaky bounded context. An architecture review of the involved bounded context will be useful in understanding the needs and examining whether the boundary of applications can be improved.

End users, external systems, and other devices require access to both infrastructure and application data. There are a few use cases where they need access to the infrastructure resources.

Use case – submit expense reimbursement request and approval

In an organization, all users are permitted to submit requests to reimburse expenses for business authorization:expense reimbursement request and approval" purposes. The financial operation team is responsible for reviewing these requests and deciding if the request should be approved or rejected.

In this setup, all users have the User role. The role is granted permissions to access these endpoints:

- `POST /expense`: This is to submit a new expense reimbursement request
- `GET /expense/{id}`: This is to see the expense reimbursement request of the given ID

Some users are assigned to the financial operations role. This role is granted permissions to access these endpoints:

- `GET /expense/{id}`: This is to see the expense reimbursement request of the given ID
- `PATCH /expense/{id}/result`: This is to either approve or reject the expense reimbursement request of the given ID

The corresponding permission control can be configured using RBAC and ACLs. Most IdPs, including cloud-native middleware, can support this setting.

Centralized or distributed authorization logic?

It is often a question among engineers whether the authorization logic should be centralized or distributed when it is related to application data.

This is not a simple yes or no question. It depends on the nature of the authorization logic. At the basic level, the user requesting a record of application data should have permission granted to read the data of the given type. If it is RBAC or ACL, it is reasonable to have a centralized service to confirm that *user X can read application data of type Y*.

Alternatively, permissions or roles can be encoded as part of the JWT custom claims. This approach reduces the time spent in resolving permissions. However, it implies the granted permissions can linger until the JWT expires, making dynamic authorization more difficult.

However, it gets complicated when deciding whether a user is entitled to see a given application's data, which is the data entitlement question of whether *user X can read application data of type Y and of ID 123*. Answering this question often requires domain-specific knowledge that should stay within the bounded context, in other words, distributed.

Moreover, other actions on application data imply that the user can read the data to begin with. The interweaving logic of permissions, data entitlement, and business logic has significantly increased the complexity of the operations. This is even more complicated with third-party API integration where data being authorized are distributed among services.

Using the same example of expense reimbursement request and approval from the previous section, a sample interaction of permissions and data entitlements business flow looks like the diagram in *Figure 14.6*:

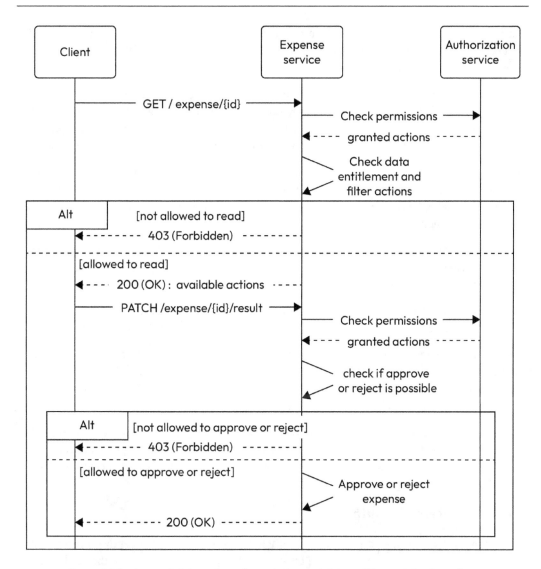

Figure 14.6 – A sample interaction of permission and data entitlements business flow

A user with a financial operations role needs to see the expense reimbursement request to decide whether to approve or reject it. So, the first request from the client is the get the expense reimbursement request by the given ID.

The corresponding service, the expense service, makes a synchronous call to the authorization service, which is dedicated to user permissions, to check whether the given user has the permissions to read an expense reimbursement request.

The authorization service resolves the user's permissions by its roles and returns a list of actions granted to the user. The expense service receives the list of granted actions, and on top of that, checks whether the user can see this particular expense reimbursement request.

There could be domain-specific business rules, such as expense reimbursement requests can only be approved by a user of the same geographic jurisdiction. The expense service also further filters which actions can be performed on this expense reimbursement request. For example, if it is already approved, then the action to approve or reject is no longer available due to business logic, not due to permissions.

Combined with the result of permissions and data entitlements, if the user is not allowed to see the expense reimbursement request, an HTTP status 403 (Forbidden) is returned to the client. Otherwise, an HTTP status 200 (OK) is returned with the payload of a list of actions available to the user on this expense reimbursement request.

Both services could have just returned a binary answer if the user could read the expense reimbursement request or not. However, returning a list of granted actions allows the list to be populated to the frontend application. The frontend application can enable and disable buttons to give the user clear expectations.

The expense reimbursement request is presented to the user on a screen, and the user has decided on the approval. The client sends a PATCH request to update the result of the expense reimbursement request.

The expense service makes a synchronous call to the authorization service to check whether the given user has permissions to approve or reject an expense reimbursement request. The authorization service returns a list of actions granted to the user. The expense service checks further if it is possible to approve or reject this given expense reimbursement request.

If the expense reimbursement request is already approved or rejected, then an HTTP status 403 (Forbidden) is returned to the client. Otherwise, the expense service updates the result of the expense reimbursement request and returns an HTTP status 200 (OK) together with the payload of the updated expense reimbursement request.

Scalability concerns for authorization

From this sample interaction, we can foresee that the authorization service is frequently synchronously called. It raises concerns about scalability. All business requests would need to be authorized, so the authorization service would be under the load of all other business-facing services combined.

Meanwhile, caching permissions locally may not be desirable, and even risky to do so. It is recommended to keep requests to the authorization service lean by designing efficient and non-chatty APIs. It is also worth considering a smaller size payload, such as a binary format.

Scaling out any business-facing service that uses the authorization service would imply scaling out the authorization service considerably too. It is advised to set up metrics and monitoring to understand the usage of the authorization service per API client, so we understand if a service scales out to handle a greater number of requests, the authorization service needs to scale out proportionately.

At this point of the chapter, we can authenticate users and authorize them with a list of allowed actions and accessible resources. Business operations on top of them would result in the system keeping sensitive data. We are going to explore the topic of handling sensitive data in the next section.

Handling sensitive data

Handling sensitive data requires careful consideration and implementation of best practices to ensure its confidentiality, integrity, availability, and compliance with regulatory requirements. In this section, we'll look at the key strategies for managing sensitive data.

Data classification

We have discussed what data can be identified as sensitive at the beginning of the chapter. It is important for an organization to explicitly classify and document which field is sensitive. There are at least three categories of data sensitivity:

- **Confidential**: Only designated persons or roles can access
- **Internal use**: Only members of the organization can access
- **Public**: Accessible to all

The documentation should serve as a guideline for everyone, including engineers, in the organization to handle them with care and caution.

Data in transit

Data in transit under TLS communication is encrypted with session keys. This ensures that even if data is intercepted or accessed without authorization, it remains unreadable.

How to prevent accidentally logging sensitive information

However, it is not safe and secure yet. It is not unusual to encounter sensitive information leaked by logging unknowingly:

- The full decrypted payload of requests, responses, or messages
- An aggregate Kotlin object that transitively contains a sensitive field
- An object of a generated class that contains a sensitive field
- Troubleshooting or debugging information that contains sensitive information
- Sensitive fields themselves

This is quite dangerous because the related code looks innocuous and the leak is often found after the fact. There are a few techniques to prevent this from happening.

A common technique adopted by engineers is to override the `toString` function of a Kotlin data class:

```
data class UserAccount(
    val username: String,
    val password: String,
    val createdAt: Instant
) {
    override fun toString(): String {
        return "UserAccount(createdAt=$createdAt)"
    }
}
```

This approach works, but it is not scalable because there are a lot of override functions to write. Alternatively, a value wrapper can work efficiently, as shown here:

```
data class Secret<T> (val value: T) {
    override fun toString(): String = "*"
}
```

The `Secret` wrapper class works on a class or a field. The `toString` override function is simple as well.

There are also open source libraries that aim to solve this issue with minimal code. For example, the Redacted compiler plugin (`https://github.com/ZacSweers/redacted-compiler-plugin`) enables engineers to annotate a field or a class to be redacted, and therefore, the values are masked when `toString` is invoked. The setup is quite simple as well:

1. The first step of the setup is its Gradle plugin:

    ```
    plugins {
        id("dev.zacsweers.redacted") version "1.10.0"
    }
    ```

2. Secondly, define a custom `Redacted` annotation class:

    ```
    @Retention(AnnotationRetention.SOURCE)
    @Target(AnnotationTarget.PROPERTY, AnnotationTarget.CLASS)
    annotation class Redacted
    ```

3. Then, configure the plugin to use this annotation and configure the mask character in `build.gradle.kts`:

    ```
    redacted {
        redactedAnnotation = "redacted/Redacted"
        replacementString = "*"
    }
    ```

We have the following data classes annotated with `Redacted`:

```
@Redacted
data class BankAccount(
    val iban: String,
    val bic: String,
    val holderName: String
)
data class UserAccount(
    @Redacted val username: String,
    @Redacted val password: String,
    val createdAt: Instant
)
```

We create one object per class and print them to the console in the main function:

fun main() {

```
    println("${BankAccount("Iban", "bic", "holderName")}")
    println("${UserAccount("username", "password", LocalDate.now())}")
    println(
        "Secret wrapper: ${Secret("email@address.com")}"
    )
}
```

We have the following result:

```
BankAccount(*)
UserAccount(username=*, password=*, createdAt=2024-10-09)
Secret wrapper: *
```

So, the sensitive information is masked as part of the `toString` function result. However, the values are not masked if the program is run from the IDE with this compiler plugin. The masked values are shown if the program is executed from the command line or Gradle tasks.

There are alternative approaches that use reflection as a means to redact or hide sensitive fields. They are not recommended due to the overhead of using reflection. Compile-time redaction is the most effective method.

As for the payload and objects of a generated class, a sensible way to prevent sensitive information leaks is to avoid logging them in a production environment.

Data at rest

Data at rest refers to the data stored on devices, filesystems, databases, and cloud environments. Data sitting in infrastructure is usually protected by MFA, RBAC, and ALCs, as discussed in previous sections. However, for sensitive information, additional steps need to be taken.

Encryption

Sensitive data needs to be stored in an encrypted state; the variations are in the *how*. Here are the common techniques:

- **Encrypted databases**: All data stored in a database is stored in an encrypted and unreadable format. The data is automatically decrypted upon retrieval without the application code. These databases usually support authorization to ensure that only authorized users can interact with encrypted data. They also innately support encryption key generation, storage, and rotation for extra security. Some databases also support encryption when data is being transmitted in and out of the database. However, encrypting and decrypting all data, sensitive or not, increases latency.

- **Encrypted fields**: Only fields identified as sensitive data are encrypted. This approach works with all types of storage, such as database columns, events in messaging infrastructure, and files. It has less performance overhead compared to encrypted databases, However, doing it at a field level implies that applications need to handle aspects that are automatically by encrypted databases, such as the following:

    - Encryption and decryption algorithms

    - Symmetric or asymmetric encryption key

    - Key generation and secret management

    - Key rotation and re-encryption

- **Hybrid**: Due to the performance overhead of encrypted databases and the additional work to handle encryption in application code, it may be justified to use a hybrid approach, in which only sensitive data are stored in encrypted databases, and the rest are kept in any type of storage.

- **Encrypted backups**: Sensitive data should be regularly backed up in encrypted format to ensure data can be restored security in case of data loss or breaches.

Data retention and anonymization

Local authorities and regulations have clear guidelines on how long data should be maintained, including sensitive data. During the retention period, it is the organization's responsibility to keep them secure and safe. After the retention period, sensitive data may be deleted.

There are also regulations (e.g., GDPR) that individuals have the right to request for privacy data to be erased from the system.

However, there may be complications for deleting sensitive data on its own. Some of the data have referential constraints and contain useful business insights, which need not identify individuals.

There are several techniques that allow sensitive data to be anonymized and become not sensitive:

- **Masking and substitution**: Replace real sensitive fields, such as email addresses and bank accounts, with known mask values (e.g., a real email address is anonymized as `anonymized@data.com`)

- **Generalization**: Reduce the precision of sensitive values so they cannot identify a specific person or record (e.g., dates of birth reduced to months of birth, addresses trimmed to cities, etc.).

- **Aggregation**: Summarize data into statistics so there is no reference to a person or a record.

- **Lost decryption keys**: Delete the decryption keys so the data cannot be traced back to the individuals.

- **Periodic anonymization**: Aggressively scan data that has passed the retention period and anonymize it.

- **Broken link**: An upfront database schema design that separates sensitive data and non-sensitive into different tables, and no tables have reference to the sensitive data table. This sensitive data record can be deleted anytime without issues (see an example in *Figure 14.7*).

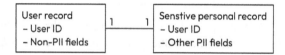

Figure 14.7 – Separation of sensitive and non-sensitive data for anonymization

The user record table has a primary key user ID and this field can be used by other tables for reference. The sensitive personal record table is merely a complimentary table to keep only PII fields.

Proactively using these techniques helps organizations manage sensitive data and protect it from unauthorized access and potential breaches. They help maintain trust with customers and compliance with regulatory requirements.

Coming next, we are going to briefly cover some practices for ensuring network security.

Network security

Earlier in this chapter, we discussed how TLS works and how it prevents eavesdropping on network communications. However, there are other malicious attacks that do not require infiltrating the authentication and authorization processes.

For example, **distributed denial of service** (**DDoS**) is a type of cyberattack in which a system is overwhelmed by multiple source systems, usually as bots and automated scripts, so that legitimate users cannot access the system. Attacks generative massive volume of traffic to saturate and exhaust the system's resources, such as CPU, memory, and network.

The following are the key strategies to protect the system from these network-level attacks.

Web application firewalls (WAFs)

A **web application firewall** (**WAF**) is a security solution specialized in protecting systems on the internet. A WAF can run in the cloud, in a data center, or a mixture of both, as a front-runner before traffic from the internet reaches deeper inside the system. It provides a few key functions:

- **Geo-blocking and IP blacklisting**: Block traffic coming from and going to the list of IP addresses linked to malicious activity and block traffic from certain geographic regions.

- **Rate limiting**: Prevent the number of requests to the server from reaching the threshold in duration as per configuration.

- **Prevention of foreign script executions**: Prevent attackers from executing scripts that are not part of the system, such as unauthorized database commands, **cross-site scripting** (**XSS**) from web pages, and trojans.

- **Policy-based or rule-based access policies**: Highly configurable and customizable rules to set up the needs of each application at a fine-grained level.

- **Frequent updates**: WAFs are updated frequently to adapt to the ever-changing landscape of security threats. WAFs address vulnerabilities outlined in the **Open Web Application Security Project** (**OWASP**) Top 10, which is updated periodically.

> Open Web Application Security Project (OWASP)
>
> OWASP is an open source project with the mission to make software security visible and accessible to engineers and organizations. It is a global community of engineers, security experts, and organizations dedicated to providing free tools and knowledge to enhance the security of the digital environment. The OWASP Top 10 is a globally recognized list of the top 10 most crucial security risks. The list is updated regularly to reflect the evolution of security threats.

A WAF is a critical part of a comprehensive web security strategy, providing essential protection for web applications against a variety of attacks. An organization with ongoing concerns should have a WAF. A cloud-based system can choose a WAF from the native cloud provider, or from a WAF that can run in the cloud. A WAF helps organizations safeguard their applications, protect sensitive data, and maintain compliance with security standards.

Traffic routing and network segmentation

In contrast to traffic blacklisting and blocking, there should be explicit traffic routing that serves as an API gateway or proxy to applications. The explicit configuration serves as a whitelist of permitted traffic routes from the external world and helps conform to the PoLP.

Explicitly configured traffic routes allow applying features such as the following:

- **Distributed tracing**: Link requests that pass through multiple components as a holistic flow

- **Metrics**: Collect metrics such as packet loss, response time, connection time, and error rate

- **Retrying**: Allow applications to retry an operation in the face of intermittent failures

- **Circuit breaking**: Disallow applications to repeat operations that have been failing

- **Rate limiting**: Overlapped with the feature of WAF, limit the number of requests over a period

So far, the traffic routing we covered here is all for ingress, that is, traffic from the external world to internal applications. Traffic egress, from internal applications to external worlds, is equally important. For example, attackers may have installed trojans that quietly export sensitive data to an unidentified destination. This can be configured by routers, network switches, network ACLs, and WAF configurations. Cloud providers also have services that manage ingress and egress routes by rules and policies.

A **service mesh** is another approach to configure and control network communications, but it focuses on service-to-service communication. It provides a dedicated infrastructure layer that defines how one service communicates with another, ensuring all routes among services are explicitly defined. Apart from HTTP request routing, service mesh can be extended to other types of transports, such as messaging, files, and databases. It automatically detects and registers new instances of the service, so engineers can focus on business logic instead of network communication. Service mesh often uses the **Sidecar pattern** in which there is a proxy deployed alongside a backend service, and the proxy intercepts all inbound and outbound traffic for the service.

Sidecar pattern

The **Sidecar pattern** is an architectural design approach where a secondary service, known as a sidecar, is deployed alongside a primary service to extend its functions but to decouple from its code base. This sidecar typically runs in the same container or VM. The sidecar handles cross-cutting concerns, such as logging, monitoring, security, and communication. This pattern enhances the resilience and maintainability of services, but without coupling with them, and thus facilitates more efficient management of complex applications.

Network segmentation is another technique that divides a network into smaller, manageable segments to limit access and reduce the risk of being attacked. This helps contain breaches and enhances overall security. It can be implemented by setting up **virtual local area networks (VLANs)** or sub-networks.

Antivirus and anti-malware solutions

Finally, antivirus and anti-malware solutions should be running in the infrastructure to scan, detect, and remove malicious software. They monitor running processes, scan stored files, and discover suspicious behaviors without manual intervention. These solutions are also automatically updated to stay with the latest threat definitions.

Most of the network security strategies involve infrastructure solutions that involve application-specific configurations. In the next section, we will cover DevSecOps in which application engineers are proactively involved.

DevSecOps

DevSecOps is a software development approach that integrates security best practices in the development process. It emphasizes that the responsibility of software security is shared among all members of the team, and security is an inseparable element in the development process.

There will still be security experts and potential security teams in an organization. They provide expertise, knowledge, tools, and guidance to development. DevSecOps embraces the following principles:

- **Shift left**: Security considerations are integrated early in the development process, as a part of the requirements. This enables the discovery, identification, and remediation of vulnerabilities before the application reaches production.

- **Compliance as code**: Include regulatory requirements in the code with automated tests to validate compliance continuously.

- **Collaboration and communication**: This encourages collaboration between development, security, and operations teams, fostering a culture of shared responsibility for software security.

- **Automation**: Automate security processes, such as code vulnerability scanning, as a part of the **continuous integration / continuous deployment (CI/CD)** pipeline to provide quick feedback on security issues, and to allow the team to address these issues early in the development process. For example, **OWASP Dependency-Check** is a static analysis tool that identifies known vulnerabilities in project dependencies. This tool integrates with build tools such as Maven, Gradle, and Jenkins.

- **Continuous monitoring**: Continuously monitor security threats, vulnerabilities, and unusual behaviors in applications and infrastructure while running in all environments.

- **Threat modeling**: Discover and identify potential threats and vulnerabilities during the early stage of development, enabling teams to proactively address security concerns.

Benefits of DevSecOps

By integrating security throughout the whole software development cycle, organizations can identify and mitigate vulnerabilities early. It reduces the risk of security breaches, the cost of fixing security issues, and the cost of remediation.

Automation integrated within a CI/CD pipeline and collaboration helps find vulnerabilities early in the process. It saves time in delivering secure applications and reduces the time to market.

Continuous monitoring and automated compliance checks help organizations meet regulatory requirements proactively and more effectively.

DevSecOps is a cultural and technical shift in how an organization approaches software development and security. The practices in the DevSecOps process foster a culture of delivering resilient applications and responding to threats effectively, leading to a more secure technical ecosystem.

A threat modeling exercise

We are going to run through an exercise of threat modeling (`https://owasp.org/www-project-threat-model/`) to demonstrate how everyone in the team is involved in this activity. Product managers, the security team, and the development team should be involved in all the steps.

Threat modeling starts with a business scenario. We are going to use the same real-life example throughout the book. This is a software system that allows households to exchange services with each other via an agreed contract. The goal of this threat modeling exercise is to identify potential security threats and vulnerabilities in the system.

Step 1 – visualize architecture and identify assets

The first step of threat modeling is to define the scope where threat modeling takes place. This includes architecture diagrams to demonstrate the following:

- Components inside the system
- Boundary of the system, entry points, and exit points
- Assets that require protection

There are a few choices of diagram format for this purpose, such as the **data flow diagram** (**DFD**) from structural analysis or container diagram (level 2) from the **C4 model**, as covered in *Chapter 1*. The container diagram for the system is shown in *Figure 14.8*:

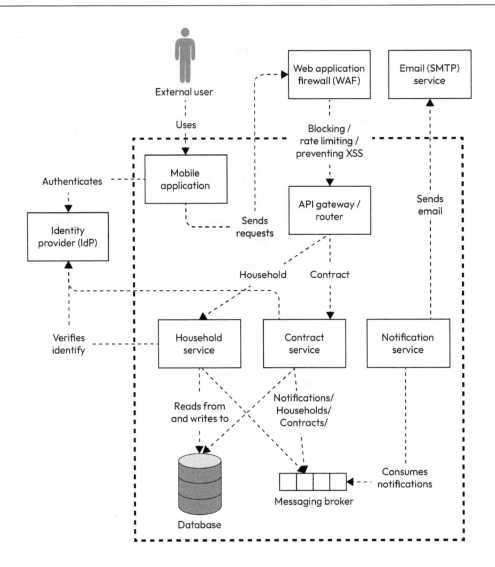

Figure 14.8 – Container diagram of the system from a real-life example for threat modeling

The dash-lined rectangle defines the boundary of the system and its internal network. We can assume the system runs in a cloud environment and it intends to use cloud-native services for cross-cutting functions. There are several components in this diagram:

- **Mobile application**: A user interface on mobile devices for households.

- **WAF**: A cloud-based firewall middleware that blocks malicious IP addresses, limits the number of incoming requests, and prevents **XSS**.

- **API gateway/router**: A cloud-based middleware that routes requests from mobile applications to the appropriate services.

- **Household service**: A backend service responsible for CRUD operations of household records.

- **Contract service**: A backend service responsible for managing the life cycle of a contract from drafted to exercised.

- **Notification service**: A backend service responsible for sending notifications to external users via emails.

- **Email service**: A cloud-based middleware that delivers email content to given addresses.

- **IdP**: A cloud-based middleware that verifies a user's identity using MFA from the mobile application and confirms if a bearer token is valid. Used by the household service and contract service.

- **Database**: A cloud-based database to allow applications to read data from and write data to. Used by the household service and contract service.

- **Messaging broker**: A cloud-based middleware that receives household updates, contract updates, and notification requests. It allows interested services to consume the messages for further processing. For instance, the notification service consumes notification messages and converts them to email requests to the email service.

From the architecture diagram, we have identified the entry points in the system. Requests come in from the mobile application, they pass through the WAF, and then they are routed to the corresponding services.

We have also identified two exit points in the system:

- Backend services request the IdP to verify an access token

- The notification service requests the email service to send an email

In addition, we have identified the following assets:

- **Household data**: Contain PIIs such as addresses and names

- **Contract data**: Private information only available between two involved households

- **Notification request**: Contain email content and email addresses (PIIs)

- **Application code**: Source code of all backend services and the mobile application

- **Infrastructure**: Servers, databases, network components, infrastructure configurations as code

With the architecture diagrams, entry points, exit points, and identified assets, the team can now examine the information and discover threats and vulnerabilities in the system.

Step 2 – identify threats

The team applies the **STRIDE** framework to categorize potential threats based on the identified assets. STRIDE is a combination of the first letters of the following six aspects:

- **Spoofing**: Unauthorized users may impersonate legitimate users

- **Tampering**: Malicious modification of household or contract data in transit

- **Repudiation**: Household users may deny agreeing to a contract with another household

- **Information disclosure**: PII, such as names, addresses, and email addresses, are exposed through vulnerabilities

- **Denial of service**: Attackers may overwhelm and exhaust the system with traffic

- **Elevation of privilege**: Users gaining access to unauthorized functions

After threats are identified, the team needs to assess the risks and determine how to respond to them.

Step 3 – assess risks and determine responses

Risks can be assessed by two factors: likelihood and impact. These two factors are multiplied to derive the risk level and thus the priority of the responses.

A simple approach is to have three levels for each factor, and each level is associated with an integer. The multiplication of the integers is the risk level. An organization can customize the levels and integers as it sees fit. In this example, the integers are assigned to each level as follows:

- **Likelihood**: 1 – Unlikely, 2 – Possibly, 3 – Likely

- **Impact**: 1 – Low, 2 – Medium, 3 – High

The numeric values of these two factors constitute the risk assessment table, as shown in *Table 14.1*:

Threat	Likelihood	Impact	Risk level
Spoofing: User impersonation	2	3	6
Tampering: Malicious data modifications	2	3	6
Repudiation: Household denying actions	1	2	2
Information: PII disclosure	2	3	6
Denial of service	2	2	4
Elevation of privilege: Unauthorized user actions	1	3	3

Table 14.1 – Example of risk assessment table

The risk levels are effectively the priority of security threats that the team needs to respond to and address, with the highest number being the highest priority, and the lowest number the lowest priority.

There are four general responses to a risk, and the team must choose one response for each security risk:

- **Mitigation**: Reduce the negative impact of the threat
- **Transfer**: Shift the risk to another party, typically by using third-party software
- **Avoidance**: Eliminate the risk by developing a new strategy or solution
- **Acceptance**: Accept and acknowledge the risk, but no further actions

For each threat identified by the STRIDE framework, a response should be outlined, as follows:

- **Spoofing – transfer**: Use the cloud-based IdP to implement MFA and to secure passwords
- **Tampering – avoidance**: Use HTTPS over TLS
- **Repudiation – mitigation**: Ensure sufficient audit trails and logging of all user actions related to household and contract records
- **Information disclosure – avoidance**: Use encrypted databases, encrypt sensitive data in messaging payload, integrate code vulnerability scanning in CI/CD pipelines, and conduct regular security audits
- **Denial of service – transfer**: Configure WAF to protect the network from DDoS attacks
- **Elevation of privilege – mitigation**: Periodically review access control settings and conduct security training with internal users

At this point, the architecture has been discussed from a security perspective. Threats are identified and their risk levels are determined. Each risk has been responded to. There are only a few steps to complete one round of threat modeling, which are covered in the next step.

Step 4 – document, review, and update

After conducting all the activities in the previous steps, it is paramount to have them all documented, preferably as a single page with rough dates when the threat was modeled. The documentation serves as a record of learning as a team and as a checklist of follow-up actions.

The security team should review the documentation and advise if there are any additional topics to discuss. Otherwise, the security team should sign off on the threat modeling document as a reviewer.

The team should convert the risk responses into work items in the backlog to ensure that the decided actions are executed.

The team should also periodically review this document and decide whether there should be another round of threat modeling. Alternatively, if there is an important feature change or an architecture change, then the team should consider whether there is a need to update the threat model.

Threat modeling is a tool and process used to help the team deliver secure software at the beginning of development. It benefits engineers, security team, product managers, and customers by having secure software products that are developed efficiently by addressing security issues early.

Summary

We discussed the importance of security in software architecture, and how sensitive information is categorized. Afterward, we covered the CIA triad for the security principles of confidentiality, integrity, and availability.

We covered authentication with the spotlight on how TLS works and how it prevents cyberattacks such as MitM eavesdropping. We delved into the details of how MFA works and its implications for software architecture.

Then, we moved on to the topic of authorization, and we covered the four major access control methods (role-based, policy-based, attribute-based, and ACLs). We discussed how authorization has impacted software architecture.

We mentioned the basic practices in handling sensitive data, including data classification, and protecting data in transit and in rest. A few approaches are highlighted on how Kotlin engineers can avoid accidentally logging sensitive data. A couple of strategies for anonymizing data are included in this chapter.

We briefly mentioned the principles of DevSecOps and its benefits to the software development cycle by having security integrated into the development process.

Finally, we ran through a threat modeling exercise with the real-life example system. We visited the details of each step, emphasized how to conclude a cycle, and when the threat model should be re-visited.

There are still some aspects of engineering that go beyond just architecture. We will cover a few miscellaneous topics that are specific to Kotlin engineers in the next and last chapters. We hope you will find them useful in supporting better software architecture.

15

Beyond Architecture

In this chapter, we are going to go through a few topics that will help engineers build better software. Some of the topics may not be related to software architecture, but consideration of their usage will support and enhance better architectures.

After reading this chapter, engineers should be equipped with a few tricks up their sleeves to boost their productivity and remove impediments when implementing software with a certain architecture style in mind. These tools are Kotlin-related if implemented in code; otherwise, some of them are general engineering utilities.

Hopefully, the conceptual understanding of all the architectural topics in previous chapters can be translated into practical and pragmatic solutions, with the aid of the toolkit in this chapter.

We are going to cover the following topics in this chapter:

- Powered by Kotlin
- Transitioning from Java
- Continuous integration and delivery
- Developer experience matters
- Final thoughts on software architecture

Technical requirements

You can find all the code files used in this chapter on GitHub: `https://github.com/PacktPublishing/Software-Architecture-with-Kotlin/tree/main/chapter-15`

Powered by Kotlin

Kotlin as a programming language has provided a lot of syntactic support for engineers to concisely express the intent of their code. Moreover, some of the features allow engineers to separate concerns and organize the code to be more manageable.

Extension functions

Kotlin extension functions allow adding extra functionalities to an existing class without modifying its source code. This feature is useful and even mandatory for the following use cases:

- Add more functions to a class from an external library, or a final class. For example, we want to extract the first letter of each word and join them by a dot, so Sam Payne would become S.P. The Kotlin String does not provide a function for this, so we can write an extension function instead:

```
fun String.getFirstLetters(): String =
    split(" ").joinToString(".") {
        it.first().toString()
    }
```

- Enhance a class to fit in certain Kotlin language features, such as operator override (+, -, in, etc.). The use of operator override will be discussed in detail in coming sections.

- Add null safety functions to handle situations such as trying to concatenate a nullable list of strings. Having a nullable receiver as List<String>? in the extension function ensures that a string will be created, whether the list is null or not. The implementation is shown here:

```
fun List<String>?.concat(): String = this?.joinToString(",")?:
    ""
```

However, there is also a use case that would support better architecture. Extension functions can be used to separate concerns of a class by isolating its functions in a different package with non-public visibility.

For example, we have the Name data class from the previous example. This data class is a domain entity that needs to be converted to different formats, depending on the operation's context.

Given that an object of the Name class needs to be converted to a JSON string, there are a few common function signature styles:

- **As a member function**: A member function on the Name class has exposed the JSON representation of the object to all usages:

```
data class Name(val value: String) {
    fun toJson(): String = "{\"name\":\"$value\"}"
}
```

However, not all usages need this function. Business logic is unlikely to need the JSON representation of the object. This approach mixes up the concerns of business logic and external representation, and worse, this external representation does not apply to all situations either.

- **As a vanilla function**: As a vanilla function, the `toJson` is now public to all projects that have access to the `Name` class:

```
fun toJson(name: Name): String = "{\"name\":\"${name.value}\"}"
```

It is functionally equivalent to the **non-local extension function** implementation; the difference is that the extension function moves the parameter to the function receiver:

```
fun Name.toJson(): String = "{\"name\":\"$value\"}"
```

The vanilla function implementation creates noise when an engineer searches for functions whose names start with `to`, especially in an IDE and if all data classes have separate `toJson` functions. This phenomenon is called **scope pollution** as we expose functions more than necessary. A quick workaround to this is to have a class or a singleton Kotlin object with a member function for this:

```
object NameJsonConverter {
    fun toJson(name: Name): String = "{\"name\":\"${name.value}\"}"
}
```

However, if the JSON transformation is only required for external integration, then it may be possible to locate the transformation functions together with the external integration code, and the function can be private as a **local extension function**:

```
private fun Name.toJson(): String = "{\"name\":\"$value\"}"
```

This approach allows engineers to extend the functionality of a class while restricting the usage only under the context that is within the same file. In other words, different concerns around an entity can be separated by having local extension functions grouped by files in the source base.

This is nothing new, as a private visibility modifier to a function does exactly that. Nonetheless, the ability to put the data class as the receiver of a function and extend its behaviors brings several benefits:

- One fewer parameter in the list

- Focus on the entity as it becomes the receiver

- Call the function as if it were a member of the class

- No need for inheritance

- Fluent call chaining with other functions that are either member functions or extension functions

Kotlin extension functions enhance the flexibility and readability of your code, by allowing engineers to add new functionalities to existing classes in a modular way. Meanwhile, there is a way to restrict the usage to avoid scope pollution and to separate concerns. After all, Kotlin extension functions promote better coding practices and make code easier to understand and maintain.

Infix modifier

A Kotlin infix modifier is another way to create more readable and expressive code. We discussed **behavior-driven development (BDD)** in *Chapter 13* on the Gherkin language. A Kotlin infix modifier enables writing test scenarios in Kotlin that deceptively look like Gherkin. For example, we define an empty singleton Kotlin object as When here:

```
object When
```

Let us define a PreCondition class and an Action class related to integer (Int) as follows:

```
typealias PreCondition = () -> Int
typealias Action = (Int) -> Int
```

Type aliases in Kotlin allow engineers to create a new name for an existing type. They also allow engineers to quickly map a name to a function type. The type alias for a function type is especially beneficial in declaring interfaces of a single function, which helps engineers implement code that conforms to the **single-responsibility principle (SRP)**, as discussed in *Chapter 2*.

It may still seem puzzling how they can look like Gherkin language for the BDD test scenario at this point. When we add infix functions, the code will start to support natural language:

```
infix fun When.number(n: Int): PreCondition = { n }
infix fun PreCondition.then(action: Action): Int = action(this())
```

PreCondition here is used as a return type and the receiver of another function. We need an implementation of Action and a function to verify the result to complete a simple test scenario:

```
object Square: Action {
    override fun invoke(p1: Int): Int = p1 * p1
}
infix fun Int.shouldBe(expected: Int) {
    require(this == expected) {
        "Expected: $expected but was $this"
    }
}
```

Putting them all together, we can produce a test scenario like this:

```
((When.number(2)).then(Square)).shouldBe(5)
```

When running this line, it should throw an exception with the following message:

```
Expected: 5 but was 4
```

The exciting part of this example is that the infix feature from Kotlin lets us omit the dots for function invocation and the brackets for the single parameter for each infix function. So, the code becomes remarkably close to natural language and the Gherkin language syntax:

```
When number 2 then Square shouldBe 5
```

Of course, it would take a long time to have a fully-fledged Gherkin-style code for BDD test scenarios from this point beyond. However, this example has demonstrated how Kotlin infix functions can make the code readable and expressive.

There are some ground rules for having an infix function in Kotlin to follow:

- It is either a member function of a class or an extension function with a receiver
- There can only be one parameter

Infix functions are usually used in building intuitive and readable **domain-specific languages** (DSLs). They are used a lot in chaining operations, such as the example we have just demonstrated.

Operator override

The operator override is another way to make your code readable and intuitive. It allows engineers to define custom behaviors for operators such as +, -, and so on. The syntax was already shown previously when we discussed extension functions:

```
data class Name(val value: String)
operator fun Name.plus(other: Name): Name =
    Name("$value ${other.value}")
fun main() { println(Name("Sam") + Name("Payne")) }
```

The `operator` modifier before the `fun` keyword indicates the intention to override a built-in operator. The return type needs to be the same as the receiver or the belonging class. All operators that can be overridden are listed in *Table 15.1*:

Operator	Function name	Example
+	plus	a + b
+	unaryPlus	+a
-	minus	a - b
-	unaryMinus	-a
*	times	a * b
/	div	a / b
%	rem	a % b
==	equals	a == b
!=	notEquals	a != b
>	compareTo	a > b
[]	get	val value = a[key]
[]	set	a[key] = value
+	unaryPlus	+a
()	invoke	a()

Table 15.1 – Kotlin operators that can be overridden

It is important that operators are overridden with compatible semantics. For example, the + operator should create a new instance of the type with the two objects of the same type combined. If the `plus` function has side effects such as updating the value of an existing object, then it is not appropriate to override the operator.

Scoping functions

Scoping functions in Kotlin execute a block of code within the context of an object. A scope starts with an opening curly bracket, {, and ends with a closing curly bracket, }, which is already natural to programming languages. We already have class scopes, function scopes, and lambda scopes, all of which use curly brackets to indicate the boundaries. Also, the inner scopes have visibility and access to the declared values and functions from the enclosing scopes. For example, a member function has access to other functions from its encompassing class.

Built-in scoping functions

Scoping functions in Kotlin provide another means to have a confined scope that focuses on a context object. There are five scoping functions provided, as shown in *Figure 15.1*:

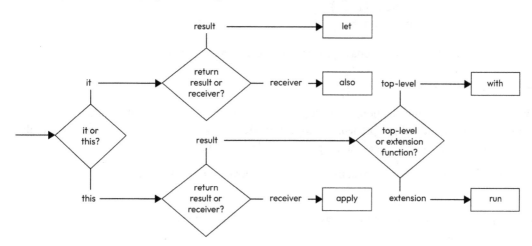

Figure 15.1 – Kotlin built-in scoping functions

Each of the five scoping functions (let, apply, run, with, and also) has its own use case and behavior. There are two main differences among them. The first difference is whether the context object is it or this.

The following three statements return the same result of "35":

```
"3".let { it + "5" }
"3".run { this + "5" }
with("3") { this + "5" }
```

The let function uses it as the context object, while run and with use this as the context object.

It is also noticeable that run and with are functionally equivalent, but the syntax is different. The run function is an extension function, while with is a top-level function. Engineers can make use of the difference to communicate the intent of the usage. Typically, the context object is the focus of the operation when using the run function. If another object is the focus of the operation, the with function can be used instead.

The second difference is whether the result of the lambda or the receiver is returned. This is like a peeking function where engineers want to insert an extra operation but do not want to alter the result. The following two statements return the same result of " 3 ":

```
"3".also { println(it) }
"3".apply { println(this) }
```

Any output evaluated in the lambda expressions is not used as return values.

Custom scoping functions

Writing your own scoping functions can bring powerful features to your system. It is particularly useful in building up a result within a predefined scope. It is often that a system is required to perform a full validation on an incoming request and report all validation failures in the response.

We need a builder class that can accumulate validation errors, as shown here:

```
class ValidationBuilder {
    private val failures = mutableListOf<String>()
    fun evaluate(
        result: Boolean,
        failureMessage: () -> String
    ) {
        if (!result) failures.add(failureMessage())
    }
    fun getErrors() = failures.toList()
}
```

The ValidationBuilder class uses a mutable list of String to collect all validation errors found in the process. Then, we can define a custom scoping function that defines the start and the end of the validation, and validation is performed within the scope:

```
fun <T> T.validate(
    build: ValidationBuilder.(T) -> Unit
): List<String> =
    ValidationBuilder()
        .also { builder -> builder.build(this) }
        .getErrors()
```

This scoping function is an extension function using a generic type as the receiver, so the validate function can be invoked on any object. It takes a lambda expression as a parameter, in which an instance of ValidationBuilder is passed as a context object identified by this. At the end of the validate function, all errors collected are returned as an immutable List.

An example usage can look like this:

```
fun main() {
    val failures = "Some very%long nickname".validate {
        evaluate(it.length < 20) { "Must be under 20 characters:
\"$it\"" }
        evaluate(it.contains("%").not()) { "Must not contains %
character"}
    }
    println("failures: $failures")
}
```

This is a simple validation on a `String` object with two rules:

- Must be less than 20 characters

- Must not contain the percent sign, %

The validation starts with the `String` object with the `validate` extension function. Inside the lambda scope, the `evaluate` function is called twice with the evaluations and the error messages. `ValidationBuilder` collects error messages if the evaluation has failed. A list of validation errors is returned and printed to the console. The console should have the following output:

```
failures: [Must be under 20 characters: "Some very%long nickname",
Must not contains % character]
```

The output has shown how full validation can be performed on a string with the custom scoping function.

Custom scoping functions are also popular with complex object building, such as a large domain object. In fact, it is used in the popular framework **Ktor** to build the server-side routing configuration:

```
routing {
    route("/hello", HttpMethod.Get) {
        handle {
            call.respondText("Hello")
        }
    }
}
```

We have demonstrated the use of a custom scoping function to perform full validation and collect all validation errors. Custom scoping functions are particularly useful in collecting elements within the scope, with the builder passed in as a context object.

We are going to cover the topic of transitioning from Java to Kotlin in the next section.

Transitioning from Java

Kotlin as a programming language was developed by JetBrains, a software company known for software development tools such as IntelliJ IDEA. The project started in 2010 and it aimed to create a language that is compatible with Java but with improvements over some of the drawbacks of Java. The name *Kotlin* comes from Kotlin Island in the Baltic Sea near St. Petersburg, Russia.

Kotlin 1.0 was released in July 2011 with features such as null safety, static typing, and type inference. It started to gain popularity in 2016 when it introduced features such as 100% Java interoperability, extension functions, lambda expressions, and higher-order functions.

In 2017, Google announced official support for Kotlin on Android. Google's collaboration with JetBrains on Kotlin supporting Android has made Kotlin a popular choice for Android developers. In 2018, JetBrains introduced Kotlin Multiplatform, which enables Kotlin code to be translated and compiled to run in Android, iOS, and web applications. Around the same time, Kotlin for backend services gained more and more attention from backend engineers, especially those with a Java background.

The 100% Java interoperability has enabled many Java engineers to smoothly transition to writing Kotlin code for commercial applications. There are a few tools and tips that we are going to share with you.

The IntelliJ IDEs from JetBrains have provided a tool to convert a Java file code to a Kotlin file code. It might sound magical, but the reality is that there are still a couple more adjustments needed to be truly idiomatic Kotlin.

Enabling Kotlin in a Java project

Given that there is a Java project already, we need to set up the project to compile Kotlin source code.

If the project uses Gradle, adding a Kotlin plugin is sufficient, such as the following code with Gradle Kotlin DSL:

```
plugins {
    kotlin("jvm") version "2.0.20"
}
```

This is the equivalent of the setting with Gradle Groovy:

```
plugins {
    id 'org.jetbrains.kotlin.jvm' version '2.0.20'
}
```

Projects using Maven would require the following changes in pom.xml:

```
<properties>
    <kotlin.version>2.0.20</kotlin.version>
</properties>
```

```
<plugins>
    <plugin>
        <artifactId>kotlin-maven-plugin</artifactId>
        <groupId>org.jetbrains.kotlin</groupId>
        <version>2.0.20</version>
    </plugin>
</plugins>
```

The preceding configuration defines the Kotlin version as 2.0.20. Also, it imports a plugin that enables the compilation of Kotlin source code.

Converting Java files and moving them to Kotlin folders

Kotlin files can be located under the src/main/java and src/test/java folders, but it is recommended to have them stored under src/main/kotlin and src/test/kotlin, respectively.

Let us convert the following Java class to Kotlin, using IntelliJ's conversion tool:

```
public class Household {
    private final String name;
    private final List<String> members = new ArrayList<>();
    public Household(String name, List<String> members) {
        this.name = name;
        this.members.addAll(members);
    }
    public String getName() {
        return name;
    }
    public List<String> getMembers() {
        return new ArrayList(members);
    }
}
```

This Java class is immutable, so all fields are private, and the list is not exposed in the getter for immutability. As you convert the Java file using the conversion tool, IntelliJ reminds you that some corrections still need to be made.

This is the Kotlin class after conversion by the tool (in IntelliJ, right-click the Java file and choose **Convert Java File to Kotlin File**):

```
class Household(val name: String, members: List<String?>) {
    private val members: MutableList<String?> = ArrayList()
    init {
        this.members.addAll(members)
    }
```

```
    fun getMembers(): List<String?> {
        return ArrayList<Any?>(members)
    }
}
```

There are some immediate changes to be made to become an idiomatic Kotiln class:

1. Update to a Kotlin data class since this class is intended to be an entity class.

2. Replace the `init` block with a constructor as much as possible. Only true initialization logic should remain in the `init` block.

3. Use Kotlin's immutable `List` interface as a member field. The same should apply to other `Collection` interfaces. Using Kotlin's collection interfaces closes off the risks of the collection being mutated.

4. Remove the `getMembers` getter function as there is no need to return a new copy of the list due to the immutable `List` interface.

5. Remove the nullable symbol (`?`) unless there is a reason to expect nullable values. This is an opportunity for engineers to eliminate null checks that become unnecessary after converting to Kotlin.

This is the result of the conversion, which started with the tool and ended with some manual corrections:

```
data class Household(val name: String, val members: List<String>)
```

If the Java entity class was using an external library such as Lombok (`https://projectlombok.org/`) to auto-generate setter and getter functions, then we would need to remove the Lombok annotations, too.

Java 14 has introduced a new feature called **record classes** that work like Kotlin data classes. An example of a Java record class is shown here:

```
public record Account(String number, String holderName) {}
```

Converting it to Kotlin is relatively straightforward, but there is a JvmRecord annotation that remains:

```
@JvmRecord
data class Account(val number: String, val holderName: String)
```

The annotation is only there to preserve some of the function names such as `account.getNumber()` for backward compatibility reasons. If this is not a concern, we can remove this annotation and let users of this class use `account.number` instead.

Idiomatic expressions, code styling, and conventions

Converting a Java file to a Kotlin file is a great opportunity for engineers to start adopting Kotlin's idiomatic expressions and conventions. It is highly recommended that the engineers pick a lint tool to unify the Kotlin style from the beginning:

- Ktlint (`https://github.com/pinterest/ktlint`)
- KtFmtFormat (`https://github.com/facebook/ktfmt`)
- Detekt (`https://github.com/detekt/detekt`) – also a static code analysis tool
- Spotless (`https://github.com/diffplug/spotless`) – also supports other languages

Picking the "best" code style is the least concern to engineering quality, but having a unified style is important for the team to focus on more important aspects such as correctness and responsiveness.

Sequence of conversion

Given an existing Java project, it is also recommended to convert Java classes in the following sequence:

1. Test classes as these represent the lowest risk. This is a safe space for engineers to learn Kotlin and make mistakes with a low impact.
2. Top-level classes that no other classes depend on.
3. If the application uses layered architectures, as covered in *Chapter 7*, classes in the outer layers (i.e., adapters, imperative shells, frameworks, and drivers) should be converted first, then go inward until reaching the code. The Kotlin interoperability with Java is smoother when Kotlin code calls Java code than vice versa.

During the conversion, engineers often start looking to replace frameworks in Java with equivalent libraries in Kotlin; we are going to discuss these in the next section.

Framework replacement

During the conversion journey, it is inevitable that someone will bring up the discussion of whether a Java library should be replaced by another library that supports native Kotlin. We discussed the paradox of new frameworks in *Chapter 1*, and on the specific topic of conversion from Java to Kotlin, there are a few things we should keep in mind:

- Everything still works! It seems obvious but the team could choose not to replace any existing framework, due to the 100% Java interoperability.

- This is likely a one-way trip. The new Kotlin library may not aim to support Java projects, except those libraries that already existed before Kotlin became popular. If the project still uses Java but needs to use the new Kotlin library with Java, the usage may be awkward.

- There are multiple Kotlin libraries that the open source community has contributed to provide a Kotlin-first library experience. Some of them look similar in terms of approaches, activities, and number of contributors. The team may fall into the paralysis of analysis, not knowing which one to use. This is more of a general open source framework adoption concern, but it affects transitioning from Java to Kotlin.

- It is not uncommon for contributors to stop some of the efforts for Kotlin-first newer frameworks. It is a natural evolution where some of the ideas have turned out to be not so viable or feasible. The team can always wait till the Kotlin-first library matures. Again, this is a concern for open source projects in general.

- Some of the existing Java frameworks have Kotlin support as an extra dependency to help engineers with the transition. The Kotlin module may just be enough and there is no need to phase out the framework altogether.

- Kotlin-first frameworks developed by popular communities or reputable organizations supporting Kotlin are likely to have stronger support and continuity.

Despite the numerous factors for framework replacement, there are a few Kotlin-first frameworks that are worth a look:

- **Client and server frameworks**:

  - Spring: `https://spring.io/`

  - Ktor: `https://ktor.io/`

  - Http4K: `https://www.http4k.org/`

  - Micronaut: `https://micronaut.io/`

  - Vert.x: `https://github.com/vert-x3/vertx-lang-kotlin`

  - Retrofit: `https://square.github.io/retrofit/`

- **Language enhancement frameworks**:

  - Arrow: `https://arrow-kt.io/`

  - Result4K: `https://github.com/npryce/result4k`

  - Coroutines: `https://github.com/Kotlin/kotlinx.coroutines`

- **Dependency injection frameworks**:

  - Koin: `https://insert-koin.io/`

- **Persistence frameworks**:

  - Exposed: `https://github.com/JetBrains/Exposed`

- **Testing frameworks**:

  - Kotest: `https://kotest.io/`

  - Spek: `https://www.spekframework.org/`

  - Mockk: `https://mockk.io/`

- **UI frameworks**:

  - Jetpack: `https://developer.android.com/jetpack`

  - Compose Multiplatform: `https://github.com/JetBrains/compose-multiplatform`

Continuous transition

One of the challenges of transitioning to Kotlin is the combination with other changes, driven by business or technical stakeholders.

It is important that the transition to Kotlin takes place incrementally and continuously. For example, a new business feature can be written in Kotlin entirely, with some usage of existing Java classes.

Engineers can also phase in Kotlin converted code when there is sufficient time and space, even during the development of other changes. The team can adopt a policy that, if a Java class needs to be updated, it is also converted to Kotlin. This policy adds a small overhead to each change, but it keeps the transition going without the need to halt.

Keeping risks manageable is the key to transitioning a Java project to Kotlin.

The future of Kotlin

Kotlin has grown out from being a better Java. Especially with Kotlin Multiplatform, Kotlin has become one of the most versatile programming languages in the market, as it can be used to write Android, iOS, desktop, web, data science, and backend applications. With the recent Kotlin V2 release, Kotlin continues to grow in popularity and usage. Engineers should keep an eye on Kotlin's emerging trends (e.g., Kotlin Multiplatform, Kotlin Native, and cloud integration) and embrace its exciting upcoming progression.

Next, we will discuss continuous integration and delivery.

Continuous integration and delivery

Continuous integration (**CI**) and **continuous delivery** (**CD**) play a crucial role in software development productivity. They are collectively named **CI/CD** in many discussions due to their close relationship.

When we discussed the cost of finding and fixing an issue with an application in *Chapter 13*, we mentioned that the cost to fix an issue is lower if it is found earlier in the development process. In a typical environment in which a team of engineers work collaboratively on a source repository, it is also less expensive to fix an issue that is caused by code conflicts from this collaboration.

CI is a software development practice in which engineers frequently integrate their changes into a shared source repository. The primary goal of CI is to detect integration issues early and reduce the time it takes to release new features or fixes. The practice of CI includes the following:

- **Frequent commits**: Changes are frequently committed by multiple engineers in a team. Each engineer also frequently updates their local source project to receive changes from other team members. The commits are as frequent as multiple times a day.

- **Automated project builds**: Each commit integrates with the source repository and triggers an automated build to compile all source code.

- **Automated testing and feedback**: Each commit also triggers an automated test suite that includes a diverse variety of tests and quality assurance metrics, as discussed in *Chapters 12, 13*, and *14*:

  - Unit tests

  - Component tests

  - Integration tests

  - Automated GUI testing

  - End-to-end testing

  - Performance testing

  - Code vulnerability scanning

  - Code style linting

  - Static code analysis

  - Code coverage by tests

  These test checks are part of the project build after code compilation. If any of the preceding checks fails the verification, the project build will fail and engineers will be notified. Engineers will then troubleshoot and fix the issue based on the feedback.

- **Version control**: CI uses a version control system to manage the code base. It supports keeping a full history of commits with audit records. It allows engineers to branch from the main code repository and later merge the branch back to the main branch.

- **Integration with deployment**: CI is the first gate of quality that certifies whether an application is good enough for deployment. Once all checks and tests have passed, then the build process can continue the preparation for deployment.

By shortening the feedback loop of *code-integrate-test-fix*, the team can deliver new features and fixes more frequently, reduce the time to market, and respond to user feedback quickly. It also improves the collaboration within the team and improves overall software quality through automated testing for each integration.

There is, however, another significant factor that would affect software development productivity. Most engineers who work in a team would have discussed the topic of branching strategies under a version control system. There are two popular strategies that keep on recurring in this never-ending debate: feature-based and trunk-based development.

Feature-based development

Feature-based development can be characterized by its higher number and longer life of branches. Engineers can work in on their own branch in isolation. Each branch contains a big chunk of cohesive work, such as a feature or a release, and therefore, it lasts for a long period to gather all the changes required. At the same time, there are other long-lived branches that represent other features. An example of feature-based development is shown in *Figure 15.2*:

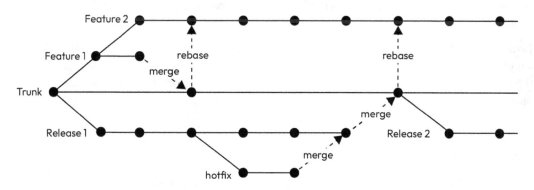

Figure 15.2 – An example of feature-based development

In this example, **Trunk** is the main branch that absorbs all changes from other branches. **Feature 1** branches out from **Trunk** and development continues in this feature branch. At the same time, the team needs to prepare a new release, so the **Release 1** branch is created from **Trunk**. The release branch is deployed to the UAT environment for acceptance testing as a release candidate.

After a few commits in the **Feature 1** branch, **Feature 2** needs to start development and it needs to make some changes from the **Feature 1** branch, so **Feature 2** branches out from the **Feature 1** branch, and the development of **Feature 2** continues in the new branch. **Feature 1** development is completed, so, a pull request is created for review, and subsequently, the branch is merged into **Trunk**.

Engineers working on **Feature 2** want to keep its branch up to date, so they rebase the **Feature 2** branch from the latest **Trunk**. The **Release 1** branch does not need to rebase because **Feature 1** is not included in the coming release.

The **Release 1** branch has been deployed to production. There are a couple of bugs found after the production release, and unfortunately, one of them is a critical bug. So the **Release 1** branch cannot be merged into **Trunk** yet. While some engineers work on the lower priority fixes in the **Release 1** branch, a few engineers need to work on a hotfix immediately and fix the critical bug in the production environment. So, a hotfix branch is created for the critical bug fix.

The critical bug fix has been completed, deployed, and verified in UAT. So, it is released to the production environment. The hotfix branch is then merged into the **Release 1** branch. Afterward, all production bug fixes are completed, deployed, and verified in UAT. So, there is another production release to wrap up this release. The **Release 1** branch is then merged into **Trunk**.

The **Feature 2** branch is not completed yet, so it needs to be rebased from **Trunk**. At the same time, engineers start to prepare a new release by creating a new release branch from **Trunk**.

Feature-based development isolates branches and keeps them focused on their purposes. The **Release 1** branch in the example has naturally prevented **Feature 1** from affecting the release. Also, the hotfix branch gives engineers a stable and safe space to concentrate on fixing the critical production bug, knowing that the critical fix can be patched as a priority without needing to consider other unrelated changes. Feature-based development uses pull requests that encourage code review and collaboration among engineers.

However, numerous long-lived branches bring the overhead of branch management. It introduces a high complexity of conflicts when merging or rebasing branches. This is particularly bad when there is substantial refactoring such as moving a file to another folder in one branch while the file is updated in another branch. This type of tree conflict often results in complex, time-consuming, and error-prone code merges. The mitigation of this issue is to rebase long-living branches frequently.

Trunk-based development

Trunk-based development encourages engineers to work on a single branch, which is *Trunk* (also known as **main**). However, each commit to the *Trunk* branch is done by merging from short-lived branches as pull requests.

It advocates small, frequent, and incremental changes to be committed to *Trunk* frequently. Each branch is short-lived and usually does not last more than a few days. There are frequent rebase or merge operations for each branch to get the latest changes from *Trunk*. An example of trunk-based development is illustrated in *Figure 15.3*:

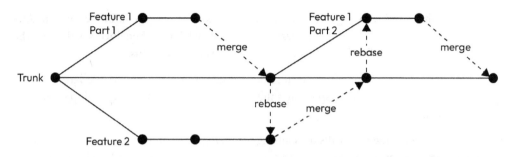

Figure 15.3 – An example of trunk-based development

In this example, the **Feature 1** branch is created from **Trunk** for development. The **Feature 2** branch is also created from **Trunk** for development.

The **Feature 1** branch has developed the code to a milestone where it is tested, verified, and releasable, but the feature itself is not completed. So, a pull request for **Feature 1** is created for review, and subsequently, the branch is merged into **Trunk**.

Feature 1 development needs to continue. So, a new branch is created from **Trunk** for the continuation of the **Feature 1** development.

At the same time, the **Feature 2** branch has detected a commit made in **Trunk**, so the corresponding engineer rebases the branch from **Trunk** to get the latest code.

Afterward, the development of **Feature 2** is completed, tested, and verified in its branch. So, a pull request is created for **Feature 2** for review. The branch is then approved and merged into **Trunk**.

The **Feature 1** branch has detected a commit made in **Trunk**, so the corresponding engineer rebases the branch from **Trunk** to get the latest code.

Trunk-based development emphasizes that the *Trunk* branch should also be good enough for a release at any time. There is no concept of a release branch. That is why all branches should be tested, verified, and reviewed by peers before merging.

To extend this concept, each commit can trigger a software release to environments, even to production. This approach fits very well with the practice of CD, where software is frequently delivered to customers, vastly reducing the time to market. It also implies that automated tests should be more rigorous and thorough in the branch to assure software quality in the early stages of development.

Trunk-based development also fits well with rapid development and short iterations that are advocated in Agile development methodologies. The quick turnarounds and short feedback loop enable the team to evolve the software product faster.

The frequent commits and rebasing also reduce the complexity of merge conflict resolution. Any integration issue can be identified and fixed early, so the feedback loop for engineers is shorter. The branch management is simplified because the *Trunk* branch is the only focus.

Having a long-living branch is an anti-pattern under trunk-based development. For larger feature development, the changes need to be split into multiple branches, and therefore, multiple commits to the *Trunk* branch.

Engineers need to make judgment calls on splitting the changes sensibly. It requires more thought and discipline from engineers to make sure each commit to *Trunk* is safe and can be released. **Feature flagging** is a common technique in hiding features in development and still allows code to be released to production. Feature flagging will be covered in the next section.

It is not uncommon for an engineer to have added changes that are not ready for production by mistake, despite the changes having been merged into *Trunk*. To make matters worse, there are other changes committed afterward. At this moment, *Trunk* is not ready for release. This situation leaves engineers with a few difficult choices:

- **Roll back**: Reverse all the commits to where *Trunk* is still safe for release. That would generate one more commit to *Trunk* for reversion. Re-apply the other required changes from new branches after the reversion.

- **Cherry-picking**: Create a new branch from the latest *Trunk* and carefully unpick the unwanted changes. Merges this branch back to *Trunk*.

- **Roll forward**: Create a new branch from the latest *Trunk* and continue to work on the change with a focus on making *Trunk* ready for release again. Merge this branch back to *Trunk*.

All the preceding choices require careful execution by engineers and none of them are easy. Many engineers would prefer rolling forward to keep the flow of development going at the cost of leaving some commits in *Trunk* unfit for release.

Comparison between feature-based and trunk-based development

The choice between feature-based and trunk-based is highly related to ways of working in the team and in the organization. This is an example of where **Conway's Law** applies, as covered in *Chapter 1*, where organization structure affects the software development process.

Feature-based development	Trunk-based development
Long-lived branches	Short-lived branches
Dedicated branches for release	*Trunk* is the branch for release
Large features developed in long-lived branches	Large features are split into multiple short-lived branches
High complexity in merge and rebase operations	Low complexity in merge and rebase operations
Slower feedback for integration issues	Faster feedback for integration issues
Development in isolation	Development with collaboration
Roll back is more common	Roll forward is more common
A hotfix branch for urgent issues	No concept of hotfix branches
The release branch is stable	Complex operations to fix unreleasable commits in the trunk
Release is less frequent	Release can be more frequent

Table 15.2 – Comparison between feature-based and trunk-based development

Both development approaches have their advantages and trade-offs. Ultimately, the choice depends on the team size, project complexity, and development practice. Some teams may adopt a hybrid approach to maximize the benefits of each approach and reduce the drawbacks.

For example, a team may decide to have trunk-based development but a release branch is created to aim for each release. It reduces the need to unpick unwanted changes for release and keeps release preparation away from the development of other ongoing features.

The preceding example can be seen as a release strategy; nonetheless, there are more release strategies that we want to cover, and we are going to cover them in the next section.

Release versus deployment versus launch

Once an application is ready for release, there is a new landscape of concerns and strategies on how it gets into the hands of customers and end users. At certain times in history, it was just a binary condition of whether it was out or not. Modern releases are more sophisticated and complicated.

Firstly, we need to make distinctions among three concepts: release, deployment, and launch. These concepts might be used interchangeably in some organizations; however, they have subtle differences that should be discussed.

Deployment is the least misunderstood concept. Deployment implies that the executable software artifact built from source code and configuration has been loaded to the target environment. This section focuses on the production environment. It is an operational and technical task that is often automated by scripts – optionally, with an approval process that involves human intervention.

Release means the application is now available to the users in the target environment. Sometimes, we might also say releasing a feature, which means the intent of making the feature available to users. Deployment is the prerequisite of release. A feature in an application, even if the application has been deployed, may still not be available to some users.

Launching an application is the least technically involved out of all three concepts. The term *launch* does not mean starting up an application. Instead, it implies the software product is marketed, advertised, and, optionally, has a launch event such as a press conference or an exhibition. Launching a software product is not part of the CI/CD life cycle. Releasing is the prerequisite of launching as users need to access the application. Launching would involve a go-to-market plan, with a variety of non-technical stakeholders involved (e.g., marketing, sales, customer services, etc.).

With these distinctions, release strategies of software products are where the complications are in relation to CD. We are going to cover a few common release strategies next.

Blue-green release

Blue-green release keeps the current version (*blue*) of an application in the production environment and has a new version (*green*) deployed to a replica of the production environment. This strategy allows the new version of the application to be deployed while keeping the current version available to users.

This strategy typically applies to server-side web-based applications and the **Domain Name System (DNS)** to route web requests to the new or current version of the application. The blue-green release strategy can be seen in *Figure 15.4*:

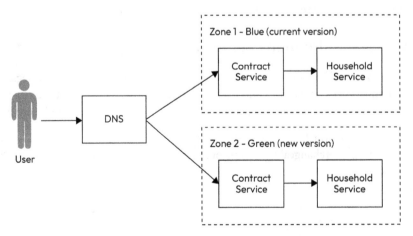

Figure 15.4 – An example of a blue-green release

The DNS, by default, routes web requests to **Zone 1 (Blue)** where the current versions of applications are running. The applications in the **Blue** zone communicate with each other only, by keeping them in the same **local area network (LAN)**.

While the **Blue** zone keeps the system available to users, engineers can deploy the new versions of applications to the **Green** zone, without the risk of causing an outage. Moreover, engineers and QAs can test and verify the new versions in the **Green** zone by using a specific domain name (e.g., `api.zone2.contract.system` in contrast to the general `api.contract.system`). Engineers can even troubleshoot and fix issues found in the new versions.

Once the new versions are verified and ready to be used by users, the traffic can be switched in the DNS, so web requests are routed to **Zone 2**. **Zone 2** is now the new **Blue** zone in effect. There is no more **Green** zone, as illustrated in *Figure 15.5*:

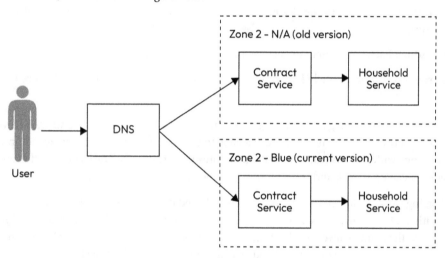

Figure 15.5 – A blue-green release (after switching)

Zone 1 is now running older versions of applications that can be shut down till the next deployment, which turns this zone into the new **Green** zone. It is important to note that **Blue/Green** is the role of the zone that is going to flip from one another over time.

A blue-green release is not the same as a rolling deployment. Rolling deployment aims to keep the service available while deployment is in progress. Rolling deployment usually takes the following steps:

1. Scale down the current number of application instances to one.

2. Deploy the new version of the application to the target number as new instances.

3. Start all instances of the new version.

4. Notify the load balancer of the existence of the new running instances, or let them be discovered.

5. Once all instances of the new version are confirmed to be running by the probe endpoints, shut down the older application instance.

Unlike the blue-green release, there is no time window in which engineers and QAs can test the newer version of the application without it being available to users. Additionally, this is a deployment technique only. It is not concerned with whether the application is available to users or not. It only cares whether the application has transitioned to the new version without outage or downtime.

Dark release/feature flagging

There are methods to verify new features without making them available to users. The new features can be deployed to the production environment normally but remain hidden from users, using **feature flagging** (also known as **dark release**).

The feature toggle can be managed in a few ways:

- **Central**: There is a central service or resource that dictates whether a feature is available to the given user

- **Individual**: Each component or service manages its own feature flags

- **Per request**: A non-publicly known request parameter is used to enable the feature to serve this request

Regardless of how feature flags are managed, this approach allows engineers and QAs to verify pre-released features before the features are available to users. The feature is only switched on when the team is happy with the verification results. In addition, the feature can be switched off even after it was made available to users, and thus it minimizes the impact of related issues.

Feature flagging works well with the practice of **trunk-based development**, as discussed in previous sections. With the feature flag switched off, engineers can continue to develop the feature and merge their changes to the trunk. However, all automated tests should pass to ensure that existing functions still work as intended with the unfinished and switched-off feature in the code base.

Feature flags mainly concern releases and making a feature available to users. Some organizations may extend feature flagging to support user segmentation and A/B testing, as mentioned in *Chapter 13*. This is not an anti-pattern, but only an enhancement of the system beyond feature flagging.

Canary release

A **canary release** is a staged release strategy that makes the newly deployed software available to a small subset of users before rolling it out to all target users. It operates at the application level, not a feature in an application. It aims for incremental availability to users, and there are a lot of variations in this strategy in the initial selection of users and strategic increase of availability. There are a few factors that would affect this strategy:

- The team might want to invite subject matter experts or domain experts to start using the application first, to gather feedback that might shape the product before the public uses it.

- The organization might want to initially release the software product to users in a selected geographic region. This could be due to the geographic context of the application, legal restrictions, or related marketing events. The organization might want to expand its geographic territory incrementally.

- The team might want to initially release the application to certain types of devices or operating systems of devices. This could be due to compatibility concerns, especially in the Android application landscape, or due to the popularity of certain devices in the market.

A canary release is sometimes mistaken for the concept of beta testing. After a software product is signed off by internal QAs, some organizations might want to invite expert users to internal testing. Testing internally, typically with **white-box testing** techniques, as discussed in *Chapter 13*, is called **alpha testing**. Testing by external users before public release is called **beta testing**.

However, beta testing is not considered a production release because the version of the software product being tested is usually not the final version. Beta testing is only for a limited period.

Feedback and suggestions from selected users are gathered to validate the product concepts, usability, and functionality. They are also used for further enhancement of the product. Releasing a non-final version of the software product for beta testing does not require a canary release strategy.

Choosing a release strategy

Choosing a release strategy is not easy or straightforward. However, it is certainly not recommended to do a Big Bang release with planned outages, as we discussed in *Chapter 6*. There are other factors involved in the decision, such as infrastructure readiness, marketing strategies, service uptime objectives, and so on. From a purely technical point of view, we can potentially use a decision tree to recommend a release strategy, as shown in *Figure 15.6*:

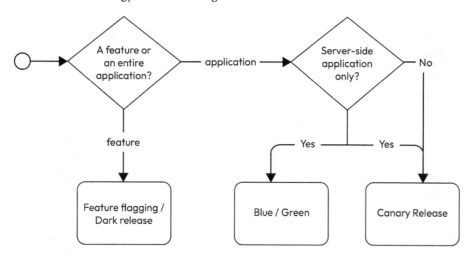

Figure 15.6 – An example of a technical decision tree of release strategies

Releasing a feature in an application should consider feature flagging or dark release first because it is the least expensive choice compared to others. If it is about releasing an entire application and it is a server-side application, a blue-green release or canary release can be considered. If the application involves desktop, mobile, or web applications, then a canary release should be considered.

Please note this is more about technical restrictions of which release strategies can be used, instead of considering which one provides the best outcome due to other non-technical factors involved.

We are at the end of the discussion on CI/CD. A well-automated CI/CD pipeline saves a lot of time for engineers in trying to integrate with other people's work and deliver the application to multiple environments. In a sense, it improves the experience of engineers working on software products. We are going to cover a bit more on the topic of the developer experience in the next section.

Developer experience

Developer experience (**DX**) is what engineers experience while developing software. It includes everything from tools, processes, environments, teams, organizations, and the culture of development. We will bring up a few suggestions for improving DX in the following sections.

Why does DX matter?

DX might, at first glance, look like the general satisfaction of any person working on a project. However, a great DX brings a lot of benefits to not only the engineers themselves but also to the software product and to the organization:

- **Productivity and efficiency**: Efficient tools, automated workflows, concise documentation, and smooth development processes remove the burden from engineers, so they can focus on coding and problem-solving.

- **Product quality**: Stable environments and intuitive tools reduce friction in the everyday work of engineers, so they can focus on delivering high-quality code with attention to detail.

- **Operation cost**: Automated tools and processes reduce the labor cost for engineers to support the system. Also, better tools lead to fewer mistakes and thus reduce the time and resources spent on fixing issues.

- **Learning curve**: Streamlined onboarding process, good documentation, and intuitive processes make it quicker for a new engineer to get up to speed and become productive.

- **Collaboration**: Good DX encourages communication and collaboration within the team and improves team morale. It also improves the interactions between engineers and stakeholders, which leads to better outcomes.

- **Innovation**: A safe and supportive environment fosters a culture of innovation and experimentation. Engineers can be creative in their solutions without the fear of failure. High-quality tools allow for trying new ideas collaboratively and learning collectively.

- **Job satisfaction and retention**: A satisfactory working environment keeps engineers more engaged and motivated. When they enjoy the work they do, employee turnover can be lowered. In return, it saves time and resources on recruitment and training.

- **Talent acquisition**: If an organization has a reputation for great DX among technology communities, it attracts top talent to join the team and improves the branding of the organization.

DX has an influential role in delivering high-quality software products, ultimately leading to more healthy organizations and better business outcomes. We are going to cover a few areas that can improve DX next.

Onboarding

Apart from the general onboarding, there should be comprehensive documentation for engineering topics, such as the following:

- Development processes (Kanban, Scrum, etc.)

- Tech stacks used in the organization

- In-house libraries and frameworks

- **Architecture decision records (ADRs)**, as mentioned in *Chapter 1*

- Engineering practices and conventions

- Specialized engineering environments set up (e.g., backend, frontend, data, platform, etc.)

These documents are best updated by each new engineer joining the organization, as it can keep the information up to date.

Having a technical peer assigned as an onboarding partner is a helpful welcoming gesture for new engineers. The onboarding partner can pair with the new engineer in setting up environments for work, requesting appropriate permissions, adding the new engineer to the corresponding communication channel, and answering questions.

Tools

Tools play a big part in an engineer's productivity. Investing in good engineering tools brings not only great DX but also tangible productivity to the engineering teams. These tools include, but are not limited to, the following:

- A **single sign-on (SSO)** portal to access all other third-party tools. Instead of having everyone remember passwords for each third-party tool, logging in to these tools via a central portal saves a lot of time. This applies to all tools beyond engineering tools.

- Streamlined method to log in to any environment or infrastructure without compromising security and auditing. Historically, engineers need to access a server using means such as the **Secure Shell** (**SSH**) protocol with a terminal tool. In modern days, there are better ways to access a server in any environment. These tools (such as Teleport, JumpCloud, CyberArk, etc.) support a simple request-approval workflow for access, wrapping around the terminal tool, establishing tunneling, restricting certain access, and logging all the activities during access to secure the environment.

- Each engineer may have their own toolkit in their pocket, such as some scripts for certain tasks. It is recommended to have a source repository to host all these scripts and small toolkits accessible to all engineers. Not only can the organization absorb the secret powerful scripts from engineers but it also establishes a standard toolkit to help engineers perform their daily tasks.

- There are circumstances where engineers need to call an API endpoint to perform certain tasks, such as rehydrating an event topic by requesting the publisher to publish all messages again. It is recommended that the organization has a shared collection of operational endpoints to reduce the time for engineers to craft these steps themselves. In addition, it is likely that those API endpoints require getting an authorization token as a bearer token to invoke endpoints (see *Chapter 14* for a detailed flow); the orchestration of getting these tokens should be scripted and shared among engineers. An example of this tool is **Postman Collections**.

- The dependencies of a Kotlin project are silently out of date over time. Use automation tools such as **Dependabot** to automatically create pull requests that update dependencies.

- Use **artificial intelligence** (**AI**) applications in multiple areas of software development. Apart from the normal syntactic code completion features provided by the IDEs, there are also AI assistants that hint at semantic code completion by understanding the existing code base. There are also embedded **large language model** (**LLM**) chatbots that provide live technical advice with example code snippets. There are also pull request bots that understand the intent of pull requests and provide useful feedback.

Development processes

Organizations should invest in tools that support software development processes. Each team could have adopted slightly different methodologies such as Scrum or Kanban, and the team would need a dashboard to run the daily standup.

As remote working has become a trend, organizations should invest in tools such as issue-tracking systems, digital Kanban or Scrum boards, and online retrospective tools to enable the team to run any software development process.

Communication and collaboration

Modern organizations will already have invested in multiple communication tools for instant messaging, video conferencing, screen sharing and pairing, and emails. It is recommended that emails should only be used for external communication. Instant messaging should be the major way of communication.

Moreover, it is recommended that each team has a channel where engineers can think out loud about their problem-solving. Members of the channel should form a habit of using threads to post messages about a specific problem. By concentrating discussion of a problem, it is possible to introduce AI bots to summarize the discussion for others to catch up.

The instant messaging system should integrate with other tools, so engineers have a one-stop shop to receive notifications and work reactively. This can include receiving notifications of a visual design change from design collaboration tools, a change of an issue in issue management tools, an alert from monitoring tools, approval in a pull request, or simply a daily meeting schedule summary.

Engineers need to have tools to immediately jump on a remote pair-programming huddle with the capability to share screens and even take over control of input devices.

Some IDEs, such as IntelliJ Ultimate, have the capability to run pair-programming sessions. These tools enhance the collaboration between engineers and encourage collective learning.

There are other tools that enhance collaboration between engineers and other disciplines in the team. For example, an online collaborative design tool such as Figma or Miro can be used as a sketchpad for engineers to work with designers and product managers to understand the requirements.

Engineers in the same specialization (backend, frontend, data, testing, platform, etc.) can have their own forum as a *trade guild* in which engineers can share their learning and discuss topics that are closely related to their work.

Feedback and continuous improvement

It is important to periodically receive qualitative and quantitative feedback from engineers to discover any room for improvement. It is recommended to conduct regular surveys, feedback sessions, or retrospective sessions to gain insights into the satisfaction of engineers and to identify areas of improvement.

As discussed in *Chapter 11*, the **SPACE** metrics provide a comprehensive and holistic assessment of the productivity and well-being of engineering teams.

Most importantly, the engineering management needs to acknowledge the feedback and implement corresponding changes to improve the DX. Being listened to and seeing feedback taken on board would vastly improve the satisfaction and morale of engineering teams.

Recognition and rewards

Engineering teams and management should recognize and celebrate achievements by teams or individuals. This can be done by explicitly shouting out the team and its members for their accomplishments or giving actual rewards for successful releases, innovative ideas, and implemented improvements. Recognition and rewards can boost morale and motivation.

Final thoughts on software architecture

As we are coming to the end of the book, I would like to share my final thoughts on software architecture. I am going to cover the current trends and how we could equip ourselves to surf on the never-ending waves of change.

Small, reactive, and independent services

Although there are a few justifications for writing a monolithic application, as discussed in *Chapter 6*, software components are getting smaller and smaller. It is less common to see a new project written with the aim of becoming a monolith these days. Instead, engineers would aggressively split out small services that communicate over APIs or events.

Small services improve scalability, flexibility, and ease of deployment. Teams can develop, deploy, and scale services independently. Microservices and nanoservices are small enough to be owned by one team, and thus they encourage autonomy and empower the team to make its own decisions. Even if a wrong decision was made (e.g., choosing the wrong framework), it is comparatively easy to pivot and refactor the service without affecting other software components.

Application logic has also shifted from imperative to reactive and from synchronous to asynchronous processing. Many new systems embrace event-driven architectures and reactive handling. Many business use cases do not require everything to be completed to receive a response. A lot of processing can be done in real-time asynchronously by reacting to events. We covered the combination of CQRS and event-sourcing in *Chapter 9*, which provides an example of responding to synchronous requests earlier and having the rest of the processes executed asynchronously.

Having a system split into small services brings the challenge of keeping overall system behaviors consistent. This leads to the discussion of idempotence, replication, and recovery, as discussed in *Chapter 10*.

This change in thinking has improved responsiveness and scalability, making it easier to integrate with numerous services and handle high-throughput scenarios. We covered performance and scalability in depth in *Chapter 12*. We also

The shift-left paradigms – API-first and security-first approaches

Continuing with software component downsizing, APIs become more important. In fact, the API-first design approach has gained popularity these days. The API-first approach advocates that APIs should be developed before the actual implementation of the features.

This approach facilitates communication and collaboration between teams. It unblocks the development of the consumer side (e.g., another service or a frontend application) earlier and allows for parallel development. Developing APIs first also gives engineers a perspective to discover corner use cases before implementing them. We provided an example of the use of OpenAPI specifications in *Chapter 4*.

The increasing popularity of DevSecOps, as discussed in *Chapter 14*, has brought security to the engineers' attention. By integrating security practices into software development (e.g., threat modeling), teams can address security concerns and incorporate them into early technical design. This approach has enhanced the security posture and reduced vulnerabilities of an application.

The influence of cloud and serverless architectures

Cloud computing and serverless architectures have changed the landscape of software development forever. Cloud providers manage the infrastructure and automatically scale resources. Engineers can focus on fulfilling business requirements in code rather than tackling infrastructure concerns. Moreover, serverless architectures are cost-effective and reduce operational overhead.

The numerous services and tooling for cloud environments, such as Kubernetes, allow applications to take advantage of cloud provider features to improve scalability and resilience.

Moreover, there is a wide range of PaaS and SaaS running on the cloud, which makes it easier to integrate these services with any application. These services include relational databases, messaging services, identity providers, email services, and even fully-fledged enterprise software systems. We discussed serverless architecture in *Chapter 6*.

Composable architecture

The idea of small services extends to breaking down software into independent modules or components that can be easily assembled or replaced. This building block approach leads to composable architecture, where each block aims to address specific concerns. These modules are designed to be cohesive to integrate with any application.

This approach increases the agility and flexibility of the overall architecture. It enables applications to rapidly adapt to a technology and to experiment with multiple options at a lower cost.

For instance, the *household service* that was brought up in many chapters can be reused in business problems other than household exchanging services. The service can easily integrate with other systems (e.g., voting, recycling, etc.) due to its modularity and high cohesiveness. We discussed in length how to define bounded contexts that result in well-defined services in *Chapter 8*. We also discussed layered and modular architectures in *Chapter 7*.

Architecture patterns continue to grow and evolve. Having composable architecture enables each pattern to independently advance and improve.

Observability and monitoring

Observability and monitoring have become an integral part of software architectures these days. Not only do engineers want to gain an understanding of system behaviors through logging, tracing, and monitoring tools but engineers also want to identify issues quicker.

Observability and monitoring tools run in the cloud and are easy to integrate, typically using the Sidecar pattern, as mentioned in *Chapter 14*, which is also an approach to composable architecture.

Auditing has also become an important aspect of software products. Having the ability to understand actions performed in the system provides insights into technical and business processes. This is particularly helpful for systems that need to comply with regulations.

We covered the topic of auditing and monitoring models in *Chapter 11*.

AI and machine learning

AI and **machine learning** (**ML**) are significantly shaping the future of software architectures. ML is a subset of AI that focuses on learning from data to generate predictions and help decision-making.

AI/ML consumes a lot of data to train its model, thus making software architectures increasingly data-centric. Systems that use AI/ML need to efficiently collect, store, and process large volumes of data.

Cloud providers provide ready-to-use AI/ML services so engineers can run them without managing the infrastructure and automatically scale them on demand. These services (e.g., AWS Bedrock, Azure OpenAI, and GCP Vertex AI) include natural language processing, behavior analysis, predictive analytics, generating recommendations, summarizing data, and pattern recognition, and the list is still growing.

Even better, these AI/ML APIs use the format and transport that engineers are already familiar with, such as JSON payload and HTTP requests. Engineers can leverage advanced AI capabilities without needing deep expertise in AI/ML. The ease of integration has sped up development cycles.

Apart from using AI/ML in business applications, they are also used in monitoring, incident response, threat detection, semantic code completion, and chat box support for engineers. The ubiquitous features powered by AI/ML are driving a transformative shift in software architecture, promoting data-centric designs, modularity, and integration of advanced analytics into applications.

AI and ML will shape not only how applications are built but also how they interact with data in real time. We are still witnessing the evolution of AI and ML, and we have not seen the full scale of them yet.

Summary

We covered a few Kotlin language features that can assist engineers in achieving better architectures, including extension functions, infix functions, operator overriding, and scoping functions.

Then, we covered the necessary steps to transition a Java project into a Kotlin project. We walked through the tools and manual correction required to convert a Java class into an idiomatic Kotlin class. We also mentioned a few opportunities to improve code quality during the conversion. We delved into the topic of transition strategies in terms of the sequence of conversion and framework transition. We emphasized the importance of continuous transition to Kotlin, and how the transition could incrementally progress in the everyday business feature coding works.

We moved to the topic of CI and CD and presented the two main integration approaches: feature-based and trunk-based development. We compared them in terms of their pros, cons, and suitability in the context of organizational structure.

We made distinctions between three concepts: the deployment, release, and launch of a software product. Then, we walked through three release strategies: blue-green, feature flagging, and canary release. We presented a sample decision tree to help engineers select which release strategy is suitable from a technical perspective.

We also covered the topic of DX, explaining its importance and how it benefits the software product, the team, and the organization.

We made numerous suggestions for improving DX, including onboarding, tools, development processes, communication, collaboration, feedback, continuous improvement, recognition, and rewards.

Lastly, we reflected on the software architecture that was discussed throughout the whole book, with a focus on current trends and future development.

Index

C

Packtpub.com

Subscribe to our online digital library for full access to over 7,000 books and videos, as well as industry leading tools to help you plan your personal development and advance your career. For more information, please visit our website.

Why subscribe?

- Spend less time learning and more time coding with practical eBooks and Videos from over 4,000 industry professionals

- Improve your learning with Skill Plans built especially for you

- Get a free eBook or video every month

- Fully searchable for easy access to vital information

- Copy and paste, print, and bookmark content

Did you know that Packt offers eBook versions of every book published, with PDF and ePub files available? You can upgrade to the eBook version at packtpub.com and as a print book customer, you are entitled to a discount on the eBook copy. Get in touch with us at customercare@packtpub.com for more details.

At www.packtpub.com, you can also read a collection of free technical articles, sign up for a range of free newsletters, and receive exclusive discounts and offers on Packt books and eBooks.

Other Books You May Enjoy

If you enjoyed this book, you may be interested in these other books by Packt:

Kotlin Design Patterns and Best Practices - Third Edition

Alexey Soshin

ISBN: 978-1-80512-776-5

- Utilize functional programming and coroutines with the Arrow framework
- Use classical design patterns in the Kotlin programming language
- Scale your applications with reactive and concurrent design patterns
- Discover best practices in Kotlin and explore its new features
- Apply the key principles of functional programming to Kotlin
- Find out how to write idiomatic Kotlin code and learn which patterns to avoid
- Harness the power of Kotlin to design concurrent and reliable systems with ease
- Create an effective microservice with Kotlin and the Ktor framework

Mastering Kotlin

Nate Ebel

ISBN: 978-1-83855-572-6

- Model data using interfaces, classes, and data classes
- Grapple with practical interoperability challenges and solutions with Java
- Build parallel apps using concurrency solutions such as coroutines
- Explore functional, reactive, and imperative programming to build flexible apps
- Discover how to build your own domain-specific language
- Embrace functional programming using the standard library and Arrow
- Delve into the use of Kotlin for frontend JavaScript development
- Build server-side services using Kotlin and Ktor

Packt is searching for authors like you

If you're interested in becoming an author for Packt, please visit `authors.packtpub.com` and apply today. We have worked with thousands of developers and tech professionals, just like you, to help them share their insight with the global tech community. You can make a general application, apply for a specific hot topic that we are recruiting an author for, or submit your own idea.

Share your thoughts

Now you've finished *Software Architecture with Kotlin*, we'd love to hear your thoughts! Scan the QR code below to go straight to the Amazon review page for this book and share your feedback or leave a review on the site that you purchased it from.

`https://packt.link/r/1835461867`

Your review is important to us and the tech community and will help us make sure we're delivering excellent quality content.

Download a free PDF copy of this book

Thanks for purchasing this book!

Do you like to read on the go but are unable to carry your print books everywhere?

Is your eBook purchase not compatible with the device of your choice?

Don't worry, now with every Packt book you get a DRM-free PDF version of that book at no cost.

Read anywhere, any place, on any device. Search, copy, and paste code from your favorite technical books directly into your application.

The perks don't stop there, you can get exclusive access to discounts, newsletters, and great free content in your inbox daily

Follow these simple steps to get the benefits:

1. Scan the QR code or visit the link below

https://packt.link/free-ebook/978-1-83546-186-0

2. Submit your proof of purchase
3. That's it! We'll send your free PDF and other benefits to your email directly

www.ingramcontent.com/pod-product-compliance
Lightning Source LLC
Chambersburg PA
CBHW060645060326
40690CB00020B/4519